THE METAPHYSICAL PASSION

"The poet . . . diffuses a tone and spirit of unity, that blends, and (as it were) *fuses,* each into each, by that synthetic and magical power, to which we have exclusively appropriated the name of imagination. This power . . . reveals itself in the balance or reconciliation of opposite or discordant qualities: of sameness, with difference; of the general, with the concrete; the idea, with the image; the individual, with the representative; the sense of novelty and freshness, with old and familiar objects; a more than usual state of emotion, with more than usual order; judgement ever awake and steady self-possession, with enthusiasm and feeling profound or vehement. . . ."

Coleridge, *Biographia Literaria*

THE
METAPHYSICAL PASSION

Seven Modern American Poets
and the
Seventeenth-Century Tradition

by SONA RAIZISS

GREENWOOD PRESS, PUBLISHERS
WESTPORT, CONNECTICUT

In Memoriam
GEORGE W. RAIZISS

ACKNOWLEDGMENTS

I am grateful to those authors who have expressly and generously allowed me to quote from their books: R. P. Blackmur, T. S. Eliot, John Holmes, Joseph Wood Krutch, Stanley J. Kunitz, Archibald MacLeish, Peter Quennell, Wallace Stevens, Robert Penn Warren, and Yvor Winters. I owe thanks also to the various publishers who have granted me general permission to use material from books under their copyright.

For special permission to reprint passages from the following books, acknowledgments are due to Henry Holt and Company for *Poems about God* by John Crowe Ransom, copyright 1919 by Henry Holt and Company, Inc.; to Alfred A. Knopf for *Selected Poems* by John Crowe Ransom, copyright 1924, 1927, 1945 by Alfred A. Knopf, Inc., *Joseph and His Brothers* by Thomas Mann, copyright 1938 by Alfred A. Knopf, Inc., *Collected Poems of Elinor Wylie*, copyright 1921, 1923, 1924, 1925, 1926, 1927, 1928, 1929, 1932 by Alfred A. Knopf, Inc.; to Liveright Publishing Corporation for *The Collected Poems of Hart Crane,* copyright 1933 by Liveright, Inc.; also, for their courtesy, to Random House for *The Contemporary and His Soul* by Irwin Edman, copyright 1931 by Irwin Edman, *John Donne: Complete Poetry and Selected Prose* edited by John Hayward, 1929, *Ruins and Visions: Poems 1934-1942* by Stephen Spender, copyright 1942 by Stephen Spender; to The Clarendon Press for *Modern Poetry: A Personal Essay* by Louis MacNeice, 1938; to Faber and Faber for *Reason and Romanticism* by Herbert Read, 1926; to The Macmillan Company for *Poetry Direct and Oblique* by E. M. W. Tillyard, 1934.

To Professor Sculley Bradley of the University of Pennsylvania I am indebted for his encouragement and direction in the preparation of this study; to Dr. Alexander Bushkovitch of Saint Louis University for kindly verifying my philosophical and scientific references; and to Gwen Campbell for her painstaking help with the proofs and index.

CONTENTS

INTRODUCTION

METAPHYSICAL POETRY defines a special poetic syndrome experienced at many moments in literary history. Only twice, however, has the designation been critically assigned to an estimable group of poets writing in English in the same period. Borrowed from philosophy, the epithet was first linked to seventeenth-century English poetry in its own time. And again, in the last two generations, the prevalence of the metaphysical impulse as a documented phenomenon has given the term eminence. Our contribution is rich not alone in this kind of verse but in its scholarship and developed criticism.[1] The present study reviews certain illustrative American poets extending metaphysical statement in the twentieth century, the relationship to their progenitors, and the cognate cultural forces of both ages.

An impressive school of critics has been examining these two literatures. Particularly attracted to the seventeenth-century metaphysicals, T. S. Eliot at one time proposed to devote to them not only the intermittent essay but perhaps a book. Eventually he abandoned his project, unable to account for their revived reputation and John Donne's "general emergence towards tercentenary fame."[2] Yet he continued to enhance Donne's renown by his own critique and poetry. Archibald MacLeish, also admittedly indebted to the Elizabethan and metaphysical poets, in more recent years moved to the literary field of social revolt and lately intellectual patriotism. Such changes should signify that the modern metaphysical impetus reached its apogee in the late twenties and early thirties. In spite of the surfeit Eliot and others may feel, a study of this verse, with its social and psychological implications, still seems useful. Critics still refer to the metaphysical tendency, and always some oncoming poets continue to exemplify it.

In 1926 Eliot conceded such an inquiry had decided contemporary significance. Our century shows an accelerated sympathy, he wrote, for seventeenth-century verse whose passions and psychology express us better than does the eighteenth or nineteenth. Not Donne alone, an increasingly important criterion, but the lesser poets of his time have been deliberately courted by our writers. Eliot apparently approved the opinion that this was a metaphysical age.[3] Three years earlier he had said of Donne and Andrew Marvell that the kinship between their minds and our own is neither local nor limited. More than a fortuitous literary fashion urges us to draw from Donne and his followers "instruction and encouragement."[4] And even "detaching Donne from his relation to a particular generation, our own, a relation which may never be repeated at a subsequent time . . . Donne will remain permanently in a higher place than he has occupied before."[5] That permanent high place is the work of our time. If we are truly cognizant of this, we should not leave "the conclusion of praise [to] another generation, not enjoying the fulness of satisfaction in Donne . . . [who] has, in the old sense . . . 'prevented' us."[6]

Representing those critics who sense an exhaustion of metaphysical usefulness for the present generation, Theodore Spencer wrote, "I would suggest that modern poetry has learnt all that it can from the metaphysicals; we need a fresher source of inspiration."[7] These words came only four years after Spencer himself had edited the tercentenary tribute to Donne. But in 1939 he found that the subject was after all not spent and saw fit to compile, with Mark Van Doren, a bibliography of studies in metaphysical poetry. The undertaking has a valedictory sound. He was nevertheless impressed by "a type of poetry which recent poets have much admired, and which was the expression of a generation faced by many problems similar to our own."[8] Spencer's critical inconsistency and the following contradictions illustrate his difficulty in writing finis to this poetic movement: "I wonder if, for our generation at least, the study has not now reached a kind of saturation point. . . . Yet [what Donne] . . .

did and wrote have been the subjects of a great deal of investigation, which is by no means at an end."[9]

The modern experience, like Donne's, is part of a "larger, a more social and religious whole,"[10] and is so acknowledged by George Williamson, who has in a sense summed it up in *The Donne Tradition,* and by many others. Our generation has had "not only a taste for mental subtleties, but also a hunger for a kind of vital consciousness which the Victorian, like the Augustan, compromise denied."[11] Modern poets and critics have discovered this kindred consciousness above all in Donne and his period. "In the history of English literature the only forces comparable to it are Shakespeare's influence, or Milton's in the eighteenth century."[12] If there is authority for this statement, our study of so vigorous a persuasion is justified. And such social conditions as stimulated metaphysical expression in the seventeenth century have set a similar imprint on our own. The intense awareness possessed by Donne and his followers of man's intellectual and spiritual passions quickens our comprehension of these poets. If, from many of Donne's poems, we remove a seventeenth-century construction here and there or revert an inversion, we discover the experience and the language of contemporary writing.

That "such qualities have been deeply felt by a whole generation of readers since 1918 is demonstrated by the fact that even a character in Hemingway's 'Farewell to Arms' can quote from a metaphysical poem."[13] Not only has Donne's poetry become familiar, but his sermons are examined, republished in extracts, and quarried for epigraphs. Ernest Hemingway had done the general reading public a service by popularizing the name and work of Donne. People who knew nothing of the passion-ridden Dean of St. Paul's began to read his early verse soon after *For Whom the Bell Tolls* became a best seller in 1940. It is true that a dozen years before, titles derived from metaphysical poets were more commonly found on the bookstands: *Angels and Earthly Creatures* by Elinor Wylie,[14] *Fatal Interview* by Edna St. Vincent Millay, and *After Such Pleasures* by Dorothy Parker. We can add the more recent *The Outward Room* by Millen Brand, a fiction title taken from Donne's "The Second Anniversary"; *Death Be Not Proud,* a 1949 memoir by John Gunther who quotes the poet's sonnet as the in memoriam note; and Robert Penn Warren's *World Enough and Time*—popularizing in 1950 Andrew Marvell's first words of "To his Coy Mistress" from the 1681 edition.

There is no lack of evidence that the seventeenth century is congenial to our tempers, minds, and poetic methods. Poets have been studying Donne's prosody as well as his relevant realism, "for Donne was essentially a modern poet. One can imagine him in complete sympathy with the realists, imagists, and *vers librists* of the last decade and a half."[15] Professors have been teaching his metrics; his anniversary and those of his colleagues are celebrated; even newspaper columnists have been making capital of him.[16] While certain critics have tried to minimize the extent of the metaphysical influence,[17] John Crowe Ransom, a practicing metaphysical, confesses that we are working with the seventeenth-century poets toward a common goal, not yet achieved: "The poetry which makes the manliest effort to be contemporary, and to retreat as little as possible upon the road that has been travelled, is like that of the so-called metaphysical school of the seventeenth century. It is being tried today by poets who are the real outposts of the poetic movement."[18] The very indecision among critics, even in *A Garland for John Donne,* redounds to his reputation. "The uncertainty comes of Donne's being still alive. . . . And unless it will again be possible for men to give themselves up to a self-contained, objective system of truths, the principles of Donne, whether we know him or not, will continue to be our own."[19] Our age has been "the sort of age that Abraham Cowley complained of—a good age to write about but a hard age to write in."[20] It is a time like Donne's which, in a dedicatory letter, he called "unlucky."

Metaphysical verse, therefore, continues to prosper, and not only as a style worn by scattered poets superficially termed metaphysicals. "The vogue of Donne rose with amazing rapidity twenty years ago. So far as the poets are concerned it seems hardly to have declined."[21] Although Henry W. Wells, who made this statement in 1940, considers scores of influences from the past in *New Poets from Old,* he finds the metaphysical among the strongest in our times. In the present work a study is proposed of the character of metaphysical expression and the nature of the conditions that stimulated it, in both the seventeenth and the twentieth centuries. Thus we can relate the quick dead to their quickened progeny.

PART ONE

*THE TEMPER OF
METAPHYSICAL POETRY*

1

DEFINITIONS

A̲ny̲ basic consideration of metaphysical poetry at once implies two insistent questions: What is the meaning of "metaphysical"? Who are the "metaphysical poets"?

The term in our sense has been used for over two centuries, often indiscriminately. There is that loose application because its intent has varied from William Drummond's day,[1] through Dryden's and Johnson's, to our own. But we are obliged to keep the name for want of another that might approximate it and at the same time contain all the connotations.[2] To saddle Donne with a school reaching from his contemporaries to Cowley, because of a common heritage, seems an imposition. Yet we make this identification because Donne's metaphysical poetry was by far the most original and significant, and because his disciples in later generations were brought close to him with the belated publication of his verse.

To begin with, there is an admitted difference between "metaphysical" as a technical expression in English literary history and its meaning for poetry with a generally philosophical bent. Because of the term's connection with philosophy, the dictionary definition of "metaphysics" is relevant:

[From *metaphysic,* n., after ML. *metaphysica,* neut. pl., fr. Gr. *meta ta physika* after those things which relate to external nature, after physics, fr. *meta* beyond, after *physikos* relating to external nature, natural, physical, fr. *physis* nature. . . . The term was first used, it is believed, by Andronicus of Rhodes, the editor of Aristotle's works, as a name for that part of his writings which came *after* the *Physics.*] . . . The primary meaning of *metaphysics* is derived from those discussions by Aristotle which he himself called the First Philosophy or Theology,

3

and which deal with the nature of being, with cause or genesis, and with the existence of God. Later, metaphysics was understood as the science of the supersensible. By Albertus Magnus it was called the *transphysical* science; and Aquinas considered it to be concerned with the cognition of God. Scholastic philosophy in general understood it as the science of being in itself. . . . In England, Bacon defined it as the quest or study of formal and final causes, contrasting with it natural philosophy as treating efficient and material causes. . . . In England, owing to the prevalence of psychological problems, it became practically identified with the analytical psychology of the time. . . . Schopenhauer and later writers have insisted that metaphysics is concerned with analysis of experience, in the broad sense, and this empirical view is largely held by modern writers.

As for "metaphysical," the adjective, the following dictionary distinctions should help clarify its meaning for verse:

1. Of or pertaining to metaphysics; according to rules or principles of metaphysics; hence, abstract or abstruse. . . . 2. Pertaining to, or having, real being or the essential nature of reality; as, *metaphysical* truth; *metaphysical* being. . . . 4. Designating, or pertaining to, a so-called "school" of 17th-century poets, whose works abound in elaborate subtleties of thought and expression;—so-called by Dr. Johnson. Donne, Cowley, Herbert, and Crashaw are of this group.[3]

One must remember that this name, as first employed by Dryden and as finally rendered fashionable by Johnson's references to the Donne school, was used without the implication of a metaphysical philosophy or system. Rather it is recent criticism that designates among the metaphysicals the "three philosophical poets" treated by George Santayana.[4] Lucretius, Dante, and Goethe also constitute the prime example for H. J. C. Grierson who suggests, however, in his introduction to *Metaphysical Lyrics,* a difference between the philosophical and the metaphysical poet. And although Eliot objects to considering Donne a philosophical poet, he makes some concession when he discusses systems of thought behind metaphysical verse. Moreover, he reverts to the Aristotelian origin of the term when he states that the metaphysical poets search for what is beyond nature, subtilizations of idea and feeling,[5] but a poet can certainly be metaphysical without being philosophical, and the converse. It is only the genesis of our term in the editing of Aristotle's works that bears on subsequent controversy. Metaphysics comes after physics, yet patently implies the presence of physics first. The metaphysical poet passionately proves this relationship. Donne is concerned with metaphysical reference when he seems most physical, and vice versa.

In reference to poetry as "metaphysical," the first critical application to be taken seriously was Johnson's in his "Life of Cowley,"[6] although the germinal idea was Dryden's.[7] Its lineage, however, dates back from Johnson to the Warton brothers, Joseph Spence, Chesterfield, Pope, Dryden of course, Drummond, and Testi, the Italian poet who died in 1646.[8] The grouping of poets into a metaphysical school is deprecated by later critics such as Wordsworth, Southey, Edward Dowden, and altogether dismissed by Felix Schelling.[9] Nevertheless, no one has offered a name more suitable or characteristic, despite the obvious confusion of philosophical and literary meanings involved. We may blame or credit Johnson for it, but his belittling epithet had become an accepted literary designation.

Even before Dryden, certain critics of the seventeenth century disapproved of metaphysical elements in poetry and of such abstractions as divorce the poet from the simplicities of the senses. Actually, Donne's verse was far more exact and palpable than that of Drummond, who disparaged poetry narrowly described as metaphysical.[10] Among others, Bishop Maxwell, Benjamin Whichcote, Cleveland, and Abercromby criticized it not only as difficult but dangerous when "abstract from sense." Of course Samuel Butler actively satirized it as nonsensical. Thus it seems that, before Dryden's discourse concerning satire in 1693, ridicule anticipating the eighteenth-century attitude paralleled mere imitation and a true understanding of the metaphysical style. Dryden himself, and Johnson, characterized Donne's and Cowley's verse as "thoughtful, speculative, and abstract," but also as "incomprehensible, vague, and repugnant to common sense."[11]

With the revived practice of and interest in metaphysical

poetry, definitions teem in our century. There is profit in their variety. To begin with, an analysis of the word in its native sense illuminates the essential dualism of metaphysical verse. In a chapter called "Abstraction" the philosopher Alfred North White-head discusses

> the standpoint of a dispassionate consideration of the nature of things, antecedently to any special investigation into their details. Such a standpoint is termed "metaphysical." . . . It is the foundation of the metaphysical position which I am maintaining that the understanding of actuality requires a reference to ideality. The two realms are intrinsically inherent in the total metaphysical situation.[12]

And conversely reference to ideality involves reference to actuality.[13] In regard to a type of poetry, some specimen definitions of "metaphysical" should show a root agreement, for all its ramifications.

"Metaphysical Poetry, in the full sense of the term, is a poetry which . . . has been inspired by a philosophical conception of the universe and the role assigned to the human spirit in the great drama of existence."[14] In view of the dignity thus accorded the metaphysical poet by Grierson, the minor "fantastic" note finds no place in his definition.[15] To Donne and his school he assigns a nobler task, the "definite interpretation of the riddle" by means of the "boldest conceptions, the profoundest intuitions, the subtlest and most complex classifications . . . passionate experiences communicated in vivid and moving imagery."[16] Terms of this high order should be applied, Grierson suggests however, only to such major figures as Lucretius, Dante, "perhaps" Goethe. But no more than one or two other modern critics characterize these titans as metaphysical in the current use of the designation. No doubt Eliot would name Dante. To Santayana they are "philosophical" poets, a description that appears more suitable. When Grierson eventually elaborates on "the peculiar blend of passion and thought," he expresses more closely the essential condition of metaphysical poetry.

If this condition is essentially a paradox, it is by that very token natural to true metaphysical verse—which is "a paradoxical inquiry" not only into "all the possibilities in a given idea"[17] but into all the possibilities of the corresponding feeling. Thus it is not metaphysical problems and ideas as such that concern the poet, but the psychological ordeal of expressing their emotional equivalents. The excitement generated by the friction of difficult meaning and human passion produces metaphysical poetry. The accompanying sensation is described by James Smith as the "metaphysical note,"[18] and by George Williamson as the "Metaphysical shudder."[19] However indefinite these expressions, they represent the reader's experience on entering the province of conflict and engaging in the "interpenetration of mind and matter."[20]

Peter Quennell is not alone among our contemporaries in objecting to a catchword that embraces Donne, Crashaw, and Cowley. But he pleads the "want of a better term. Metaphysical verse, on close acquaintance, resolves itself into an attempt by certain writers to employ the jargon and symbolism of 'modern' knowledge, and to stir the emotions by first stimulating a reader's mind."[21] Irritation with the worn but persisting name appears in Cleanth Brooks's statement that "metaphysical poetry (whatever the term metaphysical may mean or may have meant) is witty poetry." Brooks offers "one more definition of metaphysical poetry . . . a poetry in which the opposition of the impulses which are united is extreme."[22] Critics ultimately accept the use of the designation, after deprecating and redefining it:

The term *metaphysical* . . . is not altogether a happy term, since it gives the impression that metaphysical poetry discusses the nature of the universe. . . . But Donne and the poets most influenced by him were not speculating about the nature of things as [were] Milton . . . Pope . . . Tennyson. . . . "metaphysical" refers to style, not to subject-matter; but style reflects an attitude to experience.[23]

Though Joan Bennett pictures the resulting poetry as "written by men for whom the light of day is God's shadow," she finds that in secular as well as religious metaphysical verse the "intellectual bias affects" words, images, form, and rhythm. The mind moves from "the contemplation of a fact to deduction . . . to a conclusion."[24] I submit, however, that often a metaphysical poem is a problem left unsolved, notably with moderns like Ransom and Hart Crane. Donne himself often cancels one conclusion with another, or so plays them against each other that the only resolution is an equipoise.

That metaphysical poetry presents emotion intellectually—though generally not didactically—conforms with Herbert Read's analysis. "Metaphysical poetry is abstract because, like metaphysics, it deals with concepts. But, as poetry, it is no less 'emotional' than lyrical poetry . . . [and defined] as the emotional apprehension of thought . . . as thought transmuted into vision."[25] Read feels that where Johnson missed other distinctions of metaphysical poets, he was astute enough to see that "To write on their plane it was at least necessary to read and think."[26] Referring to George Chapman's verse and derivations from Dante and the early Italian poets, Read expands his interpretation to include "an opacity, or 'charged' effect, characteristic of all good metaphysical poetry; as though behind each word lurked considerable processes of thought. . . . Metaphysical poetry is determined logically: its emotion is a joy that comes with the triumph of the reason, and is not a simple instinctive ecstasy." It is, however, a kind of "symbolism in which the most abstract ideals of the intellect can be made personal and actual . . . the precise statement of such abstractions as the poet derives from his experience."[27]

This metaphoric precision implicates the distinctive, or radical, image.[28] Ransom characterizes "small-scale Metaphysical Poetry" in terms of that conceit in which the seventeenth century was so daring. Further, he finds that the pivotal image in all metaphysical verse derives from the miraculism which "arises when the poet discovers by analogy an identity between objects which is partial, though it should be considerable, and it proceeds to an identification which is complete . . . the miraculism which produces the humblest conceit is the same miraculism which supplies to religions their substantive content."[29] Definitions of metaphysical poetry variously stress its intellectual procedure,[30] or its state of mind,[31] but they invariably note the singular realistic precision of its imagery which obviates neither its intellectual reservation nor its apocalyptic mood. It has a diversiform nature: the abstract and "a scientific sharpness and an angularity";[32] it lives in two domains: "the marvelous thrust into the ineffable is followed by a quick pull-back into the world of here and now with its lucid sense-detail and its ineluctable common sense."[33]

In *The Donne Tradition* Williamson draws the general conclusion: "The nature of this tradition may be concisely defined as complex, sensuous, and intellectual as opposed to the simple, sensuous, and passionate tradition, if we remember that it does not exclude the rapture or passion of Sappho and Catullus."[34] But can one deny a characteristic passion in metaphysical poetry as such? On the contrary, there seems to be common agreement with Grierson and Eliot in their contention that the emotional element is intensified in the metaphysical "blend of thought and passion." Indeed, the seventeenth-century poets "possessed a mechanism of sensibility which could devour any kind of experience." By this means they were capable of "transmuting ideas into sensations, of transforming an observation into a state of mind."[35]

Eliot's perspicuous analyses of the metaphysical process, however informal, afford a basis for definition. Though he thinks it helpful to "exhibit these poets in all their difference of kind and of degree,"[36] he habitually refers to the seventeenth-century metaphysicals, however individual, as a group manifesting a quality of kinship. Their writing

has come to mean poetry in which the poet *makes use* of metaphysical ideas and theories. He may believe some theory, or he may believe none; but he must be a poet who experiences emotion through thought, as well as one who thinks about emotion. Of metaphysical poetry in general we may say that it gets its effects by suddenly producing an emotional equivalent for what seemed merely a dry idea, and by finding the idea of a vivid emotion. It moves between abstract thought and concrete feeling; and strikes us largely by contrast and continuity, by the curious ways in which it shows thought and feeling as different aspects of reality.[37]

Eliot's argument that this poet need not consistently maintain a belief or theory suggests again a distinction between the philosophical poet and the metaphysical. The latter employs ideas not as integers of a philosophical or religious system per se but as "aspects of reality" to be dealt with concretely. The definition of metaphysical poetry must stress its ideas not as systematic philosophy but as mental equivalents of emotional experience. Here thought is tempered into poetry by the heat of the heart, and the intellectual formula is fleshed with the body of pain and pleasure.[38] In reviewing poetry from the thirteenth century to his own time, Eliot seeks a criterion for the true metaphysical poet. Finally he selects the traits exemplifying the mean between Donne and Crashaw. In the main, metaphysical poetry signifies to Eliot "a direct sensuous apprehension of thought," an imaginative wit maintaining an "internal equilibrium,"[39] "the intellect . . . immediately at the tips of the senses."[40]

Metaphysical poetry, then, is the attempt to reconcile the body of the world with the universal mind. Its poet strives to resolve the paradox inherent in any experience by evoking simultaneously its emotional and intellectual powers. His image or his poem is the passionate endeavor toward union between the conceptual and the sensuous.

2

THE POETS AND THEIR SUBJECTS

WHO ARE the metaphysical poets? A definitive answer would help establish the nature of their art. But judgments and categories vary widely. Believing that most great poets are metaphysical, some critics take much the same view as Whitehead does in respect to philosophy: "All reasoning, apart from some metaphysical reference, is vicious."[1] This begs the question and abuses the term in its application to poetry. As immediate successors to Donne and Ben Jonson, six poets were designated by Samuel Johnson:[2] Suckling, Waller, Denham, Cowley, Cleveland, Milton. David Masson also felt Milton to be metaphysical in the philosophical sense, and was inclined for the same reason to add Fulke Greville and Sir John Davies. The roll calls of Grierson (with twenty-six names), Genevieve Taggard, and Spencer differ significantly. This confusion comes from the initial difficulty of definition. If we accept John Donne's poetry as the archetype of the metaphysical method and attitude, we shall find it hard to define the modern equivalent. An embarrassing assortment and number of poets suggest Donne in some quality or technique: Emily Dickinson, Gerard Manley Hopkins, W. H. Auden, Eliot, MacLeish, Crane, Wallace Stevens, Allen Tate, Elinor Wylie.

In contemplating the whole production of poets of this order, one finds much of it quite disparate; the metaphysical element must be some common denominator among them. What attraction exists among Lucretius, Catullus, Aquinas, Dante, Chapman, Donne, Webster, Carew, Marvell, Goethe, Hopkins, Dickinson, Eliot, Auden, Crane? What common ground is there for modern symbolists, imagists, and Fugitives? Somewhere among the fol-

11

lowing coincidences there is a fundamental clue: that Eliot respects Dante preëminently; that Dante possesses theological magnitude; that Eliot has always concerned himself with good and evil; that Baudelaire wrote *Fleurs du Mal;* that Crane understood Baudelaire and Hopkins; that Hopkins was a man troubled with religion; that Donne taught a continuity of personality from sexual love to God-love; that Crashaw expressed devotional themes in concrete erotic images; that seventeenth-century England transplanted to New England survived in specific traits; that the substratum of that New England underlies the characters of Dickinson, Wylie, and Eliot; that the Puritan explored problems of original sin, in which Eliot believes; that regardless of his official marriage to Anglo-Catholicism he continues to endure religious perturbations, as even Donne in his time; that the modern plight which produced an Eliot resembles that of the seventeenth century. Modern books abound with dedications, prefaces, references, titles, epigraphs linking Eliot with Harry Crosby, Paul Valéry, Ezra Pound, Marianne Moore, and the Fugitives, Genevieve Taggard with Emily Dickinson, Crane with James Agee. Where there are so many points of contact there must also be some persistent characteristic that patterns these writers, however scattered in place and generation. This personal and literary brotherhood suggests some common esthetic, instinctively or consciously recognized.

For similar reasons it should be instructive to examine more closely the selections and comments of those editors and critics who have grouped the metaphysical poets. Eliot, for one, finds it difficult not only to define metaphysical verse, but also

to decide what poets practise it and in which of their verses. The poetry of Donne (to whom Marvell and Bishop King are sometimes nearer than any of the other authors) is late Elizabethan . . . close to Chapman. . . . Crashaw . . . returns through the Elizabethan period to the early Italians. It is difficult to find any precise use of metaphor, simile, or other conceit, which is common to all the poets and at the same time important enough as an element of style to isolate these poets as a group.[3]

It is perhaps unlikely that any particular coterie of poets in any century constituted a consciously metaphysical school. The metaphysical is a tendency of mind, leading to a characteristic expressiveness. Given certain social conditions in a period, its impulse is likely to affect the manner of many poets otherwise quite different and to create one sort of bond among them.

In the introduction to his anthology of seventeenth-century metaphysical poems, Grierson selects Lucretius, Dante, and Goethe as representing "Metaphysical Poetry, in the full sense of the term."[4] The book itself includes the following poets: Donne, Hoskins, Wotton, Townshend, Herbert of Cherbury, Carew, Habington, Suckling, Kynaston, Godolphin, Cleveland, Davenant, Crashaw, Lovelace, Vaughan, John Hall, Stanley, King, Cowley, Marvell, Katherine Philips, Milton, George Herbert, Quarles, Sherburne, and Butler. No considerable number of these poets can be regarded as a school, for they cut well across seventeenth-century verse in time and type. Ordinarily Carew, Suckling, and Lovelace are known as Cavalier poets. John Hall is remembered chiefly as a satirist; Lord Herbert as a philosopher of sorts and a Hermetist; Francis Quarles as a crotchety writer of emblems. Milton, in the opinion of several critics, wrote only one metaphysical lyric,[5] and that insignificant; his work according to Eliot reacted against the metaphysical sensibility of his century. All this suggests that some force at work at that time caused a wide variety of writers to respond in the manner that we now call metaphysical. On the other hand, James Smith calls Donne, Herbert, and Marvell the only three metaphysicals,[6] although his selection would seem perversely narrow. By comparison, at the other extreme, Genevieve Taggard includes eighty-four poets from William Dunbar to Mark Van Doren. Her late sixteenth- and seventeenth-century group consists of William Byrd, Raleigh, Sidney, Southwell, Nashe, Daniel, Drayton, Shakespeare, Donne, Jonson, Dekker, Webster, Drummond, Wither, Carew, Herrick, Herbert, Shirley, Christopher Harvey, Thomas Browne, Milton, Butler, Crashaw, Lovelace, Cowley, Marvell, Vaughan, John Hall, Bunyan, Dryden, and William Cleland. Of the eighty-four poets included, more than one third wrote before 1700, the year of Dryden's death. Of the other two thirds, more than half are Americans and overwhelmingly in the present period. If any significance can be attached to such proportions, one conclusion may be that next to the seventeenth century in England,[7] the modern American poetic era has been the most metaphysically disposed.

Taggard's selection will be misleading, however, if one forgets that her *Circumference* is an anthology not of metaphysical poets but of poems. At that, the editor's own circumscription of metaphysical verse to "the form of an idea" should automatically disqualify many of her uncharacteristic entries. Walt Whitman surely had a cosmic outlook on life; but his style and temperament are generally remote from metaphysical considerations. Indeed, of nineteenth-century Americans only Emerson, Poe, and Dickinson are involved in such critiques. Among Miss Taggard's twentieth-century Americans, one can support the choice of Stevens, Elinor Wylie, Eliot, Ransom, Crane, and Tate. For other major and minor poets included, the argument is less cogent. E. A. Robinson, an important psychologist, and Robert Frost, a wry "philosopher" of the inner and outer landscape, are not technically metaphysical. At least one advocate has appeared for Edna Millay in this connection,[8] but the evidence is not convincing beyond a number of her sonnets.[9] Pound remains a theorist in the development of the contemporary metaphysical revival, but he is not one of its true practitioners. Though Marianne Moore has the intellectual attitude, her powers are descriptive, her emphasis on delineation rather than argument.

The dangers inherent in the Taggard approach are obviated in studies by Helen White, Joan Bennett, and J. B. Leishman who confine themselves to essential seventeenth-century names. Miss White discusses Donne, Herbert, Crashaw, Vaughan, and Traherne, of whom Miss Bennett omits Traherne and Leishman omits Crashaw. The following poets are accepted by Spencer and Van Doren as the basis for their *Studies in Metaphysical Poetry:* Carew, Cleveland, Cowley, Crashaw, Donne, Herbert of Cherbury, George Herbert, King, Marvell, Katherine Philips, Traherne, and Vaughan. Under the metaphysical aspect of the seventeenth century, Eliot examines Chapman, Donne, Herbert, Crashaw, Vaughan, Traherne, Marvell, King, Carew, Suckling, Lovelace, Cleveland, Benlowes, Cowley, Herbert of Cherbury, and Dryden. As representative of the modern metaphysical impulse in American literature, Eliot, Ransom, Tate, Robert Penn Warren, Crane, Elinor Wylie, and MacLeish are chosen for detailed discussion in this study. Other Fugitives such as Donald Davidson and Laura Riding should be considered, as well as a number of poets ranging from Anna Hempstead Branch to José Garcia Villa.

The definitions of metaphysical poetry inspected in the first chapter suggest that this poetry attempts to reconcile the paradoxical qualities of human experience. Of course, all poetry deals with experience, and that is infinitely inclusive. But it is not so much the selection of material as the manner of its presentation that marks the metaphysical. Yet there are certain topics, certain phases of experience, which are more conducive than others to the suggestive shorthand by which the true metaphysical poet expresses the passion of his thoughts. Some human experiences are more inherently paradoxical than others, and as a result there is a natural selection of themes peculiar to metaphysical verse.

As a poet Donne carries the themes of love, science, philosophy, and religion to the highest metaphysical power. But the subject of woman in certain poems is empirical as distinguished from the abstract concept of love; and the personal relation to God differs in the same manner from the more objective treatment of religion. For example, Donne's *Ignatius his Conclave* deals primarily with religion categorically considered. In "Hymne to God my God, in my sicknesse" and "A Hymne to God the Father," he makes a personal approach to Deity. "To his Mistris going to Bed," though treated metaphysically, considers sex as an earthly experience, but "Lovers infinitenesse" is a perfect syllogistic argument on love. Donne's verse letters, epithalamia, epigrams, and other occasional pieces are too scattered to be relevant here. His chief themes, then, are love and woman in *Songs and Sonets*, science and philosophy in the two *Anniversaries*, and godly considerations in *Divine Poems* and *Holy Sonnets*.

Vaughan presents childhood and nature, and such obviously metaphysical themes as eternity; Herbert struggles with God and uses church objects for his figures; Crashaw writes devotional exercises and addresses special saints, though he shows an early interest in love and other secular subjects. Attitudes of childhood to nature and the spiritual world are Traherne's special domain. Bishop King is notable for his twin treatment of love and death; while Marvell, broader in scope, considers love, death, nature, and politics. Cowley's palpable concern with nature and his friends still leaves him room for abstractions like hope, wit, destiny, and light; whereas his images draw specifically on law, science, gambling.

In Grierson's anthology the following subjects predominate suggestively in both their abstract and concrete aspects: church symbols and objects, Christ, God, the King, love, science and other knowledges, death and the afterlife, time, first principles, and ideological relationships. Nature is generally neglected except in Marvell, Cowley, and sometimes Donne. In Traherne and Vaughan childhood, as both a natural and a spiritual phase of life, has its special advocates. It appears, then, that God and religion, affection and its enemies death and distance, the old and the "new philosophy" as abstractions and tangibles, take precedence over other subjects. Seventeenth-century metaphysical verse is chiefly confined to urban and adult themes.

In the twentieth century horizons lengthen, but city and sophisticated elements still predominate. Hart Crane gives us subways, bridges, and urinals, as well as historical and legendary figures like Pocahontas, and nature, especially the sea. E. E. Cummings prefers urban materials and worldly-wise love; Marianne Moore absorbs books and pangolins into her poetry. Elinor Wylie's principal theme is love, both human and angelic, but she analyzes all consciousness even beyond death and the sublimation of sensuous experience. While the Nashville Fugitives point up history and MacLeish turns political in one phase of his poetry, Eliot from the beginning inquires into the behavior of historical and religious man. Wallace Stevens is catholic in his choice of subjects, though he evinces drawing-room tastes. Unlike those of Donne or Emily Dickinson, the themes of the contemporary poets cannot be so neatly categorized. As her editors readily decided, Dickinson treated life, love, nature, time and eternity (death and God). Hopkins' themes can also be more simply classified than those of our recent moderns. With him religion or, more accurately, man's relation with Deity was paramount; and the sea his important source of imagery.[10]

The modern metaphysicals are supplied with topics and figures from a formidable body of knowledge. This is, of course, a result of the nature of our present world, and the spectacular accumulation of facts in every field. It is also the result of the conviction, among metaphysically inclined moderns, that poets should be widely informed. Eliot, like Donne, is "charged with incorporating too much curious knowledge into . . . poetry."[11] The use of obscure information, learned allusions, and oblique statement was apparently natural to Donne, but "consciously developed in Eliot," who "gives the emotional equivalent of a large amount of reading and thinking." He "draws upon medicine, law, physics, philosophy, and . . . anthropology,"[12] and one can also add history and comparative religion. Today, with the rapid increase in human knowledge, a more learned poetry has developed, as in Donne's day when learning was likewise a living thing essential to the sensibility of its writers.

This tendency may be connected with the yearning to implement the expression of the verities: the metaphysicals were "describing the nature of the unseen world of life, love, death, and eternity."[13] If we reduce these four categories to sacred and secular love, we discover one of the essential dichotomies treated in metaphysical poetry. Yet the material substance from which the individual images are drawn is variable. We find scientific, mechanical, and scholastic references in Donne's figures, natural particulars and light in Vaughan's, sensations of the body in Crashaw's, and ecclesiastical and domestic objects in Herbert's verse. Modern poets such as "Auden, Empson, and Day Lewis build up their poetic worlds with images drawn from mathematical physics, the internal combustion-engine, or the vocabulary of psychoanalysis as naturally as the older poets spoke of a pair of compasses, the plow, or the pit of despair."[14] Where a non-metaphysical poet may shrink from the chasm between secular and supernatural affairs, a writer like Donne accepts the unity of his experience and exploits worldly trivialities as readily as the sublime, moving easily from one realm to the other.

Donne recognized contemporaneous theories and investigations as willingly as scholasticism or superstition. His practical awareness of past and present made alchemy as available to him as chemistry. Astrology, together with the increasing knowledge of astronomy, physiology, geology, and medicine, enriched his metaphors. Burgeoning psychology also contributed to his poetic resources. His passion for ideas led him to every immediate and remote field of human perception ripe for harvesting.[15] Donne's assorted learning was used to develop central motifs such as:

the identity of lovers as lovers, and their diversity as the human beings in which love manifests itself; the stability and self-sufficiency of love, contrasted with the mutability and dependence of human beings; . . . the presence of lovers to each other, their physical unity, though they are separated by travel, and by death; the spirit demanding the succour of the flesh, the flesh hampering the spirit; the shortcomings of this life, summarized by decay and death, contrasted with the divine to which it aspires.[16]

In these dual problems metaphysical propositions are involved though, as James Smith justifiably maintains, the poet need not rely on such propositions. Donne is metaphysical in many poems that do not affect the metaphysics per se, in spite of Dryden's accusation. But Eliot holds that metaphysical poetry implies a specific background of thought, systematic or fragmentary. Dante drew on Aquinas, Donne on many philosophical and theological systems before him whose articles he did not relate but used in precise and recognizable images.[17] It is illuminating, therefore, to note some of the chief concepts that often, though not inevitably, animate metaphysical poetry. The concept of the many and the one typifies the various opposing forces inherent in life and fundamental to much of this verse.

At times the individual has fought against, and depended upon, its fellow individual, much as multiplicity unity; or the individual has fought against the universal; or against the universe, or against God. Or the here-now has risen up against its natural ally the then-there, and both have risen up against eternity. Or the spirit, partaking of the universal has had nothing to do with the flesh; and the flesh, primed with the certainty of the here-now, has dismissed the spirit as a fable.[18]

The problems that sound this "metaphysical note" are as old as Plato, are as limited or infinite as life itself, as law versus mutability, the self versus the cosmos. The metaphysical poem can be tried as the bridge erected between "the finite and the infinite, the many and the one, the uttermost parts of the universe and its center, the beginning and the end, evil and good, matter and mind, past and future, the chaos that life appears and the harmony it is found to be."[19] These conflicts reside in the very stuff of existence. "It seems impossible that the nature of things should possess either one or the other of a pair of qualities: it seems impossible that it should possess both together; it seems impossible that it should not possess both."[20] A tangible instance of such straining paradox is Donne's "The Good-morrow." It is the metaphysical poet's prerogative to contrast and reconcile the temporal and the ultimate. One can view such problems as the foundation of a metaphysical poem; or as its superstructure vaulting from the buttresses of concrete subject matter—like physical love and the rites of religion.

Thus the poetry takes thought and feeling for its duplex province, a lease on the spaces of the ineffable, and furnishings from everywhere. "For what, after all," asks Herbert Read, "is the material of poetry, and particularly of metaphysical poetry, but just vaguely 'life'—*i.e.* the poet's life, the compound of all his experiences?"[21] It must therefore be their method of procedure and their general mood that distinguish the metaphysicals from other categories of poets, rather than their material which, though it shows a preference for certain meditative subjects, is drawn from everywhere.

METHODS, MANNER, AND MOOD

W E RECOGNIZE then that it is not primarily its substance which distinguishes metaphysical poetry. Love and death, two subjects handled well and often by Donne, have been favorite poetic themes in every age. What Donne's practice contributed to the versification of his day still differentiates metaphysical poetry from its neighbors. This is the technique of communication. Whatever the theme, the method evokes the intellectual apprehension as an intrinsic element in the complete emotional or passionate experience of a poem. This procedure characterizes a metaphysical poem more explicitly than its content or even its mood, of which we shall speak later. Method here involves a special consideration of the conceit, idiom, allusion, distinctive "wit," surprise in paradox and contrast, and even prosodic modifications. In other words, the metaphysical manages an image appropriate to its bold language; advantageous rhetoric; suggestive allusiveness; and an astonishing wit that results from its inherent tensions of thought, emotion, and metaphoric means.

Prominent in Elizabethan and seventeenth-century verse and the principal mark of the metaphysical method, the "conceit" has again claimed attention in modern writing. Actually this trope is a drastic exploitation of figurative language. With the earlier nonmetaphysical Elizabethan poets it was the ornamental embroidery of a sensuous verbalism, a comparison carried to the extreme limits of fancy. But as the metaphysical habit became more prevalent, this device of peculiar properties, translated to the realm of the intellect, afforded the passage between experience and idea. Brought to a superlative state of refinement by the

Jacobeans, the conceit was transmitted indirectly to the moderns, as in that familiar example of the "etherised" evening.

This specific attribute of the metaphysicals Eliot calls "primarily an eccentricity of imagery, the far-fetched association of the dissimilar, or the overelaboration of one metaphor or simile,"[1] surely a flaw if it is only an overdeveloped figure. Actually great poems of the seventeenth and twentieth centuries abound in the very effective use of conceit. Eliot himself admits elsewhere that the metaphysical mind inclines toward this functional image. It becomes a pertinent problem, however, to separate mere verbal tricks from metaphysical "habits of thought" exercised by the seventeenth century. In Europe that literary period was generally "conceited," but it does not invariably prove every poet or passage metaphysical that showed a rash of conceits. Yet prevalences in language can accustom feeling and thinking, so that a poet of conceits is more probably metaphysical than not.[2] That type of imagery, if not exaggerated or an end in itself, should objectify the idea and the emotion. Then the term is not a disparagement and the multitude of successful conceits in poetry proves no arbitrary limits to the extension of simile and metaphor. We have come to apply it to all specific figures in Donne and other metaphysicals when their use is happy as well as unfortunate, though perhaps the consummate specimen of conceit may not be determined.[3] Approximate illustrations are legion.

The following definition of the Elizabethan conceit suits equally its seventeenth-century metaphysical modification. It is *"the elaboration of a verbal or an imaginative figure, or the substitution of a logical for an imaginative figure, with so considerable a use of an intellectual process as to take precedence, at least for the moment, of the normal poetic process."*[4] The key words are "elaboration," "substitution," "logical," "intellectual process"—all of which point up the nature of metaphysical verse. Although the Elizabethan and his metaphysical descendant had traits in common, there is some difference of mind that distinguishes the balloonings, in the inflated sixteenth century,[5] from the firmer "phenomenon" of the seventeenth-century conceit.[6] The latter was first considered by Bacon and Jonson as a vehicle for thought itself, then applied to the farfetched image, and finally to Donne and his school. Such almost Augustan judges deprecated an over-refinement of thought; later critics called it "fantastic." Although the intellectual element appears to interfere with the normal poetic process, the conceit can still remain musical, as often enough in the case of Donne's "interpenetration of lyric feeling and intellectual activity."[7] Eliot likewise weaves these two functions with extraordinary skill. Both poets illustrate the desirable use of the logical, the third of Raymond M. Alden's three categories of conceit.[8] In metaphysical poetry the verbal conceit occurs least frequently. Furthermore, when a conceit is also exceptionally lyrical, the imaginative and logical types are difficult to distinguish, as with Donne. For instance, the celebrated metaphysical image of the compass is used as an example of the imaginative order.[6] If the shadow in Donne's "A Lecture upon the Shadow" can be regarded as a protracted imaginative conceit, it serves as well for the logical-metaphysical type.[6] Utilizing scholastic logic for his own purposes, Donne was largely responsible for developing the imaginative into the metaphysical conceit.[9]

We must look for this ingenious and rationalizing device also in our modern metaphysicals who are heirs to Donne's method.[6] In the seventeenth century this type of image was bold, startling, or shocking when carried to eccentric lengths. Its nature grew strange and twisted only if the poet chopped logic or was hounded to compete with his fellows. At such times the conceit was liable to become oversophisticated, through thin-spun intellectuality or an exacting metaphysical idea. These are among the common causes of obscurity in the work of recent poets also. But when successful the condensed metaphor "often has an explosive force, even before its logical implications are realized, which makes it particularly powerful and brilliant."[10]

It is the figurative device by which the conflict in metaphysical poetry is projected. The extended conceit or series of conceits, related by the theme, conveys an ambidextrous meaning. This dual quality, which William Empson studies in his *Seven Types of Ambiguity,* lends a unique strength to metaphysical poetry, provided the obscurity is not the result of vagueness. The seventeenth-century conceit has the power, in his opinion, "to diffuse the interest back on to a whole body of experience, whose parts are supposed eventually reconcilable with one another";[11] thus logically knotting a metaphysical poem. Empson draws his examples of ambiguities in imagery chiefly from Elizabethan poets; also quite naturally from the Jacobean metaphysicals and moderns like Hopkins and Eliot. The Elizabethans had a rich tradition for the art of the conceit.[12] But they overworked or watered the image and so lost the vivid exactitude of earlier and later conceits. Their "besetting sin" became "the tendency to digress upon the comparison. This fault was to be corrected by the next generation. The 'metaphysical' poets regarded the simile as a useful, not as an ornamental, device; and the conceits of their poetry were due to under-emphasis" rather than to fanciful efforts.[13] Donne undertook to discipline vagueness and to experiment with stricter metaphor. Turning his look from the attractions of nature to the inscape, he found devious corridors of psychology to explore; turning his thoughts to books and living science, he discovered the uses of astronomy and ballistics. His conceits became subject to actuality and idea, and their active contradictions. His perception of emotional experience sought relevant analogies in his rich and powerful mind; and thus he rejected the "anonymous" Elizabethan simile for figures more personal, downright, and at the same time more speculative.

By "the trial of conceits, the art of comparison was worked into the language."[14] The Elizabethan accent on the sensuous image gave way to Jacobean and Caroline sharpness and precision. For example, Marvell is "extremely suggestive, but by a quick succession of individually sharp images rather than by an intuitive fusion of dissimilars":[15] a series of metaphors strung like faceted crystals on a tough argument. The moderns, instead, play a rapid run of associations whose notes are clean enough but whose total effect depends on the after-meeting of tonal memories. As different as these methods may seem, they realize similar results. In the process, they both create what is called the radical image.[16] This is an adroit comparison of two incongruent metaphoric terms, the minor term having a low imaginative temperature, while the major term is at white heat. "The image stands, at last, in strong contrast to mere exuberance of phrase."[17] Where the conceit is found appropriate beyond the initial surprise and where the tension of the opposed elements is kept constant, the two factors maintain a just and legitimate relationship. As in the affinity between anode and cathode, the balanced forces of the image create the current. Marvell's "a green Thought in a green Shade,"[18] Donne's "her body thought,"[19] Crashaw's "free Eternity, submit to yeares,"[20] illustrate the fusion that will not allow the elements to part.

On the other hand, where opposite elements in a metaphor are not suitably associated, we get a startling but absurd conceit. Notorious examples of failure are Marvell's antipodes in shoes,[21] Dryden's weeping pimple,[22] and Crashaw's walking baths.[23] The nature of the material in a conceit is important, not as subject matter but for the companionability of its parts. "These must be such that they can enter into a solid union and, at the same time maintain their separate and warring identity. . . . It is no association of things on account of a similarity due to an accident . . . but of things that, though hostile, in reality cry out for association with each other."[24] The paradox inherent in the metaphysical apprehension of emotion is most nearly expressed by the conceit, which is a highly conditional type of image. Because of its very "difficulty and retarded communication it energizes the mind to a higher and tenser level" and prepares it,[25] by such psychological habits, to expand a word and an image into a whole system of concepts or of feelings. Eliot achieves this by the "word" passage in "Ash Wednesday." The conceit, cerebrally and structurally essential to the poem, fails only when after exacting attention it cancels the reader's imaginative sympathy instead of exciting it. "If it does not explode with a first reading, it is extremely durable."[26]

It often happens that the significance of a conceit is not apparent at once or even before the termination of a passage, when the sudden resolution of a suspended meaning transfigures the whole. This is so in "The Waste Land" where a section with its imagery may be related to the entirety and cannot readily be realized alone. Like the individual elements in a single seventeenth-century conceit, the parts in a modern poem may undergo friction that presumably gives off a sudden light. The discrete and associational images in a whole contemporary poem may comprise what amounts to one conceit of mood or situation—a sort of expanded emotional conceit of the complete poem. Moreover, individual images are scattered throughout the poem, itself an organic metaphor. This is fairly obvious in MacLeish's "You, Andrew Marvell," where the lack of punctuation emphasizes the totality of impression. The image may be either expansively suggestive as with Eliot; or as with Donne progressively persuasive by logical steps and variations that lead us through the proposition. With argumentation and paradox somewhat differently used but based essentially on the same principle, both poets often attain a conclusion dramatically reversing the initial idea or suggesting further problems. Thus the conceit is the particular instrument developed at significant foci of literary history. At the midpoint of each focus and at the nucleus of the conceit is conflict.

Conflict is the pulse of most metaphysical poetry in its content, method, and mood. Contrasts may involve contradictory ideas; juxtaposed ideas and emotions; erudite language and common phraseology; ideal vision and irony; past allusions and present realities. "The relation . . . is one of a confessed conflict rather than confused harmony."[27] In metaphysical verse Bellerophon yokes together Pegasus and a draft horse without seeming incongruity. When Eliot describes the soul as a crab at odds with its direction, or Donne fixes two people in love to the pivot of a compass, we have the typically metaphysical comparison (simultaneously a contrast) of an object with an abstraction. Realistic or scientific terms heighten the contrast, and the arrangement may be either logical or symbolic.

The paradox, in which conflicting implications compete in one figure, is appropriate for the analytic treatment of emotions and mental processes. It is a method essentially modern in attitude and psychological skill, but it is related to the seventeenth-century penchant for ratiocination. Few arguments of interest or value escape the metaphysician in verse. The poet forestalls dissent and the exceptions his opponent might take. Donne cavils until the reader is disarmed. Eliot's Prufrock anticipates ridicule by indulging in self-ridicule. Argument and dialectic presuppose conflict. The metaphysical poet then manipulates the conceit to liken dissimilarities and resolve discrepancy. He eyes a given question from all sides, justifies each aspect, and runs ahead of his ideas that no truth may be neglected. A Donnian mind will often take notes on each phase of his object and incorporate them into the poem. Truth is a multiple affair. This procedure has been characterized as mere casuistry and Donne charged with playing the mental game of the Jesuits who trained him in his youth and the scholastics whose proclivities he inherited. True, as far as it goes. But a Donne poem, though it may seem uncompromising and straitened in its several propositions, is really an exercise in liberal thought—conceived and realized with a wonderful balancing of conflicts. "The chain of passionate reasoning which links the first and last lines of so many of Donne's lyrics is itself a striking exemplar of design."[28] A syllogistic relation extends from image to image and connects stanzas as well as thoughts. Divided against itself in a civil war, thought arrives at a temporary armistice not a solution. There is a kind of justice in the cancellation of terms. "Devotion and cynicism, spirituality and license, mysticism and worldliness, morality and coarse wit, perfect taste and gross filth,"[29] are contradictions inherent in seventeenth-century adversity and our own. Such physical and spiritual coördinates presume habits of difficulty and verbal conflicts.

Both Donne and Eliot are thematically complex but compress

various levels of parallels and contrasts into a sum of experience. The effect may be that of "hallucination, but in the total context of the poem the deeper relationships are revealed."[30] If the poem apparently contradicts itself through a series of positions, their final effect settles the disturbance without always releasing an answer. "They represent dramatized instances of . . . the fundamental paradox of the theme."[31] The metaphysical poet approximates the synthesis of past and present, the universal and the regional, and so arranges the dissonant notes of experience. Emily Dickinson was expert at reconciling the perennial and the immediate, the local instance with the universal occasion. One finds the Fugitive group accomplished in expressing ironically the honest "shock of these discordant associations,"[32] and their poems functionally suited to the uniting of complexities. The operation of this sensibility, the metaphysical mechanism, can ingest all diversity, although digesting it is another matter. Eliot contends that seventeenth-century poets, before the powerful influences of Milton and Dryden, could be "simple, artificial, difficult or fantastic," but after them "a dissociation of sensibility set in, from which we have never recovered";[33] an opinion disputed by his own practice. He says, indeed, of our civilization that it

comprehends great variety and complexity, and this variety and complexity, playing upon a refined sensibility, must produce various and complex results. The poet must become more and more comprehensive, more allusive, more indirect, in order to force, to dislocate if necessary, language into his meaning. . . . Hence we get something which looks very much like the conceit—we get, in fact, a method curiously similar to that of the "metaphysical poets," similar also in its use of obscure words and of simple phrasing.[34]

Reassociation of sensibilities with the shuttle of the paradox is Donne's method revived. This two-directional operation of ironic conflict is the very rhythm of the metaphysical body. The poet strives to conceptualize his sensations and materialize his concepts. The arduousness of the task exercises the synesthetic faculty, the transmuting efficiency of metaphor and vocabulary, and the skill of fusing sensation with meaning. These abilities are related to the ambiguous method. Ambiguity can be seen as a confusion or wavering, or as a vivid consciousness of contending simultaneous meanings. If we are to accept Empson's adroit analysis of ambiguity, it is found everywhere and it works "among the very roots of poetry."[35] But Empson shows with impressive conviction that the metaphysicals are masters of ambiguity. When successfully realized it should give "a general sense of compacted intellectual wealth, of an elaborate balance of variously associated feeling."[36]

Ambiguities include the simple pun, certain types of metaphor, a seesaw syntax that may hinge on the fulcrum of punctuation, synesthesia, and conflicts of meanings. Donne's "A Hymn to God the Father" is a play on his own name; Herbert's "Pilgrimage" exemplifies pun, allegory, and emotional contrast all in one. Juxtaposition of intensity with an understated verbal style is notable in certain Elizabethans, in Hopkins, Dickinson, Eliot, Ransom, and like poets. For Empson "the pleasure in style is continually to be explained by just such a releasing and knotted duality,"[37] where significant feeling sharpened by oblique style projects both. Ambiguity of two or more meanings inheres in the very struggle of several motifs coming to expression. Aside from specific instances of verbal and syntactical ambiguity, Empson feels that seventeenth-century thinking is ambiguous because it has "a true sense of the strangeness of the mind's world . . . because it draws its strength from a primitive system of ideas in which the uniting of opposites . . . is of peculiar importance."[38] Crashaw, Herbert, Donne, and Hopkins (as in "The Windhover") are among those who present that indecision not with weakness but with power and passion through "successive fireworks of contradiction, and a mind jumping like a flea."[39] Acceptable ambiguity results from tension, condensation, "paradox to imply a larger truth";[40] but it must be differentiated from ambiguity "without proper occasion,"[41] against which the poet should guard.

Sometimes the ambiguous method edges an individual figure. Sometimes it sets up a series of meaningful contiguities.[42] Here the drama results from the dropping of connectives: the image flashes stand alone. This technique is related to cinematic cutting that also lends the flashback to the extreme associationists. The surrealist film, a dream piece like Jean Cocteau's *Le Sang d'un Poète,* uses the Eliot-Pound contrivance of associational tags. This is legitimate only if the subject, "familiar and comprehensible to the public, has for the poet certain modifications, overtones, outside references, or implicit contradictions, which turn it into a far more intricate subject" than it seemed at first.[43] The technique of ambiguity and association was familiar to the French symbolists. "In France it is at least as old as Arthur Rimbaud. Mr. Pound got it in France,"[44] Mr. Eliot got it from Mr. Pound as well as directly from the symbolists and from Donne, whose syntax was telescopic though his associative process was boldly argumentative. There are Crashaw's "daring transpositions of images which, while looking back to Shakespeare, look forward to the Symbolists" and other moderns.[45] Conflict is stressed and fusion accomplished by "word-auras" in Shakespeare, by the analytical method preceding synthesis in the metaphysicals, and by the "subtler overtones of the Symbolists (. . . the Symbolists at moments approximate to the Metaphysicals and the wheel comes full circle)."[46]

Ultimately it matters little whether one call this process fusion of contrasts, paradox and parallelism, juxtaposition, or association. The effect is much the same, the means vary according to the writer. The older metaphysicals retain the terms of contrasting relationships, our moderns—though their discrete images are exact—often omit the links. Both succeed in setting the extraordinary against the familiar and in disturbing the spirit by casual methods. The homely intimate phrase is lifted into the company of stateliness, and magnificence will stoop easily to the common experience. Such metaphysical techniques have afforded the more powerful poet an idiom in strong contrast to any prevailing tendency toward either lushness or photogenic realism. The result, among poets of the seventeenth century, the symbolists, and the modern metaphysicals, has been a new demanding brilliance.

One of the inevitable characteristics of the metaphysical method is condensation. By the apt choice of contrasts description is abbreviated, narration quickened, and analysis strengthened. By thus concentrating the structure and achieving an alliance of opposites we have "the result of intensifying both."[47] Like Herbert in a single poem, Hopkins sums up the worldly combat of the soul in this passage, one among many such:

As a dare-gale skylark in a dull cage
  Man's mounting spirit in his bone-house, mean house, dwells—
  That bird beyond the remembering his free fells;
This in drudgery, day-labouring-out life's age.

     .   .   .   .   .

Man's spirit will be flesh-bound when found at best,
But uncumbered: meadow-down is not distressed
  For a rainbow footing it nor he for his bones risen.[48]

In the "Sweeney" quatrains Eliot brings beauty and the beast together in one image, and a revelatory scene centers the mystery of the past in a positive and sordid moment of the present.

     The person in the Spanish cape
     Tries to sit on Sweeney's knees

        .   .   .   .   .

     The nightingales are singing near
     The Convent of the Sacred Heart,
     And sang within the bloody wood
     When Agamemnon cried aloud . . .[49]

This compression is the obverse of the comprehensive, the end product of allusiveness, and the intellectual symbol of the metaphysical. In the meeting of opposites we feel frequently the serious and ironic at one stroke, the lush and the commonplace tone. "Such a balance, which may not have eixsted since the seventeenth century, is one of the present needs."[50] The union of colloquial and rhetorical has been excitingly performed by Donne, Dickinson, Hopkins, and now by Auden and Eliot and their better followers. The accusation of a consequently incoherent style is in general unwarranted. The total effect of Eliot's procedure is undulant. Accomplished in lyricism as well as realism, he sees the need for arranging what is traditionally beautiful as a foil for sharp modernities. We sense the agitation of such antithesis present in the slight "Prufrock" and deeply in "The Waste Land." The consonance of the hectic or dry manner with sinuosity rounds out the latter as it points up the former. Similarly, the sophisticated seventeeth-century poets profited by the ebbing of Elizabethan lyricism and exploited its charm against a harsh counterpart.

Not only are two styles compacted, but also the "heterogeneity of the distinguishable impulses."[51] The poets in question dissect emotion for its conflicting colors and then reunite them without blurring. Johnson was unjust when he called the metaphysicals "beholders" of human nature not "partakers," when he denied them sublimity because they were particular and not general. That their methods could calibrate the spectrum of experience and also fuse it implies almost too much sensibility, not too little. By the seventeenth-century process and its modern variations, a "conjunction of feelings" is achieved which "though superficially opposed,—as squalor, for example, is opposed to grandeur—yet tend as they develop to change places and even to unite."[52] This is exactly what happens in Donne's less cynical amorous poems, where the physical and incorporeal aspects of love change places or are twisted together as the eyebeams of Donne and his beloved in "The Extasie." The complex attitudes of this poetry recognize the basic truth of human and spiritual contrarieties.

Two styles, two sensations, two moods, two thoughts, and the worst and best of both worlds are juxtaposed and joined. "Metaphysical poetry is born where the points of two cones coincide: one cone represents the real world and the other the metaphysical world, both contracted to a tiny circle or a point. Thus the images and the meanings give the sense of looking two ways."[53] All the metaphysicals knew something of this dualism, though their temperaments and styles differed. Crashaw, Catholic and mystic, and the pantheist Vaughan both felt the clash of irreconcilables. Vaughan was aware of the "actual and possible, the misery of earth and the glory of God."[54] Not only verse poets but prose

poets like Bishop Andrewes, Donne the preacher, and Sir Thomas
Browne shared this peculiar talent for opposites, for looking
before and after, and appraising heaven and earth. "It meant the
capacity to live in divided and distinguished worlds, and to
pass freely to and fro between one and another . . . [since] something of the peculiar quality of the 'metaphysical' mind is due
to this fact of its not being *finally committed* to any one world."[55]
It is capable of telescoping imaginative space by quick analogies
and by creating a correspondence between the "equipollent"
worlds in a manner that is beyond the usual poetic process.

There is corroboration in Francis Meynell's *The Best of Both
Worlds*, devoted to poems by Marvell and Vaughan. The two-
world conflict is vivid also in the person of Hopkins, whose
austere spiritual endeavor would neither yield to nor vanquish
his "natural sensuous delight."[56] Life and God are one:

> There lives the dearest freshness deep down things;
> And though the last lights off the black West went
> Oh, morning, at the brown brink eastward, springs—
> Because the Holy Ghost over the bent
> World broods with warm breast and with ah! bright wings.[57]

In Eliot the contention if muted is palpably felt: the strain, the
expectancy. We find that ambivalence powerfully theatered in the
mixed modes of the natural and supernatural worlds of *The
Family Reunion*. There the chief protagonist senses his own
dualism; and the poet plays understatement against currents of
turbulent feeling. The word "tends" is significant:

> I believe the moment of birth
> Is when we have knowledge of death
> . . . .
> Everything tends towards reconciliation
> As the stone falls, as the tree falls.[58]

If strange consonances are possible in life and felt in the aura
of the unknown, in poetry they can be made to confront one
another in a single experience of despair and yearning, of the
sensuous and the otherworldly. If there is often no solution

suggested, not to say established, in the real and cosmic problems of metaphysical verse, there is a kind of perverse condition of relief in the very expression of conflict and the adumbration of synthesis. The argument that exposes the situation even symbolically, the fertile doubt, and the irony enlighten rather than inhibit. Without solving they begin to heal the dichotomy. It is as new as the psychoanalytic couch and as old as the confessional box. The truth is in the process of discovery, not in the arrival but the passage. Therein lie the excitement and the paradoxical resolution.

4

WIT AND THE OBJECTIVE EQUIVALENT

THE CONCEIT is only one of several elements that turn about the centrifugal conflict in metaphysical poetry. Another is wit, whose home is the intellect for all its excursions into the material world. Since one of their principal objects is to heighten emotion by evoking its intellectual equivalent, the metaphysicals instead of laughter employ wit, which is a smile of the mind, a criticism of life conveyed in corrective irony. It is this balance of profound intention against a comic spirit of a high order which results in their "witty" prestidigitation. Confused in common usage, even critically wit does not come easy as an epithet for serious metaphysical poetry. Connotations have altered since the sixteenth and seventeenth centuries. Yet unless we can invent a new word with all the old weight and worth, we must be content with its original significance. This term, like conceit, is revived not because of verbal poverty but because of the metaphysical renewal.

Wit, then, is "seriousness combined with levity," a "tough reasonableness beneath a slight lyric grace" so characteristic of Marvell, and so neatly exhibited in "To his Coy Mistress." Shakespeare gave the effect of wit on a grand scale by the juxtaposition of a serious scene with a light one, or by combining the opposite implications of death and humor in such scenes as the gravediggers'. Hamlet himself is walking irony. In reduced terms Eliot's "The *Boston Evening Transcript*" and Ransom's "Captain Carpenter" employ wit to conspicuous advantage. Donne runs its whole gamut.

Especially hospitable to its subtleties are versions of satire, irony, and surprise. Satire as a form and irony as an effect were evident in seventeenth-century verse and are again today. Before the age of satire, sporadic satirists, ranging from the Elizabethans to Dryden and including Donne, Hall, Marvell, Oldham, confirmed the critical character of a poetry and a society in revolt. Moreover, the whole fabric of seventeenth-century verse is shot through with irony. Then and now wit in its various forms serves as a corrective. The very nature of conflict engenders wit, and it is no wonder that its effects, implemented by the conceit, should appear insistently in literary periods marked by a searchingly critical and rebellious attitude.

Intellectual surprise is one of wit's fine weapons shocking sensibility to attention. It is a sort of *non sequitur* that persuasively demonstrates its reasonableness. Anticipated by Donne and Herbert and Marvell, Eliot evokes surprise by the unexpected explosion of a last line, or within the poem by a sudden change of mood or the reversal of a proposed idea. By oddly associated nuances and verbal contrasts he catches the ear and the mind. Sometimes "this effect of surprise is made partly by the equally sudden shift in syntax"[1] which is one of Empson's seven ambiguities and often affected by Donne. Eliot insists on the element of "surprise which Poe considered of the highest importance, and also the restraint and quietness of tone which make the surprise possible. And in the verses of Marvell . . . there is the making the familiar strange, and the strange familiar, which Coleridge attributed to good poetry."[2]

There has been much critical effort to describe the blend called wit. Thomas Hobbes noticed fancy and judgment working together, Dryden "coolness and discretion" playing upon fancy.[3] For Johnson wit was still a grave matter but "less a spirit animating the whole of a serious composition, than the occasional dignifying and embellishment of it."[4] Though Cowley had a good sense of its function, closer to that of Donne and Carew, his practice tended to become a dry exercise. Thus from Donne to Johnson, the scope of wit narrowed until it was related to the single epigrammatic moment, rather than to the balance of intellectual and emotional elements in extended statement. Recently the meaning of wit has again been expanded. In the opinion of E. M. W. Tillyard,[5] wit may be seen as a form of the oblique, an aspect of ambiguity. Since plot constitutes the chief obliquity among this critic's categories, he stresses the satisfaction derived not only from the minor manifestations of wit in Marvell's "Mistress" but also from the tripartite plot of the poem, so to speak. There the poet's fine sense of balance controls the alternating emotions. This two-directional play of wit holds one kind of emotional tension in abeyance while the other has an opportunity to work its intent. The opening and closing passages of seduction in Marvell's poem relieve the strain of the time passage. Conversely, the playful elements would scatter as inconsequential if the haunting expectancy of death did not preserve their usefulness. That is wit at its best.

Donne's wit is not always so active, but it is more often a potential force in the background. No modernist more than Ransom inherits the Cavalier aspect of Donne's wit, considerably modified by Eliot's and his own originality. The "witty texture" shows in his "Equilibrists," "Our Two Worthies," and "Spectral Lovers," according to Williamson. I have cited "Captain Carpenter" as a further example of ironic warp working through the woof of seriousness. The macabre adds to his fantastic effects where "wit has become a poetic attitude."[6] The evocative wit of Crane, MacLeish, and Eliot—influenced by such symbolists as Jules Laforgue and Tristan Corbière—shows its diversity. Emily Dickinson invokes wit everywhere, sometimes too coyly, but more often successfully directing its "critical function upon the emotions,"[7] a telling function of the metaphysical attitude to experience.

The ironic interpretation of life is required of these poets by circumstance as well as by temperament. "Humor is the life of their poetry; wit is its language."[8] Humor is not quite the word for the seventeenth-century men, though it played wryly through their passion for life and was the light of Cavalier poetry. But the temperature of their existence toughened the humor to steely wit. And what about the mystical poets: Crashaw, Vaughan,

King, Traherne? With them wit, as also with Herbert, took the form of intense conflict between the love of earthly existence and the haunting attraction of the other world. It was at once a joyous and a painful ecstasy. Humor can be artless and seriousness naïve, but not true wit. The wit of the eighteenth century is frequently unsophisticated and gauche when used by someone less than a Pope or a Matthew Prior. The serious sallies of the nineteenth century could often be both tedious and bathetic. But the seventeenth-century poets escaped triteness by their habitual wit. Of course, they were guilty of ridiculous lapses of taste: Crashaw and Cowley and Cleveland afford startling instances. If they were sometimes silly, they were seldom boring.

For the poetry of our time too, humor in its wider meaning is used by Laura Riding and Robert Graves as an alternative epithet to wit.[9] Rather than full self-pity or emotional collapse, a commonsensical wittiness shot with pain is the sign of our generation. Its humor and heart do a mutual somersault. Its poet manages an intellectual derision forced on himself and his reader to steady both in a balancing act between despair and survival. Eliot and Edith Sitwell and Ransom, they say, make jokes against the romantic and the classic, against the standard and the sentimental, against our civilization and themselves too. It is all commonplace and therefore all the stuff of poetry. Riding and Graves come close to the psychological, the social source of wit today. They contend that no generation before theirs had turned its irony on itself in the same way. But the poet hits at society as well. This twofold action of wit was certainly not unknown to the seventeenth century. When Donne banters his mistresses, he does not spare himself.[10] Suckling laughs at his own foibles. And so the modern poet often appears the jester taunting audience and himself, but in earnest beneath his trifling. The apparently noncommittal attitude is an objective approach; it is also a passionate self-consciousness. The seventeenth-century dilemma and our own occasioned a common dualism.

For Eliot wit has come to represent "the essence of that strange period of poetry which ends with the Martyrdom and the Exile, and is as much a part of that period's religious intensity as of its levity. . . . 'Wit' stands for a kind of balance and proportion of intellectual and emotional values,"[11] so that "holy mirth" or "frivolous ingenuity" or the ironic play of "humor" is "not incompatible with the poet's seriousness, nor with his sincerity. . . . It is important to distinguish between mere *vers de société* and this poetry with its more profound repercussions."[12] The "imperturbable tact" of wit can entertain the strangest company without being disconcerted. At the heart of the seventeenth century it included the grandiloquence inherited from the Elizabethans and the caustic common sense of a Butler. Variously hospitable to these qualities were Milton the magniloquent and Dryden "the great master of contempt." Both aspects occur in Marvell's "Horatian Ode" and Cowley's Anacreontics. Popularly wit is dissociated from Puritan writers like Milton and the political Marvell. But metaphysical wit is another matter, though it may contain certain ingredients commonly expected of ordinary wit: mirth, sarcasm, surprise, even the humble pun. In the profound sense, however, wit should expose the irony implicit in thought and passion rather than in surface sound and form.[13] With the true metaphysicals, wit includes a counterpart not so much of grandeur as imaginative seriousness.

Eliot cites, among others, Catullus, Ovid, Propertius, Jonson, La Fontaine, Gautier, Baudelaire, and Laforgue as possessing wit: that crackling "quality of a sophisticated literature."[14] Certainly many of the Jacobean, Caroline, and Restoration poets belong to sophisticated literature, as well as the symbolists to whom Eliot is much indebted. He feels their wit is actually a "firm grasp of human experience, which . . . cynical perhaps but untired . . . leads toward, and is only completed by, the religious comprehension";[15] whereas there has been critical accusation of decadence against these groups. But modern ironic poets respond to the elusive virtues of the equilibrist wit: its basic sense of reason and its urbane poise can be of an intense and and imaginative order. "The wit is not only combined with, but fused into, the imagination. . . . In fact, this alliance of levity

and seriousness (by which the seriousness is intensified) is a
characteristic of the sort of wit we are trying to identify."[16] We
see the passion with which Donne advances his witty arguments,
a development beyond Elizabethan ornamentation. Where it was
an embellishment before him in lyrical verse or an extraneous
cleverness after him, in his time wit was meant functionally "to
illustrate abstractions by a surprising and concrete example. . . .
In the eighteenth century there was wit enough, but little inspiration. In the nineteenth, plenty of inspiration, but little wit. Never
since the seventeenth have the two been combined in that surprising union."[17]

Wit is not erudition alone or a cynical outlook on life; nor is it
a mere technique of language and structure. It implies also an
inspired imagination and "a constant inspection and criticism of
experience."[18] Examples come from unexpected quarters in the
metaphysical period. The fact that the Spenserians, interminable
writers of epic and homily, offer offside plays of wit confirms its
tradition. We see its operation in Crashaw's religious poetry as
well as in Carew's Cavalier pieces. Nor is it limited to poetry.
In the prose of Bishop Andrewes (beloved of Eliot), the worthy
Thomas Fuller, the character-writers Earle and Overbury, and
above all the wonderful incongruities of Dr. Browne, wit is constantly at work. We see this formula in Hamlet's puns, in Marvell's
and Donne's love poems. Today it is to be found in Pound from
his quatrains and fugitive pieces to his cantos; in Eliot from "The
Hippopotamus" to his *Four Quartets* and *The Cocktail Party;*
from the mystic simplicities of Anna Branch to the complex passions of Muriel Rukeyser.

Wherever the metaphysical mind is operative it enlarges the
borders of experience to include at once the concept and the fact,
man and God, the flower and the book, the past event and the
future chance. Wit gives these disparate elements a kind of compatibility through mutual reference. For this the method of allusiveness is requisite. Thus as Sweeney hears the nightingales,
Agamemnon dies while they sing. Such use of allusion foreshortens

time. Glory and disgrace, the coarse and the sensitive, the casual-ness of nature and the acuities of man, are juxtaposed. Allusive-ness performs a double function: revelation of conflicting human experience and relation of that conflict to conceptual form. The historical sense illustrated by the cited example belongs to more than one order of allusiveness. The poet may make cross refer-ences to any of the various senses as they are aware of place and time, and the relation between time and space. The last or fourth dimension appears to be the most metaphysical in character, but this poetry can give such import to any of the allusions, singly or in pairs; or it can effect the interpenetration of them all.

Indirection is an attribute of the allusive method. Yet its instru-ments may be precise, as with Donne. His allusions to God, to science, and to scholastic concepts are made in very exact terms. The symbolists, whose determination to comprehend all experi-ence is like Donne's and whose language resembles his in im-mediacy of idiom, are allusive by implication. Their obliquity, following modern psychological trends, is what I. A. Richards might call "the unconscious indirect method."[19] They often pre-sent automatic associations, and their feelings take a circuitous route. But the symbolist attempt to express such associations was very conscious. It is not easy to communicate the complexities of psychological poetry, and many readers lose their way. In spite of this separation between poet and public, it is likely that

poets will become not less but more allusive, that their work will de-pend more and more not only upon other poetry but upon all manner of special fields of familiarity. Many of the finest and most widely significant experiences, and those therefore most suitable for poetry, come nowadays, for example, through reading pieces of advanced research. There is nothing new in this, of course, nothing that was not happening when Donne wrote.[20]

Auden, a social poet with metaphysical and religious phases, grounds a vast number of his allusions upon his wide knowledge of psychology, sociology, and economics. The conditions that produced a modern metaphysical age are responsible for Eliot's allusions, learned and emotional, whose value for the quickened sensibility is in their interactions and "unified response." "Allusion in Mr. Eliot's hands is a technical device for compression. . . . The truth is that very much of the best poetry is necessarily ambiguous in its immediate effect."[21]

Obscurity is at times the natural result of allusion conveyed deviously, as it is the effect of the ambiguous method demanded by the poetry of conflict. Ambiguity refers chiefly to structure and meaning; allusiveness rather to subject matter and the sense experience allocated in the province of time. Both can be sources of obscurity. When Donne was intricate his concentrated syntax as well as his many philosophical and factual allusions were the occasion. The simple mass of allusions arbitrarily not emotionally associated account for much of Pound's abstruseness, while Eliot's comes from the subtlety of his unlinked references. Though he expounds the need of a traditional knowledge, Eliot is not recondite for obscurity's sake, but for the enriching values attendant on such references. Valid obscurity, which is never the result of deliberate or fashionable mystification, is a concomitant of elliptical imagery and construction, of a wealth of ideas and material in a complex age. Eliot's obscurity "can be referred to his technique, but his technique in turn can be referred to his subject-matter, that is to Eliot's own world and so to Eliot himself."[22] The metaphysical esthetic comprises configuration of thought, economy of expression, the unifying function of wit, and allusiveness of objective and subjective matter—all of which are demanded by the poet in an age of social and psychological dilemmas.

The poet himself is often the source of the difficulty of modern verse. But the source is fed by the stormy climate of the times. Many contend that this verse neglects its public duty by describing, in an almost private language, only the secret places of the poet's multiple consciousness. Involved here is the learned and allusive method of the Pound-Eliot-MacLeish school, which in turn implies aristocratic past poetry such as Donne's. A kind of compromise was evolved by the Americanizing Auden group. Even here obscurity is often present, however much Auden concerns himself with public matters. Stephen Spender, quietly and unaffectedly left of center, has been simplest and least obscure; but though a fine and moving poet he lacks Auden's versatility. Hence there is sometimes an alternative between variety and the simple virtue of straight speaking. The choice between "private faces in public places" and "public faces in private places" is not easy.[23] It is not easy in an age of intense specialization and enormous upheavals in the pure and social sciences, as well as in human conduct. Dislocations of public life and knowledge seem to be conditions under which metaphysical poetry ripens. By this very token, it tends to become involuted and personal. We find therefore a paradox matched only by the observable fact that the metaphysical poet is both subjective and objective, both an individualist and a partaker of world-wide concerns.

In 1940 Peter Monro Jack attempted to vindicate the modern poet's signal place in general affairs, his privacy touching public life at many points.

Spender broadcasts his poems and they are printed in a radio magazine. Cummings, that "isolated" poet, has his poems recorded on a gramophone. W. H. Auden, Alfred Kreymborg, William Carlos Williams and Malcolm Cowley filled the Great Hall of Cooper Union. . . . MacLeish made a popular success of his radio plays. . . . Eliot's poetic play, "Murder In The Cathedral," played to packed houses in London and New York. His "The Waste Land," even when imperfectly understood, is recognized as an event wherever a book is read. . . . Yeats was made a Senator because of his eminence as a poet. Ezra Pound may yet perhaps influence our ideas on the use and usury of money. Auden's royalties from the sale of his poem "Spain" went for medical aid during that country's civil war; he was commissioned by his publishers to journey to China and write what he saw in sonnet or stanza form. Spender . . . has fought with rhyme and reason and realism against fascism in Spain. MacLeish collaborates with the photography of Margaret Bourke-White and others in making a "sound-track" of the actualities of the American land. He is a scholar and a lawyer, but it is mainly because he is a poet that he now directs the Library of Congress.[24]

However difficult or individual, the seventeenth-century poet was likewise embroiled in the concerns of his age. The Great Rebellion, the bloodless revolution, the wars between churches and between Royalists and Roundheads, the contest of old and new sciences, all indicated the fury of the times. A great agitation upset private lives and attitudes. To be sure, a poet expressing such turbulence is often driven in on himself to find resources and restoration. But this happens after he has been enlisted physically or emotionally in struggles of very general and devastating proportions.

The problem of obscurity, and of the poetic means to deal effectively with the difficult content of a period, is controversial but not new. We have no monopoly on it. Dante contrived philosophically troublesome images and innumerable allusions; Shakespeare was rich in sinuosities of construction and material; Blake's ambiguities belong to idea and vision. If we accept the metaphysical imagination as a special unifying mechanism, we should be tolerant of a certain necessary obscurity.[25] This type, a refinement of the highest order of imagination,[26] has made use of "ironical devices, wrenched rhythms, abrupt transitions, apparent discords, non-decorative metaphors, deficiency of statement, and when successful has attained its unity only in terms of a total intention."[27] In the microcosm of the conceit, in the processes of wit, by ambiguous syntax and structure, and by the concentration of contrasted allusions, the metaphysical imagination works to objectify ideas and emotions.

And not hovering long in mid-air, it pounces on the tangible to exemplify its concepts and feed its formal passions. In that way its universals make effectual contact with particulars. The correlation between conceptualism and actuality is formulated in the "objective correlative" or equivalent, to use the clearer term. "There has not been in England another poetry quite like the metaphysical, that could translate its profoundest passions into such crisp objective constructs."[28] Its poets "start with feelings, they objectify these imaginatively into external actions."[29] And this act is a firm process of cognition as useful to actualize the theme of God as that of love. Ransom notes, after Grierson, that many seventeenth-century metaphysicals were Roman or Anglo-Catholic, and that this is perhaps no coincidence. "Catholicism is not afraid of particularizing the God, evidently believing that you cannot have 'God in general,' you must have Him in particular if at all."[30] This observation in respect to the Catholic (and by extension here, the metaphysical) imagination, trained to externalize, is borne out by Eliot in practice and opinion.[31] Actually, it is possible that Eliot's native grasp of the immediacy of the supernatural inclined him toward the Catholic state of mind. He feels that the natural and the supernatural life conform.[32] The Catholic passion for rendering the spiritual in concrete terms is seen also in Crashaw and Hopkins. But one must account for the metaphysical Emily Dickinson whose residual New England Puritanism apparently encouraged her natural inclination to objectify the life of the heart and the meanings of heaven.

The definition of the objective correlative fits the requirements of metaphysical verse where abstraction takes a concrete form.

The only way of expressing emotion in the form of art is by finding an "objective correlative"; in other words, a set of objects, a situation, a chain of events which shall be the formula of that *particular* emotion; such that when the external facts, which must terminate in sensory experience, are given, the emotion is immediately evoked.[33]

The seventeenth-century metaphysicals practiced this theory by thinking of one thing in terms of another belonging to an opposed category. "They almost tried to turn ideas into objects, so that they might make them plain; and their minds jumped from the idea to the object . . . with a rapidity hard to follow."[34] Herbert's realistic objectification, sometimes a type of aphoristic wit, is a prime example of the formula. The poet who can externalize emotion and idea is the vehicle of a mobile tradition. For carrying that tradition into the present, the historical sense, perception of time made specific, is most serviceable. A feeling for generic time was acutely developed by seventeenth-century poets: there are few lyrics so imbued with that awareness as Marvell's "Mistress" and King's "Exequy." Our modern metaphysicals, in poems by MacLeish and the Fugitives, for example, offer further striking testimony. Theirs are individual or local variations of the attitude manifested in Eliot's and Pound's more extended recourse to historical facts and past fictions.

The time continuum is implicated in metaphysical methods of compression, contrast, and allusion. It belongs to the conflict of the supernatural with the factual, the then with the now, both here and hereafter. As a specified intention of the time sense, the modern historical sense does double duty: it makes concrete the generalization of time by historical allusion, and it universalizes immediate personal experiences by reference to the large past. The poet is thereby able to extend the actual to immeasurable dimensions, and to bring all the width of historical and suprasensible time to bear intolerably upon a present instance. Even the seventeenth-century poets, to whom time as an abstraction was a more intimate theme than history, used the sense of the past as a criticism of mankind. Herbert deals with Greece and Rome; Marvell and Habington examine the course of history as well as its current application. Only at first glance does it seem "paradoxical that an age holding out such high hopes for the future should . . . look with a longing eye upon the past. . . ."[35] Donne was as troubled by the waning of established ideas and science as he was curious and eager about the new. Men like Bacon, practical enthusiast of the forward view, were exceptional. For the rest, the poets and prose writers (notably Browne) were painfully conscious of the time factor which represented past as well as future. Its connection with death was obvious at a time when plagues and wars were rampant. It was involved in a scientific revolution that gave our planet a precarious place in God's universe and even implied the very end of the earth itself. Donne's anticipatory shroud and the prospect of "the round earth's imagin'd corners," Vaughan's "eternity the other night," and the sound of time at Marvell's back are among innumerable instances relating the time sense to the obsession of death and to the upheavals in man's knowledge.

Today too the sense of the past is "a product of the 'time obsession' which is typical of a whole school of modern literature,"[36] novelists like Proust and Joyce as well as a majority of the poets. The attitude is common:

> Our framework of idea is the cultural cycle, or the awareness of the "pastness" of the past, as in the case of Mr. Archibald MacLeish. The vulgarity of the present and the purity of the past make the framework of Mr. John Crowe Ransom's irony. Even Mr. Jeffers performs a fusion of literary psychology with a fictitious primitivism that places him in the historical consciousness. Although Mr. Ezra Pound's method is a cunning imitation of the pre-historical view that seized past and present naïvely as a whole, the *Cantos* is a monument to the historical mentality. There is none of this explicitly in Donne.[37]

Yet Donne, obsessed by death and the precarious future of the soul, contemplated the body in its relation to the history of the spirit. His preoccupations lived within and beyond the bounds of time. And in his longer poems, like the *Anniversaries,* and in minor instances, like the lyric "I long to talke with some old lover's ghost," he approached the historical sense. It is a projection of the "sense of the age" and a concentration of the sense of time. That this sensibility is shared by the seventeenth century, the symbolist period, and our own, is significant. For Eliot, Baudelaire's importance hinges in part on such awareness. "And a 'sense of one's age' implies some sense of other ages; . . . Baudelaire not only reveals the troubles of his own age and predicts those of the age to come but also foreshadows some issue from these difficulties."[38] Laforgue spoke even more intimately to Eliot's generation, though eventually it was recognized that Baudelaire's sense of the ages was profounder than Laforgue's. Heir of Baudelaire and symbolism, Valéry too is a signal product of our time spirit. His originality interferes not at all with Eliot's large view of how the time spirit incorporates tradition.

Tradition implies the historical sense and that in turn involves

a perception, not only of the pastness of the past, but of its presence; the historical sense compels a man to write not merely with his own generation in his bones, but . . . the whole of the literature of Europe. . . . This historical sense, which is a sense of the timeless as well as of the temporal and of the timeless and of the temporal together, is what makes a writer traditional. And it is at the same time what makes a writer most acutely conscious of his place in time, of his own contemporaneity.[39]

The impact of any age alters the interpretation of past ages, just as every piece of literature alters, if ever so slightly, the comprehension of literature before it. The whole forms a "simultaneous order." It is past periods and previous writers that we know progressively, says Eliot, as the ages accumulate. The awareness of "the conscious present" is a heavier load at each successive step of remembering ages. Each new present must assimilate the past and feel it creatively as if vivid now.

Because the modern thoughtful poet is so deeply imbued with the time spirit, he emphasizes its manifestation as history and makes history one of his main objective correlatives. But he deals just as significantly with the issues of time, and its companion space, without direct reference to the historical. The effect on the reader is the metaphysical *frisson*. MacLeish in "You, Andrew Marvell," renders the sensation of time geographically. Louis MacNeice, in "August," represents the stone face of time as the petrifaction of our fear that we "cannot catch hold of things."[40] The still point which is timelessness needs the duration of time to give it meaning. "Only through time time is conquered" is Eliot's paradoxical expression of an elusive truth.[41] Noteworthy for possessing in our period the keenest sense of time in general, Eliot also capably objectifies it in the historical and mythical past reference. He achieves the "shudder" in such well-known instances as those of the drowned Phoenician sailor, Agamemnon dead under the desecrating nightingales, the seduction scene that carries us back to the eighteenth century, and the echo of Shakespeare's "good night, sweet ladies, good night, good night." The persuasion comes from his sensitiveness both to the sequence of tradition and to the immanence of time as a sensation in the blood. Continuities and contrasts in "The Waste Land," for example, confirm tradition and express our *Zeitgeist*, serving as devices of metaphysical irony in the general context of the human struggle.

Emphasis on the past and the time sense in the abstract is implicit in the whole background and psychology of periods of metaphysical poetry. The scientific and social cataclysms that racked the seventeenth century and convulse the twentieth carry the poet's sensibility stràight into the teeth of time. He is obliged to face the physical and moral implications of history, which is time's child. When the security of man's self—material and spiritual—is challenged, the poet is repeatedly forced to remember death. Since metaphysical poetry by its nature considers concepts of universal and perpetual concern, what is more reasonable than that it should confront time: the be-all and the end-all?

When a poet relates himself to his age and his age to history and history to time, he finds himself diminished to a representative point on the infinite plane. He is no longer a central consideration, but the object that illustrates the general proposition and illustrates it concretely if he is a good poet. The object, or actual experience, is the daily familiar counter representing the imponderable value. Time, historical allusion, and myth used as tangible correlatives test the poet's power to view the affair of life impersonally. Since Eliot is the key figure in our metaphysical period and the most important link to the Donne "school," his words regarding impersonality carry double weight. "One is prepared for art when one has ceased to be interested in one's own emotions and experiences except as material; . . . it is a recognition of the truth that not our feelings, but the patterns which we may make of our feelings, is the centre of value."[42]

Lucretius sublimated his personality in a philosophy to which he joined himself in a greater unity, and Dante's poetry made concrete the system expressing his age. In his way, Eliot externalizes the human problem and the disorderly period in which he lives in such poems as "Gerontion" and "The Waste Land." Even in the personal work of Donne we can see the "Anniversaries" as an attempt to clarify his doubting mind and the transitional temper of his century. By that "passionate act" he transmuted the intimate incidents also of his private lyrics into something very like universal experience. To read Donne is to hear his exact tone and yet to forget him in the scale of his ideas.

Another view of this "Impersonal theory of poetry" resides in the relation of the poem to the poet.[43] The illustration Eliot gives of this relationship is his now familiar one of the catalyst. The poet's personality has matured upon becoming a "finely perfected medium in which special, or very varied, feelings are at liberty to enter into new combinations."[44] An acid, goes the analogy, is formed from a compound of elements in the essential presence of a bit of platinum which is the poet's mind. But the mind, like the platinum reagent in the chemical process, does not show up in the poem nor is it affected in the process any more than is the shred of platinum. It follows then, that

the more perfect the artist, the more completely separate in him will be the man who suffers and the mind which creates; the more perfectly will the mind digest and transmute the passions which are its material. . . . And the poet cannot reach this impersonality . . . unless he lives in what is not merely the present, but the present moment of the past, unless he is conscious, not of what is dead, but of what is already living.[45]

This consciousness, with an awareness of what is alive in the past, is the historical sense: an impersonal faculty. With that cultivated taste for the many fruits of time, the poet will be able to "transmute his personal and private agonies into something rich and strange, something universal and impersonal. . . . The great poet, in writing himself, writes his time."[46]

With its genesis often in something personal, the metaphysical passion becomes objective through technique. Here is perhaps the reason why its expression adapts itself either to the romantic or the classic spirit of poetry. The metaphysical poet, whether prevailingly a romantic or a classicist, is distinguished by his method rather than by his materials or attitude to his materials. Metaphysical poetry is not so much a category as a technique of expression, applicable to special qualities of experience. This technique communicates a kind of sensibility which is receptive to the conjunction of the familiar and the strange—in association or juxtaposition. Either classic or romantic subject matter, treated realistically or ideally, can form the substance of metaphysical poetry.

Indeed, that many of its poets cannot be readily specified as romantic or classical indicates that theirs is a method not confined to any single great order of art. Historically, the important groups of metaphysicals flourished between the romantic and classical movements of the seventeenth century; and later, between the romanticism of the nineteenth century and the neoclassic realism of the twentieth. With its assimilative method, metaphysical verse participates in the aims and attitudes of all. This is true also of its prosody: it possesses romantic-extravagant traits and classical reticence, with highly realistic texture as well as idealistic moods. Without the term "metaphysical," we should be hard put to explain such poets as Crashaw, Vaughan, and Emily Dickinson. From one point of view Crashaw has romantic richness, and Emily Dickinson a classical strain. And what should we call Hopkins? Eliot insists on his own classicism, whereas his yearnings and desperations are romantic. To account for the contradictions and flexibility of Baudelaire's poetic style, we must ultimately "reconcile his classicism . . . with his achievement of a lyrical and romantic utterance carried to its furthest and most nebulous. point of attenuation. Baudeliare's classicism . . . and the attempted classicism of modern poets in general . . . is the alliance of an extreme lyrical suggestiveness and an extreme, even dogmatic, clarity":[47] a hybrid type, since the symbolist school has also been called "a second flood" of romanticism.[48] The strong resemblance between the symbolists and the English metaphysicals is acknowledged. Cleanth Brooks then offers the third term of this syllogism: that metaphysical poetry is also a romantic poetry.[49] This is only a partial truth; in another passage Brooks comes closer to the crux of the matter. "The significant relationship is indicated by the fact that the metaphysical poets and the modernists stand opposed to both the neo-classic and Romantic poets on the issue of metaphor."[50]

The seventeenth-century metaphysicals accepted neither the exuberant lead of certain eminent Elizabethans nor chose to restrict themselves to classical channels in the process of construction by Jonsonians. Yet falling heir to the inspired difficult heritage of the more imaginative Elizabethans, they used it according to their lights, and at the same time betrayed lines leading to the classical apogee. It is a fact that they moved gradually, and in some instances prematurely, toward classicism. Jonson, who was almost a century ahead of his proper milieu (Dryden's age), coached Carew, Suckling, Lovelace, Cleveland, and Marvell in marked classical tendencies. That they were also sons of John Donne is not at all strange, since he likewise evinced what later became Augustan qualities: direct and vigorous speech, satiric honesty, and packed rather than loose Spenserian structure. Advanced French rationalism and classicism influenced English expression, which sometimes lags in literary shifts by a generation or two. If the metaphysical intent was a reaction to Elizabethan romanticism and a shaping toward the Augustan age, it was also an attempt, apart from any literary movement, to devise an inclusive principle of communication.

Eliot likewise departed from the Victorian and the Georgian conventions, to draw freely upon whatever romantic excitement or classical restraint and formality suited his immediate purposes. The result was a beguiling compromise that utilized both older traditions and modernity. This is "a phenomenon not confined to any school, but noticeable most often in the purist classicism, in the seventeenth century 'metaphysicals' and in some modern poetry."[51] In 1926 Eliot claimed that the magazine he was to edit, *The New Criterion*, "illustrated a tendency toward what might be vaguely termed Classicism";[52] a tendency that was directed by the theorist T. E. Hulme and by certain French writers. Among the modern influences on Eliot and his disciples were both the imagists and the symbolists. Imagism, a discipline modeled chiefly on classical forms, was nevertheless somewhat determined also

by symbolism and by Elizabethan and seventeenth-century techniques. At the same time the symbolists were descended on one
side from the romantics and on the other from the Parnassians:
a group whose classical purposes were firmly announced and
moderately achieved.

Among the moderns the Sitwells and Stevens are most nearly
Augustan in taste and loyalty, but they retain romantic attitudes.
Their very nostalgia for more precise, polite, and decorative days
is in itself a sort of romantic yearning. According to Babette
Deutsch, the disabused Auden writes "almost with the vague
fervor of romanticism."[53] This febrile strain in Auden, admirer of
Byron, and in the classical Elinor Wylie, devotee of Shelley, is a
romantic trait found in many moderns. That does not at all pre-
clude their metaphysical expression. Indeed, their variable attitudes are implicit in the metaphysical conflict. Though Eliot
would persuade us of our classical direction, we cannot be sure
whether we are at present moving in a neoclassic current or effer-
vescing a new romanticism. Such romanticism may be a result
of the contemporary social revolution. Because of the transitional
character of our times and its consequent compromises, the poetry
of Eliot, Crane, Cummings, Auden, Robinson Jeffers, and others,
is in each case one of more or less shifting attitudes or fusions.
The synthesis of metaphysical verse, the language of nuance be-
queathed by the symbolists, surrealist experiment in the subconscious and sensational, and the slant of leftist poets, all contributed
to what some call our unsatisfactory poetry. To others these
factors represent definite achievement. In any case, it may be
said that writers of very different temperaments and attitudes
toward experience have variously employed the metaphysical
techniques of expression.

Not only is the strategic place held by metaphysical poetry in
transition periods significant, but also its intrinsic adaptability to a
numerous experience. Its essential character derives from the
abstract *use* made of an inspiring or commonplace subject. As
indicated earlier, its material may be as roaming as experience
and idea permit, and the treatment similarly diverse. Disagree-

ment as to whether a metaphysical age is romantic or classical hinges on its unique poetic function. The advantage of metaphysical wit is this very reconciliation of the two major categories of poetry.[54] "To the question 'Classic or Romantic?' the answer is surely 'Both!' "[55] Working freely in the established types of poetry, the metaphysical weighs intellect and passion, the soul and the senses, abandon and restraint. Irony is the mediating agent.

This versatility is visible in such modern prose as Joyce's but notably in poetry. Despite his critical assumptions of classical impersonality, Eliot's *décor* is "a romanticized squalor";[56] despite the fact that his methodical balance and economy of style are formal, his nostalgic moods and supernatural insight are not. The dual aspect of method and mood applies also to Stevens and to the Fugitives as a group. With Hart Crane the pull between control and impulse gives his poems a classic balance of their own. By means of inventive transports of his high art,[57] that enforced romantic exemplifies the modern paradox. The combination of simplicity and complexity, passion and poise, is accomplished by metaphysical action and the sheer pitch of its technique. It operates "between the emotionally organized form of the Romantic and the rationally organized form of the Classic: the Metaphysical seizes emotionally the idea or symbol which imposes its own logic upon the emotion."[58] The division of sensibility in either classicism or romanticism is corrected by the metaphysical fusion.[59] It must be stressed again that this intrinsically protean mode of expression is promoted during periods of transition or conflict, such as the seventeenth century or our own.

Methods of the metaphysicals have been analyzed by the poets themselves and by their critics. But the reader often recognizes a metaphysical poem or passage by its effect, without a definite awareness of the mental and technical processes involved. He feels that "note of tension, or strain. . . . The note is so distinctive that, once it is perceived, it is impossible not to recognize it again,"[60] though one may remain ignorant of the mechanics. Some of these effects have been suggested above, but it may be

useful to touch on those which the reader perceives most clearly
if figuratively. He is aware of what has been called the metaphysical "shudder," a salty or frosty tingle, an intellectual and
emotional gasp, a mystic mood of the senses, the "supernatural
music from behind the wings."[61] It is a charged effect, an extrasensory communication stretching for the upper regions and
"reaching down to the deepest terrors and desires."[62] In Shakespeare, before the metaphysical period was well established, Eliot
recognizes "a terrifying clairvoyance."[63] In Eliot himself, Elinor
Wylie—who knew the metaphysical experience too—described it
as a strange passion informed with horror, an intolerable contrast
of spirit and despair, a "frightening and beautiful murmur."[64]

The metaphysical effect is kindled, as observed, by the friction
of opposites: of two moods, of mood and language, of content
and style, of one metaphorical term and its diminished companion
term. This extraordinary counterpoint creates what has been
called the third dimension of the metaphysical aura. The infusion
of supernatural terror and conceptual passion creates also the
ineffable dimension. That intellectual agitation emotion can give,
or the sensuous reaction to intense intellection, is deeply moving
to the imagination. "The distinctive note of 'metaphysical' poetry
is the blend of passionate feeling and paradoxical ratiocination."[65]
Both are subtly elaborated into uncommon areas of sensitivity.
Their single impact affords the reader a simultaneous experience
of the real and the super-real worlds, or in such exciting succession that there is the effect of living at once in two worlds.
It is "analogous to a dissonant chord, or . . . to the clouded
resonance of a Chinese gong."[66] The simultaneous or successive
complexity can be indefinitely protracted. The "amazing *timbre*"[67]
of any typical Donne passage continues as a reverberation in
subsequent passages, producing delicate or extreme dissonance.
This elusive quality of the metaphysical manner accounts for
image-making in critics who attempt its description, and for the
fact that many metaphysical poems might be found, in Genevieve
Taggard's opinion, but not many poets who are consistently
metaphysical. For her, "the metaphysical is a mood assumed for

the moment, or one manner of approach, not a constant quality."[68]
Yet the prevailingly metaphysical poet is distinguished by the persistence of a tone throughout much of his work. Donne, Dickinson, Crane, and Eliot, for example, indulge in no momentary mood. Their manner presupposes an emotional disenchantment, spiritual earnestness, and the irony that controls both. The characteristic mood of metaphysical verse is recognized by its repeatedly sardonic quality, restless disillusionments, irritable surfaces and stinging effects—and its terrible intuitions.

It is this concentration of mood in such verse which accounts for the charged effect that Herbert Read assigns to all good metaphysical poetry and Ezra Pound to all good poetry. To express the terror and wonder of that tension, like the older metaphysicals the moderns resort to complex effects of wit and passion, and attempt the unexpected conjunction of the two elements. The emotional shock creates overtones in the mind. The intellectual explosion scatters fire over the senses and the feelings. "This term 'explode' is significant: it conveys the sense of everything happening at once,"[69] a state that demands the attention of the whole self. In Dante and Donne, Herbert and Marvell, Hopkins and Eliot and Auden, are found not only alternate tension and relaxation but the sudden result of their proximity. Furthermore, "the making the familiar strange and the strange familiar," can as a single achievement be credited again and again to the metaphysicals.

PART TWO

SOURCES OF THE
METAPHYSICAL IMPULSE

5

TIME OF TRANSITION

THE PREDICAMENTS of a troubled epoch, as well as subtle crises in the personality of an individual artist, are stimulants to metaphysical expression. In their time of contending faiths, speculation was a spiritual necessity for Donne and his followers, as for Eliot in current circumstances. Somewhat different conditions produced the great poetry of Dante and Shakespeare. But Dante's metaphysical interest was also the culmination of a culture, and many Shakespeare passages have analogy with Donne's characteristic idiom.

Both ages that concern us here are notable for scientific advances and for world disorders. England has never before or since suffered such religious reversals as during the Elizabethan period and the seventeenth century. Our own age is the immediate and unhappy heir of unprecedented industrial, technological, and political upheavals. At such times easy statement and style prove inadequate. The difficult idiom, the hard epithet, the mental effort, coöperate toward a more complex utterance. Writers develop an attitude in which the heart does not exclude the mind, and the head and the heart learn life with special anxiety. Although some critics, like Grierson, insist that all great poetry is metaphysical, not all metaphysical poetry will be good, let alone great, writing. But when poetry turns metaphysical and when it is great, he contends, it is the voice of its tumultuous day.

During transitional and particularly turbulent crises in history, "advanced" poetry has generally been metaphysical in a loose sense: witness Dante, Marvell, Goethe, Blake, Hopkins, Dickinson, Baudelaire, Yeats, Crane—to take token names at random.

59

The problem is to ascertain the reasons for this tendency among the poets of a given place and time. As for the Jacobean-Caroline period Eliot says: "On all sides, it was an age of lost causes, and unpopular names, and forsaken beliefs, and impossible loyalties . . . the beauty of life and the shadow of martyrdom are the background."[1] Any study of the seventeenth century, our own, and comparable periods, suggests that metaphysical poetry is a sign of such times as know acute discomforts of body and soul, as well as fundamental and rapid changes in belief, science, psychology, and artistic expression.

There are periods other than the seventeenth century with which the modern world has a significant correspondence. An inspection of this correspondence should help to characterize metaphysical poetry and the conditions that give it impetus. Whitehead,[2] Eliot,[3] and Tate[4] have each intimated that metaphysical expression occurs at the rise and decline of romanticism but not in the heart of it; and before or after a collectivist impulse such as appeared in the Middle Ages, the social eighteenth century, and the twentieth. Dante betrayed a sense of the conflict between the individual and his conformity to the state or the hierarchies. Donne represented a triple struggle. Eliot revolted against the standardization inflicted by our culture; he subsequently moved toward the absolutes of royalism and Anglicanism. Clearly, the metaphysical poet did not thrive in the eighteenth century, whose intellect and "enthusiasm" were separated and uncritical of each other, nor even in the potential nineteenth when the philosophies were too poetical for the poetry.[5]

The literary fusion of metaphysical symbols with their appropriate and precise emotional equivalents was effected in the thirteenth century by the late Provençals and Dante; the phenomenon occurred again in the seventeenth century, and once more through the agency of Baudelaire and later Laforgue. We ask what social circumstances cause groups of poets to seek such statement at a given time, and if their poetry distills a special "quality of a civilization."[6] Just as Dante "became the voice of the thirteenth century," so Shakespeare represented "a turning point in history."[7] It was a turn that led directly into the metaphysical period already adumbrated in Shakespeare's day and marked a moment "in human history, or progress, or deterioration, or change."[8] These poets and these periods are frames of reference for the condition and consciousness which obtain in our own day. At such historical points the mind of men is more sensitive, the heart more critical, and the poetry a metaphysical essence of the two.[9]

The seventeenth century served as a battleground between two eras, itself an age of violent loyalties and hates. To its lot fell the onus of exceptional protest and struggle. It suffered contests between the ancients and moderns, the individual and authority, divine and human rights. If some poets showed no clear symptoms of the turbulence, strain is evident in the very fact of their metaphysical verse. The casting for longer horizons, the sleepless spirit of inquiry, and the resultant eager activity proved a general uneasiness. Revolution was not confined to ideas alone. On the physical side there were wars and exiles, persecutions and martyrdoms, explorations, travels, and colonizations. However promising the uncharted areas of the New World, the Indies, and fresh frontiers of commerce, the universe was of more disturbing interest, more difficult to visualize in the bright light of the latest astronomical advances. Kings lost their heads and the Roundheads found theirs in a new sociological orientation. Movements of stars and the circulation of the blood were exciting discoveries of an accelerated science sloughing old concepts of astrology, alchemy, and medicine. In this complex of forces the metaphysicals sought cosmic significance for a fluctuating universe.

The seventeenth century issued from the querulous 1590's and neighboring decades. But where the Elizabethan period was national in purpose and integrated by a common effort, the later period broke up into conflicting endeavors. The spontaneous confidence of the first announced itself in a versatility of talents and expansiveness of personality. Its successor, for all its quickened activity, was on the other hand a time of cross-purposes that assembled nothing so much as doubt of man and God. After the disintegration of Elizabethanism in plays as in lyric poetry, "fastidiousness and excess replaced the old spontaneous ease and freedom."[10] Confident integrities fell apart, and for them was substituted a more penetrating intellectual thrust to the heart of things. In the last years of the sixteenth century there was "a sort of intellectual and emotional paradise. In the seventeenth century the race fell from its paradise into the realities of the modern world."[11] A franker pursuit of truth was hereafter the driving impulse.

For the first time history, science, and language were methodically investigated. Progress was first consciously named as a social and biological goal. The overthrow and precarious restoration of the monarchy established its limits. The church passed through vicissitudes from the reign of Henry VIII until Dryden's period, when Dryden himself veered between one faith and another. Education broke away from the scholastic system. Puritan expulsion of music from the church ultimately promoted its secular use. Man's traditional relations to God and knowledge had to be readjusted. These new relationships were seriously studied, satirized, deplored, welcomed. It was the age of Bacon, Galileo, Kepler, William Harvey, Descartes, Cowley, Evelyn, Pascal, Boyle, Spinoza, Newton, Milton's *Areopagitica*, the Invisible College of 1645, the Royal Society of 1660, the Act of Toleration, Locke's *Letters on Toleration* and *An Essay Concerning Humane Understanding*. There was abroad a factual sense tempered by a desire for just, as well as exact, estimates of matter and mind.

Many were exhilarated, but others were deeply hurt by the rude happenings of the day. Yet Vaughan for one saw their instructive value as well. "We could not have lived in an age of more instruction, had we been left to our own choice."[12] The turmoil suffered by this age is reflected in the following lines prefixed to his *Olor Iscanus:*

This was my shaking season; but the times
In which it fell were torn with public crimes;
I lived when England against England waged.[13]

If Vaughan was chiefly distressed, Donne was also perplexed.
He was the mirror that showed a shocking blow. Though sporadi-
cally a man of action, he nevertheless recruited himself to report,
in poem and sermon, the general discordance. Like his age, he
was a divided man. His nature welcomed the enormous changes,
and his curiosity hungered for the new satisfactions. Yet he was
profoundly disturbed and felt a great need for order. That order,
so difficult to achieve in the turmoil of physical actuality, he
sought to formulate in the metaphysical relationships of his
art. The perplexity of "the worlds condition now" was focused
in the lines:

And new Philosophy calls all in doubt,
The Element of fire is quite put out;
The Sun is lost, and th'earth, and no mans wit
Can well direct him where to looke for it.
And freely men confesse that this world's spent,
When in the Planets, and the Firmament
They seeke so many new; then see that this
Is crumbled out againe to his Atomies.
'Tis all in peeces, all cohaerence gone;
All just supply, and all Relation . . .[14]

The intense will of Donne and his like, imposing itself on the
conflicts of the seventeenth century, pulled its character into
the formal distortions of an El Greco. In the internecine vehemence of the time unusual characters were created, and the poets
produced strange beauties and blatancies unequalled before in
English literature. Between the ultimate disintegration of medi-
evalism and the establishment of the new science, Donne effected
a meeting in literature of the scholastics' deductive method with
the empiricism of Bacon. Despair and faith, disillusion and
scientific hope, were joined in a century that, as Grierson affirms,
saw the greatest changes in concepts since man first began to

think. It is no surprise, then, that Donne's philosophical and realistic wit should blend the human, inanimate, and supernatural, and that his imagery was "drawn from all the sciences of the day, from the definitions and distinctions of the Schoolmen, from the travels and speculations of the new age, and . . . from the experiences of everyday life."[15] Discoveries on land and in the sky, anatomies of man and his mind all contributed to his work and that of fellow writers.

The literature from Spenser to the Restoration is private and upperclass for the most part. Here can be included Donne, Jeremy Taylor, Thomas Browne, Milton, and the host of Cavalier poets who at various times inhabited the ivory tower. But they are likewise known to have taken active part in the field, the church, and verbal combat, as well as in government affairs. Writers privately immersed in books also participated publicly in the scientific adventures of the Royal Society. Others, engaged in a personal struggle for religious faith, made public attacks on state and church that sent them to prison and into exile. Much writing was thus acute and lonely; but even in its seclusion this writing reflected the divisions tearing the outside world.

Naturally such poets resorted to the self as a sanctuary from external dilemmas. The Elizabethans, the romantics, and the Victorians entertained what might be called a world philosophy, but if it was wide it was also shallow. The metaphysicals, except for a respectable body of satire that ramified into every subject, could in contrast be termed surveyors of the private terrain. But their world view was just as often realistic and critical. The tension that seems to be limited to internalities actually is stretched between past and future. Marvell's "To his Coy Mistress" is ostensibly a poem of seduction. Within that frame the references are of a cosmic nature: it becomes also a seduction toward a philosophy—or better, an attitude. Behind this almost Cavalier poem, behind much light Cavalier verse, stood an ominous inner conflict. Thus political and intellectual civil war sometimes turned poets to "a sort of quietism,"[16] a sublimation in poems about love, gardens, and God. Epicureanism, with its retinue of littérateurs and libertines, jostled devotionalism; the Cavalier was sometimes a pietist. For many metaphysicals, the hope of heaven was the last available refuge. When the permanence of the state in the shape of King or Protector was uncertain, the unifying principle of God was invoked. Ideas of harmony differed radically. The Quakers, the Cambridge Platonists, Davies in *Nosce Teipsum,* Hooker, Archbishop Laud, Hobbes—each was faithful to some reconciling form in the period's protracted unrest. Bacon found his answer in a proposed House of Learning and a mythical Atlantis; Hobbes discovered a mechanical solution; Newton saw a compromise between religion and science. Others, like the critic Henry Reynolds in *Mythomystes,* gave a metaphysical reply, as the Platonists in theology, the bishops Corbet and King in high-minded oratory, Donne in sermon and verse.

Between two cultures, one that had achieved self-satisfaction and one proud of the order of its common sense, men questioned themselves as well as the world. The satire of Raleigh, Donne, Marston, and Hall; the disturbing drama of Shakespeare, Webster, Middleton, Ford, and Tourneur, told the times. Men looked for the home of the passions, and "character-writers" felt their way toward psychology in an era that demanded an analysis of all things apprehensible. The multiplicity of events and ideas impelled poets to "try on various metaphysical caps."[17]

It was a marvelous and untidy time, a "century of genius."[18]

The crowded stage of this hundred years is indicated by the coincidences which mark its literary annals. At its dawn Bacon's *Advancement of Learning* and Cervantes' *Don Quixote* were published in the same year (1605), as though the epoch would introduce itself with a forward and a backward glance. . . . Shakespeare and Cervantes died on the same day. . . . In the spring of this same year Harvey is believed to have first expounded his theory of the circulation of the blood. . . . Newton was born in the year that Galileo died (1642), exactly one hundred years after the publication of Copernicus' *De Revolutionibus.* One year earlier Descartes published his *Meditationes* and two years later his *Principia Philosophiae.* There simply was not time for the century to space out nicely its notable events concerning men of genius. . . . [There was] world important work within these limits of time: Francis Bacon, Harvey, Kepler, Galileo, Descartes, Pascal, Huyghens, Boyle, Newton, Locke, Spinoza, Leibniz.[19]

The result of the work of Galileo, Newton, Descartes, and Christian Huyghens alone can well claim for that century "the greatest single intellectual success which mankind has achieved."[19] In a review Eliot outlines six of the most significant changes or developments by which F. J. C. Hearnshaw measures the period:

The increase of the power and pretension of kings; secondly, the decay of the feudal aristocracy, the rise of the capitalist middle class, and the increase of a pauper proletariat; thirdly, a revolution in the art of war; fourthly, an extension of geographical discovery, accompanied by the founding of colonies . . . resulting in the expansion of Europe into the New Worlds; fifthly, the spread of the Renaissance, with its essential secularism and its fundamental individualism, into fresh countries and into hitherto prohibited spheres of thought; and finally, the development of natural science.[20]

With the substitution of dictator for king, capitalist for feudal, technological for natural, much in the above summation is remarkably true for today. But that age possessed "a kind of equilibrium and parity,"[21] scales weighing tremendous confusions and great clarifications. It could associate morbidity with imaginative passion, intellectual pride, with spiritual humility, vision in the least of the Cavaliers with realism in the best of the mystics. Truth varied in their grasp like Proteus without acknowledging its identity. In spite of its quaint habits, we see how close we have come to that age, which because of a kin crisis of great changes is more puzzling than any century but our own.[22]

Although Donne was the foremost rebel against convention in literary style and content, he was neither the first nor the only one. Among the more important predecessors of his revolt were Raleigh, Chapman, and Fulke Greville. "The Passionate Man's Pilgrimage" by Raleigh anticipates not so much Donne's complexity as Herbert's crisp style and forthright attitude. But Marlowe's passionate manner suggests the later Donne who "will purge, not decorate his soul."[23] Among Sidney's bucolics his

Arcadian "Song" and some of his sonnets—chiefly the first and best known in *Astrophel and Stella*—sound the fresher note of fervor and intensity. Greville has already an intellectual turn and penetration that were to become common qualities among the lyricists. In his sonnets and Drayton's called *Idea*, in Chapman's *A Coronet for his Mistresse Philosophie* and Barnabe Barnes's *A Divine Centurie of Spirituall Sonnets* appear glints of an exacting independence as to problems of love, thought, and religion. The paradoxes scattered through them now assume a difference from those of the routine Elizabethans. There is a possible rationale for the preliminary and sporadic vigor shown by certain poets. After all, Thomas Wyatt wrote sonnets of hard substance and exact tone. Therefore Donne was perhaps merely rejecting the prevalent Italianate influence and effecting a return to the closer English tradition.[24]

Yet it was a more serious change. E. K. Chambers shows how seventeenth-century disenchantment began its insidious work in the very bloom of the Elizabethan period. After the loosening of medieval ecclesiastical bonds, after the dynastic feuds and Roman intrigues in the time of Henry VIII, the Elizabethans enjoyed an age of continuous efflorescence climaxed in the defeat of the Spanish Armada. Every human enterprise felt like an adventure. Literature showed a look of unity in success and a destined eagerness for the future. "Elizabethanism then is sensuous, comprehensive, extravagant, disorderly, thirsty for beauty, abounding in the zest of life . . . but it is not the whole truth."[25] Already disillusion and doubt darkened the edges of the great bouquet. Economic, religious, and political intrigues disturbed the last years of Elizabeth. Even Spenser, the representative figure, wrote the acidulous *Colin Clouts Come Home Againe* as well as *The Faerie Queene*. Among others, Edward Dyer and Chidiock Tichborne gave preliminary notations of discontent as correctives to the general self-satisfaction. John Harington wrote his disenchantment into his diary, Raleigh into the poetry of "The Lie." Thomas Pound was the disappointed dancer who turned Jesuit and wasted himself in prison. But the recusants are not alone in their disillusion: "it is a constant undersong in the full strain of court poetry itself."[26]

The coming chaos was imminent in the Elizabethan era, though the tumult broke much later. In such dissolution metaphysical and mystical moods prosper, for "any emotional attitude which seems to give a man something firm, even if it be only the attitude of 'I am myself alone,' is eagerly taken up."[27] If Shakespeare is nevertheless a highly integrated writer in outlook and style, it is because he "*is* the unity, that unifies so far as they could be unified all the tendencies of a time that certainly lacked unity."[28] In general the Elizabethans were "eager" and "zestful" for physical action and bright song. The more searching souls of the emerging metaphysicals began to apply these adjectives to truth and thought. The Elizabethans, "even at their most physical, retained a gloomy, almost rabid fear of the flesh. The seventeenth century rationalized this conflict."[29]

There were winds before the storm. A late Elizabethan in time but an *avant-garde* in science and common sense, Bacon reacted against the expansive credulities of the waning age.[30] Like Raleigh, who tried to summarize the past in a great and final history; like his friend Chapman, who led in the attack against primitive attitudes and stale attractions, Bacon refreshed Aristotelianism with facts and experience. Entertaining a theory of tragedy more definite and didactic than Aristotle's, Chapman was an "augury of what the metaphysical might be."[31] His poetry had the uneasy charged effect, hectic and troubled, of a type that would soon overtake the more agreeable and richer Elizabethan verse. His feeling is sometimes quite close to that of Donne, himself a late Elizabethan. Eliot sees the affinity between the two poets, whose roots lay in a medieval metaphysic but whose growth was stimulated by the distressed atmosphere of their day. The same climate brought forth the morbid mind of John Webster. An earlier example of that concern with psychological matters is Davies' *Nosce Teipsum*, first published in 1599, which attempted a reconciliation of the world and the soul. Davies might have been a truer forerunner of "metaphysical ingenuity and argumentative imagination,"[32] had he not depended chiefly on the old solemnities of the soul and disregarded the churning ideas of the day. On the other hand, Greville showed a decided respect for science in *A Treatie of Humane Learning* though he attacked its vanities. Both Greville and Raleigh, who were also influenced by Martial, anticipated the outburst of Donne's 1593 *Satyres*. The contemporary Juvenalian satirist Joseph Hall admired Donne's *Anniversaries*. Hall's connection with the second anniversary was recorded in conversations between Jonson and Drummond,[33] a seventeenth-century Spenserian who suggests the metaphysical spirit only in his contemplations of death and his reflective flair.

Obviously the common conception of Donne as a one-man revolution is wrong. There were the precedents of earlier work by Wyatt, Marlowe, and Chapman; the new sardonic clarity in Raleigh and at odd moments in Sidney and Spenser; the thoughtfulness of Davies, the acrimony of Marston and Nashe, the serious satire of Greville. That Shakespeare comprised the one real synthesis of Elizabethan lyrical exuberance and seventeenth-century disenchantment is of a piece with his unique greatness. His own rebellion was implicit in the progression of his plays and his poetry from *Venus and Adonis* to the passionate sonnets, from *Titus Andronicus* and *The Comedy of Errors* to *Hamlet* and *The Tempest*. Jonson's dramatic reforms were as explicit as Shakespeare's were implied in the ripening of a personality that paralleled the maturing of the times.

Where earlier Elizabethans marked the coming trend, it was above all Donne who disposed of the conventions of Platonic courtship and the laxness of post-Spenserianism. He discarded those Petrarchan and "romantic-chivalric" elements which impeded fresh statement. Before the sarcastic question and the rude retort became conventional in turn, Donne worked out his own personal and poetic truths. He was essentially a realist of both sacred and secular loves. Herbert's question might well have been his:

> Who sayes that fictions onely and false hair
> Become a verse? Is there in truth no beautie?
> Is all good structure in a winding stair?
> May no lines passe, except they do their dutie
> Not to a true, but painted chair?[34]

However, it is only fair to add that in other lines of the poem Herbert attacks mental sinuosities. Despite his own thwarted career and nettling doubts on the way to God, Herbert was annoyed by poetry so complex that its meaning is "at two removes." But Donne's revolution prevailed against current objections because it was founded upon a sure need of the new times. They demanded some technique by which to present the more complicated qualities of experience in a more complex age. Many Jacobean and Caroline poets had become contemptuous of the fluencies in the ebbing period. Even "a minor poet like Habington could be moved by the spectacle of a starry night to ideas which seem to us both more modern and more profound than any to be found in an Elizabethan poetry except Shakespeare's."[35]

Without perhaps contemplating a whole new prosody, Donne rebelled against the facile or decorative metrics which had become a convention. For all the acrimony of Marston and the brilliant bombast of Marlowe, it was Donne who effectively dismissed the more popular platonics, the dress parade of patriotic verse, the costumer's pastorals, the sweet artifices of the madrigals. On his death Thomas Carew said of him:

> The Muses garden, with Pedantique weedes
> O'rspred, was purg'd by thee; The lazie seeds
> Of servile imitation throwne away;
> And fresh invention planted, Thou didst pay
> The debts of our penurious bankrupt age;
>
> .   .   .   .   .
>
> Since to the awe of thy imperious wit
> Our stubborne language bends, made only fit
> With her tough-thick-rib'd hoopes to gird about
> Thy Giant phansie, which had prov'd too stout
> For their soft melting Phrases.[36]

To this one might add lines perhaps by Donne:

> Here sleeps House by famous Ariosto,
> By silver-tongu'd Ovid, and many moe,
> Perhaps by golden-mouth'd Spencer too pardie,
> (Which builded was some dozen Stories high)
> I had repair'd, but that it was so rotten,
> As sleep awak'd by Ratts from thence was gotten . . .[37]

The insurrection against jaded platitudes is perhaps most readily symbolized by the change in verbal love-making. Before his "fatal interview" with Anne More, Donne the emancipator of sex poetry boldly acknowledged infidelity to his mistresses. But subsequent poems showed his respect for the honest, not formal, emotion of love. In both situations he looked into his mind and heart, and wrote. Several poems preceded Donne's in plain speaking. Michael Drayton's sonnet, "Since there's no help, come let us kiss and part," suggests how the poet could at moments "in bare words paint out my passions' pain."[38] The following lines tell something of the emancipation:

> No far-fetched sigh shall ever wound my breast;
> Love from mine eye a tear shall never wring;
> Nor in "Ah me's" my whining sonnets drest.
> A libertine fantasticly I sing.
> My verse is the true image of my mind . . .[39]

Though the libertine attitude grew fixed in its turn, poetry now declared independence from the Italianate fashion. So in "The Dreame" Donne leaves the "time-hallowed recipe of the love-dream"[40] and substantiates his sense of realism where fact faces fancy:

> Thou art so truth, that thoughts of thee suffice,
> To make dreames truths; and fables histories;
> Enter these armes, for since thou thoughtst it best,
> Not to dreame all my dreame, let's act the rest.
>
>   .   .   .   .   .
>
> I must confesse, it could not chuse but bee
> Prophane, to thinke thee any thing but thee.[41]

An instructive contrast to our acceptance of Donne as a modern iconoclast is in the view of C. S. Lewis. He concedes the affinity of our psychoanalytic attitude toward sex with Donne's; but, Lewis continues, his rebellion against the Spenserians is a return to the medieval cult of the lover with its concomitant sense of sin. Joan Bennett's reply to Lewis makes the probably significant connection between Donne and the moderns in this matter.[42] She denies that Donne was medieval in his sense of sexual sin: he did not express distinctions between marriage and adultery so much as the deeper difference between love and lust, good and evil. And his imagery was an expressive patina over psychological and metaphysical meanings.

Chiefly it was his "love of ideas" which fostered his phrasings of sexual love; he felt these ideas "as a form of voluptuousness,"[43] not derived from any fashion or school but from his own obsession with thought which ruled him all his years. His ego could not escape this passion "even in the ecstasy of sexual love or the glory of contemplating the divine."[44] Both man's soul and man's body, walking and in the grave, were worthy of minute study. Whatever past inheritances contributed to his philosophical attitudes—the medieval Jean de Meung's cynical gaze at chivalry, the Pyrrhonism of the Renaissance, and Montaigne's naturalistic skepticism[45]—they became a personal and modern idiom of the mind of this "revolutionist in love."[46] His metaphysical inclinations related sex to other considerations in a relativist balance of values.

The great stirring of thought and imagination in the seventeenth century was paralleled by travel: in the name of politics, conquest, and study. Men came and went as exiles, as pilgrims, as explorers. Often it was not any leisurely impulse on the part of the individual that sent him wandering. In Elizabeth's reign, the Queen dispatched her emissaries to colonize or to prove the freedom of the seas for England. Buccaneers like Drake were driven by an imperial ambition that was part of the prevalent exuberance. This fever of exploration spread from the Portuguese, Spaniards, and Italians to the English. They took their trade, piracy, and literary passion to Spain and Spanish America, to Samarkand and Eldorado, to the Indies, Constantinople, and Nineveh. Journeys were often undertaken by men of letters, like Raleigh, or by travelers turned belletrists, like Thomas Coryat—in a time when everybody wrote and writers ranged over territories both intellectual and real.

Donne good-naturedly satirizes Coryat's exploratory prowess:

> Venice vast lake thou hadst seen, and wouldst seek then
> Some vaster thing, and found'st a Courtizan.
> .   .   .   .   .
> . . . And thou
> This Booke, greater than all, producest now.
> Infinite worke, which doth so far extend,
> That none can study it to any end.[47]

To the well-known 1611 *Crudities* were added his letters from India called *Traveller for the English Wits*, and others to his mother and to his friends in England. In 1601 appeared William Parry's *New and Large Discourse of the Travels of Sir Anthony Sherley*, the enforced exile who passed through Africa, Constantinople, and Persia. This man was pirate, diplomat, traveling businessman, and archeologist all in one. Translator of Ovid's *Metamorphoses*, George Sandys also wrote *The Relation of a Journey begun an. Dom. 1610* and touching Egypt, Turkey, Palestine, and America. To cite Richard Hakluyt's various *Voyages* and Samuel Purchas' *Pilgrimes* is superfluous. Other testimonies to the fashion of travel and the fashion of recording it include *The Observations of Sir Richard Hawkins, K^{nt} in his Voiage*, Walter Raleigh's *Discoverie of Guiana*, John Smith's *A true Relation of . . . Virginia*, and Gabriel Thomas' *An Historical and Geographical Account of . . . Pensilvania*—which carry us from such great Elizabethan adventures as those of Richard Eden, Humphrey Gilbert, Francis Drake, through the seventeenth century to 1698.

Thus English colonial expansion and victory on sea and land promoted considerable communication between British and foreign literatures, between thought abroad and the science and philosophy of England. The period was also increasingly troubled with the shuttling of political and religious exiles. It was an age of pilgrims' progress in a literal sense too. The movement between England and France was liveliest during the Exile. And not only courtiers but literati were assigned to diplomatic errands. Conversely, ambassadors of long standing were also known as scholars and men of letters, as in the case of Henry Wotton, to whom Donne addressed an appropriate poem.[48] Movements of religious men, colony-bound ships, and fighting troops were mirrored in specific poetic references, analogies, and in the disturbed spirit of the literature as a whole. Marvell refers to Bermuda and America in fact and metaphor. Donne speaks of his mistress' treasures as "my America." He says in a verse letter that "we 'have added to the world Virginia,' and sent/Two new starres lately to the firmament";[49] and shows everywhere how he "learned from traveling, and reading about traveling, that his own mind had its west and east, its distances, mountains, rivers."[50] An emotionally curious Coryat, a mentally bold Drake, Donne voyaged into the unknown as well as to the continent and on the high seas. As to his soul, "like a Prince she sends her faculties/To all her limbes, distant as Provinces."[51] His poetry was enlarged by many successful allusions to geography, as in the poem-long analogy of "Hymne to God my God, in my sicknesse"—

> Whilst my Physitians by their love are growne
>   Cosmographers, and I their Mapp, who lie
> Flat on this bed, that by them may be showne
>   That this is my South-west discoverie
> *Per fretum febris,* by these streights to die,
>
>   .   .   .   .   .
>
> Is the Pacifique Sea my home? Or are
>   The Easterne riches? Is *Jerusalem?*
> *Anyan,* and *Magellan,* and *Gibraltare* . . .[52]

And voyaging in itself was no uncommon exercise for writers. Browne visited Iceland; Ben Jonson took Walter Raleigh's young son to Paris; Lord Herbert of Cherbury was in Paris for the first time in 1608, was ambassador to France in 1619, and traveled in the interim; Carew was in Florence and The Hague in 1613 and 1616, and in 1619 went abroad again, this time with Lord Herbert; Lovelace left England to escape political imprisonment; Suckling was acquainted with France where, as suggested elsewhere,[53] he may have come in contact with the *précieux* poet Vincent Voiture; Crashaw visited Paris before 1646, and at last came to rest in Italy where not long after his conversion he died. As Rome was a religious destination, so Paris was the intellectual Mecca then—as it has been in our own time for more than one generation.

Besides his brief expeditions to Cadiz and the Azores and later visits to Italy, Spain, and Germany, Donne went to France on military matters and wrote some of his poetry there. We have the evidence of "To the Countesse of Bedford *Begun in France but never perfected*" and "A Letter to the Lady Carey and Mrs. Essex Riche, from Amyens." While in France with the Drurys he composed "The Second Anniversary."[54] But Montaigne had already infected him with the urbane and rational humanism of a skeptic. This "first of modern psychologists" acknowledged the limits of man's reason and by his mild, civilized understanding tinged his time with rational doubts. "He succeeded in giving expression to the scepticism of *every* human being."[55] Donne represented in England Montaigne's and Théophile's agnosticism and naturalism, already a tradition among certain thinking poets of the day. French freedom of thought and the stress on skeptical reason suited the younger Donne as Pascal's attention to faith was answered in the older Donne. Even his metaphysical manner, for which the causes are many, was somewhat colored, according to Sir Sidney Lee, by Du Bartas.[56] The French *Semaines,* translated by Joshua Sylvester into English, had their effect also on Quarles, Cowley, and the grand manner of *Paradise Lost.*

The later seventeenth century, during the Protectorate and the Restoration, experienced a somewhat different and perhaps more intimate contact with France. By the time Malherbe and Boileau's *L'Art Poétique* dominated the critical field, England had been independently prepared for French classicism by such native classic influences as Jonson and the crisp compact style of the metaphysicals. Thus the impression made by French literature and thought was transmitted through the early skepticism of Montaigne—apparent from Shakespeare to the Earl of Halifax—and later via the literature and life at the French court for which the English Cavaliers had a decided taste.

Here the French *précieux* must be taken into account. This epithet and the term metaphysical have been equated by a critic who speaks of the "French 'precious' or 'metaphysical' poets of the period 1600-30" in a discussion of Pierre Motin.[57] Katherine Philips, a student of French poetry, preferred French books to English and went so far as to translate four acts of Corneille's *Horace*. The salon which this Matchless Orinda made artificial efforts to maintain in England was a pale reflection of the brilliant Hôtel de Rambouillet, with its courts of love and its witty elegances of style. One of Madame de Rambouillet's most sparkling ornaments, Voiture made his impression on Suckling and on Lovelace, Cavalier par excellence.[58] Thus preciosity, nicely exercised on French soil, quite naturally had its modified counterpart in England. After all, English seventeenth-century verse, including the metaphysical, was frequently aristocratic and personal because of the social stratum to which many of the poets belonged, as well as the abstruseness of their expression and the private problems of emotional adjustment. Yet the kind of metaphysical verse that Donne wrote cannot be said to correspond to preciosity, since it stressed content and method over elegance. No doubt there is some rapport between these two types of wit as well as between French preciosity and Italian Marinism.

A fair example of French salon verse domesticated in England was that of Cowley, affected by such inflated prosaic poets as Saint-Amant. His wit was certainly French rather than Italian, his rhetorical style moreover a half-hearted imitation of Corneille, Racine, and other French classicists. What he failed to acquire from Racine was psychological acumen.[59] Cowley's letters, his essays, and his way of life suggest an Epicurean taste sharpened by contact with the French. As royal secretary to the English Court in Exile, he lived in France between 1644 and 1656—at a time when Epicureanism, skepticism, and the libertine posture prevailed in French literary life. Whereas the whole-souled Puritan Milton deflected it, his friend Marvell felt the French spirit and more nearly represented the age, assimilating whatever tone harmonized with his own wit.

It is evident that at the outset of the seventeenth century English literature had for some time been well disposed toward anything Italian. The titles of plays, reworking of Cinthio's tales, Castiglione's influence, pastoral and erotic literature, and sonneteering attest to its popularity. From the importation of the sonnet by Wyatt and Surrey to Milton's personal contact with Charles Diodati and his own Italian poems, the Italian impress was deep. In the interim, Roman Catholicism turned men like Crashaw to Italy.[60] And Marinism confirmed the English conceit in obscurity, complexity, and a certain harshness. That Crashaw and Cleveland were Italianate is a commonplace. It was Crashaw's temperament and religious tastes that inclined him toward the lush Giovanni Marino, the first book of whose *Strage degli Innocenti* he translated into his version of the "Sospetto d'Herode." His transcription of spiritual ecstasy into erotic symbols had conscious and involuntary kinship with the Italian literature of that time.[61]

Granting Pope's and Johnson's belief that Marino's fustian influenced it,[62] metaphysical verse is not synonymous with concettism.[63] Whatever fascination Italian conceits did exert over English verse, they supplemented the metaphysical mode of the age. In the same way Italian Neo-Platonism reinforced the casuistry of such poems as Donne's "Extasie."[64] It was perhaps also prompted in part by a motif in *Il Cortegiano*. Castiglione's courtly precepts as well as his realistic approach, Tasso and Ariosto, together with Marino, constituted the most powerful Italian influences of the time.

The Spanish equivalent of the Marinist style, Gongorism was

found a ready support to English "conceited" verse. Góngora was related in spirit and intention to the extravagant aspect of the metaphysical. Both resorted to mental gymnastics to avoid vulgarity. Garnering suggestions from every available source, Donne is said to have been well read in Spanish literature. Although even Herbert, so native in style and temperament, felt the influence of Spanish mystics, it was Crashaw whom they warmed with their devotionalism and fired with their ecstasy. Expressive of the European baroque tradition, Crashaw was particularly taken with the great Spanish mystic St. Teresa.

6

SEVENTEENTH-CENTURY CONFLICTS

THE CULTURE of the seventeenth century was stimulated and modified by political and religious struggles. Politics was then as intricately involved with religion as it is today with socio-economics. The social or class problem became a factor in the tug of war between Parliament and King. The major issue was not class privilege so much as the divine right of kings in a last stand against political liberty. Simultaneously the Anglican church and the Puritans were in deadly combat, both meanwhile relentlessly persecuting the Catholics. Where religion was concerned, science entered the lists. It is thus scarcely possible to examine seventeenth-century politics without touching theology, science, philosophy—all threading through social and military events. The tangled situation is paralleled in our own age. Today the contention between theoretical science and religion is subordinated as an issue to the practical application of science in peace and in war; the public religious problem is the persecution of minority groups and the suppression of churches by certain nations. Otherwise the seventeenth and twentieth centuries are kin as eras of enormous unrest, considerable speculation, and universal revolution.

Most of the struggles culminating in the seventeenth century originated in the disorders of the late sixteenth century. Spain and England exchanged shocks in Elizabeth's reign. The Rebellion in England had repercussions in other lands. On the continent the Thirty Years' War eventually involved most of western Europe—Germany, where it began, and subsequently France, Sweden, Denmark, Austria—a débâcle greater than any until

79

our own times. Such desperate religious wars, with their genesis in the Reformation and in the persecutions under Henry VIII, Bloody Mary, and Elizabeth, grew acute in the twenties and thirties of the following century and stimulated the Counter Reformation.

When the metaphysical poets took up arms in the flesh or in spirit, for the most part they supported the King's side. Donne, who expresses no preference in his satires, in his private life moved among the intellectuals and aristocrats. The King's men were among his acquaintances. Whether it was political advancement he desired or the deanship of St. Paul's which he finally accepted, such preferment could originate only from nobility or King James. At least in his poetry, Donne in turn influenced mainly two upper-class groups: the courtiers and the divines. George Wither, Bunyan, Milton, and Marvell were the principal exceptions in their political sympathies, though Marvell had no very hard words for Charles at the time of the Restoration. The majority of Protestant poets, however, supported the aristocracy. On whatever side the writers ranged themselves, they were ardent participants of the manifold struggle between zealous Royalists and intransigent Puritans. "The great civil war was a metaphysical war. . . . Cromwell's army was not inspired by any passion for the constitution; it fought to found the Kingdom of the Saints. Butler's *Hudibras* is a savage record of what the human spirit had suffered under the tyranny of metaphysical saints."[1] Had Cromwell's objective been purely political, religious enthusiasm in that age would still have inflamed his adherents.

In the opposite camp also, philosophy was employed as an instrument to justify the cause of monarchy and the Cavaliers. Theory was a weapon against the growing strength of constitutional parliamentarianism. Hobbes for one grounded the need of monarchy on a moral basis. Since God, he argued, does not reveal the true moral state to secular man, we must turn to some tangible evidence of moral law, namely the monarch. Furthermore, since the king depends on the people for his well-being and power, he will not jeopardize his position by opposing the people's will and welfare. This is the social contract that Rousseau later interpreted in another way. Hobbes's ethics is essentially expedience, one that equalizes moral law with a dubious sovereignty. However, his aim—and as much has been said for Machiavelli—was to strengthen the divided nation and provide security and peace. His philosophy, or "nominalist metaphysics,"[2] is nevertheless disturbing to many. Today men and nations are again so perturbed by an anxiety to calm the turmoil that they resort to moral contortions and ruthless ways. Ezra Pound, erstwhile iconoclast and reformer, turns to fascist ideals, "the new synthesis, the totalitarian."[3] In their ardor to resolve doubts and to right an off-balance world, many advocate methods abhorrent to others.

The Civil War in England and the harsh measures used by the Puritans depressed Vaughan, if not to the point of rebellion. His reaction was a return to nature and childhood, in delicately passionate expressions of both; he went outdoors for light and turned inward for innocence. Milton on the contrary entered the mêlée with vigorous prose tracts and a twenty-year devotion to government affairs when Cromwell was in power. Milton's prose is often remarkably modern in thought and projects his views on church government, regicide, the freedom of the press, and other matters in no uncertain terms. He rejected every divine right but God's and his words echo in the conscience of man's heart and in the agile reason of his mind. The dispute over authority between church and state was satirized as early as 1611 in Donne's *Ignatius his Conclave,* partly inspired by the Gunpowder Treason of 1605 and the Oath of Allegiance in the following year. Attempted and actual assassinations (Henry IV of France and the English Charles) contributed powerful scenes to the drama of the seventeenth century. The bewildering pressure of political and religious events in those years engendered a mood "which has chiefly made the national temper of England since the Commonwealth a different, and a less youthful, thing than that national temper was before the Civil Wars."[4]

To consider economics as the fulcrum of society is compara-

tively modern. In the seventeenth century it was ideologically
not so central a consideration: the rights of men were then more
nearly related to political, moral, theological issues. Yet these
disputes fostered economic changes, as in the struggle for freedom of the seas. The Civil War in itself signified a shift of influence from one class of society to another. At least it corrected
certain abuses of economic privilege. No serious civil war can
shake a nation without economic dislocations—after which the
doctors will offer philosopohic panaceas. The Royal Society and
Hobbes are conspicuous examples. Hobbes's "moral" argument as
set forth in the *Leviathan* was perhaps sincerely intended for
the good of the people, but the sovereign and his satellites would
nevertheless profit by its acceptance. The embattled middle
classes, verbally less articulate, expressed themselves by way of
the Reformation, the Great Rebellion, Puritanism, and regicide.
In spite of the Restoration, the eighteenth century was nevertheless admittedly a more middle-class period than had been the
seventeenth century wherein the issues were bitterly contested.

The stages of the change were not so noticeable in literature
as the final realities. Elizabethan and Jacobean drama, and even
that of Congreve and Wycherley, gave slight evidence

except in so far as it records the rise of the City families, and their
ambition to ally themselves with needy peerages and to acquire country
estates. Even that rise of the City, in *Eastward Hoe* and *Michaelmas
Terme*, is treated lightly as a foible of the age, and not as a symptom of
social decay [sic] and change.[5] . . . [Yet] the transition from Eliza-
bethan-Jacobean to later Caroline comedy is primarily economic: . . .
the interest changes from the citizen aping gentry to the citizen become
gentry and accepting that code of manners. . . . Middleton's comedy
. . . marks . . . the transition between the aristocratic world which preceded the Tudors and the plutocratic modern world which the Tudors
initiated and encouraged.[6]

In Bunyan himself, in tracts, satires, and studies by "character-
writers," there were certain decided indications of the economic
position and problems of writers and their subjects. But the
poetry as a whole stood apart from the economic implications of

the day. Whatever class distinctions appeared in the verse were evidenced in the homely themes and images of a Herrick or a Herbert. Otherwise, if poets took part in the struggle, it was sooner in the name of politics or religion or philosophy.

How a people should be governed and by what rights, civil or divine, were argued by philosophy as much as by sociology, economics, and politics. Political philosophy was then a species of general philosophy including religion, psychology, and science. None of these many crosscurrents can be followed separately. Whitehead accepts the Reformation and the scientific revolution as perhaps the two essential changes in the seventeenth century—the final efflorescence of the Renaissance. The scientific movement from Copernicus to the founding of the Royal Society and beyond to Isaac Newton belongs to "natural philosophy," often as speculative as it is specialized and technical. Again, when Donne refers to some branch of science such as astronomy, he calls it the "new philosophy." When Hobbes discusses the rights and duties of the sovereign, he is a philosopher engaging in moral and ethical considerations. "For a philosopher like Hobbes has already a mixed attitude, partly philosophic and partly scientific . . . and by his metaphor of Leviathan he provided an ingenious framework on which there was some peg or other to hang every question of philosophy, psychology, government, and economics."[7] Economics then is as much a department of Hobbes's philosophy as is science. At the same time natural philosophy and theology formed one image in men's minds. Truth was put to many tests of linked significance. For some it derived from external sources; for others the source was the inner man. To Hobbes authority meant an objective trust in the sovereign; for Descartes it was a subjective deduction; a matter of empirical value for Bacon, of conscience for Milton and Fox.

It was the need of the age to establish a new orientation of philosophy. Plato, Socrates, Augustine, and Aquinas had accepted the responsibility of the thinker. Now Bacon, a natural evidence of the times, saw that inductive investigation of materials was necessary to truth. "It was unthinkable that any mind of the first order should concern itself with mere mechanical ingenuity and it did not become thinkable until certain high views concerning human dignity and importance had been reluctantly abandoned."[8] It was Bacon's role to divert men's attention from Platonism to empirical knowledge, and to prepare a program. He virtually drew up a bill of divorcement between man and God, though nothing of the kind was overtly concluded. Still temporizing and cautious of obstructive criticism he, like Descartes, reconciled fact, research, and religion. In the same oblique way, Galileo professed to aid mariners while developing his methods and instruments for wider purposes. Browne cited authority after authority, but by this means tested each by invoking the next.

With physics, mechanics, and causal laws in mathematical form creating skepticism, Descartes attacked epistemology by dividing its source into two: matter and mind. Copernicus' and Galileo's dynamics flung Descartes back on himself. Since authority and sense data were both doubtful, since one philosophy supplanted the next with devastating completeness, he returned to knowledge by way of *cogito ergo sum*. The "I" was discovered by ontological proof. Thus an abstract, almost geometric, reasoning fixed the soul and objects in extension. The body was related to the soul through the agency of the animal spirits which "though material, were sufficiently rarefied to be able to communicate directly with spirit."[9] The "Extasie" of Donne embodies a similar if traditional form of this theory:

> As our blood labours to beget
>   Spirits, as like soules as it can,
> Because such fingers need to knit
>   That subtile knot, which makes us man . . .[10]

Though God was an essential element in Descartes' philosophy, its dichotomies tended to separate man's new approach to fact from his traditional religion, and prose from poetry. This hastened eighteenth-century deism, as well as verse with the properties of prose. Meanwhile Cartesianism supported the trend toward mathematical proof of metaphysical theories. Before the division between thought and extension—mind and matter—influenced philosophy and the later seventeenth-century writer, literature was able to feel in prose with Browne and think in poetry with Donne.

The stress on matter rather than metaphysics gradually suppressed scholasticism. Degradations and disruptions of civil war urged Hobbes toward a pragmatic order too cynical for some. In the general vein of Descartes, Bacon, and Galileo, Hobbes hoped to fix the principles of temporal matters before approaching ultimate issues. He did not credit the separate existence of the soul but circumvented a denial of immortality by relying on Judgment Day and the universal resurrection. Meanwhile he placed both heaven and hell on earth. He was an early determinist who referred "free will" to the battle of appetites and aversions. His philosophy of appetencies has an interesting resemblance to Freudian insistence on the various drives. In both cases, the stress is laid on the factual basis of human conduct. Hobbes is an excellent instance of hard logic at odds with the suprarational imagination of the seventeenth century. Metaphysical poetry, still possessed of this esoteric imagination, had nevertheless prophetically utilized the scientific, psychological, and prose virtues of the advancing age. The blend often proved most fertile.

John Locke summarizes another aspect of seventeenth-century thought and, as an enlightened liberal, stresses reason, education, and the perfectibility of man. The two decisive revolutions of the eighteenth century were nuclear in his thinking. With Descartes, Locke initiated one important phase of modern philosophy. *An Essay Concerning Humane Understanding* augurs the closer study of psychology. In the very nature of mankind he discovered the privilege of the enlightened individual to be himself. His general articles of faith are eighteenth- and nineteenth-century in character, but his stress on the individual is more typical of the seventeenth century than of the Augustan ideal of man as a manifestation of society. Much of his argument, with its essentials of sensation, demonstration, and intuition, reminds us of Donne. Locke compromises between traditional religious beliefs and the new philosophy—a conflict and a compromise inherent in the whole epoch. For all of his *tabula rasa,* mathematical strictures, and jostling atoms, Locke attempts to certify God metaphysically: a seventeenth-century occupation. A representative of his own century's dualism, he was a rationalist and a critic of rationalism, thus anticipating both the age of common sense and the romantic revolt.

By Locke's time, for all the sparks of an earlier fire, there is no longer the "metaphysical flicker from world to world, none of the old imagery struck out in the heat of struggle or in the ardour of discovery."[11] No longer is there quite the same imaginative desire to relate soul and body, the universal and the particular, which appears in Donne's verse letters, his *Anniversaries,* even his sermons—that rare blend of physical and metaphysical curiosity coloring almost every line he wrote. His excitement over the revolutions of Copernicus, Tycho Brahe, Galileo, and Kepler, was of a different tone from the sober effects of later writers. In a way his imaginative reaction to news in astronomy and philosophy flared like ours to Marx, Einstein, Jeans, Freud, and Frazer. Already our literature seems to show a cooler and more complete assimilation of their contributions, such as are not discarded. A questioning quality in Donne allowed him to be both avid and doubtful of novel things and economical of the old.

The changes in the wake of a new philosophy were agitated by an intellectual inheritance from elder systems of thought. For example, the old juxtaposition of microcosm and macrocosm acquired a modern significance with the development of the microscope and telescope. Meanwhile the ancient concept added figurative interest to cold fact. From a psychological standpoint, moreover, the mind of man was being newly explored as a miniature community of universal concepts. Donne derived his microcosmic ideas in part from Paracelsus, that still-medieval Swiss physician who materially influenced Donne's thinking. Through the poet's manipulation, the idea was altered in his sermons and verse from an ancient pedantry to a concept heightened by imagination. "Under the name of 'an anatomy of the world,' he gives us an anatomy of himself" projected against a cosmic background,[12] and he utilizes a traditional notion for modern ends. That he did not present a systematic or progressive philosophy, any more than did Shakespeare, is not in his disfavor. They were humanists in a loose but sufficient sense.

The devotional and humanistic elements produced a new suspension—in the same way that Puritan fanaticism and naturalism, Platonism and realism, the ascetic and the sensuous in religion, were concentrated in one literature. As expressed by Mario Praz, Mary Magdalene was a symbol of the age: sinner and saint, a luxurious penitent, libertine contrite after indulgence, beauty in sackcloth. There were worked into one extraordinary fabric the tolerance of humanism and certain intolerances of religion. The quarreling religions of the epoch assumed the new pattern of Anglicanism. Many antagonistic aspects of life joined issue or sought compromise. In spite of anti-Platonists like Bacon, a revival of Platonism took place. It was a spiritual era, but Hobbes's materialism gained territory. There was progressive objectivation, but Descartes offered a subjective solution by mathematical proof. Chemical knowledge was increasing, but alchemy acquired new adherents in the Hermetists, among whom was Herbert of Cherbury. In the body of Donne's work alone, we find Jesuitical weapons used against the Jesuits themselves in *Pseudo-Martyr* and *Ignatius,* Pythagorean and Platonic concepts side by side, Paracelsian doctrines and contemporary scientific ideas made vivid.

Because of our own concern with the dramas in science, interest has returned to the next most important period of scientific discovery. Prepared for its tumultuous traffic of ideas by the earlier Copernicus, the seventeenth century began at high tension. Bruno's death in 1600 "ushered in the first century of modern science in the strict sense of the term. . . . The new mentality is more important even than the new science and the new technology." It was "the most intimate change in outlook which the human race had yet encountered."[13] Imagination was being oriented to the Copernican position of the earth among the universal bodies, as confirmed by Galileo. Before the century was very old, this adjustment was followed by a mental revision regarding three significant conceptions about stars and stellar movements: size, distance, and number. Infinite space, plurality of worlds, and the factor of time acquired a new reality as themes for the poets. Comets and "new" stars were the talk of the town. As the century advanced in age, knowledge, and gradual application of mathematical and physical theories, religion and philosophy were affected at every turn in a revolution of the first order.

But the liberalized attitude of curiosity and dispassionate thought prepared the ground. Both this mood and the less temperate reactions of religion were synchronized by the writers. They participated in the intellectual changes imaginatively, though doubt and disapproval struggled with the welcome accorded the new men of science. Opinions differ as to who were then the true warders of Salomon's House.[14] Bacon contributed the inductive experimental method; Galileo applied it to solving problems and inventing mechanical apparatus; Descartes brought mathematics to bear on physical experiments and phenomena of the senses; William Harvey utilized these methods in the discovery of blood circulation. Finally in Newton were "combined all the elements of the new science. He used the latest and the most improved mechanical apparatus; he tested his own theories by numerous experiments, . . . he demonstrated his conclusions by mathematics."[15] The staid Ptolemaic-Aristotelian tenets of immutable perfection in superlunar regions were confounded by Brahe, Galileo, and Kepler. By 1610 such alterations troubled men less and less but continued to enthrall them as the fellowship of discovery united generations and cut across nationalities. Born thirty years after Copernicus' death, Kepler confirmed his findings with the encouragement of his senior, the Danish astronomer Tycho Brahe. In Italy Galileo saluted Kepler as a colleague in the large

laboratory of truth. Results as concrete as the telescope, calcula-
tions of comet orbits, the evidence of gravitation and the circulation of the blood were actuated intrinsically, however, by the new
independence of mind.

These international discoveries stirred men, particularly Jonson
and Robert Burton, to curiosity and literary activity. But Donne
is the most remarkable single instance of the effect of Galileo's
book in the year 1610—after which references to the telescope
were legion.[16] Donne's verse letters first tell his awareness of
the inflaming new implications. Among the fictions which appear
often in his imagery are the four elements. But now, through
Kepler's persuasion, they are subjected to scrutiny. In *Biathanatos*
Donne refers to Kepler; in *Ignatius* (1611) to Brahe and Galileo
as well, and treats Copernicus as a character. The idea of a trip to
Galileo's moon and other celestial bodies comes quite early in
Donne's work, where greater interest is manifested in new worlds
than in the position of this one. By the time of his *Anniversaries,*
the apparent fickleness of stars and the decay of nature cease to
be mere figures of speech. In these poems such concepts take on a
harsh dignity as cosmic symbols of disproportion and mutability.

Representative of his century, Donne proves to be a triple
ironist. In turn he indicts the astronomers, those who distrust
astronomers, and those who, like himself, at times dread the inroads of science. What were men to make of all this? Bacon stood
almost alone in encouraging unequivocally the conquest of nature, and his ideas helped create "the 'climate' of opinion which
eventually subdued the vapors of melancholy that rose from a
decaying world."[17] Burton anatomizes the effects of mutability
and decay, but the preachers and the poets are especially concerned. In his characteristic metaphysical figures Donne typifies
the still uncertain attitude toward astronomy and describes
the dissolution that attacks love as well as other constancies
with Pythagorean change. The philosophical regret over its decline is elaborated in "An Anatomie of the World,"[18] and even
more seriously in "The Progresse of the Soule." In these twin
vehicles of his deliberations, the poet is seen most anxious to

fasten his faith among fickle worlds of relative values. Relativity is both a medieval philosophical and an ultramodern scientific concept accompanying shifts in human knowledge and its validities. In the seventeenth century the uncertainty became almost an obsession. When new ideas are so rapidly engendered as to appear superficial and corruptible, doubt permeates every thought. Donne wished to establish a modicum of truth if not of peace, relationships if not finalities, and an honest skepticism as well as hopeful faith.

Doubt was fertile ground for despair, the concept of decay for thoughts of death. The distressing changes that bewildered the brain encouraged inquiry into human and universal humors. In 1621 appeared Burton's *Anatomy of Melancholy*, whose theme suggests the tone of the times. Drummond in *The Cypresse Grove*, a work devoted to death, complains in 1623 that the imagination is led into "a thousand Labyrinthes. What is all wee knowe compared with that wee know not?"[19] Browne is provoked to expose a doctor's religious credo in *Religio Medici;* and his *Hydriotaphia: Urn Burial*, in a mixture of Latinity and imaginative English prose, expresses the pity and necessity of physical alteration. Change was the great traducer of faith and established beliefs in the seventeenth century. Among the fierce campaigns then raging was one between reason in support of faith (scholasticism) and reason in support of science (Baconianism). The scholastic interest centered in *being*, Bacon's in *becoming;* the former in final causes and final order, the latter in intermediate causes and the properties of immediate matter. The scholastic *why* was opposed to the Baconian *how*. Bacon and Galileo illustrated the epoch's scientific struggle on the one hand, and Donne demonstrated on the other how scholastic methods could be enlisted to satirize the very attitudes that generated them. The vestiges of scholasticism lent to the seventeenth century an added intellectual cast that was congenial to Donne's very character. For the cosmological poetry of his day the careful, universal, and formal qualities of scholastic reasoning comprised a useful *modus operandi*. Its contentiousness prepared him for the rigors of modern reasoning. He was accessible to every source of thought, ancient and new. The combat was useful if distressing.

With Donne, Bacon and Browne afford three eminent examples of the dichotomies splitting their age. Donne is perhaps most nearly the transitional figure between the scholastic methodologist and the rebellious empiricist in both love and science—a man whom he pictures in a famous image as valiantly scaling the mountain of truth in a spiral and tortuous effort. Where the other two labor for metaphysical solutions, Bacon attempts the scientific. But Bacon's reputation oscillates between that of the father of modern science and empiricism and that of a scholastic of the early seventeenth-century type. Impeded by the religious passions of the age with which he was obliged to temporize, he remains a pioneer philosopher of the scientific method. He provided later experiment with its first great theoretic impulse, establishing that characteristic seventeenth-century connection between the practical and the theoretical, between knowledge and life.[20]

Himself "his own 'great amphibium,'" Browne is in another way representative of "the double-faced age in which he lived, an age half scientific and half magical, half sceptical and half credulous,"[21] half factual and half fantastic. Browne writes of gorgons and crystal, and creates their fusion. He thinks out his sensuous reaction and feels his philosophical excitements in the favored Eliot manner. He is as visionary and emotionally involuted as he is detached by a sense of the concrete. That sensitivity which can accept dissimilar experiences is revealed in this Donne passage:

I throw my selfe downe in my Chamber, and I call in, and invite God, and his Angels thither, and when they are there, I neglect God and his Angels, for the noise of a Flie, for the ratling of a Coach, for the whining of a doore; I talke on, in the same posture of praying. . . . A memory of yesterdays pleasures, a feare of tomorrows dangers, a straw under my knee, a noise in mine eare, a light in mine eye, an any thing, a nothing, a fancy, a Chimera in my braine, troubles me in my prayer. So certainly is there nothing, nothing in spirituall things, perfect in this world.[22]

It is just this sort of leaping imagination that moves from a straw to God, from a woman's shoe to a strange star in the sky,[23] which Eliot understands thus:

A thought to Donne was an experience; it modified his sensibility. When a poet's mind is perfectly equipped for its work, it is constantly amalgamating disparate experience; the ordinary man's experience is chaotic, irregular, fragmentary. The latter falls in love, or reads Spinoza, and these two experiences have nothing to do with each other, or with the noise of the typewriter or the smell of cooking; in the mind of the poet these experiences are always forming new wholes. . . . The poets of the seventeenth century . . . possessed a mechanism of sensibility which could devour any kind of experience.[24]

The writers then knew a freedom and an inclusiveness of comprehension, like Browne's. Insofar as his refutation of vulgar errors suggests Bacon's overthrow of the "idols," Browne was Baconian: alert and inclined to intellectual currents. But he stopped far short of the determinism toward which his age was fast moving. And here older schools of thought had a reinforcing influence.

The two-way character of the times allowed for a merging of past systems with new ideas that looked to the future. Such was the case of atomism. Rejected for some time, the ancient atomists now regained honor. It was natural for Bacon to accept most sympathetically the teaching of Democritus as altered by Epicurus and transmitted by Lucretius. In the process of refuting their moral implications, Lord Herbert summarized Lucretius' argument and admitted its consistency. Greville offered a mystic Neo-Platonic critique of Epicurus, but demonstrated the current knowledge of atomism, as did Kenelm Digby, who supported Aristotle. This familiarity is proved likewise in Burton and Browne: in the first by quotations, in the second by a defense of Epicurus against indictments of atheism. Through denouncing the popularly erroneous conception of Epicureanism, Edward Benlowes goaded further interest. John Hall's "Epicurean Ode" took the atom for imagery. It was Donne[25] who recognized Lucretius' kinship to the new science of the day in typically casual references to atoms.[26] These instances suggest the tentative attitude of the first half of the century.

Later, in spite of Hobbes and Boyle, Epicurus still provoked hostility and fear. But now the general approach to the atomists was less crude than before. While confuting the anti-Christianity of atomism and defending the soul's immortality, writers employed Lucretius' expository method of argument. The second half of the century saw many verse paraphrases of Lucretius and four English translations, accompanied by commendatory verses. Whereas Katherine Philips merely admired Epicurus, Cowley was actually something of a Lucretian, and his essays were decidedly friendly to Epicurus. Cowley's mind was in general congenial to the advances in science, to the materialism of Hobbes, and to the revived interest in atomism. It is only natural that Thomas Sprat, historian of the Royal Society, should have gone to Lucretius for the subject of his longest poem. As for Dryden, he did Lucretius the "greatest service, both in elucidation and in praise,"[27] thus finally acknowledging with determination the century's progressively scientific temper.

Science was being increasingly implemented by mathematics, an exact though abstract means of demonstration. Whitehead submits that the "paradox is now fully established that the utmost abstractions are the true weapons with which to control our thought of concrete fact."[28] This observation elucidates the dual nature of seventeenth-century life—at once abstract and concrete in its thought and its literature. Did not Donne, the geometer of the imagination, join the ultima Thule of scholastic thinking with mathematical claims? At the debut of that mathematical century he already epitomized its general development. He put to his own uses in poetry the mathematical symbolism of the day,[29] and thereby conveyed the vaster abstractions of his spiritual meanings. Something of the same sharp methods is noticeable in Herbert too, whose mathematical inventories are more intellectual than a Whitman catalogue. There is a delicate exactitude in Marvell, a sort of pliable precision in the movements of his mind as in style. This mathematical sense was poetically extended to the geometry of the skies and the geography of the earth, as indicated by the following passage out of a sermon by Donne:

> Here is a new mathematics; without a change of elevation, or parallax. I that live in this climate, and stand under this meridian, look up and fix myself upon God, and they that are under my feet, look up to that place, which is above them, and as divers, as contrary as our places are, we all fix at once upon one God, and meet in one centre. . . .[30]

which compares for feeling and concept with MacLeish's "You, Andrew Marvell":

> To feel creep up the curving east
> The earthly chill of dusk and slow
> Upon those under lands the vast
> And ever climbing shadow grow . . .[31]

The metaphysical-scientific approach defines a visionary mode and gives it sharp outlines. "To make this vision acute Donne has drawn into use the science which devises 'quantities and dimensions' to symbolize reality."[32] The reader constantly meets Donne's insistence on external facts and the individual's personal interpretation of those facts. Dogma and traditional authority, unsupported by experience, serve him chiefly as metaphoric suggestions for his poetry. The deductive rationalities were being undermined and actualities substituted for axioms. We cannot deny the syllogistic reasoning in Donne's writing, but his cancellations of one argument by another and the final sense of suspended judgment suggest that he implemented scholastic rationales with instances drawn from experience. To Mary Ramsay, Donne appears therefore in a medieval light, but to most critics as emancipated and independent.

The scientist and the poet have struggled individually and together toward the same end: penetration of the mysteries. They have been driven by a common curiosity about universal phenomena and human experience, and by a common hope to establish relationships and relevancies. In *De Rerum Natura, La Divina Commedia, The Anniversaries, Faust, In Memoriam,* and

The Waste Land, the poet has shown decided if not fervent cognizance of science in some form. Wordsworth pronounced a past and prophetic ideal when he said that the poet "will be ready to follow the steps of the Man of Science, not only in those general indirect effects, but he will be at his side, carrying sensation into the midst of the objects of the science itself."[33] Contrary to the tenets of positivism, science itself often bears implications beyond the fact: "No science can be more secure than the unconscious metaphysics which tacitly it presupposes."[34] As the root was often factual, so the flower of Donne's ardor was metaphysical—forever leaning toward a comprehensive unity. In spite of an ostensible capitulation to theology, his fever remained unabated. His doubts and suspicions were less unsympathetic than tentative, like the tumultuous state of the "new philosophy." If Donne's astronomy is uncertain, his mathematical attitudes essentially religious, his sense of time superior to his sense of space, he is not alone. The scientists themselves were at once pious and probing, and a feeling of suspense ran through the whole century. Donne's pessimism struggled with his enthusiasm. Our febrile moderns are similarly discouraged in the face of great social and scientific events.

In spite of Bacon's precocious hopes, we cannot expect of Donne and his contemporaries the same confidence that characterized Davenant's *Gondibert,* Cowley's 1661 *Proposition for the Advancement of Experimental Philosophy,* and his odes to the Royal Society,[35] to Harvey and Hobbes. Even this later scientific preoccupation and liberal interest did not escape Thomas Shadwell's and Butler's satire. We still find countermovements and exceptional attitudes to God and church—in Richard Baxter, George Fox, Traherne, and even in the Earl of Rochester, that true Restoration type. More, we find Bacon, Hobbes, Boyle, and Newton vacillating between loyalty to facts and respect for metaphysical problems. In varying proportions, a dual allegiance to religion and science troubled the men of that time. The opposed areas of interest had certain common impulses, each borrowing thought and imagery from the other.[36] "The metaphysical poets . . . particularly admired the methodology of science, and in fact they copied it, and their phrasing is often technical, spare, and polysyllabic,"[37] while their poetic synthesis is still highly imaginative. Even the structure of line and stanza was influenced as the processes of their minds were directed by scientific impulses. The colliding systems of thought and religion engendered a vivid sense of the metaphysical paradox.

It was the role of the epoch to make use of the century-long litigation between science and religion, between fact and feeling. At the start of the century, the opening guns of the new science announced the conflict to come; at the end they vanquished the more imaginative activities of tragedy, metaphysical verse, and religion. In the interim were ranged protagonists on either side who not only contended with one another but experienced the duel of fact and faith in themselves. The breakup of a whole system of thought is manifested throughout Donne's work, from his *Paradoxes and Problemes* to the metempsychotic "The Progresse of the Soule."

War was waged not only between science and religion but among the religions themselves. It was Rome against Canterbury, Anglicanism against Puritanism, Oxford against dissenting Cambridge. A pivotal problem was the interpretation of the Bible in the light of the "new philosophy." Bacon put religion as a faith in one category and science as tangible evidence in another. Together with supernaturalism and the unscientific Scriptures, he relegated religion to a lonely but safe retreat. The Bible was accepted literally by the fundamentalists, allegorically by others. There was also extant a comprehensive approach akin to Dante's fourfold meaning for his *Divine Comedy:* literal, historical, allegorical, and moral. Such was Browne's plural attitude, like the conflicting responses of his day. Milton resorted to inner authority instead of traditional interpretations. Everywhere there was a personal combat for truth. Hobbes with his "destructive biblical criticism" made superficial concessions to religion;[38] rational theologists like the Cambridge Platonists based their argument on the religious view but used reason to do battle for their conviction;

the Quakers turned inward for instruction. Often one camp borrowed the enemy's ammunition to defeat him.

Lord Herbert illustrates the complex, when not temporizing, character of the religious and philosophical feud. Brother of one of the best metaphysicals and a metaphysical poet himself, Herbert of Cherbury was a Hermetist, a Platonist, and a comparative religionist. At the same time he anticipated Descartes and deserved in a sense the title of "father of Deism." Interested in classical mythologies and in oriental religion, he ultimately reduced all religions to the individual's internal evidence, supplied by reason or by nature. Since to him reason was a natural instinct and the common heritage of mankind, he advocated "natural religion." With a somewhat different emphasis, the Cambridge Platonists resembled Lord Herbert in their reliance on individual reason and like Descartes trusted the ultimate answer within themselves. Actually they were Puritans who abandoned the Reformation's fanaticism for the "explanatory spirit" of the age. In harmony also with the growing pragmatism, they desired the real effects of goodness here and now. Their insistence on the *spirit* of God and the devil, and not their forms, reminds us of Hobbes—whose figurative heaven and hell existed in living man and not in some assigned external locale.

The play of forces made this era at once a religious and a skeptical,[39] a poetic and a practical medley, engaging men's hard effort toward compatibility or explanation. People were inclined therefore either to dispose of the case of God by apologetic rationalizations or to parallel natural laws with spiritual laws to which they gave precedence. To spiritual minds substance was explained as a manifestation of soul. God was thus the essence of organic and inorganic matter. This attitude is implied in Henry More, Traherne, and Vaughan—whose speculations included Neo-Platonism, Western theosophy and Oriental magic, Hermetism and cabalism. Separately or in conjunction these faiths attempted to integrate God, the estranging mind of man, and nature, which had been largely a confused mystery. Some personal unification was required to withstand the chaos. A man like Vaughan, pantheist and physician, could contemplate eternity and the grasshopper with the same penetrating eye. But whatever theory or creed a poet supported, doubts as strong as his passionate loyalties were bred by "the logical severity of the seventeenth century."[40] There was above all no room for complacency.

Passions flared and polemics shook the century end to end and engaged many nations. But in England the religious crosscurrents were most noticeable not only in the serious church differences, but also in effects on poets and divines, on prose and poetry. Donne, Browne, Walton, Taylor, Fuller, Marvell, Cowley, and even the Royal Society "represent the combination of culture and seriousness, a love of literature and a sober piety, to which the Anglican *via media* conduced."[41] Pelagians, Arminians, and Calvinists, Puritans and Laud's Anglo-Catholics, Anglicans and the High Church adherents of Ferrarism do not exhaust the list of participants in the conflict. What looks like apostasy, a passage of renegades—from Vondel's and Crashaw's conversions, Donne's abandonment of his family's religion, to Dryden's changes of faith —is actually an unhappy but fruitful competition of beliefs and interests. These clashes stimulated the metaphysical habit of equivocation, and created the intermediary of the Anglican Church. The middle way, the meeting ground for contradictions, typified the method by which the seventeenth century endeavored to mend discord and join opposites. It entailed analysis before synthesis, a tracing of connections, an articulation of controversy.

Theological argumentation thus helped to stimulate the metaphysical art of exchange. It referred religious things to the mundane and arrived at spiritual meanings by approaching objects critically. Skepticism was a mark of such investigation, for a mind free of anxiety will not persist in spiritual and intellectual inquiry. The effort to explain and fuse extremes afforded in itself some measure of relief. The critical attitude that pursued religion as relentlessly as everything else provoked men to clarify the Word to their own satisfaction. Fighting for supremacy, doubt and the passion for belief encouraged the study of psychology. And a

growing concern for psychological truth in turn ripened the understanding of mind and soul.

This meaningful interest of the late sixteenth and whole seventeenth century enriched Elizabethan drama, reinforced the lyric,
and ran through all varieties of prose. It took the explicit form of
"character-writing" with Thomas Overbury's studies and John
Earle's *Microcosmographie*. Here were rude Theophrastan types
pointed up in customary verse and prose satires of the age by such
as Donne and Joseph Hall, whose *Characters of Vertues and Vices*
are human as well as allegorical. Essays, epigrams, biographies,
and books with conscious purpose (*Psychologia*, 1590) had already dealt in character and its more obvious shadings. We have
the fine example of Bacon's essay "Of Youth and Age" and his
study of Henry VII while the century was young, and Locke's
greatly developed essay late in the epoch. Joseph Beaumont produced *Psyche*, the longest English poem and virtually a treatise
on "loves mysterie," and Edward Benlowes a poem of mystical
psychology called *Theophila*. The *Anatomy of Melancholy* is a
storehouse of oddities in human conduct and expression. Between
the *Psychologia* and Locke much of the strongest literature of
the age showed a self-conscious regard for the psychological background of individual act and emotion.

Among the "characters" are somewhat primitive specimens, on
the order of Jonson's "humours"; but in the plays of Shakespeare
and his fellows,[42] in the introvert poetry of Donne and other
metaphysicals, we find some of the closest and profoundest pres-
entations of man's psychology in the range of all English literature. "Thus the evolution of thought in the seventeenth century
coöperated with the enhanced sense of individual personality
derived from the Middle Ages. We see Descartes[43] taking his
stand upon his own ultimate mind,"[44] Shakespeare approaching
character in dramatic objectivity, and Donne ascertaining the
subtleties of the subjective. In both his prose and poetry Donne
was a supreme researcher into the personal psyche. Though his
concern is chiefly himself, yet it is to be seen as an illumination

of the sources of human personality: the senses, the mind, and the emotions that are affected by both. His sermons alone are a study of "the psychology of weakness . . . a masterpiece of the stream-of-consciousness ethics."[45] His own tantalized being, of which he was so painfully aware, was the ground for worrying the problem of the complex consciousness. Yet Donne's psychological interest was as much a product of participation as of private converse with himself. Woman was his mistress before religion, and from both he learned a good deal about human reactions. He moved among men at war, in the city, and in his parish. From them he gathered material for his satires and sermons and his poetry too.

Herbert is a psychologist of an apparently simpler and more direct kind. His pungent observations of a man troubled by the world and the relationship to his God are seen again in the Dickinsonians and heard in such disparate voices as the early Ransom and Anna Branch. With Herbert the study of his reactions to God was spurred by the frustrations of his career and by the tingling temper of the hour. But "his problem is always universal," and as both introvert and extrovert he left us the "autobiography of a mind with a rich and difficult content."[46] Traherne, often relying on intuitions that precede mature consciousness, dealt nevertheless with "certain basic human needs . . . in terms strikingly anticipatory of some of the main emphases of contemporary psychology."[47]

Intuitively and with rudimentary psychology, poets labored through falling concepts and the confusion of rising structures toward a knowledge of the individual consciousness along with an understanding of conscience. "When the world is ablaze, only those can express themselves who stand aside."[48] The introversive poets of the seventeenth century bring to mind such later psychologists as Baudelaire, Rimbaud, Hopkins, and Crane. From the lonely investigation into the mind, into religion, and eventually into social ways, the psychological and the metaphysical comprehension developed side by side. "More than that of any other science, the history of psychology is interwoven with that of metaphysics,"[49] a view that could account for the interrelation in the seventeenth century of philosophy, religion, and the study of human behavior. No doubt there is meaning in the coincidence of arriving psychological knowledge with religious and scientific upheaval, and with metaphysical expression.

The psychology of that age was a phase of its promiscuous curiosity and tangled tensions, of its serious need to find order. With the collapse of Rome's sole authority following the Reformation, religion played into the hands of politics and submitted to new philosophical forces. The "truth," once comparatively calm at the heart of a single church, was now struggling for its life. The mother church on her part and the schismatic churches on theirs must plead passionately for their respective views. For this, new psychological means were developed. To win over supporters that had previously been obedient and unquestioning, another kind of proselytism arose—on the order of the democratic political campaign. In the astute maneuvers of a legal-minded Donne were combined the self-consciousness of the Jesuits, the rationalizations of the Neo-Platonists, and the Cartesian attitude to objects, subjectively reached. Current differences in ideas made common use of psychology for the purpose of influence.

The cultural structure of the seventeenth century thus exhibits the scaffolding upon which was built a metaphysical poetry. One may conjecture the ideal condition for such verse. But here are suggested some actual circumstances that produced the metaphysical writing generally considered most typical. Because of the massing in one epoch of essential materials—political, social, economic, ecclesiastical, philosophical, scientific, and psychological—poetry was confronted with an unusual obligation. There came a supreme need to find in the encounter of these energies some order, or at the very least some rationale. Each of the forces attempted to create a suitable decorum. And within each category of the convergence accumulated an internal complex.

Politically the clash between the "divine right of kings" and the right of the Commonwealth to self-determination, chiefly through the Commons, resulted despite the Restoration in a shift toward greater parliamentary power and a limitation of monarchy. Appropriate to this was the shift of interest from aristocracy to the middle classes, whose economic status improved and whose importance in literature and society increased. In religion, a three-part coercion took place. Catholicism had ultimately to account to the Reformation and reacted by means of a Counter Reformation. The waves of leniency and harshness toward Catholics and Puritans in turn, depending on the character of the monarch and the fortunes of war, settled at last in the comparatively quiet compromise of Anglicanism. The by-product of this long struggle among the papacy, the individual conscience, and the *via media* was the religious emigration to New England: a chapter in the story of American metaphysical poetry. Lastly, old theories and old masters in the sciences retained certain loyal partisans, while the "new philosophy" acquired eager and sometimes intransigent adherents. Ptolemy and Copernicus fought it out in the universities. Aristotle and Plato, alchemy and chemistry, astrology and astronomy, mechanism and free will, the subjective and the objective—the air rang with their collisions. An impassioned interest in facts moved in two directions: objectively toward visible and calculated reality, reduced to experiment and mathematics; subjectively toward a comparable concern with the individual's experience. The ego was for the first time a companion implement to the test tube. Hence, to see the rival presences of materialism and mysticism in this period is not so anomalous as it might appear superficially. The junction is expressed in a poetry quite matter-of-fact in its very transcendentalism. The century was at once lyrical and erudite, direct and esoteric. This composite period, a physical and spiritual transition to a new world—from the Elizabethan to the Augustan age, from the Renaissance to modernity—still retains a look of its own. From the very mixture of strains appears a personality of peculiar poise.

ANALOGIES

That climacteric in human history which was the seventeenth century returns in our time with a greater and more general vehemence. Society and the individual live in the furious and common element of controversy. Like Donne, the indicative twentieth-century poet is at once highly self-conscious and objective. Yeats, D. H. Lawrence, Eliot, Auden, and Crane exhibit the adjacent contrasts of the material and the spiritual, the primitive and the subtle. The headlong temper of modern development has bred contradictions exacerbating those in the seventeenth century when "the uncomfortable antithesis of matter and mind in the Cartesian scheme seems to have made inevitable both the materialist and the idealist solutions."[1] England then grappled with philosophies, religions, revolutions, and restorations. Lately political and economic wars subsume religious considerations: republican Spain versus Catholicism, Nazi neopaganism versus Christianity, and Russian materialistic atheism.

There are critics of both periods who believe that the poets have been too little concerned with the movements of contemporaneous culture. It is true that the metaphysicals then and now have been highly subjective. Yet that very subjectivity has usually been caused by the pressure of events. The metaphysical penchant in many of these poets argues that they were fiercely aware of the restlessness of their age. The poets, indeed, were Cassandras of imminent clashes in thought, science, and public affairs. Their apprehension of impending events is in the very mood of their writing.

The Royalist poets rallied tangibly to their cause, witness Love-

lace and Suckling (the latter with his absurd but gallant enlist-
ment of a private cavalry). Among others, Crashaw and Cowley
were exiled for religious and political reasons; Cromwellians like
Marvell and Milton labored in behalf of the Commonwealth. Poets
in general answered the challenge. In modern parallel Hulme,
Pound, and Eliot—as even earlier, Hopkins—observed and noted
the portentous flashes before the storm of the world wars. American expatriates for a time sought futile assurance in Europe. The
reversed traffic is now enriching America with a run of political,
religious, and literary exiles who must influence our intellectual
life. The spirit was at great expense three hundred years ago, as it
is now. Machiavellian and martyr attitudes were at cross-purposes
when Hobbes and Milton walked, and are again met in mortal
struggle today.

To the frontier areas of psychology in the seventeenth century
our era has added new states of the unconscious and subconscious.
To the profound changes in science then, our perversion of technological developments has brought another disillusionment. The
consequent irreligiosity impelled Baudelaire, Rimbaud, Eliot,
Auden, and many others to turn all the more fervently to spiritual
interpretations. These, like Spenser, Donne, Crashaw, and Herbert, abandoned their earlier secular preoccupations in favor of
devotion or escape. The dramatists responded similarly, as Eliot's
interest in them indicates. Shakespeare,[2] Marston, Webster, and
Middleton betrayed a tension that was aggravated after the
Armada incident. The same questioning of knowledge, morals,
and human activity has disturbed us "in a sense that the men of
the nineteenth century, that fierce battleground of new and old
ideas, never dreamed of."[3] The summary poem "The Waste Land"
—reflecting even as it deplores the disruption of sanctions throughout our times—recalls in its Elizabethan allusions the declining
sanctions, royal and supernatural, at the end of the Renaissance.
The breakdown of an established mode of life is common to the
metaphysical periods.

The altering concept of humanism is a touchstone. Since science
has belittled man in the scope of the universe, humanism has

come to place him not at the center of the world so much as at the center of our immediate activities and investigations. With the recognition of a new cosmology at the beginning of the seventeenth century, there was a revolutionary shift in man's metaphysic. Man was no longer indisputably the physical or moral center of the universe. Since then, Dante's meticulously elaborated assurance of the soul's ultimate destiny has been both dissipated and enlarged into space-time considerations. After a series of philosophical protests from thinkers like Berkeley, Hume, Kant, Fichte, Hegel, James, and Bergson—who desired either to restore man's earlier place in the scheme of things or to devise an approximate equilibrium between his apparent fate and his inveterate will to be—we have again come to crisis. Either we are to accept the depressing conclusion inferred from the second law of thermodynamics, or we must construct another philosophy to assert a personal survival. Some prospective theory or metaphysic may be in the process of formulation. Metaphysical poetry again assumes the duty of assimilating new skepticisms. For historical clarification of changes in science and philosophy, thinkers are returning to the seventeenth century.[4] Modern poets naturally explore the same source for inspiration, example, and sympathy.

We set our own distress beside that of the seventeenth century, whose conception of an incorruptible and changeless heaven was so roughly shaken and the harmony of two worlds shattered. Man's life was at the same time narrowed to the orbit of one star and dispersed into ever-widening infinities. The Copernican and later the Newtonian systems replaced the Ptolemaic and Dantean certainties with increasingly mechanistic implications. By the end of the nineteenth century these were in turn suspect. Quantum and other theories have dislodged certain formerly accepted phases of determinism while making room for speculations of atomic chance and accident in a closed universe. In the seventeenth century faith was challenged by science; in the twentieth, on the contrary, our faith in science is being qualified. "Nor is it simply in its larger aspects, in the fundamental metaphysics underlying scientific inquiry that science has become self-critical and revolutionary. . . . Authority has ceased to exist for an essentially homeless generation."[5] Even in the matter of relative values we take comfort in Donne's sympathetically modern attitude. To him "the relativity of the best human learning" was a principle that led to "an appreciation of the sanity of suspended judgment" and a respect for paradox.[6] The metaphysicals and the symbolists have been confronted by such a multiplicity of concepts and data, that the relative measure is the best they can afford. That is one function of metaphysical wit: to formalize a plethora of experience or suggest manifold meanings by allusive auras, as in the case of the symbolists.

Such related attitudes are both an escape and a conquest by means of irony: yielding and obdurate. "The contumacious poet is one who finds himself ill at ease in life, unable to accept current valuations, urged to mock, to flout, to outrage; he is hurt by life; he will harden, but cannot rot into cynicism."[7] Eliot is such a one. He is the heir of Catullus, Villon, Skelton, Baudelaire, Laforgue, Corbière, Marvell, and of course Donne, also called the poète contumace. Among other defiant poets who today flash the very weapons they often scorn are Graves, exploiter of the psychological findings of Freud, Jung, Rivers, Butler, and Frazer; and Auden, who utilizes also political economy, sociology, and the sciences.

The rebellious poet is one who either turns to swim against the tide or directs into channels the expansiveness of periods like Elizabethan England, Tennyson's England, and the France of Hugo. His third option in times of stress is to isolate himself. The first choice is illustrated by Rimbaud and Hopkins; the second by Donne, Eliot, Baudelaire, Yeats; the third by some of the religious poets of the seventeenth century, by Blake, and by Emily Dickinson. In chaotic times, then, poets have bluntly revolted; or attempted to order a civilization that has got out of hand; or withdrawn to religion, cults, and technique.[8] None of these three responses need exclude the others. An intensified life of the mind and the emotions follows exuberant epochs, all the more so when material disintegration engulfs the spirit. Thus, after the amplitude of the Elizabethan age, there came a period of religious anguish, regicide, and intellectual revolution. The modern analogy is, of course, the reaction succeeding opulent Victorian progress and its laissez faire. This reaction was patent in Thomas Hardy's pessimism, the social irritability of Shaw, mechanical utopias proposed by H. G. Wells, the wit and cynicism of the Decadence.[9] At last, the devastating wars and depressions of the twentieth century exposed the shallow promise of the nineteenth. Before "the physical and the rational could be reconciled in a spiritual, a completely human, ideal, a dreadful battle had necessarily to be fought. . . . It was Donne's great and tragic destiny to experience the worst agonies of that inconclusive battle. . . . The battle still persists."[10]

The mental make-up of the late English Renaissance distinctly resembles that of the twentieth century "both in clash of thought and in clash of political interest."[11] Its intensely critical attitude never seemed more significant and congenial than in the testing time of our two world wars. In both periods the established classes have been shaken from their position. In both, science has taken issue with credulity and religion. Though the seventeenth-century scientists, from the martyrized Bruno to Newton, for the most part respected religious sanctions, the trend was largely scientific. The historical revolt at the end of the Renaissance had substituted the empirical method for the metaphysical and rationalist. Now another metaphysic is struggling to stand beside, if not in place of, the purely factual and mathematical. While science is universally promoted, the scientists themselves and certain modern philosophers like Henri Bergson and Whitehead are questioning its sheerly material values. Without repudiating the validity of the physical sciences as such we were, in 1929, "entering upon an age of reconstruction, in religion, in science, and in political thought."[12] The divorce between the material and the ideal, between realistic necessity and ethics, has exaggerated many of our problems. In the seventeenth century, religion was fighting for its traditional place; today spirituality is struggling to renew its function. From opposite directions, the two epochs reach a

common ground. That despair over a present chaos and that trust
in the future dividing the seventeenth century from Bacon to
Dryden speak also for us in Dryden's words:

> All, all of a piece throughout:
> Thy Chase had a Beast in View;
> Thy Wars brought nothing about;
> Thy Lovers were all untrue.
> 'Tis well an Old Age is out,
> And time to begin a New.[13]

Whenever we approach seventeenth-century poetry we feel
that "we have crossed the threshold of the modern world and
catch a persistent echo of familiar voices,"[14] and familiar problems. Not even the singing and hard-riding Cavaliers, busy with
court and courtship, escaped the *Zeitgeist*—often less remote from
us than the nineteenth-century spirit. For all their worldliness they
were intimates of mystery; they talked the common language of
bitterness relieved by images of wit. Harried, desperate with
time, and afflicted with the cold touch of death, the poets experienced a kindred restlessness. "They too lived under the
shadow of corruption and disintegration,"[15] in a time as uneasy
almost as our own. To consider the multiple conditions affecting
all seventeenth-century Europe, the English mind in particular,
and to note the similarities in modern culture is to account in part
for the development of the metaphysical sensibility.

This sensibility worked between the decaying luxuriance of
Elizabethanism and the triumph of hardheaded propriety in the
Augustan age. The metaphysical effort strove with the Puritan inter-
regnum, the zeal of the Protectorate, and after the Exile with the
roughshod reaction of coarseness. Finally, scientific good sense
and "natural" thoughts suppressed the pregnant doubts and suggestive "enthusiasms" of metaphysical expression. So far we see
the twentieth-century metaphysical peak between the first two
world wars. The impulse began at the close of the Victorian era,
which is comparable to the Elizabethan in its expansion, imperial-
ism, and overconfidence. Swollen with industrial success and
crowded by mental pressures, the spirit of our age collapsed into

drastic disappointment. The result has been an esoteric literature resembling the intense idiom of the seventeenth century. Now the zeal of the leftists, the reaction of the right, and a mutual simplification attempt to suffocate the metaphysical impulse with pragmatic attitudes.

In such cousin circumstances the traits of the two radically transitional epochs appear markedly alike, although separated by three hundred years. These inevitable features are experimentation, wit and satire, obscurity, difficult intellectual content, self-consciousness, preciosity, the dualism of doubt and faith, the death obsession, and an acute sensibility maturing under stress. It would be strange to find an easy poetry amid the mingled agonies of death and birth. Rebellion and hope for the future move hand in hand with despair, and are expressed in writing by the most daring techniques.

Experimentation adopted the satiric slant in both ages, and the accident of events supplied materials terribly suited to witty derision and bitter contempt. One can adduce the satires of the early defiant Donne, the "railings" of Cleveland, Suckling's light irony; the sardonic melancholy of Eliot's first poems, the critical attitude of Yeats, the direct sarcasm of Auden, and the indirect thrusts of Ransom. This poetry, "tough enough to reject the easy solutions of the human predicament that arise in every age,"[16] is not coarse or arrogant but sinewy in Eliot's sense of intellectual resilience and emotional inclusiveness. It supports the pressure of external and internal criticism and the convergence of many points of view. Difficult in conception, oblique in progress, complex in implication—it is man's response to overwhelming knowledge of himself and the universe, whether it be at moments when the Ptolemaic and Copernican systems are supplanted by the Newtonian or when Newton is displaced by Einstein. This poetry naturally offers increased intensity at the expense of clarity, and a music of ideas to which a tortured diction must comply. The listener is eventually convinced of its hard propriety. The circumstances of the age push the poet into a complex idiom that accommodates the rhetorical and the rude, the lyrical and the learned phrase. In *A Dialogue on Modern Poetry* its defender believes "that modern poetry would have been no less difficult if Eliot had never existed or had been dumb. Its difficulty is due, not to Eliot's influence (great and salutary as that has been), but to the nature of the times and other causes beyond any man's control."[17]

The conditions may be beyond the control of any individual but not beyond his imaginative grasp. Lacking external unity, our age developed a remarkable self-consciousness. Whether our poets derive from the seventeenth-century metaphysicals or are metaphysical through independent necessity, they unmistakably suggest the earlier group in their expressive means of communicating a run of intense experience. As self-conscious ironists they accede equally to mind and emotion: wit must balance opposed experiences and contrasted ideas. To resist a facile satisfaction, to expose conflicting problems, and to strive for order is to suggest an adult approach. The mature attitude escapes cynicism as it does thorough-going confidence.

True of both ages, therefore, and engendered by their disturbances, is the struggle between doubt and belief. Modern sympathy for Donne is quickened by "the quality of his doubt, of the doubt that led him to a hard won faith in his wife and his God, and his doubt is at least part of his Christianity. It is in fact inseparable from his faith."[18] The play of question and answer suggests a suppressed yearning for faith. And belief walks with doubt which, according to Eliot, is the handmaiden of faith. Indeed, the poet who suffers "private uneasiness" is more the poet and particularly he may become more the metaphysical poet. Perhaps just such expectancy of spiritual order and the rejection of it, if too accessible, are the very materials for his poetry. David Daiches astutely analyzes the fundamental relationship between doubt and belief which led the poets of our generation and of the seventeenth century to express themselves metaphysically:

It would seem also that in an age of multiple faith, where the symbols become not meaningless but ambivalent, the dialectic can become most brilliant and most subtle. . . . [For Donne] differences did not mean

mutual exclusiveness as it came to mean in times that were intellectually more settled. There comes a point at which multiple belief can
scarcely be distinguished from confused belief; the metaphysical influence on the younger English poets of the 1930's, for example, can be
interpreted as arising from the latters' intellectual eclecticism which
has something in common with Donne's Janus-faced quality. But
multiple belief itself often implies tolerance, and tolerance is often—
if unconsciously—based on skepticism, as the case of Sir Thomas
Browne will show, so that, paradoxically, skepticism can be the basis
of multiple belief as well as of the rejection of all belief.[19]

Conviction stands attacked on all sides in the violent life sur-
rounding our poets. Small wonder that where there is no peace of
mind they are beset by dubieties, and in the midst of wars they
pursue the theme of death. It would surprise a literary historian
not to find in our age such works as *The Waste Land*, *The Hamlet
of A. MacLeish*, *Ulysses*, and other morbid reminders of doubt
and death. A like quality of horror, "the same disabused, acid
world view" in the older metaphysical poets, and "the sense of the
abyss in the French symbolists, all reflect the same thing in
different manners."[20]

History repeats itself with mutations. Obviously, we cannot
parallel without marked exception the events of the seventeenth
century with those of today, nor the reactions of its poets with our
own. The fundamental similarity exists nevertheless. Apparent
differences are sometimes also the basis for a resemblance. For instance, critics who extol the fusion of faculties achieved by the
earlier metaphysicals regret the lack of unification today. Yet it is
just this aptness to integrate human sensibility which characterizes much of our poetry as metaphysical. The difference is one of
degree not kind. Our very imitation of seventeenth-century verse
is a proof of kindred sensibility. If the intellectual climate of the
two periods is necessarily not the same and the religious emphasis
has shifted, the acuteness and multiplicity of problems nevertheless establish a basic affinity. The tumbling worlds of Donne and
Eliot impelled them both to see "unity in diversity" and to seek
"order out of chaos."[21] Though our awareness of a mutable world

is more general and complete, the awareness of predicament in late Elizabethan and Jacobean literature is bitterly evident. It is said that Donne's skepticism was concerned with a *choice* of faiths, ours with faith in general. It still holds that dubiety was the mark of his mind, as it is of ours. It still holds that Eliot, Auden, and others have been seeking a way to belief. If Donne's attitude toward current science was tinged by scholasticism while ours is naturalistic, we cannot skim the fact that Eliot's recoil from the implications of science is akin to Donne's distress. And where their affinity is strongest is in the liberal impress of scientific and psychological suggestions. Both men possessed the metaphysical aptitude to test innovations and to relate them to spiritual significance.

The logical sequence of concrete images was surely more clearly presented by seventeenth-century poets than by those today. The symbolist influence may be in part responsible for the tendency of the modern poet to prefer the severed association. This is true notwithstanding the formal appearance of many stanzas by Eliot and the Fugitives which approximate seventeenth-century logical structures. Although the modern associative process in imagery encourages a superficial dissociation of meanings, the contiguity of discrete figures follows an internal logic. The cohesion of modern poetry lies in the comprehensiveness of its experience. In this respect we have much in common with the seventeenth-century poets, from whom our means of expression differ but not our total communication. If, moreover, our images have not the typical flavor of the seventeenth-century conceit, they are amazingly reminiscent. The "fantasy" of Herbert or Marvell may not be the "fantasy" of Graves or Ransom. Yet the processes of wit today have created the closest thing to a conceit in the history of literature since Donne's time. The vehemence of his intense age produced a figurative medium of exceptional worth. Today we have found it useful again for our drastic feelings and imagery. Much that made the poetry of the seventeenth century brilliant and terrible, exacting and suggestive, is with us again.

Our variations from that period are laid chiefly to the difference between the integrated sensibility of the seventeenth century and the disruption of our emotional grasp. The cause of present disunity is referred to economics (Tate), religion (Eliot), loss of the tragic sense (Krutch), use and misuse of science and technology (Ransom), the separation of the poet from society (Donald Davidson), the schizophrenia in the poet between thought and feeling (Richards)—among them a fairly complete account of the divisions of the modern soul. If there were greater personal convictions in the seventeenth century, the age itself provided numberless conflicts among men and within the individual. Our times are analogous in many ways, and our dissociations have nevertheless produced a similarly inclusive poetry.

TWENTIETH-CENTURY TENSIONS

W$_E$ $_{ARE}$ terribly aware of a radical dislocation in society, in man himself. Driven by "opposing winds of doctrine," our poets must strain to stand firm, believing that "at the present time the problem of the unification of the world and the problem of the unification of the individual, are in the end one and the same problem; and that the solution of one is the solution of the other."[1] From the central affliction of disunity radiate the disintegrating forces of political catastrophe, religious dryness, dissociation of sensibility, disorder in poetry, mechanical standardization, and the general meanness of our life as Eliot sees it. Our problems are so complex that politics or metaphysics, for example, cannot always be considered separately. The dubieties in our culture beget books like *Metapolitics*.[2] Polemicists and poets both tend to approach social, political, scientific affairs "in terms of essences and abstractions,"[3] as Delmore Schwartz says of Wallace Stevens. But like that of others, Stevens' rarefied poetry, especially of late, is affected by the palpable desire to discover a correlation between the soul of man and the commonweal. Such philosophies as deny dualism— on the one hand that of Marxian environmentalists and on the other of emotionalists (Nietzsche, William James, Dewey, Bergson); Catholicism (Eliot, Maritain, Dawson, Péguy); and concepts like transcendentalism and humanism are different approaches to the same double objective: order in the world and integrity of the individual.

These philosophical paths cross and deviate. Eliot repudiates the new humanism (though he was influenced by Irving Babbitt), is dubious of Marxism (though the Catholic Charles Péguy in corporates the best of Marxism into his prose and poetry),[4] and scorns Bergsonism (though he was directed in his ideas by Hulme, an inconsistent disciple of Bergson). Eliot on the other hand is taunted by those who see Anglo-Catholicism as an equivocal solution to spiritual problems, a worldly authority with a defeatist view of human nature. This much he claims for the Catholic answer: that it goes straight to the fundamental (the moral) struggle in man and that esthetically it gives every human experience a universal frame of reference, as in the case of Dante's *Divine Comedy*. In a more general sense we are "all consciously or unconsciously seeking some form of catholic unity to correct the moral, artistic, and political chaos that has resulted from an over-development of protestant diversity" in modern times.[5] Though as a control over our intellectual anarchy Eliot requires some authoritative discipline, he stops short of the Catholic solution in his best-known work and many earlier poems. Until he found his personal sanctuary in religion, he was a sardonic prophet of disintegration. Tradition soon became his first antidote, and religion one of its chief ingredients. Whatever the remedial measures might be, disorder is the primary diagnosis. And whatever virtues or faults Eliot's personal theory offers, at least "The Waste Land" as a poem represents the spiritual condition of the 1920's with imaginative cogency.

"Eliot insists upon metaphysics as giving depth to literature, and he tries to persuade us that literature which is not metaphysical is shallow."[6] He is the most prominent among those in a generation of writers who promoted this tenet. His poetic successors, including a number of revolutionary poets, have couched their meanings in symbolic-metaphysical style. The self-conscious poet is the introvert, though he feels also a sort of personal responsibility for the spiritual integrity of his age. Frederic Prokosch hears the detonation of the bomb but sees its searing flame on the poet's page. Without denying his social conscience, Rolfe Humphries emphasizes the inner man and his need of intenser awareness. His "Statue" is symbolic of a spiraling back to self after the 1930's.[7] Further testimony to this renewed introspection is heard in Spender:

The violence of the times we are living in, the necessity of sweeping and general immediate action, tend to dwarf the experience of the individual. . . . For this reason, in my most recent poems, I have deliberately turned back to a kind of writing which is more personal, and I have included within my subjects weakness and fantasy and illusion.[8]

But the inner activity of the poet echoes the tumult in the world of politics, science, and society. Men like Auden and Stevens and Ransom have concerned themselves with disorder because of the need of order and have made "a poetic liability into a poetic resource, limited but real."[9]

Our poets have lived through "a season in hell," in Rimbaud's words. Their faith in any social corrective has been affected, as have their febrile temperaments. The writing of approximately the last half century has shown this nervous tension, relieved by the high promises of Marxism, psychoanalysis, anthropology, and time-philosophies. There have been three obvious stages within this period, all of them influenced by the metaphysical attitude. Before 1914 the optimism of the nineteenth century lingered. Socialism, evolution, and a flourishing science still nursed utopian hope. Soon, as in the late Elizabethan period, premonitions of failure inaugurated a debunking decade marked by biographers like Lytton Strachey, novelists like Hemingway and John Dos Passos, and poets like Wilfred Owen, Pound, and Eliot. The second phase—from the end of the First World War to the thirties—was characterized by irresponsibility mixed with feverish disillusion. The third, declining swiftly toward the Second World War, was agitated by a brief but militant social effort to resurrect mankind.[10] A return to more personal if clearer notations is now struggling in the latest apprehension of disaster.

As a whole the period has been skeptical, intellectually intense, stinging with irony, and shadowed by doubt. "If poetry is conditional and ironical, affirming and denying in one breath, what response could be more natural to a world which has changed so rapidly that no one knows where he stands?"[11] Realities are being shattered in crisis after crisis. Two wars, labor upheavals, suffragism, technical advances and specialization, prohibition, boom, depression, relativity, Freudianism, behaviorism, inhibitionism, Bergsonism, Buchmanism, Marxism, Dadaism, defeatism, fanaticism, and fear, all tumble about us so madly that there is no time to recover from catastrophe or to assimilate change.[12] "The whole of the modern temper has been a fretful canvassing of the conditions of the soul of man" and of society.[13] With the incessant pressure of external circumstances, the metaphysical poet's inner tension paradoxically resists the smashing impacts. Profiting by its modern formulae, he yet repels the more painful implications of science. The metaphysical ordering of the personal spirit will exploit equally contemporary data and traditional lore. The resulting poetry offers both a refuge and a testing ground for current problems. It constitutes the last step in transition, or the first move toward a new integration.

As the seventeenth century against Elizabethanism, so now contemporary thought, feeling, and expression reacted against the exaggeration of the nineteenth century. Expansion in the provinces of industry, technology, and sociological activity was paralleled by national and empire growth. In America it took the form of prosperity and self-indulgence. Evolution and materialism promised more than they could fulfill; they ran ahead of moral and sociological responsibility. Tariffs, economic and emotional, erected barriers over which pride was to fall. Men sensed this before it happened. Poetry matured swiftly and with pain. In one of the greatest epochs of development the world has known, material experiment was extensive as psychological and poetic experiment was already intensive. Less than fifty years ago vistas were wide and hopeful. But very soon after, the artistic mood altered to a profound discontent that nevertheless produced a vital period of creativeness. The powerful influences are the intense influences, though they be deficient in confidence or credulity.

Overflowing the nineteenth century into the twentieth, the large liberating and confounding forces—Darwin, Thomas Hux-

ley, Marx, Freud, Jung, Pavlov, Einstein—hurled infinite possibilities and anxieties into the lives of men. The flush of excitement
and optimism gave way to dark disappointment, and reaction
was automatic. "It was too good to be true. . . . The depth of
the despair of the present is the measure of its defeated expecta-
tion."[14] The new poetry turned wary and skeptical. What it found
lacking in affirmations and purpose it made up by intense vision.
Yeats's later poetry had that "combination of immediate exactness
with potential expansion" and that "control of focus,"[15] attributes
of much latter-day writing. Yeats, Valéry, Joyce, and Eliot are
representative of an effort at reprisal against a spreading external
menace—by means of myth, symbol, and a metaphysical grasp of
the mind's action. For Eliot this action is productive of spiritual
unity, for Valéry of the principle of life, for Yeats of a fertile myth,
as in the inevitable encounter of the Swan with Leda.

In the early decades of the present century, the habit of travel
among Americans denoted both the epoch's still unconstrained
character and its discontent. The accompanying phenomenon of
self-exile had the same origin. Among the significant and typical
writers who remained abroad for considerable periods, or actually
expatriated themselves, were Henry James, Gertrude Stein, Laf-
cadio Hearn, Malcolm Cowley, John Reed, H. D., John Gould
Fletcher, Crane, Pound, Eliot, MacLeish, Jeffers, and even the
quasi-regional Frost. The thoughts and artistic methods of a generation of writers were enriched by this experience, and in some
cases a strong American feeling was confirmed. There occurred
an exchange of ideas especially among the younger writers of
England, France, and America, though other countries shared in
the new developments: Italy, Germany, and Belgium. If there was
something amiss with America—with the world at large—perhaps
a cultural "cure" could be got from a change of air.

By means of this restless transience, the American poet learned
and practiced poetic habits that might otherwise have remained
alien. In France he became acquainted with symbolism, impressionism, surrealism; in England with imagism; while in his studies

he met Chinese, Japanese, Provençal, and Old English influences. Naturally contacts of this sort, once they were established, reached far beyond the place of origin. At Harvard and in England, Eliot was impressed with symbolism by way of Arthur Symons, Hulme, and Pound.[16] Early in his career Pound knew the French writers, and later cultivated an interest in Chinese forms and Japanese drama. Imagism had its season in England and America at once, in magazines like *Poetry* and *Blast*. A return of the poets to primitive forms coincided with the work of André Gide and D. H. Lawrence, the popular study of African art, Hulme's concern with the Byzantine, and the revival of Old English alliterative and accentual verse.

Primitivism is a recurrent phenomenon in literature, not confined to the romantic. For his day there was a sort of primitivism in Donne's very sophistication. A return to childhood and nature characterized Vaughan, and particularly Traherne. "For a moment, a breath of the coming primitivism of a more exhausted and complacent time comes into the sophisticated civilization of the seventeenth century."[17] A form of Rousseauism, this interest in the primitive may be the effort to find the good answer in the beginnings of mankind, in original innocence. The contrary philosophy, the Catholic belief in original sin, is supported by Eliot and his disciples. Yet these poets have also shown a most determined regard for tradition, which is in itself a return to the past— essentially romantic in attitude. Certain of his absolute (Catholic) and traditionally classic values Eliot inherited from Hulme. In the following lines the latter exhibits his philosophical interest in primitive and Byzantine art,[18] a concern not unrelated to his incipient imagism and to ideas of abstraction:

We neglected Byzantine art, for example, just as we neglected scholastic philosophy. . . . Both Byzantine and Egyptian art spring from an attitude towards life which made it impossible to use the accidental shapes of living things as symbols of the divine. Both consequently are geometrical in character. . . . The only thing the new period will have in common with mediaevalism will be the subordination of man to certain absolute values.[19]

Yeats's poems on Byzantium confirm this contemporary interest in older forms, as do the primitive implications of his astrological convictions.

There are clear instances of our cult of primitive places, peoples, objects, and idiom: Sherwood Anderson's "dark laughter," the fad of African masks and archaic statuettes, our infatuation with Mexico and Harlem, enthusiasm for the "primitives" of the painter Henri Rousseau, American rural artists, and the expressionists. The outstanding exponent of pristine panaceas for contemporary conflicts is of course Lawrence, who resorted literarily to basic sex impulses and finally to self-exile among the Mexicans and American Indians. Gertrude Stein's cult of automatic and quasi-automatic writing denotes not only subtle psychological curiosity and an objective attempt to free the writer of self but a concern with abstract primitivism. Here also may be cited Pound's use of Chinese ideograms, the typographical experimentation of Cummings, and Guillaume Apollinaire's emblematic stylizations—reminiscent of the seventeenth-century shaping of poems to suggest their content. These, like the emblems of that time, are experimental in nature but primitive in effect.

Sometimes regarded as an evasion of our dilemma, primitivism is a natural anomaly of the modern mood. "Twentieth century amateurs of savage art exhibit a legitimate craving for an imperilled spontaneity while duping themselves with the notion that by satisfying this craving they can satisfy also the more complicated wants of mankind."[20] But this interest afforded, besides escape and a kind of panacea, an extension of knowledge into comparative religions and cultures. Ernest Fenollosa, searching in an unknown art for motives and principles, looked for fundamental esthetics. To that end he paralleled and compared Eastern and Western art, expecting from the contact an American Renaissance. Pound was impressed. He completed Fenollosa's essay on the Chinese written character and his work on the Japanese Noh plays. Pound's repeated notice of the primitive is seen in his memoir of Henri Gaudier-Brzeska, a sculptor of ultramodern tendencies whose art is both primal and abstract. His sculpture and writing attempted a synthesis of severe abstraction and massive primordial contours: an austere subtlety joined to the intrinsic character of whatever material he worked with. In referring to Jacob Epstein's form in comparison with Gaudier's, Pound approached a definition of metaphysical "austere permanence: some relation *of* life and yet outside it."[21] Like his generation—Picasso, Epstein, Hulme, Gaudier, Eliot—Pound has been interested in the concept of form. That concept would prove the appositeness of primal meanings and their subtle present significance, as in Gaudier's sculptural "appreciation of masses in relation."[22] The double quality of this sculptor's work shows that there is a point at which the primitive and the decadent touch.[23] For Eliot, "the purpose of reascending to origins is that we should be able to return, with greater spiritual knowledge, to our own situation."[24] In the so-called primitive, there is "the operation of a social-religious-artistic complex which we should emulate upon a higher plane."[25] Primitivism is only one of several responses to a period of intellectual and physical turmoil. Its opposite is an uneasy, obsessive, but strangely inert concern with the shape of the future. An evasion of either is recourse to the inner self for safety or consolation.[26]

Among the many current reactions has been that against the romantic nineteenth century generally; against Victorianism more specifically; against Georgian placidity; against the so-called Decadence, itself a retaliation for Victorian virtues; against the group of social utopians at the turn of the century whose one-sided nostrums were doomed to failure; against the free-verse rebellion, an event of the poetic revolution. The more slovenly freedoms and loose forms of the vers librists precipitated the most potent reaction, the Eliot movement: a synthesis of radicalism and tradition. This movement hurdled its nearer predecessors and found itself in the seventeenth century. Its sympathy has been extended also to the borders of the metaphysical age—the Elizabethans and the early Augustans, including Dryden and in some cases Pope—and by analogy to the ideation and feeling of

Dante and the symbolists. The welcome accorded the seventeenth century excluded Milton until his recent partial reinstatement. The distaste has been for the style rather than the man. Our poets respect the seventeenth century (excepting Miltonic grandiloquence) for its middle style,[27] after Elizabethanism became astringent and before Augustan convention turned stale.

From Wordsworth to Tennyson and Matthew Arnold, from the Pre-Raphaelites to the "mauve" decade and the Georgians, the poetic process was a gradual vitiation of romantic poetry, finally no more than minor streams between placid Georgian banks. When didactic, it was naïvely explicit or solemnly general. Moderns prefer implicit symbolism but the exact image, oblique manner but the precise form, important implication but the immediate response. The proper nuances have a psychological function for us, imperfectly appreciated by the nineteenth century. Few poets today can write of romantic love or patriotism or simple nature without looking anachronistic. "The passions which swept through the once major poets no longer awaken any profound response, and only in the bleak, torturous complexities of a T. S. Eliot does it find its minds given adequate expression." There "impends for the human spirit either extinction or a readjustment more stupendous than any made before."[28]

The resort of the present age is the same ironic realm visited in the seventeenth century. There has been again a key transposition in the psychological attitude toward certain values like love. Many Victorian dogmas were already weakened before H. G. Wells or Havelock Ellis, but even these iconoclasts preserved a transcendental attitude toward love which was destined to be further modified. The scientific approach freed the love theme of taboos, but at the same time weakened its connection with the great themes of sin and romantic dedication. Still the need for a deep passion remained. Meanwhile, some of the most influential writers cleared the way for it: Aldous Huxley, Hemingway, Lawrence, Joyce, Eliot. The analysis advocated with different motives by grandfather Huxley terminated in a destruction of illusion by grandson Huxley. Modern writers stress abstract design in art and intellectualism in literature, "since both represent a reaction from that diffusion of sublimated sex through all the arts which is one of the chief characteristics of romanticism."[29] At the same time there was an effort to reëstablish other values and processes in place of those that had fallen. Among these have been William James's "will to believe," Bergson's "élan vital," Hans Vaihinger's "defense of workable 'fictions,'" the English "emergence," and the German "Gestalt."[30] To escape the consequences of late nineteenth-century mechanism and twentieth-century disenchantment, a number of scientific and metaphysical roads were indicated. It became apparent also that "a revolution in the imagery of poetry is in reality a revolution in metaphysics."[31]

The poets' critical attitudes suggest many forms of modern poetic revolt. They have rejected Victorian operatic effects and refused to compromise thought for its more agreeable postures.[32] Their dry and inquiring assumptions incline them to the satiric periods as well as to certain Elizabethan qualities. Strictures against the nineteenth-century deficiency in "cancelling power" are significant. Also significant is the shift in emphasis from English classics chiefly admired by the Victorians—Chaucer, Spenser, Shakespeare, Milton, Burns—to others that also attract recent poets: Peele, Kyd, the less familiar aspects of Shakespeare, Webster, Marvell, and Dryden.[33] Ransom disparages the "heart's desire" poetry of the romantics which idealizes and therefore fails to adapt itself to reality. He scorns its "furtive libido" and its ways of escape. Critic-poet of the same school, Tate calls obscure a romanticized emotion by Edna Millay but not Donne's "Second Anniversary." He admits that Cleveland and Cowley fathered bad verse, but not so bad as James Thomson's "The Vine." Cowley's "Hymn. To Light," firm verse in spite of its poor lines, was written in "an age that produced some of the greatest English poetry."[34] Logical extension of imagery is well used, he believes, in Donne's "A Valediction: forbidding mourning," but to poor advantage in Cowley's hymn. Yet Cowley's failure here is less obnoxious than

Thomson's because of the seventeenth-century resolute use of language. Tate, like Laura Riding, condemns the romantic exploitation of "poetical objects." He says:

> I am·not attacking the great Romantic poets. Romanticism gave us the "Ode to a Nightingale"; decadent Romanticism is now giving us the interminable ballads and local-color lyrics of Mr. Coffin and Mr. Stephen Benét. . . . The more we track down the implications of . . . the imagery in the best verse of Donne, Marvell, Raleigh, Milton, Hopkins, Yeats, Eliot, Ransom, Stevens, the richer the meaning of the poem.[35]

The revolt against the nineteenth century consisted probably "only in the discarding of the increasingly blurred expression of the century, its stale grandeurs, stale terrors, stale little intimacies, but not fundamental poetics."[36] Our poetic revolutionaries "pour mieux sauter" returned to Elizabethan and post-Elizabethan rhetoric. After romantic laxness they felt the need to tense their nerves. It is true that in the nineteenth century Browning and Emily Brontë were psychologically advanced, that Tennyson and Arnold were troubled by religious doubts, that Hopkins was prosodically and otherwise precocious for his time. It is further true that Baudelaire, Rimbaud, and Mallarmé were prepared to understand a difficult period emotionally and intellectually. But it was Eliot's generation and the generation he molded which as a group took full inventory of the changes.[37] Although Yvor Winters has some unusual loyalties, such as to Jones Very, he is no lover of loose romanticism, meaningless descriptive verse, or incoherent motivation. "If the convention of a poem is badly defined, the poetry is vague. This is one of the many things wrong with most of Shelley, Byron, Hugo, De Musset, Lamartine, and the other typical romantics."[38] Winters states, moreover, that though on the contrary Verlaine's life was a confused affair, the precision with which he calculated his limited range of meaning sets him above those romantic predecessors "who smeared everything with a consistent texture of falsity."[39]

Of course, there has been more than enough in twentieth-century poetry that is attitudinizing or tiresome. But it must get credit for being disabused, observant, and intense. MacNeice makes these points:

> Our diction should be masculine but not exhibitionist. After the feminine writing of most of the nineteenth century . . . and after the neuter writing of the Georgians we are working back towards the normal virile efficiency of Dryden or Chaucer. . . . [Our poets] should write honestly . . . neither lagging behind in an obsolete romanticism nor running ahead to an assurance too good to be true.[40]

Spender observes a like esteem for the sinewy writing of the best of seventeenth- and eighteenth-century literatures. Among the important admirers of early Augustan effects, Edith Sitwell shows more than usual scorn for Victorianism: "The power of English poetry had been much weakened by such poets as Matthew Arnold and Dr. Bridges. . . . [But] the silvery tintinnabulations of tea-spoons left over from the tea-parties of the Victorian Aunts of Poetry" have been discarded at last.[41] Such signal exceptions as Hopkins and Yeats remain high in our regard. Swinburnian vagueness resulted in part from nineteenth-century slighting of mathematical precision.[42] The seventeenth and twentieth, on the contrary, are mathematical periods maintaining a "fundamental duality, with *material* on the one hand, and on the other hand *mind*."[43]

It was not the scientific optimism of the Victorians but our scientific probity that directed the exploration of matter and mind "reaching deep down into the unconscious and even perhaps into the blood."[44] In revolt against a Wellsian world, Eliot questioned inventions and progress whose claims slurred means of securing the integrity of the spirit. His reactions are not always personal crotchets regarding perfectibility, undisciplined liberalism, and conventional welfare. Shared by others, these displeasures were early encouraged, perhaps suggested, by Hulme's speculations. His and Pound's corrections were resistance to the latterly enervating values of romanticism: its flaccid art and intellectual relaxation. As a result, much of Eliot's "distaste for the romantic poets was owing to the lack of correspondence between their beliefs and a mature understanding of experience."[45] He deplores their lack of perspective and their vulnerability to irony. "I have long felt that the poetry of the seventeenth and eighteenth centuries, even much of that of inferior inspiration, possesses an elegance and a dignity absent from the popular and pretentious verse of the Romantic Poets and their successors."[46] Compared with Donne and Chapman, "almost every nineteenth century poet is in some way limited or deformed."[47] Tennyson's blank verse is more callow than that of "half a dozen contemporaries of Shakespeare; cruder, because less capable of expressing complicated, subtle, and surprising emotions."[48] Where Dryden "fails to satisfy, the nineteenth century does not satisfy us either; and where that century has condemned him, it is itself condemned."[49] Wherever virility of style or intensity of emotion and mind is found, there one finds our poets rediscovering affinity. Whether it be in Hopkins, Emily Dickinson, Browning, Dryden, Marvell, Webster, Chapman, Raleigh, Douglas, Chaucer, Dante, or the Anglo-Saxon rhythms, the modern rebel admires a crisp economy or subtle fervor. The whole of the romantic tradition, waning in its Victorian, Edwardian, and Georgian aspects, has failed of approval with many moderns.

The Georgians were in their time hailed as "new" poets who would refresh the Victorian practice and clear the Decadence. Most modernists, however, rejected their lead. Simplicities of theme and manner that ignored the severe issues of the interior self very soon grew irksome to the speculative war and postwar poet. Since Tennyson or Longfellow or W. H. Davies, poetry has perceptively moved away from the idyl and the rural lane to the man in the street and the machine. Prufrock walks the pavement and listens at the beach, but his rhapsodies are scornful of himself and other men; he is a private and a public symbol in a very special new synthesis. His passions are thin but the irony bites hard. Even A. E. Housman's sardonic melancholy has not been sufficient to satisfy the modernist critic, to whom he is also a romantic, "a term not exactly of abuse, but of pity and impatience."[50] A D. H. Lawrence, who expresses the modern intensity, seems almost out of place in a Georgian anthology. To him real thought "is an experience. It begins as a change in the blood."[51] Exposed to salutary influences, most of the Georgians remained unaffected by such ardor. Where Swinburne was too facile, Browning was too difficult for them. Critically accurate in recognizing Hopkins' genius and in promoting experimental ideas, Robert Bridges was too timid and academic in practice. Hopkins' truly germinal talent lived concealed until it was too late to exert a personal influence. Posthumous publication of his work energized English poetry by its revival of accentual Anglo-Saxon prosody and that contact of vibrant inner life with verse. His excitements, though also turbulently romantic like Crane's, appeal to contemporary taste for abstruse, difficult cognition. Even to the skeptical mind an emotional catharsis is salutary. Therefore Hopkins' religious poems are useful to those who wrestle for understanding. Finally it was Pound and Eliot and the Sitwells, with their strange intense landscapes, that provided "a challenge to the almost embarrassingly nude forms of the Georgians."[52]

In a double review of Grierson's Donne edition and of *Georgian Poetry, 1911-1912*, Walter de la Mare, though himself a Georgian, sets up a juxtaposition in itself prophetic. He found Donne's poetry lean of description but full of meaning in his "profound, self-plaguing penitence." He was never an escapist or a sentimentalist, from his early love poems to the "holy sonnets." Apparently De la Mare wants this quality of emotional directness in the Georgian anthology—which includes poems by Abercrombie, Gibson, Davies, Stephens, Flecker, Chesterton, Brooke, Bottomley, Drinkwater, Monro, and Lawrence. Though Brooke's reputation has not vindicated the reviewer's estimate, what De la Mare had to say is otherwise significant:

There are many influences perceptible in this volume; but that of Donne—Donne in his headlong, rebellious youth—is traceable only in the work of Mr. Rupert Brooke. He is more self-centered than the rest, more analytical and intellectual. He is also more impatient of tradition. . . . His verse keeps unusually close to actual experience and is yet imaginatively in focus.[53]

Representing a reaction against the Victorian worship of science and progress, the Georgians limited their themes to acceptable generalities like love and the landscape, youth and age and the milder natural world,[54] until the war ruffled their poetry. But eventually it relapsed to a choice of several sentiments either delicate or daring. Echoes of Cavalier lightness lacked its prickling quality, and the daring was superficial.[55]

More exactly it was a retreat from Victorian issues and the deeper meanings of the World War, just as the Decadence was a flight into conventional pessimism from the preceding optimistic period. "The Georgians, in opposition to the aesthetes, professed to bring back happiness into poetry, but their happiness rings no more true than the fastidious gloom of their predecessors."[56] Georgian poetry manifested enough variation, such as De la Mare's symbolic mysticism; W. W. Gibson's interest in the workingman; Lawrence's passion and mastery of subtler emotions; Masefield's superficial muscularity and storytelling gift; Owen's, Edward Thomas', and Sturge Moore's understanding of war, men, and nature respectively. Yet as a whole the movement seemed, in the retrospect of metaphysical critics, to be quiet, simple, ignorant and evasive of the real issues involved in industrial life and in the cunning passions. The counteraction of the metaphysical poets was directed against what they deemed false or insufficient. They were "faced with the problem of communicating on several levels at once . . . of building something to replace the Tennysonian tradition." Where the seventeenth century had complexity and versatile imagery and the nineteenth at least philosophical support, "the Georgians had neither multiplicity nor philosophy, for neither was allowed them by the conditions of their time, and they tried to compensate by naïveté."[57]

Together with the change in attitude, there came a change in poetic form. Imagists and writers of free verse had already experimented radically with novel patterns. Against both these groups, constituting two stages toward verbal independence, the Pound-Eliot school took some exception. Technically the free verse movement in this century was a great liberating force. It was accompanied by a vigorous return to regional and human realism. Interest in places localized the realism; interest in people expanded it. The freedom of the new verse ran riot in America, but its expressive nuances were not sufficiently subtle to speak for the new age, which demanded " 'metaphysical' irony . . . constantly aware of alternative approaches to the situation."[58] Even Whitman, whose authority had been strong in the first stages of the revolt, was inadequate for the metaphysicals. He had begotten the free-verse generation, and his reputation declined with theirs. He was found to be neither intellectual nor adroit enough in the latter-day sense. He was mostly sun and wind and flesh; but the shadows were not there though he embraced death, and he seemed to have missed the nerves. His good optimism was uncomfortably reminiscent of the Victorian, and his love could not overwhelm subsequent cataclysms.

Emily Dickinson approached the temper of the new types, and her delayed influence steeped the twenties and thirties. Her American idiom differed considerably from Whitman's enormous language. She also saw nature, but meticulously. She also disregarded the traditional in rhythm and rhyme if not in stanza, but her temperament was metaphysical and her writing at times came close to "pure" poetry. Published posthumously, like Donne and Hopkins, she reached her vogue only thirty years after. This belated appearance stimulated the technique and sensibility of our times with an imagistic yet abstract poetry. She and Hopkins were precocious expressions of the modern metaphysical era.

If they were the vanguard, Eliot became the leader of the metaphysical revival. His followers were legion, and almost every new poet owes him a debt. Distortion of his tenets and methods, and multiplication of echoes, have not deterred others. Though this writing surprised the reader out of his wits and enticed him beyond his depth, the virtues of an intellectual, emotive poetry became a stern corrective to much frowzy free verse. The rigors and subtleties of associative poetry demand the devoted attention of the reader. There is nothing soporific about Pound, MacLeish, Cummings, Crane, or Stevens. Their poems were meant to and naturally serve to irritate the mind into taking notice. Modernist idiom and prosody, supported by appropriate past examples, offer a spicy mixture of fact and abstraction, of intellection and feeling. The age gradually grew susceptible to a complex poetry express- ing the central vortex around which the furies fly. The reaction represented by such poetry can become highly rarefied and re- mote.[59] At its head Eliot, already channeled by French symbolism, was impelled to stem not only a prolonged romanticism but also the lax standards of free verse, of which he was heir. His acknowl- edged master Pound had been an early champion of free verse and had cultivated its offshoot, imagism, when free verse was still not generally acceptable.[60] But though Pound wrote the tenets of imagism, he himself reproved vers libre abuses and eccentricities by the example of *Hugh Selwyn Mauberley* whose cadence taught other poets Gautier's *Émaux et Camées*.[61]

So we arrive at the full development of the Eliot period after a number of rebellious phases, expressions of one general revolt. What might appear to be a reactionary move by the Pound-Eliot reversion to traditional literatures and techniques could be inter- preted equally as radicalism. Perhaps as Eliot says "a step in the opposite direction is not, here, a step backwards."[62] In the case of Hopkins, for example, his exploitation of Old English alliter- ation and what he came to call sprung rhythm was so advanced that even acute readers would scarcely have taken to him in his lifetime; nor has the average reader reached him yet in sensibility, technique, or meaning. This still applies to Shakespeare, for that matter, and post-Elizabethan metaphysicals.

Dissociation of sensibility—meaning from matter, mind from emotion, sensation from sense—is commonly attributed to certain processes that began in the late seventeenth century. One action of science was to stultify the sensibilities while it honed the mind; common sense alienated the faculties, one from the other. Among the stylists who more than Dryden or Pope limited the potenti- alities of poetry was Milton, who had "not been able to think and to imagine at the same time."[63] The vital English of Shakespeare was "split into two components one of which was exploited by Milton and the other by Dryden. Of the two, I still think Dryden's development the healthier,"[64] insists Eliot, to whom the philosopher and the poet in Milton seem not well integrated. With the conscious revolt of the present, the blank verse that had been molded for a long time on Miltonic proportions reassumed Shakespearian and Websterian elasticity and conversational tones. To the modernist,[65] Milton's conventional and artificial musicality weakened his sensuous (especially visual) imagination and subordinated psychological acuteness of thought to the sound of words. His aural sense was developed out of proportion to his other faculties. In addition to Góngora and *Euphues*,[66] Tasso and Du Bartas are held guilty for what is regarded as pompous in Miltonic beauty. Milton "forgets himself to marble" in the manner of Poussin, his contemporary in art, and both "spoke a dead language."[67] Though rhetoric has been revived in modern times through the influences not only of Dante and the late Elizabethans but of Hopkins, Whitman, and Crane, this rhetoric has not been either Miltonian or Latinic in tone.

With the subsidence of other reactions, Milton is again being defended. Pound initiated Miltonoclasm in particularly abusive terms, supported by Eliot's obliquely sniping criticism. He calls Milton's rhetoric an "abominable dogbiscuit" and is cheered by Eliot's use of Dryden as "a good club wherewith to smack Milton."[68] Had we been more familiar with Dante, there would be less need of Dryden as a counterblast, since "Milton resembles Dante in nothing";[69] the one being a "windbag," the other a precise image-maker. Specifically Pound sees Dante as metaphysical, Milton as "merely sectarian." Other critics followed the trend: Middleton Murry, Read, Bonamy Dobrée, F. R. Leavis, and F. L. Lucas. But Logan Pearsall Smith,[70] after candidly reviewing the attitudes against Milton, attempts to refute his modern detractors.[71] The prominent accusations have been his unlovable character; the overabundance of verbal music and ponderous proper names in his verse; his use of foreign idiom and syntax, a stricture first submitted by Johnson. The modern shift of taste toward a stark and harsh poetry accounts for much of the (now receding) shadow on Milton.

In general the aversion to ways of thinking and techniques of writing contrary to our extreme inclinations has somewhat waned. As to Victorianism, there is even at moments a regret that we have lost so completely its comparative calm and security. But if recent poets envy what passes for Victorian smugness and confidence in the now modified verities, they cannot honestly employ in literature those qualities of which life itself is again devoid. Modern criticism no longer emphasizes our points of superiority over the Victorians so much as our differences from them. The Victorians may have entertained doubts about their doubts; we are unhappily certain of ours. We are inhibited as to the "simpler expansive developments of emotion" and its expression. If the cause is "the increasing indefiniteness of our beliefs and disbeliefs,"[72] the cause behind it is the accelerating frequency of modern crises.

9

PHASES OF THE MODERN CRISIS

Incipient before the First World War, political disorder
was widely augmented in the twenties and thirties; and the conviction became general that the previous generation had failed
to establish a more secure and civilized society. "The absorption
of certain of the young modern poets with politics may be considered in two ways: as a reaction from the Georgian decline,
and as an indication of the social unrest" which existed in Europe
at this time.[1] While under his technical influence, these poets
condemned Eliot for lack of participation in the political struggle.
Yet historically he has not been altogether isolated from socio-
political issues.

Here Hulme, his ideological progenitor, had a particular concern with the problems of class and party stressed by Georges
Sorel, some of whose work he translated into English. Hulme
desired the establishment of such political thinking as might
promote a return to classicism in literature and the other arts, his
prime interests. The connection between literary classicism and
socialism appears in Sorel's exposition of the class struggle. Sorel,

the most remarkable socialist since Marx . . . expects a return of the
classical spirit through the struggle of the classes. . . . Given the classical
attitude, he tries to prove that its present manifestation may be hoped
for in working-class violence. . . . There are many who begin to be
disillusioned with liberal and pacifist *democracy*, while shrinking from
the opposed *ideology* on account of its reactionary associations. To
these people Sorel, a revolutionary in economics, but classical in ethics,
may prove an emancipator.[2]

Hulme also believed that ethical concepts are absolutes, and further that the idea of just equality among men offered "something to all men." He and Eliot envisioned a society with a classical or revolutionary authority, either of the church or the state. The "liberal" democratic process to them constituted a romantic and disordered condition of society. These thoughts are obviously related to the present world struggle, and Hulme was prophetic of that conflict if not of the outcome.

In his 1915 translator's preface to Sorel's *Reflections on Violence*, Hulme attempts to explain and justify the author's antidemocratic thinking by reference to the fall of man and original sin. These concepts theoretically separate democrat from antidemocrat. The former relies, with Rousseau, on man's original goodness and the resulting evolution toward perfectibility. The democrat is by assumption romantic, rational, and relative. Believing in original sin, his opponent is classical, pessimistic, and absolute. The conviction that man has a very limited ability to improve implies his attendant suffering and ultimately breeds a kind of mystic faith. This belief, whose influence on Eliot has been so considerable, is self-contradictory in several ways. Its classic absolutism is only the reverse side of the coin, since romanticism has its own absolute faith—not in authority but in man himself. There is, moreover, the incongruity between democratic Catholicism by very definition and Eliot's aristocratic views. Granting the traditional basis of his creed, his disappointment with the democratic principle, or practice perhaps, results from the present state of society. Likewise Sorel's "disillusionment with *democracy*" runs in the history of much modern disillusion. "The belief that pacifist democracy will lead to no regeneration of society, but rather to its decadence, and the reaction against romanticism in literature, is naturally common to many different schools."[3] We might correlate this social disenchantment and literary reaction with the extensive revolt against nineteenth-century ideals, with the two devastating wars (to date) of the twentieth century, with the apparent failure of democracy to fulfill its brilliant promise, and finally with its strenuous efforts to be reëstablished in the world.

We have recognized the analogous situation in Shakespeare's

time and after, and made a pertinent historical comparison between those writers and ours. The late Elizabethans and Jacobeans

were seeing and hearing, not the fabulous Renaissance and the revival of classicism, but the other side of the Renaissance: the political intrigues, the murders, the violence of cardinals, princes and politicians. Eliot, feeling himself in a Europe of cultural decay, unbelief, mass-murder, torture, political intrigue, usury and faithlessness, made the discovery that the late Elizabethans were describing a world which had much in common with our own.[4]

This is a significant acknowledgment from Spender who has a right to say that "there is, in our modern literature, a consistent tradition of writing that has a political-moral subject."[5] The political stress applies to the originally leftist Auden-Spender school, the moral to the older Eliot-Pound group, but neither neglects the reciprocal meanings. Modern writers are divided by Spender into three groups as to their social and political, essentially moral, attitudes: those who express no overt belief such as the earlier Eliot, Virginia Woolf, and Yeats in his briefer poems; those like Lawrence who maintain a private individualistic program; those who interpret an existing belief or foretell a future one. In the last group we find exponents of potential progress and success: Shaw, Wells, and J. B. Priestley; the communist writers; the psychologists.

Among others, Eliot has contended that the social laissez faire of bourgeois democracy can cause a lack of vigilance and a selfish indifference to the future. The past laxness of democracy eventually led to disaster and brought about an assault on the liberals and the middle classes. While "liberalism did not know what it wanted of education, radicalism does know; and it wants the wrong thing. Radicalism is, however, to be applauded for wanting something."[6] Eliot blames the middle class for moral corruption, for debasing education, and for stimulating thereby the radical slant of contemporary thinking. With Dante he feels that evil is better than a mere suspension between good and evil, and adds that radicalism of the left is better than nothing at all. This much he finds in favor of communism: its realistic fundaments and its passionate ideal as a "religious" education. Such is the attitude of certain rightists, among whom Eliot would no doubt place himself. From a leftist point of view,[7] middle-class culture (implying Eliot also) is condemned for its indifference and exhaustion, its lack of spontaneity, and its self-conscious fear of being duped, wrong, or ridiculous.

Yet even the more subjective of its (metaphysical) poets are often or finally involved in the politics of our century. Some of them, like MacLeish and Genevieve Taggard, whose earlier themes were personal and speculative, eventually acquire an ardent interest in social developments. Pound and Eliot view their conflicts in historical perspective; Crane superimposes the industrial on the personal problem; and the Fugitives offer regional economic criticism. In many cases the social poets themselves have borrowed heavily from metaphysical attitudes and techniques. Conversely, when the metaphysical poet devotes his verses to such verities as love, God, and time, he still cannot divorce himself from his age and his social or economic environment. Indeed, the poet of this age has increasingly responded to its intellectual and social climate. Literature even implicitly has felt and reported our accumulating difficulties.

Assaulting a generation at a highly vulnerable moment when it was ready for new candor, the First World War quickened both its aggression and self-retreat. People put on a defense of doubt and questioned wholesale the established rules: of nation, religion, morals, and mind. The mold was broken for what had been and skepticism saw no easy pattern for what was to be.[8] The historical sense and a "professional self-consciousness" were needed to equip our poet to express such complicated social maladjustments. The war and postwar generation was driven in spite of itself to the use of irony and oblique attack both metaphysical and psychological, to the grotesque, the quizzical, the intellectual, the symbolic. Those not engaged in actual warfare were still in the presence of death. Self-consciousness and social consciousness became fellow soldiers. "The brutality and humanity demanded by Synge both came into poetry at once—with the

War."[9] Since propaganda is a temporary expedient, social optimism must be implemented by concern with the deeper issues aggravated by external conflict. Thus, in the wake of the First World War, literature became more metaphysical in attitude and more strikingly ambivalent in expression.

Poets looked for "more violent sources of imagery" in their efforts to express the latent brutality in life;[10] violence was employed as much for the description of the inner scene as for the revolutionary and communal. While the public crisis challenged them, individual requirements made commensurate demands. On the other hand, even so aloof and special a poet as Wallace Stevens has felt the enormous hurry of social forces, particularly with the Second World War. He says that "in speaking of the pressure of reality, I am thinking of life in a state of violence, not physically violent, as yet, for us in America, but physically violent for millions of our friends and for still more millions of our enemies and spiritually violent, it may be said, for every one alive."[11] Men forget themselves in such times, and yet remember themselves acutely.[12] The indirect artistic reaction is as significant in such situations as the direct. Franz Werfel's mysticism or Lawrence's primitive revolt or the Sitwells' *mise en scène* is no mere irrational coincidence. Self-exile, intricate technique, the complex of emotions, and social valedictories in Proust, James, Chekhov, and Eliot are the profound effects of unrest. As Henry James well and early understood:

The plunge of civilization into this abyss of blood and darkness . . . is a thing that so gives away the whole long age during which we have supposed the world to be, with whatever abatement, gradually bettering, that to have to take it all now for what the treacherous years were all the while really making for and *meaning* is too tragic for any words.[13]

The premonitory retreat of certain writers began before World War I.[14] At first Yeats took to the countryside and Irish legends. Pound remembered Provence and China. For a time Eliot continued to present the contemporary scene with sardonic astuteness, but his retreat came later. "Yeats, Eliot, and Pound in various degrees then have used history as a standard by which to show the nature of their own time."[15] Others felt it their duty to effect changes as well as to observe them. The "generation of Auden and Spender could no longer see any choice but to hasten the process and work for a new order."[15] Without active participation in a new order, the men who gave us the fiery journal *Blast, Ulysses, The Ambassadors,* and such telling poems as "The Hollow Men," were nevertheless *"the first men of a Future that has not materialized."*[16] In a general mobilization, the arts were likewise recruits. For several years before the first great war, they were affected by the ferment in society. Political changes in England and in its constitution, the numerous strikes, the suffragette movement, the Irish agitation, and mounting international differences created a tense atmosphere. "There was, indeed, a sense of rebellion in the air, against convention, against accepted codes of morals,"[17] a refractory sense demanding voice. The wars—those of the seventeenth century, those of the nineteenth in France, and again the world-wide wars of the twentieth—not only gave writers new themes but heightened their sensibility, stimulated their mental processes, cross-fertilized current literary types and methods, and prepared new integrations of experience and expression.

Our wars are the brutal offspring of sociologic, mainly economic and political disorders. Specifically, socio-economics interested Eliot as standardization, Pound as usury. In the *Cantos,* Pound devoted some of his sharpest passages to diatribes against usury, affecting all society as exploitation and monopoly, both industrial and imperial. He describes elsewhere how even the mild Georgians reacted to adversities occasioned reciprocally by finance and war:

The world war startled a few of them into thought, the Russian Revolution and the later fiscal calamities have perhaps clouded their declining years with a vague adumbration. . . . [Harold Monro, for example,] had chosen the worst time to live in, he had gone through the two darkest *lustra,* or the three or more as you figure it: 1902 to 1908, 1920 to 1930. . . . Our generation was brought up in absolute economic illiteracy. Only the most tortured and active among us have been driven to analyse the hell that surrounded us. Monetary infection has penetrated the inmost crannies of mind; the virus has been so subtle that men's minds . . . have been strangled before they knew it.[18]

Pound's conclusions are always questionable, yet he did provoke some economic consciousness in modern poetry.[19] Today almost all poets have been modified in temperament and in theme by the sociological experience of our time, though their methods may derive from the previous generation. Genevieve Taggard pursued social sympathies after the period of Elinor Wylie's metaphysics. Kenneth Patchen became for a time the mystical symbolist of the revolution; Horace Gregory the radical intellectualist. Conrad Aiken, MacLeish, Crane, Stevens; Josephine Miles, Kenneth Fearing, Muriel Rukeyser, Norman Rosten—older and younger poets alike—are concerned in various degrees with the social landscape. The whole English group associated with Auden when he was still in England was frankly sociological in its main subjects. The Fugitives proposed at first to cure the South of its maladies by advocating a return to agrarian economy: a sort of insular reprisal against the encroachments of the North and of industrialism.

Political and abstract philosophies have in this century been reëxamined with an intensity that carries over into literature. Whitehead summarizes what civilization has endured intellectually in the last three hundred years and how philosophy has tried to converge on factuality:

The seventeenth century had genius, and cleared the world of muddled thought. The eighteenth century continued the work of clearance, with ruthless efficiency. . . . A scientific realism, based on mechanism, is conjoined with an unwavering belief in the world of men and of the higher animals as being composed of self-determining organisms. This radical inconsistency at the basis of modern thought accounts for much that is half-hearted and wavering in our civilisation. . . . In the nineteenth century, some of the deeper thinkers among theologians and philosophers were muddled thinkers. Their assent was claimed by incompatible doctrines; and their efforts at reconciliation produced inevitable confusion.[20]

In our time, while positivism with its fidelity to fact governs scientific thought, philosophies like Bergson's reject static materialism. "It is this union of passionate interest in the detailed facts with equal devotion to abstract generalisation which forms the novelty in our present society."[21] Thus the inheritance of materialism and mechanism from the sixteenth and seventeenth centuries, sustained by the half-explored positivism of the nineteenth century, has led to conflicting spiritual reactions today. Scientific philosophy has paralleled the struggle of political philosophies: material and ideal. And metaphysical poetry has been found eminently fitted to reflect that dissension by inquiring into opposing concepts with a hope for their integration.

In one form or another, a number of philosophers and poets have purported to discover their own need—and by analogy that of society—for spiritual regeneration after positivism; for an affirmation superior to the tentative success of Victorian science; for hope after the material pessimism of Housman and the surface progressivism of Wells. Such Neo-Scholastics and religio-intellectualists as Hulme, Maritain, Eliot, Michael Roberts, Ransom, and Tate condemn as modern heresy the secular effort toward a (false) perfectibility based on undisciplined values. Because modernity has been forced to view life and knowledge as relative, complex, and fluctuating—as Donne anticipated—these men desire a limited and absolute simplicity of final values. Hulme's and Eliot's politico-religious objectivity, in the philosophical sense, is grounded on a "higher absolute" and opposes the empirical objectivity of science and positivism. The opposition constitutes one of the paradoxes of the modern world. To some extent men have been aware of this paradox and have endeavored to confine conflicting elements to their respective categories, in the manner of seventeenth-century "new philosophers" when confronted by a like predicament. But in art they have on the contrary assumed the task of organizing the discord imaginatively.

Hulme quite early regretted our "failure to recognize the *gap* between the regions of vital and human things, and that of the *absolute* values of ethics and religion. We introduce into human things the *Perfection* that properly belongs only to the divine,"[22] and by reflection to great art. The doctrine of the futility of human existence is characteristic of the reaction to nineteenth-century confidence and sounds repeatedly in "Gerontion," "The Waste Land," "The Hollow Men," and "Sweeney Agonistes." As a symbol of the limits of humanity, Hulme and his disciples counsel renunciation of personality rather than its glorification in progress and humanism. Their allegiance, given to a universal and yet static hierarchy of values, looks for the absolute in external and divine (not humanistic) perfection. But Hulme offers a philosophy of "intensive manifolds" that refer to the inner self: an interpretation of Bergson's intuitions for which Hulme actually should have had little sympathy.[23]

The contradictions in modern philosophy are mirrored in literature. The creative "self" of Bergson, with its conscious and subconscious activity in time and space, is psychologically germane to the symbolist literature which Eliot has absorbed. Thus obliquely, divergent schools of philosophy and psychology have appeared in related writings. For example, Proust gives the fictional equivalent of Bergson's metaphysics. Like the symbolists he embodies in a round drop of human experience all that is "relative to the person who perceives it, and to the surroundings, the moment, the mood."[24] The world has a four-dimensional perspective, much like Eliot's world in his poetry. Yet he would presumably deprecate the influence of such philosophies as Bergson's that set personality at the focal point of interest. Whether they are romantic or profess to be classical in attitude, modern writers of conflict have often forced a detached absolutism on their work and thoughts. This has been done with an uneasiness that must account for the equally powerful influence of relativism. In Cummings there is a strong categorical strain. Marianne Moore shows a conscientious effort to discover what poetic condition can carry the absolute. Yet historical relativism is everywhere apparent, not the least in Pound and Eliot and Crane —a romantic absolutist to Laura Riding.[25] Natural for the Bergsonian, the relative idea is infused with romanticism; and, paradoxically, so is absolutism. In Hulme the absolute is sentimentalized pessimism, despair in the abstract. And his romanticism is betrayed in unexpected allusions to and regard for Bergson.[26]

With all such ideological vicissitudes, the real significance is that poetry has found philosophy returning to a place of honor beside science. And though a young and fragmentary thinker, Hulme supplied one generation with an elementary metaphysic of the arts. He created a fellowship of minds; he stimulated a new vocabulary; he stressed the importance of coördinating human experience and statement. Though Eliot may have formed his ideas before Hulme's speculations were published, their influence perhaps reached him by links of conversation. There is a paradox in these men's poetic and rational position. Like many other moderns they are intellectualists, and yet they repudiate the radical philosophies based on the continuous adventures of science. Their argument may well be that they do not reject scientific intellection but wish to synthesize an appropriate philosophy of matter with spiritual meaning. Eliot "views with dismay the disintegration of culture caused by modern scientific liberalism, the school of thought rendered popular by the Darwin-Huxley-Bergson-Bertrand Russel [sic]-Eddington-Whitehead group, which has to-day a very large and intelligent audience."[27] Philosophies pertinent to this group aim to advance our minds and spiritual resources toward infinity and therefore are, in the view of the Eliot bias, irresponsible as to the limits of human ability—an irresponsible liberalism deriving from the expansiveness of the Renaissance.

Eliot's theory of suffering refers spiritual regeneration to the supernatural. His resistance to humanism had early encouragement in Hulme's view of the new Renaissance attitude "as a heresy, a mistaken adoption of false conceptions." Humanism "deserves no admiration," asserted Hulme, "for it bears in itself the seed which is bound inevitably later to develop into sentimental, ultilitarian romanticism."[28] The lack of community today between humanist and other intellectual attitudes, and likewise among the detractors of intellectualism, repeats the situation in Donne's time. And Hulme recognized those historical inconsistencies. "It seems as if no sooner had Copernicus shown that man was not the centre of the universe, than the philosophers commenced for the first time to prove that he was."[29] Such contradictions now also generate a striving but confused esthetics—advanced and inconoclastic, scientific and psychological in its argumentation, but unsettled in its philosophy. An impressive number of moderns discovered disillusion in science and humanism as once men had become disappointed in metaphysics. Their argument goes that if science has no ends in view but factual knowledge (the positivist aim) then it denies something that differentiates us from the animal. The animal and the primitive conform to nature's concern with the means, but human beings have developed a desperate interest in the ultimate beyond immediate recognition. It would seem that humanism on one side limits this supernatural interest and on the other restricts the natural impulses.[30]

In order to reëstablish metaphysics, Hulme emphasized the relation between matter and thought, between mores and morality. Held responsible for the discontinuity between them, are the quantum and the "emergent" personality theories, among others. But the new metaphysicians have split up into various groups, tenuously related by opposition to the positivist premise of science. Since this pure premise is insured for the present, some reconciliation with the inevitable process of science has been attempted by writers like Ransom. The metaphysician now can believe in a pragmatism *not inconsistent with the known facts*,"[31] and admit like William James the relation of physical fact to metaphysical speculation. Santayana is a modern philosopher whose classical compromise between the physical and the spiritual offers one answer to the dilemma. A metaphysician who would eliminate naturalistic considerations in human destiny would be guilty of his own brand of discontinuity. It would be sheer anachronism today to postulate our values on a pure metaphysic, or rely blindly on a "phantom called Certitude." Krutch questions the feasibility of a retrogressive system of metaphysics in our time and Eliot's resort to dogma.[32]

When Eliot attempts to reaffirm the certitudes, he nevertheless uses the contemporary instruments of skepticism, knowledge, and irony. His striving for integration of values is ill at ease with dualistic conclusions, of whose existence he is certainly aware. In this dualism he is not so much troubled by the suppression of facts as of the supernatural. "Culture, after all, is not enough, even though nothing is enough without culture."[33] Influenced by Babbitt's humanism but disturbed by its logical extension and by the breakdown of contemporary civilization, Eliot relied on skepticism before he reached a resting place in religion. To him this is not an inconsistent stand. He maintains that skepticism and disillusion lead to religious understanding. And he admits that "Catholicism *without* the element of humanism and criticism . . . would be a Catholicism of despair."[34] But for the ultimate support of the soul humanistic reason does not suffice him or his predecessor. "It is to the immense credit of Hulme that he found out for himself that there is an *absolute* to which Man can *never* attain. For the modern humanist, as for the romantic, 'the problem of evil disappears, the conception of sin disappears.' "[35] The problem thus invariably returns to that of original sin, of good and evil. Where philosophy touches on religion, these themes as related to humanism have stimulated metaphysical exercise from the seventeenth-century poets through Baudelaire and the symbolists to Hulme, Eliot, and the Fugitives. The conduct of modern civilization has materially augmented such speculation.

Counter to the dogma of original sin, the contention as proposed by Rousseau gives mankind an unlimited opportunity for improvement. This implies that society, which imposes evil on the innocent individual, will not interfere with men to a point *beyond* repair. Vaughan, Traherne, and Wordsworth would subscribe to the idea of original innocence shadowed gradually by social invironment. The child comes from God whole and good, but is imperceptibly alienated from his perfect origin. He can, however, by a partial return to the ways of nature be somewhat redeemed from evil influences. The noble savage and the innocent child are closer to perfection than the corrupted civilized man. Proper education of the individual and education of the human race would also—in the opinion of eighteenth-century rationalists, nineteenth-century progressivists, and modern humanists—carry us ever nearer to perfection. This has been the resort to reason. Reversion to nature and progress toward the highest rationality appear incompatible. But the romantic perfectionists found a meeting ground in the belief that man was once good and could be good again by a process of enlightened training.

Their opponents believe in an original state of sin, a dogma correlated with the "classical" attitude. Evil is necessary to good, and men have a responsibility toward evil. This responsibility consists in the knowledge of sin and in recognition of the limits set to human goodness. There exists an absolute good of the supernatural order to which mankind can only approximate by much hard trying. The rest is a matter of faith in salvation. Pride in the limitless potentialities of man crowds out the ultimate dependence on divinity. Such dependence should lead to humility in the sight of God, since suffering is the human condition. Where man ends and God begins is necessary human knowledge. For Baudelaire the experience of sin and introversive suffering were prerequisites to faith. Eliot has been sympathetic to this attitude. That evil forces today have not been checked by the proper processes of culture has confirmed his argument: civilization cut loose from the supernatural is in the way of disaster. The wrestling with good and evil is preliminary to the experience of faith. Experience is man's *modus vivendi:* the rhythm of evil and good, the pulse of a beating world.

> The world turns and the world changes,
> But one thing does not change.
> In all of my years, one thing does not change.
> However you disguise it, this thing does not change:
> The perpetual struggle of Good and Evil.[36]

A state free of this contest is death in life. He says of the heroine in *The Changeling:* "Beatrice is not a moral creature; she becomes moral only by becoming damned."[37] Innocent before, she matures in the moral sense only after the murder.

The discovery of good through evil appears in Baudelaire, who has been called "a fragmentary Dante." Eliot sees him rather as "a later and more limited Goethe."[38] The comparisons exhibit a shared concern with the great moral issues in life and beyond it. Eliot finds Baudelaire important for his experience with satanism and Christianity.

Indeed, in his way of suffering is already a kind of presence of the supernatural and of the superhuman. He rejects always the purely natural and the purely human; in other words, he is neither "naturalist" nor "humanist." . . . In the middle nineteenth century, the age which (at its best) Goethe had prefigured . . . Baudelaire perceived that what really matters is Sin and Redemption. It is . . . this which separates him from the modernist Protestantism of Byron and Shelley.[39]

By his reading of Baudelaire's character and career, Eliot exhibits his own distaste for romantic attitudes and tokens of modern civilization, and his preoccupation with dogma as well as morals. He quotes an apposite passage from Baudelaire: "La vraie civilisation . . . n'est pas dans le gaz, ni dans la vapeur, ni dans les tables tournantes. Elle est dans la diminution des traces du péché originel."[40]

Pleading his major and minor models, Eliot has done much to educate our poets in the perception of good and evil. If moral values have not been appreciably strengthened, a consciousness of their absence and desirability has. The "number of the half-alive hungry for any form of spiritual experience . . . high or low, good or bad, is considerable."[41] In all forms of political, philosophical, and religious beliefs today is implied an infatuation with something that might have absolute value, to which a man could hold as to a rock in fast waters. For those who do not believe as Eliot believes, his interest lies in the fact that he is realist enough to depict the evil in which we stand lip-high. Furthermore, the spiritual struggle implicit in all his work is congenial even to those who accuse him of surrendering to a faith that allows no verification. His poems mark the arduous way of the soul through doubt and disbelief toward faith, which he contends is a difficult haven to find. To him "intellectual freedom is earlier and easier than complete spiritual freedom."[42]

We are goaded today to find salvation collectively or as individuals first because of war frequency and the attendant evils. Second, the rush of new knowledge—psychology not the least— has declared man's precarious and pluralistic nature in a dangerous world. Third, we confirm the understanding of human misfortune and our own discoveries by reëxamining the past and its mind. We observe how the three philosophical poets analyzed by Santayana were all deeply absorbed in personal and universal dilemmas. In Lucretius the contest between Venus and Mars is that between creation and destruction: good and evil. Goethe's Faust "thirsts for all experience, including all experience of evil";[43] and Dante's Ulysses says:

> nè dolcezza di figlio, nè la pieta
>   del vecchio padre, nè il debito amore
>   lo qual dovea Penelope far lieta,
>
> vincer poter dentro da me l'ardore
>   ch' i' ebbi a divenir del mondo esperto,
>   e degli vizii umani e del valore . . .[44]

In spite of his fixed system, Dante was psychologist enough to suggest the concurrent presence of hell, heaven, and periods of purgation in the life of men on earth. His stress on the personal history of a man and on the spiritual exploration of his experience is most congenial to our poets. A type of spiritual journey is the scheme also of the *Anabasis* of St.-J. Perse, translated by Eliot in 1930.

Preoccupation with this theme has sent us again to the late Elizabethan and seventeenth-century contest with evil, as it appears in drama, lyric poetry, and the work of divines and philosophers. Hobbes's quasi-Machiavellian advocacy of external control and other pragmatic suggestions for virtue intimate the dogma of original sin. His cogent statements on the appetencies are, however, remarkably close to our analyses of the subconscious drives whose innocence often results in evil. Psychologically these drives constitute the modern version of original sin. The difference lies here: modern psychologists draw no moral conclusions, but a man like Hobbes demanded a moral set of controls. In his time, Bunyan and Milton spent the energy of their work on the problem of evil, the alternating revolt and submission of the spirit, and its progress toward good. To Milton the tasting of the fruit of the tree of knowledge was no sin, since such knowledge affords a moral distinction between good and bad. Before the fall, freedom was a negative virtue and only after it a positive condition of reason. The seventeenth-century preoccupation with man's basic struggle begins early in Donne, who was "already in his reckless youth meditating on such profound subjects as the nature of good and evil, . . . the arguments for and against the being of God."[45] *Biathanatos* considers the problem of sin at length; the lyrics take up the dual nature of man in imaginative detail; and in his sermons, Donne exploits his own passions and those of humanity at large to illustrate the dual principle, the sins of the body and of the soul. From the relations of the two, the great metaphysical question at once arises: the origin of moral evil. The insistent moral reckonings of late Elizabethan dramatists and the poets of the next period have helped—with Dante and Baudelaire—to direct contemporary insight to the root enigma of good and evil.

The moderns find ramifications of the problem not in religion alone, but also in politics, social questions, and the universal themes of love, death, and time. MacNeice asserts that the rhetoric of Auden and Spender presupposes good and evil as concepts in their scale of values.[46] Spender connects Henry James with the period when these notions were of crucial importance: *The Golden Bowl* "has the stain of evil in it which one finds in the Elizabethans. It might be the Duchess of Malfi claiming Antonio."[47] The metaphysical fairy tale of *Dr. Donne and Gargantua* by Sacheverell Sitwell exploits the trial between good and evil. It is seen as the essence of human consciousness: a perpetual activity whose cessation would constitute death-in-life or limbo.

"To see boundless good on the horizon, to see it without the limiting discipline of the conviction of evil, is in poetry as in politics the great stultifier of action."[48] Dante's attitude thus re-appears not only in Eliot but in this statement by R. P. Blackmur, and in Ransom's dictum that adult poetry is created by the "fallen" mind.

Though the dogma of original sin has had its source and its longest survival in Catholicism, it is relevant also to fundamental Protestant ideas of predestination. It was a tenet of seventeenth-century Puritanism in England and carried bodily to New England where the mental and moral climate was suitable for its incubation. The tradition of Calvinism is discussed by Winters in *Maule's Curse*, which deals in part with issues of sin and pre-destination as they appear in New England allegory. There is indeed a strong correlation between the uses of allegory (Bun-yan's primitive and Hawthorne's subtle form) and the artist's preoccupation with sin. Allegory eventually develops into the symbolism of Emily Dickinson and Eliot. The New Englander, whose roots wind back to the Reformation, is possessed by the passion of morality. In seventeenth-century England the theo-cratic state was of great importance, and in the New England of America "it acquired an unchecked social and political influ-ence."[49] For Emily Dickinson, Melville, and Hawthorne, products of a culture that gave us transcendentalism also, "it dramatized the soul."[49] The puritanical criticism of life runs, moreover, through James's novels, and an inverted puritanism is found in those of William Faulkner and Hemingway.[50] In spite of Eliot's later Anglo-Catholicism, his New England experience has been considered by some critics a significant factor in his work and personality. That tendency has always been strong with the poet who as "a tireless Calvinist" has "formulated Catholic plays and harried his pagan English public with Godliness."[51]

Thus has a quite ingenious theory been evolved to connect Eliot's metaphysical penchant with seventeenth-century England. In spite of his expatriation and final allegiance to English royal-ism and Anglo-Catholicism, Eliot retained the seeds of New

England Puritanism which was his derivation. The Puritans were incessant arguers and garnered countless instances of the play of sin from their own and vicarious experiences. This argumentation made for close scrutiny and vivid language in prose and poetry. "Eliot is a better poet than Pound because in Eliot the dialectic is more exacting. . . . It is Eliot's Christian morality (his morality, I think, rather than his creed) that gives drive to his poems. His family were New England puritans."[52] His attitude toward the disordered present takes a regional bias from this background: "that combination of practical prudence with moral idealism which shows itself in its later developments as an excessive fastidiousness and scrupulousness."[53] But the recoil from aspects of life's vulgarity to be seen in much New England literature is counteracted by curiosity and suppressed passions. The two extremes in Eliot's poetry, of Bostonian refinements and the roughneck insensibility of the Sweeneys—like the contrast of past and present—perhaps typify his debates with himself as well as the play he stages between indulgence and asceticism, evil and good, man and God, the common and the higher life. They are heard in his latest play as in "The Waste Land" whose "sterility we soon identify as the sterility of the Puritan temperament." The "desolation, the aesthetic and spiritual drouth, of Anglo-Saxon middle-class society oppresses London as well as Boston."[54] In Eliot's "taste for Baudelaire and Laforgue as well as for Poe, the wheel has simply come full circle." The mind's "absorption in the problem of belief and its trust in moments of vision; its dry, unexpected wit; . . . its severe self-discipline and sudden, poignant tenderness,"[55] inform this kind of poetry from Herbert to Emerson and Emily Dickinson, from Marvell to Elinor Wylie and Eliot. Spencer sums up the hypothesis that Eliot represents Yankee Puritanism carried across the centuries:

Perhaps it is a way of writing which comes naturally to Americans, or at least to New Englanders, whose colony was founded at the time when this style, since called "metaphysical," was at the height of its popularity in England. It would give Yankee wit an interesting genealogy if we could prove that its father was the poetry of Donne and its descendant the poetry of Eliot.[56]

As sin and its conquest provide the action of religion, so conflict is the drama of metaphysical poetry. It may be in the form of death and life, damnation and salvation, good and evil systems, or purpose and obstacle. The analogy is important not alone for the basic relevancy but insofar as a substantial number of poets discussed here have made religion their career or their very personal concern. Though Dante's politics materially affected his life, his love and his masterpiece were conditioned ultimately by the religious attitude. In the seventeenth century most of the metaphysicals were theologians or strongly attached to religion. Marvell was a notable political exception, but even here Puritanism is an inseparable adjunct. The best poems of the physician Vaughan are religious if not devotional. Lord Herbert's philosophical divagations are related to theology.

As we approach modern times, we see the germane poets preoccupied with themes in the province between metaphysics and religion: William Blake, Christina Rossetti, Francis Thompson, Hopkins, and Emily Dickinson—who writes of love, nature, death, and eternity often in terms of God. If we center the French influence transmitted to our metaphysicals in one person and that person Baudelaire, we find him pertinent (aside from his style) for his stress on sin and redemption. Among contemporaries religion has had an urgent function. Eliot's concern is a commonplace. Not only Maritain obviously, but Ramon Fernandez, Hulme as esthetician and poet of some half-dozen imagistic pieces, and the Fugitives as a group accept the "religious" orientation. This is not inevitable, however, for metaphysical poems are frequently nonreligious. The reader can easily find in Emily Dickinson or Elinor Wylie, in Crane or MacLeish, the topics of love, time, nature, and their emotional equivalents treated in metaphysical terms apart from religious connotations.

Nevertheless, religion has been a rich and critical source for metaphysical writing. The reasons are patent. In times of cultural and material chaos men experience a two-way reaction. They both question religion and make gestures of acceptance toward God and the church with the hope of sharing the difficult responsibilities. In such times it is natural to find men asserting that "the categories which ultimately make up the religious attitude, are the *true* categories and the *right* way of thinking."[57] In the recent crisis, religions have been subjected to attack and suppression not equaled since the persecutions of the seventeenth century. Oppression often results in an effect opposite to its objective. Quickened sympathy for the church or a free religious life springs behind the tread of persecution. In 1931 Eliot could write that "whereas twenty years ago a young man attracted by metaphysical speculation was usually indifferent to theology, I believe that today a similar young man is more ready to believe that theology is a masculine discipline, than were those of my generation."[58] The world has been "trying the experiment of attempting to form a civilized but non-Christian mentality. The experiment will fail";[59] a prediction that has already been in a measure justified. Though Eliot's personal interest is partisan, he feels the religious position wherever found, even in communism, is desirable and indeed inevitable. "A system of ethics, if thorough, is explicitly or implicitly a system of theology; and to attempt to erect a complete theory of ethics without a religion is none the less to adopt some particular attitude towards religion."[60]

Theological and moral care is activated by convergence of enemies all around, or by some disappointment in science and culture. The superciliousness of science and suppressions of religion by political ideologies have simply increased the social awareness of spiritual values. "Ours seems to be the day of the loosening of moral authority, and, on the other hand, as if by way of compensation or natural provision, the day of the rise of many distinguished moralists to give a content and a ground to moral principle."[61] Winters, for example, is a critic "capable of metaphysics and eschatology." A moralist of poetry, he discusses MacLeish, Crane, and the surrealists from the standpoint of spiritual strength and mysticism.[62] On behalf of science and its recent self-questioning, Whitehead evinces regret over the disagreement between scientific results and religious beliefs. He intimates that a *rapprochement* might be possible between a spiritualized scientific philosophy and a religious satisfaction cleared of transient fact.[63] And even in a pessimistic account of the modern temper, Krutch betrays a hope for some stay against contemporary storms of thought. Since man has an ethical inclination and the moral order is his "most fundamental myth," he requires some authority for ideas of wrong and right. Along with intellectual development emotions still demand ineffable symbols. "Time was when the scientist, the poet, and the philosopher walked hand in hand."[64] It seems that the present dilemma has again invited, at least in the metaphysical poet, the coöperation of science, religion, and metaphysics.

We have searched for salvation in nationalism, a new ordering of the classes, psychoanalysis, and now in a rejuvenation of faith— with or without ritual. Thus "perhaps since the early seventeenth century there has been no age of such acute theological controversy as is our own. . . . We have a different attitude towards science—we have had Einstein and Whitehead—and a new attitude towards religion—we are brawling over Thomism and the Liturgy."[65] Accompanying a return to established beliefs, dissatisfaction with conventional theology has promoted also strange new sects and high-minded movements reminiscent, in their multiplicity, of the seventeenth century. The growth of Christian Science, the Ethical Culture Society, the Oxford Movement, spiritualism, cults on the order of Madame Blavatsky's, a revival of black magic and astrological systems, all suggest the variety, extravagance, and ardor of religious and moral hopes. Defense of religion and qualities derived from simple devotion or from picturesque ritual often intensify the patterns and passions of literature, as in the prose of Bishop Andrewes and the poetry of Herbert and Crashaw. Words became weapons in the seventeenth century when Catholicism, Puritanism, and Anglicanism were put on their mettle. Shrewdness of attack and self-scrutiny are needed equally when issues join battle, today more than yesterday.

The return of contemplative artists not only to religion but to ritual has disturbed many minds. Others defend what seems like evasion and an easy submission to authority. Spender describes Eliot's surrender as a final step in humility, a difficult intellectual concession. By degrees he moved from an esthetic stand involving moral values, to a moral one involving conquest of personality, to the last position requiring church authority.[66] In the process great mental, emotional, and stylistic talents must be exercised. However suprising the outcome, his mind has revealed power:

The worldliness of its prose weapons, its security of posture, its wit, its ability for penetrating doubt and destructive definition, its eye for startling fact and talent for nailing it down in flight, hardly go with what we think of today as English or American religious feeling. We are accustomed to emotionalism and fanaticism in religious thought and looseness in religious feeling; the very qualities which are the natural targets of Mr. Eliot's weapons. It was probably these very qualities which, after the demolition of the pretence of value in post-war society, drove him into the Church as the one institution unaffected by the pretence or its demolition.[67]

Apologists for Eliot attempt to understand the critical pass to which we have come and the meaning of the religious position in periods that suffered analogous misgivings. Eliot shows perspicacity in taking literary and spiritual cues from the seventeenth century, the self-damnation of Baudelaire, Dante's purgatorial symbols. The mental hesitations and the purgative devices are true to his time also. Descriptive of its decade, "The Waste Land" was also in a sense prophetic of further devastation. In the same way "Ash Wednesday" threw its light forward as well as back, and has been justified at least in the augmented Catholic and Anglo-Catholic trend. Eliot has represented our psychological preoccupation, too, as it touches not only religious but other human expression. Notably his major poem, in its statements of myth and psychology, unites sex and religion—the two important passions in Donne and two of the prime considerations in our psychological poetry.

From its amorphous views of the personal and social conduct of man, psychology has in this century stepped toward the more exact sciences. As an extension of the seventeenth-century *nosce teipsum,* it is a study in extraordinary popular favor and exerts a general influence on the literature, painting, and plastic arts of the modern age. Scarcely any serious fiction or poetry is innocent of psychological complexity. To speak of Joyce, Proust,[68] James, Huxley, Wyndham Lewis, Virginia Woolf, Dorothy Richardson, Crane, Cummings, Aiken—is to occasion talk of the psyche. Surrealism, symbolism, associationism, stream-of-consciousness, and dream techniques, all echo the terms and forms of psychology. Various knowledges are called on to explain the self: anthropology and comparative religion, sociology and sexology. Where Lawrence made a religion of sex, the Freudians rediscovered sex in religion. Thus the investigations of Freud, Jung, Ellis, Malinowski, and Pavlov have fed our literature and art as they in turn have drawn on our unconscious and articulate experiences to stimulate their scholarship.

It is strongly recommended by Richards that we continue "the development of a psychology which will ignore none of the facts and yet demolish none of the values. . . . An account of poetry will be a pivotal point in such a psychology."[69] This has already been happening. Empson, illustrating his points with text and context, gives a distinct psychological turn to his phraseology. Quite evidently he is a disciple of Richards. He speaks of synesthesia, a conscious or unconscious device, used by Poe, Edith Sitwell, the symbolists, and Marvell. "It throws back the reader upon the undifferentiated affective states which are all that such sensations have in common . . . like those due to migraine or epilepsy or drugs like mescal."[70] Poe was interested in color and sound sensations: his approach to them as critic, technician, and psychologist of the morbid had a bearing on the development of the French symbolists.[71] No doubt the symbolists have been good psychologists of sense data and emotion. In their active period, psychology was beginning to probe the unconscious and subconscious. The symbolists exploited these findings with an acuteness and persistence that have not been matched by any single group, except perhaps the modern metaphysicals who inherited their techniques. Elusiveness of music, childhood and dream equivalents of vowels in terms of color, the margins of the conscious, the performance of the nervous system and the mind, were captured in verbal nuances. Not only the aura of immediate experience, but references to its origin in remote myths and mores expanded the potentials of art.

One can correlate a poet's ideas with the method by which he shows their action in the mind. That is, psychology and metaphysics can work together to produce the poetry of Donne, Crane, or Eliot. Hart Crane was aware of the shorthand connectives between concept and perception—a syndrome of intellectual and sensory complexes. In that light "The Waste Land" is a noteworthy psychological study of human consciousness. Students of psychology have investigated experience from visual apperception and visceral sensation to the historical sense, from the reflex to the metaphysical concept—a total knowledge attempted instinctively by Donne's age and consciously by ours to fix if not solve some of its many problems.

With this advantage, literature has made curious notations on the agonies of the modern complex. Ibsen, Hauptmann, Maeterlinck, D'Annunzio, and Yeats are among those who employed allegory and symbols in a new mysticism of psychology. Although vastly different in style and also their attitudes to life, both Jeffers and E. A. Robinson have dealt with psychological behavior. The ideas of Hartmann, Charcot, Janet, and Freud reached writers through books and universities. They were emotionally prepared: the air was already charged with passion and imminent disturbance. Gertrude Stein, as a student who came to the notice of William James, conducted experiments in automatic writing. At Harvard, Aiken and Eliot were introduced to studies that served them well, Aiken continuing to be fascinated by aspects of individuation, identity, and change. Various psychical phases have been probed: negation, the sense of unreality, dissociation, and other results of the disintegrative forces of modern civilization.

It should be noted that not only writers but critics have been using philosophical, psychological, and metaphysical terms about the literature produced under such tension. The critics and the poets are often one and the same. The significance of their inter-action is in itself a subject for psychology and no doubt relevant to the great stir in knowledge during trying times. Empson is the psychological critic, Edmund Wilson historical, Ransom meta-physical or ontological (to use his term), Auden sociological, Winters moralistic, and Eliot a repository of many types.

Eliot's concept of a poem as singular in emotion and pluralistic in feeling, and Ransom's as "a *logical structure* having a *local texture*" are both psychologically motivated.[72] The poets now apply to the analysis of verse the psychological data and terms used in the study of human personality. Eliot's conceit of the sky as a patient etherized is thought to be related to the interest at Harvard (when William James and Josiah Royce presided) in " 'anesthetic revelation' of metaphysical truth."[73] Involvement of the inanimate with a mental state or process is a psychological as well as a metaphysical habit. The climbing of the stairs in "Pruf-rock" may be considered as "an important kinaesthetic image of effort."[74] Even more suggestive is this observation: "The curious splitting of Prufrock in two [you and I] . . . and the intimacy of the two selves have obvious parallels in schizophrenia . . . (in-vestigated by Morton Prince and 'the Boston School' at the time Prufrock was written)."[75] The separation between the two selves is an immemorial and often normal phenomenon, but contem-porary self-consciousness has intensified its importance. The over-burdened mind of modern man tends to self-division.

Certainly, of the many directions taken by thought today, the psychological is among the most prominent. Even political con-sciousness is greatly modified by the psychological, as seen in propaganda and social poetry. Auden attempted a synthesis by applying the clinical method to social conduct. He presented a complex political view of society, the apparatus of the individual, and a combination in his "analytic account of the collective uncon-scious."[76] There are even categories of psychological poetry, such as associative versus behavioristic, for example. Of course, meta-physical poets are particularly aware of variations and in their way resemble technical psychologists. Not only our literature but our very emotions seem to have been modulated by the new in-formation regarding their activity. This corroborates Eliot's state-ment that the difference between us and writers before us is our knowledge of them. Though the basic human personality may not change, increased self-consciousness is in itself a mutation, so to speak. The extended knowledge of the psychological method acts as a check on its very overemphasis: Eliot has already hinted at its easy abuse. As so often, therefore, metaphysical wit is pre-pared for the ironical correction of its own excesses.

"The Waste Land" is a complete illustration of the sardonic and serious use of psychology in its relation to anthropology and com-parative religion. Such scholarship Eliot assimilated to the point where his sources are not always traceable and only wryly acknowledged. There are of course a number of direct references like those to *The Golden Bough* and *From Ritual to Romance*. The traditional and current learning possessed by poets like Donne and Eliot exemplifies Hulme's belief: "Humanity ought therefore always to carry with it a library of a thousand years as a balancing pole."[77] Yeats, Pound, and Aiken are notable for profiting by primitive cults, folk lore, and medieval symbolism. And MacLeish brings images from geography, geology, astron-omy, as well as anthropology. In all these we watch the conces-sions of Victorian morality to frank scholarliness. Ellis and Mali-nowski, Jessie Weston and Frazer, have illuminated present civi-lized conduct as well as its origins. On the shelf or reading table of the informed it is not unusual to see *Psychopathia Sexualis* or *The Sexual Life of Savages*.

> There he found always the excellent books
> Of Talmage, Martineau, Beecher, and Brooks!
>
> .   .   .   .   .
>
> Culture our watchword, and this is what it means—
> Einstein, Eddington, Millikan, and Jeans![78]

The jingle opposes older reading matter to the more recent parade of intelligence reaching the poet's mind. The naturalism that Darwin and his apostle Huxley contributed to the unsettlement of religion and philosophy has been extended to the physics and astronomy of Einstein and other scientists. Religious predestination had given way to the determinism of science. Now damnation becomes a physical possibility as the thermodynamic conclusion to the history of our planet. And even mankind's possible suicide is conditioned by the timeless potentials of matter. The mental transition from religious doom to the mercy of a mechanical universe is painful at each step. "The flourishing of science has been so vigorous that we have not yet had time to make a spiritual readjustment adequate to the changes in our resources of material and knowledge."[79] The reaction has long set in. Writers who "have made literature a training-ground for science" have turned to questioning the ultimates of science which, "in the last few decades, has been a training-ground for literature."[80]

Nevertheless, there are signs of a reconciliation between science and the life of the spirit. Self-examination has been the first move. In 1925 Whitehead acknowledged that a turning point had been reached in the progress of science: "Time, space, matter, material, ether, electricity, mechanism, organism, configuration, structure, pattern, function, all require reinterpretation."[81] This should give some satisfaction to the poets who are challenging science.[82] They for their part recognize this age of material investigation as a clearing-ground for the future. The scientist, the Marxist, the primitivist, the behaviorist, all propose to search and answer the demands of the here-and-now. Tangible evidence is being explored; even dreams are brought to the clinic. In their fashion the symbolists and the surrealists may be thought of as probing further unknown areas of humankind and, with other investigators of our age, examining the physical basis of the metaphysical. Besides its material effects, our age has studied the implications of time. For the philosophers James and Dewey, time signifies progress, change, the encouragement of the pioneer spirit. It has meant for the courageous searcher, for the vanguard minds in the seventeenth century, a vista of adventure and not a hopeless prospect. As the sole reality, time may represent to someone like Bergson a source of organic creativeness; for Proust or Thomas Wolfe it represents nihilism, a river in which "ourselves must drown."[83] In every crucial epoch, hope and despair are twins born of conflict.

Despair and confidence continue their grappling through the materialistic optimism of Wells, through the disillusion of *The Decline of the West* and "The Waste Land,"[84] through revivals of faith and ever new notions of science—until some balance is struck. The conciliations and the clashes are both important. Though the center does not yet hold, the various syntheses of the present age are highly illuminating.[85] Man's unappeased curiosity pursues information with increasing speed, but he shows an equal need to know "about the nature of things in an ultimate sense."[86] Intellectuality is the emotion of our times, though we question it together with everything else. Darwin, Freud, Marx, and Einstein have successively distilled the modern poem.[87] Poetry is the fairest blend of all these theories and researches; and a concern for the spiritual fate of the personality has recently added a new essence. The psycho-metaphysical poetry of the last quarter-century and more—drawing on the social, physical, biological, and mathematical sciences, on economics and religion—has most nearly dealt with "the whole turnip." The competition between incontrovertible knowledge which we refuse to surrender and the desire for some ideal not limited to a life-and-death cycle adds to our dilemma.

Though ideologically Eliot may refuse to arbitrate with scientific progress, his poetic method has made many concessions to past learning and present scholarship. The anthropology behind the myths, the use of race memory, and psychological association are all evident in "The Waste Land." Moreover, as a poet he makes use of science for its terms, and as a critic for its analogies. In an age investigating the biochemical, biophysical, astronomical, and psychoanalytic, Eliot owes science a debt for its exact training of poetic and critical procedure. He holds, however, that together with knowledge the creative instinct and the reconciling faculty are indispensable to join the matter, the milieu, and the moment in a condensed and spiritual significance. From the start Eliot believed in the extensive education of the poet because a poet, "like a scientist, is contributing toward the organic development of culture":[88] he is himself a living proof of this contention. Anesthetic images, the analogy of the catalyst, the neurological figure of the cortex, the suggestion of the combustion engine for modern poetic rhythms, are mere instances of the functional and figurative uses in his criticism and verse of technical information.

His work has been impressed by the industrial aspects of the machine age as well as the scientific. Like Donne, Eliot is an urban poet. Both are Londoners in the large sense. The city is the chief source of their inspiration for imagery. This does not mean that natural objects and the fact of nature (as a metaphysical concept) have not engaged their attention. Perhaps because Eliot has always been surrounded by city civilization he is acutely aware of its pressures and unquiet life, mechanical and mental. His ironical reflections and metaphysical queries have the centers of machine-age culture as frames of reference. "For a long enough time we have believed in nothing but the values arising in a mechanised, commercialised, urbanised way of life":[89] an uncompromising view. But Pound has a special word in praise of the meaning of the machine for art: "The lesson of machines is precision, valuable to the plastic artist, and to literati."[90] The values of time-space machinery are best transmitted by music in Pound's opinion, as in the case of George Antheil. His interest in the geometric art of Gaudier-Brzeska also emphasizes that relationship to mechanical forms. Pound's own poetry, in all but its early phase, liberally reproduces effects of contemporary life. The universal tendency to reflect the industrial age in our poetry may be accepted almost without demonstration. The younger schools of poets are particularly ready with analogies and rhythms deriving from the piston, the dynamo, the airplane.

Revolutionary writers are more apt to utilize the machine age in all its manifestations than the more traditional or the purely metaphysical poet. As socio-metaphysicals, the Auden-Spender-Day Lewis-MacNeice-Isherwood group has been quite successful in representing our local experiences in rhythm, structure, and imagery. Pound and Eliot,[91] in spite of a critical position toward our industrial culture, can reproduce its atmosphere masterfully. Jazz in "The Waste Land" and "Sweeney Agonistes," the cinema and headline technique in Pound's collage cantos, are vivid evidence. The work of Crane is a highly implemented romance of modern sights, sounds, and associations. Although Marianne Moore and Stevens exploit the garden, the amenities of the living-room, and the bookshelf—the perennial masquerade of life—their favorite forms are unmistakably urban in the contemporary manner. Stevens' Pierrot, after Laforgue's, is very well adapted to the present scene. Certainly the heirs of symbolism and the surrealists have skillfully availed themselves of the technological age. Apollinaire

stretched a new nervous surface to the industrial landscape and the business of the world, and claimed the new components of nature, machines and placards and scientific discoveries as the stuff of poetry. He wanted for the poet the new universe of scientific, microscopic, telescopic, radiographic vision; for the poet the courage to leave accepted logic for new untried chains of relations; for the singer the compression of business thought.[92]

As Pound and Apollinaire appropriated business idiom and symbols, so Cummings profited by the typewriter for visual suggestions. The precision of modern instruments, the novel elements of the machine, and the enriched activity of our life afford the general poet stylistic examples and material for metaphor. The metaphysical poet no less—from Donne to Auden—has proved capable of using the minutiae of science and urban conditions for vivid contrast with spiritual issues. Not only suggestive modern effects but the distress they engender provide him with substance and idea and a spur to seek a rationale for existence.

Although the personality of this modern poetry may appear chaotic, certain features make themselves clear. The coexistence of paradoxical traits is dramatically expressive of metaphysical dualism, and irony arises naturally from any effort to resolve the conflicts. The action implies at least two protagonists in most situations: past and present, belief and doubt, the vulgar and the recherché, the material and the ineffable. Such components, as in Donne, "are pitted against one another like characters in a play."[93] The double mood is thus the essential mood of modern metaphysical verse. To be aware—as it is—of two or more situations, potentialities, or facts, presupposes a fairly mature comprehension couched in an often trying style. When poetry is overconscious of competing elements, it tends to preciosity and leaves the province of legitimate obscurity. The true virtues, therefore, of modern poetry—intellection, metaphysical maturity, the realistic drama of dualism, and intense sensibility—become vices when they are overtaxed. The difficulties of verse at present derive from these qualities and from experimentation with their possibilities. The contact of intellection with feeling, the revolutionary use of traditional material and forms, resulting divergent moods, come together in a contracted area of experience. It would seem then that the ambiguities of an Empson or a Ransom derive from a double source: concentrated ideas of varied ancestry and symbolical associations of feeling. When the two are crossed by experimental methods there is further complexity.

Such poetry is troublesome not because of wayward purposes, but because the poet exerts himself to mediate contemporary discord. When environmental conditions are hard to focus, inevitable methods are allusiveness, structural ambiguity, the symbol, and the metaphysical debate. A plural attitude becomes necessary for the support of two or more elements. This attitude is naturally characterized by irony, or metaphysical wit, which is a criticism of one mood by its opposite. The satiric thrust and parry play against society and the poet with equal zeal. There is the effort to deal justly with mixed idea and emotion and to correct one attitude by juxtaposing it against another. In an age of psychological revolt and widespread experiment, in a time of high tension, mental processes are revised. To tell the change, a new idiom is developed and the abrasive metaphor contrived. The sensibility that requires such an image contains "the destructive element" and stands a chance to survive future irony. Metaphysical poetry strains to neglect no experience in its near-total consciousness of contemporary personal and public crises. Complacency is not for such times.

Where intellect and emotion check and extend each other, we find the active presence of doubt. Intellect, depersonalized and disabused, measures emotion with fact and reason. But the emotions in turn impassion the mind with a hunger for belief. In such debate and rebuttal a dialectic is developed which employs passionate ratiocination and vigilant feeling. The resulting poetry is full of the interest of contrast and exchange. In a dissonant age, our metaphysical poetry attempts to convey the essential conflicting experience—through conjugations of the heart and mind.

PART THREE

SEVEN POETS: TEXT AND CONTEXT

10

T. S. ELIOT

THERE IS NO ready or exact critical measure for the modern metaphysical. Few poets in any period have been exclusively that, and some outside the tradition have produced true metaphysical poems. And the twentieth century experiences more diverse esthetic influences than any comparable previous era. But those who are first of all mystics, symbolists, surrealists, or imagists, shall we say, have been modified by the metaphysical trend. Conversely, authentic metaphysicals are sometimes diverted into other channels of expression by circumstances or by a change in their interests. A few figures, therefore, who have in our day made a special and affinitive contribution to the metaphysical idiom should suffice illustratively.

Eliot stands head and shoulders above other poets as a major influence, more or less consistent in practice. Of the Fugitive group, Ransom, Tate, and Warren may be regarded as representative. The whole work of Hart Crane and Elinor Wylie can already be seen in the round. MacLeish's provocative career parallels the lift and peak of the metaphysical impulse and its decline in the 1930's, when various poets were swept into a mood of intense social participation by the imminence of World War II. Thus in these seven poets one may approach a composite portrait of the modern metaphysical.

Undoubtedly, many others could be chosen for a different or a fuller treatment, from Louise Imogen Guiney to José Garcia Villa. Laura Riding and Donald Davidson take their place in a more complete discussion of the Fugitives. Though primarily a symbolist, Stevens has a decidedly metaphysical turn of mind.

167

Furthermore, in addition to some fifty disparate names (including surrealists, objectivists, expressionists, and those with no tag at all),[1] a good many better-known American poets have been marked by one critic or another as metaphysical to a degree: Aiken, Cummings, Frost, Jeffers, Edna Millay, Marianne Moore, Pound, Robinson, Genevieve Taggard, Mark Van Doren, and William Carlos Williams. In England and America, social poets have often given the contemporary scene a metaphysical depth, and among these Auden and his colleagues and Muriel Rukeyser are conspicuous. Other categories also cut across the metaphysical: the intellectualist (Blackmur, Huxley, Read, the Sitwells); the symbolist (Yeats, Valéry, Dylan Thomas); the mystic (Blake, Christina Rossetti, Thompson, Rilke); the philosophic and transcendental—terms that characterize, better than metaphysical, certain poets from Lucretius to Wordsworth and Emerson. With so scattered and trailing a potential catalogue, it serves as well to consider a limited group of relevant neometaphysicals.

While Pound afforded a manifold impetus for the modern experimental movement in poetry, Eliot became the poetic synthesis of its best qualities. In a minimum of lines, Eliot accomplishes what *il miglior fabbro*[2] fails to do in a mass of suggestive material. Eliot profited by the mentor's ideas, but he was furthermore able, as Pound was not, to formulate a consistent expression. Pound's variety and vigor, his restless curiosity, and his genius for experiment, were vivid instigations. But while Pound continued his trials, the profound artist in Eliot perfected a technique that adequately conveys his perception of life, with the result that his work has achieved a homogeneous effectiveness, while Pound's remains a collection of specimens. The coördination in Eliot's art between idea and emotion derives from his singular metaphysical penetration. It is Pound's failure in this of which Eliot makes a point while he admits a serious obligation to his master and says: "just when I am most pleased with myself, I find that I have only caught up some echo from a verse of Pound's. . . . His eye is indeed remarkable, it is careful, comprehensive, and exact; but it is rare that he has an image of the maximum concentration, an image which combines the precise and concrete with a kind of almost infinite suggestion."[3]

Parallel passages from Eliot and Pound hint at the difference between a metaphysical and a nonmetaphysical handling of like material. Each is obviously indebted to both past and present in technique and material, but Eliot uses common sources with a subtle power of his own. The following passage from Pound stirs only a pensive sentiment, touched with sarcasm:

> I have gone seeking for you in the twilight,
> Here in the flurry of Fifth Avenue,
> Here where they pass between their teas and teas.[4]

Also in an evening scene Eliot insinuates meaning and excites the imagination:

> Let us go, through certain half-deserted streets,
>   .   .   .
> Streets that follow like a tedious argument
> Of insidious intent
> To lead you to an overwhelming question . . .[5]

Pound's Canto IV offers a fine classic reminiscence in these lines:

> Dew-haze blurs, in the grass, pale ankles moving.
> Beat, beat, whirr, thud, in the soft turf under the apple trees,
> Choros nympharum, goat-foot, with the pale foot alternate . . .[6]

But Eliot adds a slight metaphysical *frisson* in the comparable—

> I heard the beat of centaur's hoofs over the hard turf
> As his dry and passionate talk devoured the afternoon.[7]

In Canto VII Pound speaks of an "old voice" and "ghostly visits" and the turn of the stair;[8] these phrases bob in a flotsam of history off the contemporary beach, whereas in "Gerontion" and "Ash Wednesday" Eliot develops them in poems of high tension, intellectual insistence, and metaphysical conflict. Again, if we compare a further passage in the same canto where Pound gives us "thin husks" of men "speaking a shell of speech" and a "dryness calling for death,"[9] with reminiscent phraseology in "The Hollow

Men" and "The Waste Land," the advantage is all in Eliot's favor. Whatever difference one finds between Pound's "These fragments you have shelved (shored)"[10] and Eliot's well-known "These fragments I have shored against my ruins"[11] lies therefore in the meaning Eliot develops for the whole poem and Pound does not. Although "Eliot's Sunday Morning Service" and "The Cooking Egg" suggest Pound's "Mauberley" sequence in tone and stanzaic structure, although Burbank and Mr. Apollinax bring to mind Pound's Hecatomb Styrax,[12] Eliot succeeds by a line or a phrase in disturbing the spirit as well as the ear and the brain. "The Love Song of J. Alfred Prufrock" recalls Pound's "Villanelle: the Psychological Hour,"[13] if only in single words like "middle-ageing" and in the homesick conversational tone. But the emotional suggestiveness of "Prufrock" makes of it something much more than a scene of self-seduction. Where Pound speaks of "So many hours wasted!"[14] Eliot gives us "time yet for a hundred indecisions,/And for a hundred visions and revisions,"[15] where Pound's "Youth would awhile forget,"[14] Eliot's has seen "the eternal Footman" hold his coat.[15]

Both poets have been critical of society, conventional art, and jaded romanticism. However, Pound's realistic iconoclasm neglects the inscape,[16] while Eliot's logic wrestles with the god.[17] Pound's drama is external, but Eliot achieves an inner tension; he is also visionary, but Pound merely critical. In short, though the two were similarly influenced and closely connected in their poetic beginnings, Pound remains the useful instigator and experimenter, while Eliot, through his superior skills of fusion, has become a major figure in our poetry.

From his early pieces to his latest work, Eliot's metaphysical development has been consistent. Moving in the direction of the ineffable, though by explicit means, he looks for the principle and implications beyond the fact, to which Pound almost always defers. Even in *Old Possum's Book of Practical Cats*, primarily a pleasant book in the satiric vein, Eliot alludes with wry humor to the mental difficulties of definition:

His mind is engaged in a rapt contemplation
  Of the thought, of the thought, of the thought of his name:
      His ineffable effable
      Effanineffable
Deep and inscrutable singular Name.[18]

The poet conducts an endless "raid on the inarticulate," aware
that for him and for us, "there is only the trying."[19] He uses
tangible reality judiciously, always in relation to the inner event.
There is a continuous exchange among areas of consciousness.
We feel the projection of the senses in the life of the mind, and of
the mind's unappeased interest in a fourth-dimensional existence.
The effort to express the contact between the actual and the un-
utterable creates the metaphysical bias in his poetry. "It is only
because of what you do not understand/That you feel the need to
declare what you do."[20]

Commerce between the concrete and the abstract is required
of the genuine metaphysical poet. Here are instances of the ineffable reduced to fairly exact notations:

Destiny waits in the hand of God, shaping the still unshapen:
I have seen these things in a shaft of sunlight.[21]

    . . . One thinks to escape

For a momentary rest on the burning wheel . . .[22]

I said to my soul, be still, and let the dark come upon you
Which shall be the darkness of God. As, in a theatre,
The lights are extinguished, for the scene to be changed
With a hollow rumble of wings . . .[23]

One may accept two meanings for "the burning wheel," that of
temporal destiny and that of the turning earth whose hot marrow
is fluid. In "hollow rumble of wings" is another example of ambiguity: the wings can be interpreted as actual theater props and
also as spiritual wings from the beyond. These moments demonstrate the poet's ability to fix a sense of the remote or a mental
concept to a sudden physical apprehension, or on the contrary to

promote an experience of daily life into the unknown by imperceptible twists of phrasing or imagery. The poetic operation of giving the extrasensory in very palpable terms is related to synesthesia,[24] the expression of one sense in terms of another or the concurrent stimulation of both. The following passages illustrate such fusion, together with a suggestion of the abstract:

> ... all the admonitions
> From the world around the corner
> The wind's talk in the dry holly-tree
> The inclination of the moon
> The attraction of the dark passage
> The paw under the door.
>
> . . . . .
>
> Do you feel a kind of stirring underneath the air?
> Do you? don't you?   a communication, a scent
> Direct to the brain . . .
>
> . . . . .
>
> That apprehension deeper than all sense,
> Deeper than the sense of smell, but like a smell
> In that it is indescribable, a sweet and bitter smell
> From another world. I know it, I know it!
>
> . . . . .
>
> They don't understand what it is to be awake,
> To be living on several planes at once
> Though one cannot speak with several voices at once.[25]

Eliot's communication with the world around the corner, his simultaneous recognition of several planes of existence, give him hints beyond all data. His sensory knowledge is immediate and goes direct to the brain.[25] But it comes also "from a very long distance" like a voice "between two storms."[25] He experiences both "a wink of heaven," and "the stifling scent of despair."[26] Not only by applying intellection to the senses; not only by using the concrete as a foil for the abstract; not only by treating metaphysical themes as elements in conflict—but by adding as well a strain of the mysterious, Eliot achieves a mean between the reality of this world and the presence of some secret world. In *The Family Reunion* and sometimes in *Murder in the Cathedral* he evokes supernatural beings: the Eumenides, voices, ghosts. But he need not resort to the supernatural to effect a transition between two worlds. In "East Coker," "The Waste Land," "Ash Wednesday," even in "Sweeney Agonistes" and in the early "Prufrock," he approaches the "margin of the impossible"[25] and communicates from there the supernal sense. This intention to apprehend conditions here and hereafter,[27] now and through all time, is the attribute of the metaphysical researcher into human and extrahuman properties.

In spite of his own fundamentally religious answer to the great questions of life—to be found in his personal history, his critical works, and in poems like "Ash Wednesday" and "The Rock"— Eliot's poetry in general is based on the premise of doubt. Doubt is an essential of metaphysical poetry and differentiates it in part from the assurance of the mystic's vision and from the declarations of philosophical poetry. So for all Eliot's hankering after order and pattern, his poetry is full of struggle and the trembling of the scales:

> End will be simple, sudden, God-given.
> Meanwhile the substance of our first act
> Will be shadows, and the strife with shadows.[26]

The son of man can neither give nor guess the answer, for he knows only a "heap of broken images."[28] And he admits through the poet that his lost erring soul knows very little of the future and is "homeless in earth or heaven."[29] Only "The fool, fixed in his folly, may think/He can turn the wheel on which he turns."[30] Even "good and evil in the end become confounded."[31]

He who develops his poetry on the principle of doubt will naturally be given to paradox. Sometimes this degenerates into a device to insure surprise, shock, and other dramatic effects. Indeed, the excess of paradox in Eliot occasionally defeats its own ends, and surprise no longer results. Nevertheless, when skilfully used, the method of paradox enhances metaphysical interest.[32] Thomas Archbishop explains the simultaneous rejoicing and mourning at the Christmas Mass that celebrates at one time the Nativity and the Passion of Christ.[33] The Christian paradox inheres also in the joy and sorrow suffered at the memory of a martyred saint. "Ash Wednesday" is a masterpiece of both religious and metaphysical paradox. Its oppositional nature thus derives from two sources.

> Teach us to care and not to care
> Teach us to sit still.
>
> . . . . .
>
> End of the endless
> Journey to no end
> Conclusion of all that
> Inconclusible
>
> . . . . .
>
> And the light shone in darkness and
> Against the Word the unstilled world still whirled
> About the centre of the silent Word.[34]

Such an equivocal word as "still" (virtually a pun) harmonizes with the poem's fundamental paradox, which is a type of ambiguity indispensable to conflict. Opposed statements and passages persist throughout Eliot's work from *Prufrock* (1917) to *Four Quartets* (1943).

> We have lingered in the chambers of the sea
> By sea-girls wreathed with seaweed red and brown
> Till human voices wake us, and we drown.[35]
>
> Neither fear nor courage saves us. Unnatural vices
> Are fathered by our heroism. Virtues
> Are forced upon us by our impudent crimes.[36]
>
> The only hope, or else despair
>   Lies in the choice of pyre or pyre—
>   To be redeemed from fire by fire.[37]

Paradox is seldom a mere formality with Eliot, or a stylistic trick. Under its superficial effect lies often a truth to be discovered in the context of the whole poem or in the very context of life as the metaphysical sees it. The first and last lines of "East Coker" express the paradoxes of birth, death, and the afterlife:

In my beginning is my end. Now the light falls

．　　．　　．　　．

We must be still and still moving
Into another intensity
For a further union, a deeper communion

．　　．　　．　　．

. . . In my end is my beginning.[38]

At times Eliot admits candidly his reliance on the church, and in
"The Rock" we find a submissive attitude that precludes the metaphysical play of argumentation. In one passage he may seem in-
curious of good and evil and content to be led, one step at a time,
by the religious light.[39] Yet another passage will prove again that
he is in the main intellectually restless and one "who knows how
to ask questions."[40] Even of the church—from "The Hippopotamus"
to "The Rock"—he demands a constant self-questioning and re-
building.[41] As a poet he is concerned not only with the "right relations of men" and the "relations of men to GOD,"[42] but with all
relationships. As a result, the two-way paradox by its nature takes
to a rhythmic design:

> For Man is joined spirit and body,
> And therefore must serve as spirit and body.
> Visible and invisible, two worlds meet in Man;
>
> ．　　．　　．　　．
>
> The visible reminder of Invisible Light.[43]

The metaphysical poet is intrigued by paradox and conflict as
they allude to the order which he hopes to find. Unlike the pure
scientist, as the positivists describe him, the metaphysical has a
supranatural purpose behind his investigative zeal. It is true that
"The masters of the subtle schools/Are controversial, polymath."[44]
But dialecticians like Lucretius, Donne, and Eliot, are interested
in controversy for the sake of a harmony envisioned. Had they
found order about them or within them, there would have existed
no terrible need to search "matters that with myself I too much
discuss," no need to dispute "What Precisely/And If and Perhaps
and But."[45] The arrangement that Eliot covets is implied in the
very disorder where he beholds

> ... many creatures moving
> Without direction, for no direction
> Leads anywhere but round and round in that vapour—
> Without purpose, and without principle of conduct
> In flickering intervals of light and darkness.[46]

> Shall we lift up our feet among perpetual ruins?[47]

The poet pictures himself "in the middle way, having had twenty years—/Twenty years largely wasted, the years of *l'entre deux guerres*—"[48] and in the person of Harry he insists that it is not his "mind, that is diseased, but the world I have to live in."[49] As the world becomes more complicated in the historical relationship of the dead and the living, the theme of order is with ever greater difficulty "developed and resolved in the pattern of time."[50] Life

> ... begins to seem just part of some huge disaster,
> Some monstrous mistake and aberration
> Of all men, of the world, which I cannot put in order.
>
> . . . . .
>
> Accident is design
> And design is accident
> In a cloud of unknowing.[51]

Effort is directed toward discovering some scheme among the shored fragments, some center that will hold: in religion, or in an equilibrium of the mind and spirit, or in art perhaps.

> ... Only by the form, the pattern,
> Can words or music reach
> The stillness ...[52]

The patterns are formed, dissipated, and perpetually reassembled by the poet whose verbal effort is put to the strain. Feelings, concepts, and words are stretched, compressed, dislocated, and re-created to withstand the burden and to match the vision.

The metaphysical assumes the obligation of "such a vision of the street/As the street hardly understands";[53] thus might he meet the times and his own requiring nature. He wrestles in the shadow that divides what we know from what we strive to know with insinuations of some "other" faculty:

Between the idea
And the reality
Between the motion
And the act
Falls the Shadow

.   .   .   .   .

Between the essence
And the descent . . .[54]

are the hour and the place of both hope and doubt. He belongs to
the poets who are pursued by "the imperatives of 'is and seems,' "[55]
by the finite and infinite, death and love, men and the gods, Christ
and fate. Even in less likely poems such as "Prufrock"

There will be time to murder and create,
And time for all the works and days of hands
That lift and drop a question on your plate . . .[56]

The question is not limited to the surface problem of whether or
not Prufrock should marry. The lines have deeper implications and
are charged with Eliot's later probings of the social and moral
scene. His least *vers de société* seems impregnated with intellectual and visionary disturbances of a time that has stopped in
the dark. It is no ordinary moment.

In life there is not time to grieve long.
But this, this is out of life, this is out of time.
An instant eternity of evil and wrong.[57]

And the past is about to happen, and the future was long since settled.
And the wings of the future darken the past, the beak and claws have
desecrated
History. . . .[58]

The violent story of the poet's epoch sends him to study also the
soul's history. Despite his passion for order and his hope of
sanctuary, he is not deceived by the events of the external or the
inner world. Even in death, imaginatively, he has "lain in the soil
and criticised the worm."[59] At the moment of birth, the poet begins to have knowledge of death; and neither the knowledge nor
fear of it ends his concern. Disturbed and awed by it, or reconciled to what is beyond death, his discontent is not stilled.

Oppressed by thoughts of time and dissolution, Eliot has been in a sense the consciousness of his generation's "unhappy family,/ Its bird sent flying through the purgatorial flame."[60] He has watched the wheel turn faster and throw up the perpetual question. "For who knows the end of good or evil?"[61] The alternation of sin and innocence is reflected in the natural seasons and in the seasons of man. April can be "the cruellest month" and May "depraved." In a correspondence between the actual and the abstract, the poet finds himself united "to the spiritual flesh of nature,"[62] where fact becomes extradimensional. His multiplane experience apprehends natural phenomena, human history, and the abstract faculty that finds their further significance. The operation of the psyche is of great importance to the poet who sees there the microcosmic reflection of the universe and the laboratory for good and evil. Eliot's understanding of it is deep if not wide. His observations are sharp and often uncanny. They are seldom superficial. For example:

> In a world of fugitives
> The person taking the opposite direction
> Will appear to run away.
>
> . . . . .
>
> Perhaps my life has only been a dream
> Dreamt through me by the minds of others.[63]

The two selves of Prufrock and the divided self of Harry in *The Family Reunion* are only two expressions of the psychological purgatory investigated by Eliot, as by Donne in his time and Baudelaire and Rimbaud in theirs.

Many Eliot passages merge symbolist clairvoyance with the unmistakable inflections characteristic of late sixteenth- and seventeenth-century poetry from Campion to Waller, from Chapman to Cowley. There is a note that is heard in the unmetaphysical Herrick, the classical Jonson, the Cavalier Suckling, and in the most metaphysical play of Marvell's wit. It is heard in

> The chill ascends from feet to knees,
> The fever sings in mental wires.
> If to be warmed, then I must freeze

And quake in frigid purgatorial fires
Of which the flame is roses, and the smoke is briars.[64]

I have lost my sight, smell, hearing, taste and touch:
How should I use them for your closer contact?
These with a thousand small deliberations
Protract the profit of their chilled delirium,
Excite the membrane, when the sense has cooled,
With pungent sauces, multiply variety
In a wilderness of mirrors. What will the spider do,
Suspend its operations . . . ?[65]

The passage from "Gerontion" suggests Shakespeare, Webster, and Donne. The last two are indicated by name in "Whispers of Immortality," which is the concentrated evidence of Eliot's affiliation with the seventeenth century.[66] The beginning and the end of the poem are molded closely on the tight prosodic frame used by Donne. This intellectual and rhetorical cohesion appears in certain model poems by Pound and is largely affected by the Fugitive group. The style of the middle section of the poem is eased by echoes of modern symbolists, with stanzaic strictures retained. This symbolist-metaphysical poem imbues thought with sensation and gives the physical an abstract significance. In short, metaphysics is made to breathe and move between death and life.

And even the Abstract Entities
Circumambulate her charm;
But our lot crawls between dry ribs
To keep our metaphysics warm.[67]

The rhetorical device of juxtaposing learned words with simplicities and ambiguous syntax with clear idiom is used with authority. In Eliot's poetry there is achieved a fine amalgam of the supersensitive symbolist style, the associative ellipsis, and metaphysical speculation. The result is physical excitement together with an "ecstasy not of the flesh."[68] Experience ranges from the submarine to the astral:

The trilling wire in the blood
Sings below inveterate scars
And reconciles forgotten wars.

> The dance along the artery
> The circulation of the lymph
> Are figured in the drift of stars . . .[69]

As his seventeenth-century model would have been inclined to do, our poet sets "lymph" in a biological image that includes contact with the stars and so knits the universe together. Such an image is the revived conceit.

Quite as provocative as the overworked specimen of modern conceit, the "patient etherised" to characterize the twilight sky,[70] are others exercising more surely the metaphysical notion:[71]

> I will show you fear in a handful of dust.[72]

> The worlds revolve like ancient women
> Gathering fuel in vacant lots.[73]

> Every street lamp that I pass
> Beats like a fatalistic drum . . .[74]

> This broken jaw of our lost kingdoms . . .[75]

> And other withered stumps of time
> Were told upon the walls . . .[76]

> My life is light, waiting for the death wind,
> Like a feather on the back of my hand.[77]

Eliot has, moreover, a distinct flair for the single adroit epithet which by its nature is related to the metaphysical conceit. In the first example below, an abstract adjective is coupled with a concrete noun; in the second the adjective specifies the image. In both instances the effect is startling and true:

> A curse is like a child, formed
> In a moment of unconsciousness
> In an accidental bed . . .[78]

> Not here the darkness, in this twittering world.[79]

The aggregate of metaphysical images and passages in Eliot is considerable indeed and confirms the intrinsic mood permeating his language and thought.

There are fewer works to be described, however, as exclusively metaphysical in the formal sense. *Murder in the Cathedral* and *The Family Reunion* are rather fully developed in that direction. Poems such as "Whispers of Immortality" and those that comprise *Four Quartets*[80] may be singled out as metaphysical in their very character and structure. But the early satiric poems, as well as "Gerontion," "The Waste Land," "The Hollow Men," and "Ash Wednesday" are more symbolist than metaphysical—though they are repeatedly charged with metaphysical implications. If we accept a Donne poem like "The Extasie" or "A Lecture upon the Shadow,"[81] or Marvell's "To his Coy Mistress" as the type of the metaphysical, then the better-known Eliot poems do not conform. The pursuit of a thought or image through all its involutions and the insistent progression of logic are absent. With the seventeenth-century poet the discipline was an open exercise. With Eliot the casuistry is more elusive and the antiphonal fervor muted. The expected structure gives way to another logic, the notional ellipsis, where expression is symbolical and reasoning inferred rather than demonstrated step by step. The form is impressionistic, not declared.

Yet in the range of Eliot's poetry is every evidence that he was seriously under the spell of seventeenth-century verse: dramatic,[82] lyrical, and satiric. The impress of a whole period is felt in his critical and creative writing. Specific cases serve merely to point up a debt he acknowledges everywhere. When he writes "And the unseen eyebeam crossed,"[83] the image could be directly ascribed to Donne's "Our eye-beames twisted . . ."[84] When Eliot writes "The dancers are all gone under the hill./O dark dark dark. They all go into the dark,"[85] the emotional cadence at once suggests Vaughan's nostalgic "They are all gone into the world of light!/ And I alone sit lingering here . . ./Or else remove me hence unto that hill,"[86] a parallel pursued less readily than this:

> Would it have been worth while,
> To have bitten off the matter with a smile,
> To have squeezed the universe into a ball
> To roll it toward some overwhelming question . . .[87]

in comparison with Marvell's lines from "To his Coy Mistress":

> Let us roll all our Strength, and all
> Our sweetness, up into one Ball:
> And tear our Pleasures with rough strife,
> Thorough the Iron gates of Life.[88]

From the same celebrated poem Eliot borrowed phrases for deliberately ironic effects in "The Waste Land."[89] Other lines in Marvell's poem, "then Worms shall try/That long preserv'd Virginity,"[90] appear as

> For I know, and so should you
> That soon the enquiring worm shall try
> Our well-preserved complacency.[91]

Passages from "Gerontion" have been frequently cited as illustrating Eliot's skill in reproducing the sound and complex passion of language that ripened toward the end of Shakespeare's career. Here the idiom of Webster, Tourneur, Middleton, and Ford—the rich idiom of the late Elizabethan theater before it closed—returns and blends into modern expression.

Late sixteenth- and seventeenth-century writing left repeated echoes in the corridors of Eliot's mind and in the tones of his style. "Marina" and the line, "Desiring this man's gift and that man's scope,"[92] ring out the name of Shakespeare. "Journey of the Magi" begins with a paraphrase of Bishop Andrewes, and "Gerontion" and "Ash Wednesday" both develop Andrewes' theme of "the word within a word."[93] The speechless Word and the Word made flesh are powerful symbols obsessing Eliot and appearing in poem after poem, most markedly in "Ash Wednesday" where it is one of the chief motifs. That in so signal and concentrated a work as "The Waste Land" the literary references are preponderantly Elizabethan and metaphysical is, to say the least, worth noting.[94] Only Dante and the French symbolists can compete with that period for effect on Eliot, to whose temperament it has been naturally congenial in tone, intensity, and intellectual mood. But from the earliest pieces in his college journal to the present, Eliot exhibits an amazing synthesis of many past literary influences from Dante,[95] through the meta-physicals, to the French symbolists.[96] On these major influences were quite naturally imposed the material and idiom of his own insistent civilization.

Whatever he is not, Eliot is at least a representative of the twentieth century in one of its strongly characteristic phases. Its irritated sensibility is continuously apparent in his symptomatic writing. Its social experiences, accelerated knowledge, and self-conscious torments have been raised to a high power of sugges-tion. His scattered choice of literary affinities is not at all alien to the temper of our age. In the persuasion still widely exerted by his critical and poetic work, he has demonstrated that Dante's particularized vision, the mystic and sophistic wit of the meta-physicals, and the evocations of the symbolists, all appeal power-fully to the poet of our times. He has established a connection among them, and a tension between technique and spiritual perception. There is a certain proportion to be found in his poetry between the distractions of our time and the synthesis of its needs. The divided spirit has been eager to end hostilities, but neither the emotions nor the mind would accept an uninquisitive peace. Eliot has given us what the seventeenth-century poets gave their readers in comparable circumstances: rebelliousness, conscien-tious doubt, yearning, and the terrifying suggestion of two worlds. Exact imagery and taut inflections are adequate to both the mind and the heart. This complex is a type of the modern race, a kind of contemporary Tiresias, who combines opposed characteristics that are nevertheless complementary. The symbol compresses opposite impulses of experience and a great range of time wherein flux and permanence plague us.[97] If there are reasons to place Eliot among modern symbolists, they are offset by his successful cross-fertilization of symbolism with the metaphysical tradition. According to the metaphysical process, he integrated the move-ments of the mind and the passions; and symbolism aided his psychological inquisition of the senses. In general his work real-ized our response to the metaphysicals and the causes of that re-sponse, in a time when public and personal passion runs high.

THE FUGITIVES

The fugitives have been the most nearly integrated poetic group in America. They do not constitute a movement so much as a coterie unified by convictions about the South and by common literary opinions and practices. Since metaphysical poetry often responds to the mental climate, we must regard the economic and social ideas of the Fugitives as factors in their writing. Personal history and place brought these poets together, and their later development has perpetuated a certain sympathy among them. In an anonymous foreword to its first issue *The Fugitive,* a magazine appearing in April 1922 in Nashville, Tennessee, protested against the state of life and poetry in the South at that time: "THE FUGITIVE flees from nothing faster than from the high-caste Brahmins of the Old South." The South shares in the destiny of America, and therefore its economic and intellectual life needed rehabilitation. By common consent, the Fugitives began early to show in a set of social and poetic tenets their distaste for the ideas and methods which they eschewed. "The group mind is evidently neither radical nor reactionary, but catholic and perhaps excessively earnest, in literary dogma."[1]

John Crowe Ransom, Donald Davidson, Merrill Moore, and Allen Tate were among the initial members of a literary enterprise that in spite of its short life left an impress on our current literature and numbered among its contributors (besides Warren) Robert Graves, J. G. Fletcher, Hart Crane, and Laura Riding. Ransom had already published a volume of verse, and in the second issue of the magazine Tate gave incipient evidence of originality:

God took a crayon in his hand
And sketched a swift line of distress.

. . . . .

The ringing canticles of hope,
The azure rhythms of his brain,
Threaded the years that else were blind.[2]

Here God enters as the classical gods recede, time becomes one of the strongest motifs for the Fugitives, and their imagery begins to reveal metaphysical and symbolist tendencies. In the third issue Tate's "Horatian Epode to the Duchess of Malfi,"[3] like his "Non Omnis Moriar," already exhibited an interest in Elizabethan and Jacobean dramatists. This interest harmonized with the early realization of Eliot's importance, whose continued influence indicates the group's position in the history of twentieth-century American poetry.

Once the pseudonyms were dropped, whatever was written for *The Fugitive* in verse or in prose manifestoes took on a more serious aspect. An editorial signed by Ransom illuminates the later work and objectives sponsored by the group as a whole and individually:

These poets acknowledge no trammels upon the independence of their thought, they are not overpoweringly academic, they are in tune with the times in the fact that to a large degree in their poems they are self-convicted experimentalists. . . . In America the inroads of sophistication are early, and it is American gospel to indulge it. . . . The poets abhor the thought of changing the considered phrase that perfectly expresses them in the interest of an irrelevance called meter.[4]

Tate also points up their common history and indicates the establishment of the new tradition under Eliot's accepted leadership:

We are told that we evince a uniformity of outlook, of tone; that we have the earmarks of a School. . . . I believe that the unique virtue of the contemporary revolt is its break, in a positive direction, with the tyranny of representation. . . . Mr. Eliot has demonstrated the necessity, in special cases, of an aberrant versification. . . . Perhaps T. S. Eliot has already pointed the way for this and the next generation, . . . the

Moderns have adequately arrived, and their claim is by no means specious.[5]

Obviously encouraged by the example of Eliot, the Fugitives early in their career urged a fresh start for Southern poetry on the course of a new discernment and more original prosody—yet carrying the best of certain approved past traditions. They were determined to invigorate verse and to "create from what is nearest and deepest in experience—whether it be old or new, North, South, East, or West,"[6] an adequate form to express the more intense qualities of their response.

No doubt what may sound like uneasy derivative echoes of Eliot in Tate's "Perimeters,"[7] Ransom's "Good Ships,"[8] and Warren's "After Teacups,"[9] were now in general fashion. In the magazine version of "First Epilogue to OEnia," Tate might have borrowed from Donne for his conceit of "a body dissolved into thought."[10] In a later issue he gives us Baudelaire's key poem as "Correspondences."[11] References to Propertius, Donne, and Elizabethan dramatists, translations and adaptations of the French symbolists, and efforts to establish the Eliot mode, were auguries confirmed by later practice. That about two dozen poems by Ransom, appearing subsequently in *Chills and Fever* and *Two Gentlemen in Bonds,* were first printed in *The Fugitive* suggests the early importance of the journal and the present consequence of a fellowship that very nearly constitutes a school. Individual as poets, the Nashville group has maintained a consistency of idea and, with the exception of Merrill Moore, a characteristically intense style—signatures of a literary entity.

"One Escape from the Dilemma" by Tate is at once a résumé of their common history and an introduction to the nature of his own verse. He clarifies the position of the group and names some of its fundamental tenets: the revolt against the nineteenth century, the limited approval of imagism, sympathy for the metaphysical period and the symbolists, a natural affinity for methods promulgated by Eliot. Tate analyzes the paradox of modern verse—the traditional nature of its radical development. The reason he assigns is the disillusionment of the age, which leads to the conflict of truths in a new sophisticated poetry. The chaos echoed in this poetry, he says, will not allow for an easy style. That is why Elinor Wylie means more than Sara Teasdale. That is why the emotional content must be sharp and differentiated rather than expansive or musically familiar. Baudelaire's theory of correspondences has combined with a defined English tradition and selected values of free verse to influence modern diction. Our metaphysicals may be radical as poets, but their sensibility and intellectual consciousness are too severe for a wholly relaxed free verse, and too abstract for past representational poetry. In 1924 Tate already sums up the situation:

Thus the Moderns, impressed with what Mr. Santayana calls "curious and neglected forms of direct intuition," are driven . . . to modifications of the standard forms of diction. . . . We think of this as Decadence, but . . . it is Elizabethan. It is not direct continuity from the immediate past of English poetry. It is a development out of the whole of it under French direction; and it is no more startling than the progress from Wyatt to John Donne. . . . [Our poet] can't write like Homer or Milton now; from the date of his experience he infers only a distracting complexity.[12]

From this we can approach Tate's poetry guided by his own signposts. It is complex because it must be, from the evidence of his argument; it is classic and satiric in the modern manner; it is highly realistic and yet has romantic impulses; its critical observation of the senses, the intellect, and the emotions is desperately intent. The control of the recondite and the spontaneous reflects the modern attempt at order. But not only has Tate to deal with the difficult environment of twentieth-century man, he assumes as well the burden of the South's dilemma. One finds him, therefore, interpolating Confederate memories and potential Southern values into the context of metaphysical problems of time and place. The sins of history against the South are joined with the vice and virtue of general mankind in "God's hatred of the universal stain."[13] Like many moderns, the poet is profoundly concerned with death as a theme; particularly as to Southern history is he "instructed by the fiery dead."[14] The sense of loss in regard to his region of the country competes with the proud responsibility of resurrecting its better past. Where Eliot remembers traditional splendors common to a whole civilization, Tate emphasizes a special sectional recollection. The historical sense is doubly demanding in Tate's consciousness.

Here is, then, an additional source of paradox in his poetry. A generally sardonic quality is sharpened by a local irony. His haughty but realistic wit utilizes the encounter between present fact and the stale fancy of a dead period. With intellectual impatience he shakes off the marks of decadence of which he is well aware. Like an eagle his mind

> Beats up the scaffold of space
> Sick of the world's rot—
> God's hideous face.[15]

He pursues a continuous and almost intolerable argument with himself, or alter ego, feeling time's implacable will and hearing "the dark pounding its head/On a rock, crying: *Who are the dead?*"[16] The overlong period of complacence and nostalgia suffered by the South led inevitably to a realistic reaction. This revolt has been directed not only against itself but also against the contemptuous tolerance of the North and the results of the whole country's shortsightedness during the feverish boom years. Remonstrance takes two forms. In a violent realism, Faulkner and Erskine Caldwell, for example, expose whatever degeneracy has needed excision. Parallel to the fictional expression, operates the relentless poetry of the Fugitives. The self-esteem of these poets, however, defends whatever qualities of the South could be preserved and nurtured. A keen sense of the past and present to be used in behalf of the future has been substituted for "a duller sense that cannot/Smell its own mortality."[17] The agrarian panacea formulated by the Nashville group and the half-acknowledged compromise with science and technology may be unsatisfactory to many. At least the Fugitives have promoted an unsentimental irony and the courage to see peril. Tate speaks from "the deep coherence of hell,"[18] and the South is no island. Its mere local loveliness perished long ago.

> The man in breeches, all knowledge in his stare
> A moment shuddered as the world fell.[19]

> Our gain's the intellectual sound
> Of death's feet round a weedy tomb.[20]

Tate is a susceptible member of the whole unhappy race of moderns.

In "Sonnets of the Blood," the poet propounds an extensive metaphysical inquiry into his ancestral heritage. Yet reference to a specific past is merely a point of departure for intricacies of the conceptual imagination. The first sonnet invokes the aid of science. The third sonnet debates the principle of circumstance and the concept of death. Throughout the series the poet searches provinces of the blood, time, and the grave—without finding much more than paradox. Old and new values of the South possess him, but he is equally haunted by the universal mysteries. Like the Elizabethans, whose inflection is heard in his sonnets, the poet of the unlucky South aches with concatenated human failure. "There is no man on earth who can be free/Of this, the eldest in the latest crime."[21]

"Ode to the Confederate Dead" marks Tate's highest expression of his heritage. Even so the poem demands the larger context of general human frustration in nature and time. The immediate subject matter radiates lines of vision. An intelligent Southern poet speculates not only on the cultural defeat of the South but on the regenerative aspects of any defeat, even at the hands of death. The motifs and occasional symbols—crab, wind, jaguar, old man—recall Eliot without detracting altogether from Tate's originality. Likewise the conflict between "the beginning and the end" and the intense diction:

> You who have waited for the angry resolution
> Of those desires that should be yours tomorrow,

> You know the unimportant shrift of death
> And praise the vision
>
> .   .   .   .
> And in between the ends of distraction
> Waits mute speculation, the patient curse . . .[22]

Tate's lines "sough the rumour of mortality," but the "com-memorial woe" of those who fall feeds the future as their "in-exhaustible bodies" feed the grass.[23]

If the historical sense is inordinately developed in this oppres-sive day of human history, where in America should it be better occupied than among the Fugitives, whose dead seem to walk beside the living? With Pound and Eliot the invasion of the past is in a way artificial and transplanted, though they have made a great living presence out of it. With the Nashville poets it is an expected preoccupation. The contact with the past is not limited to the South by any means. In "The Mediterranean" Tate reaches back into antiquity in an attempt to "locate our blood."[24] Similarly in "Aeneas at Washington" and "Retroduction to American His-tory," the historical distance is considerable. Often the sense of time is localized, but as often it is of more general dimensions. Indeed, the emotion aroused by the contemplation of time is usually made very personal—that is, universalized as a feeling belonging to any man.

It seems the disenchantment of stepping beyond youth was a contagion passing poetically from the symbolists to Pound and Eliot, from them to MacLeish and the Fugitives. Meditating on the proverbial thirtieth year,[25] Tate considers history and time itself. He moves from himself into an ever-widening metaphysical perspective: this anxious

> Station where time reverses his light heels
> To run both ways, and makes of forward back;
> Whose long coördinates are birth and death
> And zero is the origin of breath:
>
> .   .   .   .
> Yet in a year, at thirty, one shall see
> The wisdom of history, how she takes
> Each epoch by the neck and, growling, shakes

It like a rat while she faintly mews.
Perhaps at the age of thirty one shall see
In the wide world the prodigies to come:
The long-gestating Christ, the Agnulus
Of time, got in the belly of Abstraction . . .[26]

In these lines time is personalized, yet the poet has become an impersonal focus of vision. Birth and death are correlated in abstractions made active as animal life. The figurative language of Christianity is not the sole expression of the "religious" attitude in metaphysical poems, where it intimates an unnamed horror and that "inhuman ecstasy."[27]

Tate's "after-wit of knowledge" allows for an afterglow of feeling. He appears to understand Donne's dual passions and suggests his very phrasing, as here:

The going years, caught in an accurate glow,
Reverse like balls englished upon green baize—
Let them return, let the round trumpets blow[28]
The ancient crackle of the Christ's deep gaze.
Deafened and blind, with senses yet unfound,
Am I, untutored to the after-wit
Of knowledge, knowing a nightmare has no sound . . .[29]

The conceit of years reversed "like balls on green baize" is in the tradition of Donne's compass image. By a homely analogy borrowed from a famiilar game, Tate objectifies one of the universal abstractions. The mind retains the figure of the play while transferring its emotion to the almost felt movement of the years. Another deft conceit is a true native of the South and could have derived from nowhere else with the same natural feeling: "His shadow gliding, a long nigger / Gliding at his feet."[30] This comes as a startling but casual inspiration and shows greater inventiveness than echoed images such as "the leaning man drowned deep" and "the wind speaking / Destiny, the four ways."[31]

It is not easy to avoid the recognizable sounds of Tate's masters in the intellectualized projections of contemporary life.[32] For example, "Idiot" once more adapts a familiar cynicism to a familiar nostalgia. Expected irony etches a timeless mood with lines too

reminiscent of Eliot and a cadence heard in MacLeish. The mad-
man shaking memory like a dead geranium becomes the idiot who
"Covers his eyes with memory like a sheet."[33] The panther sub-
stitutes for the leopard, the julep glass for the teacup. Similar
metaphoric counters are worn a little thin by the symbolists and
the school of Eliot.[34] Thus Tate's emulated affinities provided him
with ready and congenial matter.[35] "The Meaning of Life" and
"The Meaning of Death"[36] are exploited in poem after poem.[37]

In company with his masters and his fellow Fugitives, he cher-
ishes "a passion for time." The sense of continuity is very strong—
"It has all been forever."[38] His emotion relates man's season to the
supernatural where "After dog silence howls his epitaph."[39] Tate's
consciousness of time's wrong against humanity links him with
Pound, Eliot, Crane, MacLeish, with those who have experienced
the terrible hour.[40] And like them not only does he use physical
details for the abstract with convincing adroitness, he is furthermore beguiled by the fashion of transposing the senses. We find
such "correspondences" as the symbolists recommended by their
brilliant example: "The bleak sunshine shrieks its chipped
music";[41] "The windy apple, burning . . . / The apple wormed,
blown up / By shells of light";[42] and there are sounds in his lines
of those other poets who have guided the metaphysicals, such as
Dante[43] and of course Donne.[44] But he takes fair advantage of their
type of intellection and intriguing combinations. Worthy of Donne
is the subtle ambiguity of "Time begins to elucidate her bones."[45]
Gradually the verbal exactitude becomes clear: time's physical
process in cleaning the bones of flesh, and the mental process
illuminating the idea of death.

In many instances Tate falls into place among his colleagues
and models. The kind of argument that progresses by way of
paradox and repetition is developed in "Shadow and Shade," a
poem that Donne would have understood and comparable to his
"Lecture upon the Shadow" and certain passages in "The Extasie."
Tate even indulges (one can assume) in the seventeenth-century
pun on the word "die." In "The Subway" we find an example of
a modern structure treated metaphysically. Mechanics and mys-

tery come to a meeting point: "I am become geometries"[46] could
be a line from Hart Crane. Dedicated to Archibald MacLeish,[47]
"The Traveller" is written in closely constructed tetrameter quatrains. The form recalls Eliot's quatrains, the theme and lack of
punctuation resemble MacLeish's "You, Andrew Marvell." The
related subjects of the two moderns and the acknowledgment to
Marvell comprise a neat packet of kinships. Corresponding to
MacLeish's circling of the sun, Tate's poem describes man's
spiritual journey to the grave. Here the traveler's quest moves
through "swarming dark" toward death. In the final sense the
traveler falls to earth to understand at last—not MacLeish's passage of hours around the world—but the accomplished cycle of
man who joins the "secret ones" in a common fate, the unity that
gathers mankind one by one: "And a dark shift within the bone /
Brings him the end he could not find."[48] If MacLeish is the source
of inspiration for this poem, Tate nevertheless makes it a real
contribution to metaphysical expression.

So in "Last Days of Alice"[49] there is an even more individual
conception of the human dilemma. With that subtle childhood
classic as a starting point, Tate develops a bitter commentary
applicable to the adult personality. Particularized by mathematical terms, this poem is passionate with "abstract rage." It ends
in the religious paradox consonant with the theme and the mood.

> The All-Alice of the world's entity
> Smashed in the anger of her hopeless love,
>
> .   .   .   .
>
> —We too back to the world shall never pass
> Through the shattered door, a dumb shade-harried crowd
> Being all infinite, function depth and mass
> Without figure, a mathematical shroud
>
> Hurled at the air—blesséd without sin!
> O God of our flesh, return us to Your wrath,
> Let us be evil could we enter in
> Your grace, and falter on the stony path![50]

"Inside and Outside" likewise concerns the immediate and final
fate of man. Here is a very bodily description of the dead with

the living looking on. The poet pursues the theme beyond the experience of the eye, though sustaining the abstraction on an exciting plane equal to the physical comment. Concept is galvanized by strong concrete language:

> While the body's life, deep as a covered well,
> Instinctive as the wind, busy as May,
> Burns out a secret passageway to hell.
>
> . . . . .
>
> There is no word that death can find to say
> Deeper than life, savager than their time.
> When Gabriel's trumpet ends all life's delay,
> Will crash the beams of firmamental woe:
> Not nature will sustain the even crime
> Of death, though death sustains all nature, so.[51]

Tate vies with Ransom as equilibrist. After an apparent conclusion to "The Paradigm," the vibrations of the argument continue to hum. Donne would have admired the twisting contention between hate and love. The parallel experiences are drawn so tense and plausible that the reader finds the argument irresistible. This manner of discourse entangles the emotions and surprises the mind into consent. By the compression of the exacting syntax, many phrases come to resemble Donne's typical style:

> So fades out each heart's looking-glass
> Whose image is the surface hurled
>
> By all the air; air, glass is not;
>
> . . . . .
>
> For in the air all lovers meet
> After they've hated out their love;
> Love's but the echo of retreat
> Caught by the sunbeam stretched above
>
> Their frozen exile from the earth
> And lost. Each is the other's crime.
> This is their equity in birth—
> Hate is its ignorant paradigm.[52]

This poem, and the more ingratiating "Pastoral,"[53] exemplify the metaphysical approach to problems of love and hate, life and death, sin and innocence. The "Pastoral" is a modern blend of Donne's "Extasie," Marvell's "To his Coy Mistress," Eliot's "Conversation Galante," and the more intense examples of the sixteenth- and seventeenth-century bucolic love debate. Tate's contemporary pastoral has a timeless setting for a modern idiom. It is much more than a descriptive piece: it is an argument betweeen love and time. Here it is not coyness and desire in conflict, but the moment and the eternal condition, the male and the female principles. The discourse is advanced, moreover, by the forward weaving of the Dantesque *terza rima*. Though "Pastoral" is an excellent instance of the tradition concerned, it digresses somewhat from Tate's chief preoccupations.

In "Causerie" you return to the "essential wreckage of your age."[54] This poem is more in his accustomed vein of intellectual passion at odds with circumstance and conscience both: a token of the tormented race.

> They waited. I, who watched out the first crisis
> With them, wait:
>   For the incredible image. Now
>
> .   .   .   .   .
>
> A jagged cloud is our memory of shore
> Whereon we figure hills below ultimate ranges.
> You cannot plot the tendency of man . . .[55]

The poet speaks "To the Lacedemonians" from one of the most important sources of his experience. Though like others of his stature he has been beguiled into assuming the accents of Eliot's viewpoint and Pound's estimate of civilization, Tate has more than one wellspring for his agitations. Had there been no Eliot to show the way and supply the methods so variously adaptable, the acutely conscious modern (and the sensitive Southerner) would undoubtedly have tackled the local and universal problems with the instruments of metaphysical wit. In Tate's poem are the bitter lees of a long homesickness. Yet the history that Tate arraigns is fitted into a sharp present mood from which the future is not excluded. As an "exile utters the creed of memory,"[56] so this poet is morbidly attracted to the fate of the Confederacy.

Feeling this subject personally, he nevertheless relates the problems of the South to American civilization as a whole and to all mankind. The inclusiveness of tragic destiny and death exempts no one. The poet employs the "skill of the interior mind" to understand the local in universal measures, and not let "the mere breed" absorb the generation.

> Because I am here the dead wear gray.
>
> It is a privilege to be dead; for you
> Cannot know what absence is nor seize
> The odour of pure distance until
>
> .   .   .   .   .
>
> Huddled sublimities of time and space,
> They are the echoes of a raging tower
>
> That reared its moment upon a gone land,
> Pouring a long cold wrath into the mind . . .[57]

In the work of Robert Penn Warren there is an observable tension which, like Tate's, recalls the seventeenth-century state of mind and its response to the turbulence of the times. Warren's critical contemplation of modern man's predicament in general still gives him room to utilize his particular surroundings for color and detail. There is a strong impression of the South in his poetry, but it is in a sense less absorbed than the verse of Tate and less plainly regional than Davidson's. The symbolic imagery and intellectual transpositions in Warren are sometimes abstruse: because his locale or some specific experience is a mere point of focus for the psychological condition which contains his real, and always imponderable, subject. When his imagination materializes a forest where the hunting dog bays and echo answers, where flame flies and the shadow answers, it is the reflection which affords his true theme:

> And always at the side, like guilt,
> Our shadows over the grasses moved,
>
> .   .   .   .   .
>
> Our mathematic yet has use
> For the integers of blessedness:

> Listen! the poor deluded cock
> Salutes the coldness of no dawn.[58]

For each mortal occasion described, he knows a further relation—as did Donne in regard to love or a five-pointed flower or the progressive shadow. In the discernment so demanded, personal guilt is as relentlessly confronted as public crime in the guise of war and other human dilemmas.

As might be expected, with Warren the sense of time philosophically extends the setting of an ordinary human scene. Personal history and the tale of time are involved in a difficult dispute:

> All our debate is voiceless here,
> As all our rage, the rage of stone;
> .   .   .   .   .
> I do not love you less that now
> The caged heart makes iron stroke,
> .   .   .   .   .
> We live in time so little time
> And we learn all so painfully,
> That we may spare this hour's term
> To practice for eternity.[59]

The seventeenth-century English poets and our own metaphysicals like Emily Dickinson were under compulsion to weigh conduct and conclusions in the scales of time. Since they moved on much the same mental planes their words have similar inflections. In Warren's lines just quoted we hear Lovelace: "I could not love thee (Deare) so much, / Lov'd I not Honour more."[60] There is also here a sound of Dickinsonian passages, and of one in particular:

> How conscious consciousness could grow,
> Till love that was, and love too blest to be,
> Meet—and the junction be Eternity?[61]

Such echoes do not diminish Warren's originality nor the intensity of his equivocal mind. They serve to confirm him in the metaphysical faith.

The Fugitives have returned something of their debt to the tradition that inspirited their style. No reader, acquainted with the Jacobean poet, can fail to hear his tight harmonies in such love lyrics as Tate's "Pastoral" and "The Paradigm," Ransom's "The Equilibrists," and Warren's "Love's Parable"—

> That time, each was the other's sun,
> Ecliptic's charter, system's core;
> Locked in its span, the wandering one,
> Though colder grown, might yet endure
>
> .   .   .   .   .
>
> For joy sought joy then when we loved,
> As iron to the magnet yearns.
>
> .   .   .   .   .
>
> Your power, that slack is, but again
> May sway my sullen elements,
> And bend ambition to his place.[62]

It is obvious that Warren admires his model's use of science and technology to implement meaning. Warren's magnet in this poem corresponds to Donne's compass:

> And though it in the center sit,
>   Yet when the other far doth rome,
> It leanes, and hearkens after it,
>
> .   .   .   .   .
>
> And makes me end, where I begunne.[63]

When mental processes agree, material and methods and the resulting images are likely to bear a resemblance. We thus find elements, mathematical symbols, instruments of measure used; colors abstractly conveyed; theories defined concretely; homely sense experiences agitated by doubt and hope; problems prolonged by some contiguous thought; substance and its ideal meaning repeatedly alternating. Compare Donne's

> As 'twixt two equall Armies, Fate
>   Suspends uncertaine victorie,
> Our soules, (which to advance their state,
>   Were gone out,) hung 'twixt her, and mee.
> And whil'st our soules negotiate there,
>   Wee like sepulchrall statues lay;
> All day, the same our postures were,
>
> .   .   .   .   .

> For, th' Atomies of which we grow
>   Are soules, whom no change can invade.[64]

with Warren's

> We stood among the painted trees:
>
>   .   .   .   .   .
> So steady, that our substances,
> Twin flies, were as in amber tamed
> With our perfection stilled and framed
> To mock Time's marvelling after-spies.
>
>   .   .   .   .   .
> Or are we dead, that we, unmanned,
> Are vacant, and our clearest souls
> Are sped where each with each patrols,
>
>   .   .   .   .   .
> Love's limbo, this lost under-land?[65]

Metaphysical poets then and now have grappled with the indefinable and with their own inability to apprehend fully the elusive realities. The incredibility of time past and the terror of time future for the ego, such as haunt Tate in "The Wolves," for instance, and Eliot in much of his poetry, are persistent themes with Warren.[66] In every effort to extract its essence, Warren feels the fourth-dimensional presence: "But there it stood, after all the timetables, all the maps, / In the crepuscular clutter of *always, always,* or *perhaps.*"[67] The obduracy of a subject viewed abstractly and yielding its meaning so grudgingly (if at all) leads Warren to advance on it usually by way of paradox, in terms of its opposite, or from another time plane. Eliot believes that the moment of birth occurs "when we have knowledge of death."[68] And Warren maintains that "In separateness only does love learn definition,"[69] a sentiment he shares with Donne. In the same way Warren attempts to fix the meaning of other imponderables, with magnetic abstracts and metaphoric precisions:

> Happiness: what the heart wants. That is its fond
> Definition, and wants only the peace in God's eye.[70]

> Summer's wishes, winter's wisdom—you must think
> On the true nature of Hope, whose eye is round and does not wink.[71]

But "the unformulable endeavor" or "the immaculate itch" to define history, time, distance, life, death, or God,[72] does not in itself supply the answer or polarize the "iron of despair."[73] Warren sees apparently that "history held to your breath clouds like a mirror."[74] And the distraction of passing faces does not "suffice you, born to no adequate definition of terror."[75] Whether highly subjective or communally interested, a poet of this psychological order knows the futility of demanding

> Of the wave-lipped, sea-tongued sand
> Answer,
>
> .   .   .   .   .
>
> For all repeat
> In mirrored-mirrored-mirror-wise
> Unto our eyes
> But question, not replies . . .[76]

These passages, illustrating Warren's metaphysical restlessness, may slight his concrete imagery. Without being passionately sectional, despite a special allegiance to Kentucky, his poetry is enriched by regional associations: sounds, colors, and odors of the South. The reference in the following is not so much to a soldier or a Southerner as to any life-weary person anywhere who slumps,

> And wears infirmity but as the general who turns
> Apart . . .
> At dusk when the rapture and cannonade are still,
>
> .   .   .   .   .
>
> Where like an old possum the snag-nailed hand will hump
> On its knee in murderous patience . . .[77]

Warren's suggestions of some universal significance by plain, provincial figures affect us like metaphysical surprise, as in his reference to "That head which hooped the jewel Fidelity, / But like an old melon now, in the dank ditch, seeps . . ."[78] As a matter of fact, the Nashville poets share in common the ability to employ local color and dialect in their verse with minimal affectation and without limiting the generic sense of their writing. Tate on occasion slips in a localism: "it warn't in my time, by God, so / That the mere breed absorbed the generation!"[79] Or consider the effect of patois in the midst of the following sententious question: "So: Man, dull critter of enormous head, / What would he look at in the coiling sky?"[80] This flair for combining homely idiom with learned terms, the vernacular with sophisticated or philosophical implications, tokens the daring but usually discriminating wit of successful metaphysical poetry. The Fugitives' surprise effects can be much broader than those cited. In the following passages Warren juxtaposes blood and brain, modern mechanics and ancient sin, inconstancy and belief:

Blood splashed on the terrorless intellect creates
Corrosive fizzle . . .

You know, by radio, how hotly the world repeats,

The crime of Onan, spilled upon the ground . . .[81]

A change of love: if love is a groping Godward, though blind,
No matter what crevice, cranny, chink, bright in dark, the pale tentacle find.[82]

Here are distinct neo-Elizabethan flavor and form. Warren suggests also the seventeenth-century manner not only in temperament—discontented, searching, unappeasable—but in the syntactical arrangements and abrasive quality of his verse. Moreover, like the Jacobean poets, he can maintain this tone or temper by the entire design of an individual poem or by the homogeneous impact of a series of poems, considered as a whole. Many in his first group, called *Thirty-Six Poems,* are thematically related to the apparent antipathies between man and the forces of the universe, animate and inanimate. In the resultant drama the common destiny of all these elements becomes the motivation, and even nature itself is given an almost metaphysical faculty of apprehension. At the same time, the fate of human beings is seen as a mere aspect of the turning "planet's tilt."[83] This is not Wordsworthian pantheism, with its resigned and exalted compliance. It is a knowing horror of the world's destiny, and a sorrowing consciousness of man's involvement. Within the cyclorama of the cosmos, the poet is moved by "the stately perturbation of the mind."[84] Troubled by "the accident of flesh and bone, / or principle of thief and rat and moth,"[85] he probes the meaning of that course which seems always to carry human and animal life back to the condition of the inorganic,

> Where the blind and nameless bones recline.
>   they are conceded to the earth's absolute chemistry
>   they burn like faggots in—of damp and dark—the monstrous
>   bulging flame.
>   calcium phospate lust speculation faith treachery
>   it walked upright with habitation and a name
>   *tell me its name . . .*[86]

Warren contemplates the American pioneer story, childhood, time, as elements of fate which revolve with the turning earth on its slant axle thrust unseen through nature. The grief of man is paralleled by the pangs natural objects suffer. Reciprocally, the lives and deaths of men take on the properties of inanimate nature. This is in part the pessimistic attitude that results from modern naturalism and, as in present fiction, from the impact of scientific thought. The "little flesh and fevered bone" perhaps attain in death "the sweet sterility of stone," but stone itself may suffer "eternal agony of fire."[87] A common spirit informs them all and threads the human and inhuman on the same mysterious filament. The poet speaks of "the shuddering and sweat of stone"[88] and its "bitter tendons."[89] So the human brain is to him at once a problem of anatomy and metaphysics:

> Do those dead hear
> Earth lunge in its dark gyre . . .[90]

> What years, what hours, has spider contemplation spun
> Her film to snare the muscled fact?[91]

> Mortal, you ought
> Not dread fat larvae of the thought
> That in the ogival bone preform
> The fabulous worm.[92]

The circumstances of his early development, the personal and literary friendships Warren formed were all congenial to the kind of poetry under discussion. He himself says, "The seasons down our country have a way / To stir the bald and metaphysic skull,"[93] to excitement. "Eidolon," "Pondy Woods," "Genealogy," "History," and "The Ballad of Billie Potts" present the blood-and-terror aspect of the South on which the novelists have seized, and the poet can ponder directly and parenthetically:

> (O Time, for them the aimless bitch
> —Purblind, field-worn,
> Slack dugs by the dry thorn torn—
> Forever quartering the ground in which
> The blank and fanged
> Rough certainty lies hid.)[94]

"Memory's gelded usufruct"[95] of the old South is questioned by the "fangèd paradox"[96] and shocked into a different use by an intellectual, not a romantic, fervor. The modern intellectual is forced to admit that he is "gun-shy" of the banging, brutal epoch,[95] although he has the courage at least to investigate all areas of life in the present "blunt experiment of Time."[97] As much as he respects decisive action, he is a victim of the double plague of thought and emotion, and he sees as in the clarity of a dream the sometimes subterfuge of straight attack and the paradox at the root of life. To free it of this snag would require an almost inaccessible trust that "from evil bloometh good."[98]

Its guises varying with each versatile exponent and often transmuting into faith, skepticism plays an active role in metaphysical poetry. In the Nashville group none is natively more original than John Crowe Ransom, whose misgivings are set in subtly intentional terms. Though later more ingenious and satiric, the deceiving simplicity of his style was already in the making before the coterie assembled:

> I will be brief,
> Assuredly I have a grief
> And I am shaken; but not as a leaf.[99]

At first faintly suggestive of Eliot, many poems by Ransom appearing in *The Fugitive* were later incorporated in books of a decided independence:

> His grave eye subduing the outrageous red tie at his throat,
> Considering if he should carry his dutiful flesh to the ball,
> Rather than open his book, which is flat, and metaphysical.[100]

Since the Fugitives constituted a reaction against the older simplicities, Ransom's wry humor and apparent forthrightness cannot be mistaken for mere good nature. His whimsicalities are involuted and persuasive; they are a sly modulation of metaphysical phraseology. It is often by way of character studies and small sharp scenes that Ransom makes his criticism of life. He is as sensitive as any to controversial feeling and paradoxes of thought. Such dissonances are conveyed in the sketches, at once tense and deliberate, which are Ransom's indirect and inventive manner of approaching the human predicament. Like all metaphysicals he knows that truth (one prime object of poetry) is so obscure or protean that it can be only momentarily illuminated even by the exactest delineation of character, meaning, and word. This may account for the caustic incisiveness of his speech, which cuts through superficial meanings in search of an absolute. Like a Cavalier of the intellectual order, Ransom finds the hidden nerve with the objective selectivity of the skilled thrust.

The nature of God has provided poets with their most metaphysical mystery and Ransom's first book is *Poems about God*, born of the First World War:

> Most of these poems about God were completed a year ago, that is about the time when the great upheaval going on in God's world engulfed our country too. . . . God . . . was the most poetic of all terms possible; was a term always being called into requisition during the great moments of the soul, now in tones of love, and now indignantly; and was the very last word that a man might say when standing in the presence of that ultimate mystery to which all our great experiences reduce.[101]

Ransom's words on God, however, were neither pleasing nor angry. He already was perfecting a technique that teased the reader's mind into responsibility. Sometimes he evokes a critical response in his audience by the device of oversimplification: witness the easy sarcasm about a time "When God was centuries too young / To care how right he worked, or wrong . . ."[102] Thus the gullible reader is trapped by the poet's apparent ingenuousness. Or again, Ransom may achieve sardonic effects from the contrast between verbal plainness and the bitter obduracy of his implications—a trick that the seventeenth century knew very well:

> An easy thing to improve on God
> Simply the knowing of even from odd,
>
> . . . . .
>
> Simply to follow curve and line
> In geometrical design.[103]

As has been suggested, Ransom often takes the familiar tone with God that we hear in Donne, Herbert, Vaughan, Quarles, and even in Crashaw. A poet then, by consensus of that period's versatile temperament, could carry on an earthy conversation with an unearthly presence. In the same way, and with the added flippancy of the modern approach, Ransom speaks of "twinges of some godly gout"[104] and freely admits that a man may find God "sweetest of all / Discovered in a drinking hall."[105] He questions without qualms the invariable presence of God in the sacramental chalice and suggests a divine exaltation in "the foam of a crockery stein."[106]

When Ransom seems to be more serious, his portentous irreverence still recalls lines such as these by Quarles:

> O, I am dead: To whome shall I, poore I
> Repaire? To whom shall my sad Ashes fly
> But Life? And where is Life but in thine eye?
>
> . . . . .
>
> Speake, art thou angry, Lord, or onely try'st me?[107]

and Herbert:

> Is the yeare onely lost to me?
>
> . . . . .
>
> Not so, my heart: but there is fruit
> And thou hast hands.[108]

Profiting by this deceptively naïve quality, Ransom fosters a cunning characteristic spark intended to touch off an inquiring flame:

> Now, Lord, I die: is there no word,
>
> .   .   .   .   .
>
> No word. But tight upon his arm,
> Was God, and drew not once away
> Until his punctual destiny.
> To whom could God repair to pray?[109]

Ransom's God is innocent and knowing at the same time. The effort at proportion between opposing attitudes, between flesh and the thought that comes through flesh, between the divine idea and the physical fact, shows in the agile art of Ransom as it was wont to do in the seventeenth century. Donne says of Elizabeth Drury—actually of the pure notion of woman—that "one might almost say, her body thought";[110] and Ransom speaks of "The invincible emanations of her white body."[111] And elsewhere he compounds (like Anna Branch's "The Monk in the Kitchen") a homely chore with spirituality, the flesh with intelligence:

> The broom was busy in her hand,
> The goodness in her face.[112]
>
> Her broad brow meant intelligence
> And something better than a bone,
> Her body's curves were spirit's tents,
> Her fresh young skin was innocence
> Instead of meat that shone.[113]

No comparison is below Ransom's respect as a metaphysical poet; no height of exaltation above his aim. The artless style of his first book has a little of the devil in it. In *Chills and Fever* his more distinctive artistry is a sophisticated crisp mixture flavored with sugar and vinegar. Once Marvell could speak of a "vegetable love" and mean something incredible by it. In one of his reckless pieces Donne includes the surgeon's probe, the priest's reverent sacrifice, madness, "the sweet sweat of Roses," and the following daring images:

And like a bunch of ragged carrets stand
The short swolne fingers of thy gouty hand.
Then like the Chymicks masculine equall fire,
Which in the Lymbecks warme wombe dothe inspire
Into th' earths worthless durt a soule of gold,
Such cherishing heat her best lov'd part doth hold.[114]

In a striking love poem Ransom gives us a bold conceit which one is tempted to call a derivative of Donne's "ragged carrets."[115]

Think not, when fire was bright upon my bricks,

. . . . .

I glowed like them, the simple burning sticks,
Far from my cause, my proper heat and center.

. . . . .

Dear love, these fingers that had known your touch,
And tied our separate forces first together,
Were ten poor idiot fingers not worth much,
Ten frozen parsnips hanging in the weather.[116]

The sense of separation in the very presence of the lover and, on the other hand, the spiritual intimacy which can conquer absence and distance constitute a paradox that tormented Ransom and his progenitors.[117] Their particular emotions lend color to amorphous images of space, time, and death. Donne chiding the sun, Carew contemplating the gifts bestowed by Jove on beauty, Suckling's pale wan lover, Lovelace at war, and Marvell in the garden, are all obsessed by mortality and the desire to give it significance beyond the hour and the grave. The exigencies of human fate drive them to testify to a sense of the soul; obversely to immaterial values of the senses. Also facts and forebodings of science discourage the poet and at the same time enhance his imagination, as in the following passages from Ransom's "To a Lady,"[118] so rich in analogies to seventeenth-century poetry:

Too quick the annual sun returns,
Mounts to the ledge and scans the pillowed face
Whereon four seasons hardly have writ the trace,
Though even he on his timeless circuit mourns
That faintlier his fire burns.[119]

> Bring proper gifts to beauty then:
> Bring topaz, emeralds, gold, and minerals rare,
> Musk that will ever be sweet on mortal air,[120]
>
> .   .   .   .   .
>
> Dear love, rise up and proudly sing
> For even foreboding soldiers deep at night
> Make up no prayers against to-morrow's fight;
> They fling sweet oaths on high, not honouring
> The dismal nearing Thing.[121]
>
> .   .   .   .   .
>
> What can a virtuous poor pale lover do
> Who's prey to dissolution quick as you?
> This day smells mortuary more than most
> To me upon my post.[122]

The antinomies of life and thought are edged in Ransom's verse by a poignant irony. In "Vaunting Oak" occurs a moving debate between death and deathless love. There the girl, "who had been instructed of much mortality,"[123] tries to persuade herself with nature's example that love like the oak is forever. But the "sorrowing lover" knocking at the cadaver tree "drew forth like a funeral a hollow tone."[124] Many evocative scenes describe Ransom's search for principles intimating that "leaves and lovers have in common" something surer than the drying skeleton.[125] To him a principle can be sufficiently concrete to have gender, and he may see how "carrion telleth truth!"[126] A reciprocity is thus developed between the physical and the metaphysical, between mortality and the supernatural: "It was a sign had puffed up great the mortalest worm that dies,"[127] a statement with a decided Elizabethan spice. Ransom gives fact a bearing on fancy and makes the abstract sound empirical. To accept this special turn of mind requires a sympathy with the restless formulizing endeavor.

The poet does not apologize for his kind (lonely but typical of an age), whom learning has stuffed with lore and who are impelled by some mysterious daemon:

> With reason, friends, I am complained upon,
> Who am a headstrong man, sentenced from birth
> To love unusual gods beyond all earth,
>
> .   .   .   .   .

And if an alien, hideously at feud
With those my generation, I have reason
To think to salve the fester of my treason:
A seven of friends exceeds much multitude.[128]

Ransom is of the breed that is not easily pacified intellectually or emotionally. In a periphrastic satire he traces the progression from the tried simplicities to an inclusive and "jauntily designed" plural sentience:

> And who can tie the miscellany,
> Plato, Scythian, dog, and wart?
> One is One, but these be Many.
>
> .   .   .   .   .
>
> —Aforetime there was one God only,
> Simplex was his name, none other.
> Ah, but Simplicity was lonely . . .[129]

Had not Eliot arrived sooner, Ransom might have assumed the first role of social satirist expressing himself in the metaphysical manner. His mind is brave, his penetration acute, and his caustic wit relieved by subtle humor. Though a phase preliminary to his religious metaphysics, Eliot's early ironies are so telling in themselves that he may be more readily remembered for these. Any satiric verse paralleling or following his is therefore suspected of being derivative. In Ransom's 1924 volume he ridicules the ubiquitous tea, the bitten macaroon,[130] à la Eliot:

> These hailed each other, poised on the loud surge
> Of one of Mrs. Grundy's Tuesday teas,
>
> .   .   .   .   .
>
> A macaroon absorbed all her emotion . . .[131]

One of a sophistical bantering breed,[132] Ransom makes an estimate of famous poets in a "Survey of Literature" from the anti-romantic, at least antisentimental, viewpoint the Fugitives have taken. Wordsworth is too abstemious, Milton flatulent, Tennyson dousing with gravy, and Shelley drowned in "pale lemon jelly."[133] Finally he asks God's mercy on those who write with "No pewter and no pub, / No belly and no bowels, / Only consonants and vowels."[133] Apparently he feels that in America and in our time generally "It goes not liquidly for us."[134] The nightingale's note sounds flat indeed.

Ransom himself is sometimes involved to the point of preciosity. But his modulations of feeling and complex insinuations at least look pliant and brisk. He is, moreover, able to disturb the reader's thought and effect the metaphysical thrill:

> From the deep thickets of his mind the train,
> The fierce fauns and the timid tenants there,
> That burst their bonds and rushed upon the air . . .[135]

From these delicate if strict passions the poet can swiftly transfer his mood to the ironic and can exercise his listener's wit by a multiplication of thought. He can speak of the "astronomied Oes of eyes"[136] and tease the dog as "the bitch's boy."[137] But often he carries wit beyond the level of "acid gayety,"[138] as in the Robinsonian "Eclogue" and the Donnian "Equilibrists."

> It happened. For Time involved us: in his toils
> We learned to fear. And every day since then
> We are mortals teasing for immortal spoils,
> Desperate women and men.
>
> .   .   .   .   .
>
> . . . We are one part love
> And nine parts bitter thought. . . .[39]

"The Equilibrists" must be taken whole, it is so homogeneously designed. Individual lines and phrasing recall Donne's "The Canonization," "A Valediction: forbidding mourning," "The Funerall," and for structure Marvell's "To his Coy Mistress." But for remarkable adroitness and bitter inevitability, this love poem stands as a modern model of its kind.

Ransom's language is at once simple and learned; his attitude at the same time impudent and reverent of human agony. The vehicles for his allegory are often characters briefly etched in scenes economically staged. These people, alternately strange and familiar, are parables of his ideas on discontent, terror, and the sublime hungers. He pursues his arguments in symbolic sketches. The meaning of the allegory may be remote, but the persons are immediate even when odd; they are hardly mere personifications of qualities. With close attention they become still more accessible, but the method remains indirect and the passion elusive. These traits make for an intellectually, rather than an emotionally, metaphysical poetry. One type of the Ransom manner is "Captain Carpenter,"[140] a character once more of allegorical proportions who suffers balladlike vicissitudes. It is man methodically shorn of limbs and heart and brain in his passage through life—and the effect is cunningly and wittily weird. This objective poem is modern in tone, ambiguous in construction, emotionally strange and relevant at once; the surface is light while the implications are directed into deep and distant channels.

12

MACLEISH—WYLIE—CRANE

THE METAPHYSICAL period of Archibald MacLeish is interestingly represented by his collection, *Poems, 1924-1933.* Since the publication of that volume MacLeish's expression, like his subject matter, has altered. It is perhaps more than coincidence that the years covered by MacLeish's collection are also most conspicuous in the American metaphysical movement. They betray the poet's experience of World War I and portend the subsequent emotional crisis. The years of truce between two unspeakable wars aroused the restless intellectual activity and charged the social conscience of writers like MacLeish.

Since his metaphysical statement was heard chiefly in the decade between 1925 and 1935, it will answer our purpose to examine primarily the volume of collected poems, which includes the books *The Pot of Earth, The Hamlet of A. MacLeish, Einstein, Conquistador,* and many pieces from *Streets in the Moon* and *New Found Land.* Of the three early volumes excluded from this collection, *Tower of Ivory* is academic and negligible. But *The Happy Marriage* and *Nobodaddy* contain themes and exhibit a technique that indicate the poet's inclination developed more fully later. His work after 1935 showed an ebbing of this metaphysical tendency. When the financial storm, one of the several crises preliminary to World War II, broke over the United States and other nations, MacLeish was impelled to deal directly with immediate social problems. Such materials demanded a treatment appropriate to their satiric or expletive character, rather than the subtleties previously so effective for the analysis of spiritual unrest. MacLeish's subject matter in *Panic, Public Speech, The*

212

Fall of the City, Air Raid, Land of the Free, and the more optimistic *America Was Promises,* was now topical rather than suggestive; and his forthright methods, via verse plays for radio and photographs to the melody of a poem, were those he considered more serviceable at the time than indirection and paradox. These books, except for the occasional examples they supply, must necessarily stand outside the problem of metaphysical communication.

Of course one cannot determine the exact conditions, but it may be assumed that in a time preparatory to or consequent upon great public ordeals and cultural conflicts, a highly sensitive poet will often respond metaphysically. MacLeish illustrates two successive or alternative aspects of the reaction to predicament in society: one, introspective and analytic; the other, active and explicit. Both attitudes had their single root in his susceptible social awareness. After the First World War his generation found itself in a plight of emotional disillusion and intellectual uneasiness. Although his metaphysical phase was construed by some as an evasion of issues, it more likely indicated how deeply if obliquely he engaged at the time in spiritual concerns of civilization. As the public ordeal clarified in the light of great events moving toward the forties, MacLeish sought other ways of expression.

It has been his nature to share in whatever mental or social activity his times suggest. He was precipitated from the university into World War I: as an ambulance driver he witnessed its ravages and as a soldier he saw action in the Marne offensive. Some of these encounters were echoed in "Hamlet,"[1] an ostensibly personal poem with cosmic implications. The war affected him and left an aftermath of restlessness. Abandoning the practice of law, in 1923 he returned to France for five years, extending his travels to the Mediterranean region and as far as Persia. In these years of expatriation MacLeish was touched by those French and English poets who had stimulated Pound, Eliot, Crane, and a host of other moderns.[2] Not only the disillusioning war experiences but also his later membership on a League of Nations' commission conditioned the poet for his period of doubt and inquiry—as well as for his later period of social revolt and action. His real and vicarious participation in public matters, in the manifold developments of scientific, psychological, and literary ideas, matured his sense of the age as a growth of his historical sense. The play of metaphysical imagination had every sort of incitement.

It was in this earlier period that MacLeish was most subjective and introspective. Not even those who designated him as a Decadent—together with Pound, Eliot, Crane, and the French symbolists—could maintain, however, that he was aloof from the commotion of life around him. In his metaphysical poems he was alive to the contemporary scene as well as its universal inferences. During this phase his material was fairly extensive, but his themes were more important. Cosmic as to frame of reference and contemporaneous in their scientific and brooding reflections, they comprise destiny and death, a mechanistic universe disastrously determined, the implicit irony of man's relation to nature, the complexities of consciousness, the elements of time and space. His continuous objective was to define the forces rocking the human race, and express the disillusioning corollaries. The quality of the resultant poetry is at once morbid and vivid, reflective and nervous. To realize his moods and speculation, he took the expected methods: ways of wit, surprise, paradox, and contrast. Shrewd use of the conceit and the phenomenon known as the metaphysical shudder are repeatedly observed in the middle period of MacLeish's poetry. Even his lack of punctuation in a number of poems and the particular prosody by which he varied the music of his verse are well suited to his metaphysical motivation.[3]

Although the practical exigencies of propagandistic writing suppressed much of his former contemplative and skeptical tone, MacLeish never quite lost the metaphysical mood. Characteristically introspective even when concerned with outer realities,[4] it looks not only into the individual's mind but the activity of the generic mind as well. Such simple assurance as stated in "Open your eyes! There is only earth and the man!"[5] is not the natural language of the metaphysicals. But having been decisively impressed by the Eliot-Pound attitudes,[6] MacLeish carried certain devices of the "school" through his public-speech period. For example, intellectually transcribed sensations such as Marvell's "green Thought in a green Shade"[7] tinge his experience of silence and sound.[8] This correspondence between the senses and the mind, and the metaphysical apprehension of time, appear in varying degrees in all the phases of his work. Indeed, urgent public matters continued to recall the cosmic equivalent of the "terror that stands at the shoulder of our time."[9] MacLeish has stood in the very pulse

> Of ratcheted revolving time
> Repeating its repeated beat
> .   .   .   .   .
> Of seconds scissored by the clock.[10]

Though in his works of social propaganda he treats of death not speculatively but in its immediate aspects of air raid and starvation, the habit of the metaphysical conceit brought him to see the dead as "Blown clean to the arrow-heads under the centuries" where the "long harangues of the grass in the wind are our histories."[11] His ethic indignation still perceived "the luckless look that / Makes the dying dangerous and strange."[12] The expressive intriguing idiom influenced his language even when he thought he understood more directly how the "living inherit the / Hard speech of the dead like the seed of a pestilence."[12] Such lines have the ominous dramatic accent of the Elizabethans, others the sometimes quaint daring of the seventeenth century: "Covered with / Gable of God's love" and "The camphor taste of fear."[13]

So through his phase of social poetry certain metaphysical overtones hung remotely in MacLeish's figurative language and dramatic technique. Here is evidence that this mood was all along congenial to him. In two books prior to his collection that temper was prefigured. The long title poem of *The Happy Marriage* suggests Donne's intuition of sex psychology, as well as his use of the figurative paradox. There are already many hints of thought action on the senses and on the emotions of love:

> This was not love but love's true negative
> That spends itself in passion to be spent,
>
> .   .   .   .   .
>
> A woman was no lawyer's brief
> Compounded to persuade the sense
> Of things beyond experience
>
> .   .   .   .   .
>
> So should his body be his subtle brain
> And thought be sense and sense be thought again.[14]

In *Nobodaddy,* whose title derives from Blake, we find a dramatic prologue to the poet's chief metaphysical theme: consciousness. This important modern motif of course subsumes love and life, death, time, and divinity. *Nobodaddy* is an engaging variation of the parable of Eden and the genesis of sin. Here the primitive and the self-conscious have their initial encounter. At first Adam and Eve are pure body, growth without self-knowledge. At the moment of the serpent's temptation, question begins to take form. This is the setting for "the dramatic situation which the condition of self-consciousness in an indifferent universe" presents to Mac-Leish.[15] The Voice suggests that after Adam's rebellion the man would see what? "You would see Adam—"[16] After the Fall, Adam and Eve become two separate personalities in a new world of loneliness. She is

> Eve and not Adam, Adam's other self
> And therefore not himself. We are not earth
> Although the dust of earth is in us. . . .[17]

The psychological struggle of selfhood and submission continues in the persons of Cain and Abel. Theirs is a parable, in this poem, of modern individualism and the concurrent retreat into some protective belief. Cain possesses a godlike sufficiency, whereas Abel by priestly ritual and obedience to external decree shuts out the teachings of doubt. Yet Abel symbolizes another aspect of the man Cain:

> You are the flesh that wraps me and your fears
> Darken about me as an unknown something,
> Touched in the night, darkens the scared brain . . .[18]

This physical and spiritual duel between the first two brothers remains unresolved in the play as it does in the poet's and in modern man's duality.

In *Poems, 1924-1933* the themes that were of greatest concern to MacLeish at that time are developed in the longer poems and quintessentialized in the short lyrics. "The Pot of Earth" has its point of reference in a pagan myth of death and the generative powers of the sun.[19] Contemporary psychological and anthropological interpretation of myths is admitted at once by the introductory quotation from *The Golden Bough*, a familiar source book. Whether mythical or scientific, the explanation of the cyclic behavior in nature and man does not suffice the poet: he is distraught in the presence of inexplicable destiny. In this poem woman is the symbol of death breeding life only to die again. But the "impulse of intolerable loins" is impatient of death, even "burgeoning from your bones" and the very winter of the earth.[20] Such seasonal rhythms cannot satisfy the poet's skeptical turn of mind:

> What is this thing that sprouts
> From the womb, from the living flesh, from the live body?
> What does it want? Why won't it let you alone
> Not even dead?[21]

One would wish to "Attribute a significance perhaps / Not ours to what we are compelled to be,"[22] but the poet leaves the theme suspended by a question. Circling and clinging to the mystery for no finally apparent reason, each man is the "climbing ivy-tip of time."[23] That all men die says really nothing about death. In an illuminating moment of consciousness the soul lies awake wondering why it was given and why it will be taken away, why the seasons are incessant.

> Yes, wake, and of the close, unusual dark
> Demand an answer, crying, What am I?
>
> . . . . .
> . . . What do they mean
> The red haws out there underneath the snow,
> What do they signify?[24]

The Hamlet complex of the inquiring spirit dominates that phase of MacLeish's work where action waits upon conviction: the doubting and contemplative phase, perhaps the most nearly metaphysical.[25] Together with "The Waste Land" of Eliot, "The Hamlet of A. MacLeish" characterizes a period with whose disposition we sympathize even today. Intellectual sarcasm and scornful phraseology, leveled at the world and at the self, are modified by melancholy and the vivid illuminations of nightmare. The poet can hear from the

> Westward greying face of the wandering planet
> The voices calling the small new name of god,
>
> .   .   .   .   .
>
> And hear within the hollow room
> The clock tick Hurry! And behold
> Our eyes grow older in the glass.
>
> What is it that we have to do?[26]

MacLeish's "Hamlet" and Delmore Schwartz's "Coriolanus"[27] illustrate the particularly suggestive values felt by our poets in Elizabethan verse and drama. They serve very well as frames for contemporary analyses of psychological states. The cutback to the original plays in marginal notes or interpolated passages is more than a dramatic device: it gives meaning to MacLeish's claim that "It seems / I have the sense of infinity!"[28] This is said as naturally as Vaughan's "I saw Eternity the other night."[29]

In the second decade of MacLeish's verse appear some memorable comments on the infinities of time and space, the mysteries of death and creation. Hours are linked endlessly around space, with man "face downward in the sun / To feel how swift how secretly / The shadow of the night comes on . . ."[30] The intimate experience of time is at moments potently capsuled in MacLeish's briefer poems. "The Too-Late Born," "Lines for a Prologue," and "L'An Trentiesme de mon Eage,"—a signpost year—carry a concentrated weight of time. The poet swiftly recapitulates the ages of mankind and the world in a compression at once personal and impersonal. The taunting distance at which MacLeish stands

affords a poignant view of his past, of the universal past dissolved in the secret future. Although Eliot might be speaking
more than once in "L'An Trentiesme," MacLeish has fixed this
moment into a kind of signature:

> And I have come upon this place
> By lost ways, by a nod, by words,
>
> . . . . .
>
> And here above the chimney stack
> The unknown constellations sway—
> And by what way shall I go back?[31]

In the last three lines appear at least three metaphysical devices.
There is contrast of the chimney stack (a homely object) with the
infinitude of constellations, of plain language with scientific fact.
There is parallelism of personal emotion with objective idea.
There is surprise effected by the sudden simple question in the
last line.

Here and elsewhere MacLeish makes masterly use of the poetic
shorthand residing in this method. Condensed into nine lines, the
whole history of one man's existence symbolizes the world's history as well:

> The earth rolled over in the void.
> My head heaved up into the sun.
> The rue Saint Jacques advanced, deployed,
> Contracted. Two resemble one.
> Eating. His hands shooks hands. I have enjoyed—.
> The street swung open, seemed to run
> Two ways to darkness, was destroyed.
> My head reeled backward from the sun.
> The earth sagged over in the void.[32]

Beginning and end, or spiral movements, do not dispose of man's
intolerable question leading "Not to, not ever to, but toward."[33]
The poet looks into the "puzzled eyes"[34] of dreamers and contemplates "the eager dead."[35] Their withheld knowledge leaves
the old ironic query intact—"And do you think / Death is an
answer?"[36] MacLeish senses the life-and-death succession as the
silent shadow pursuing the sun, as the tireless imperceptible turn-

ing of the planet in "You, Andrew Marvell." This and the short pieces already cited, and a score of others,[37] are endowed with these stinging perceptions. The metaphysical shock occurs again and again in such lyrics,[38] and in this lightly derisive quatrain where the poem constitutes at the same time a single conceit:

> Around, around the sun we go:
> The moon goes round the earth.
> We do not die of death:
> We die of vertigo.[39]

Metaphysical wit is nimble here, as it is in the form of macabre humor in "The End of the World" where a side show exemplifies the absurd and at once awful fate of men's activity. Reflection upon the great verities that are likewise the great enigmas brings MacLeish quite naturally to the province of science where it borders on metaphysics.

He could have chosen, then, no better subject than Einstein for training his emotions on thought. In "Einstein" we see presented the all-dimensional being whose mind signifies physics but whose extra-cortical self bears a different and further meaning. The physicist is shown to possess material properties, but immaterial attributes irreducible to physical formulae. His feet press against the earth's sphere; yet when his mind contemplates it, suddenly he feels

> The planet plunge beneath him, and a flare
> Falls from the upper darkness to the dark
>
> . . . . .
>   He lies upon his bed
> Exerting on Arcturus and the moon
> Forces proportional inversely to
> The squares of their remoteness and conceives
> The universe.
>   Atomic.[40]

The choice of the Einstein symbol is short of inevitable: a man physical down to his shoes and metaphysically capable of grasping our shuddering planet with his mind. Before his skull is emptied by death, he must attempt the "pure and single factor of all sums— / Solve them to unity."[41] By the evidence of the philosophers and scientists themselves, there is poetry in the very infinity of mathematics. The concept is the span thrown between the scientist and the metaphysical poet where "spin within his opening brain the motes / Of suns and worlds and spaces."[42]

Many modern writers have shared this sensibility:[43] the awareness of mortality winding along the tangled "Immortal Helix."[44] Though ineluctable, it has seemed to them no simple effort to focus time, place, and personality in a telescopic vision. But in the midst of an exacting hope, the poet may see "in the sudden blackness the black pall / Of nothing, nothing, nothing—nothing at all."[45] The effect of such lines is the weird quality found in King or Marvell or Eliot. Social or amorous particulars, factual commentary or strong sentiment, may be followed without warning by appalling considerations. The metaphysical is hardly complacent.

Even in "Conquistador," ostensibly a minor epic of action and scenic impressions, the intellectual technique carries one around the curved edge of time. The poet wakens the dead from "sleep's thickets," and they become companions of current thoughts and passions. That MacLeish chose the locale of Mexico, mysterious land in time past and time present, has its own significance. His unchanged preoccupation with this element is confessed in a description of a visit to Mexico:

I have always been obsessed—perhaps that is too strong a word, obsession, or perhaps not strong enough—obsessed by time. My strongest consciousness is of time. In poetry it is the rhythm. . . . In Mexico you are most conscious of time, more so than in Persia even, probably because of the contrast between the modern and the ancient, the eternal.[46]

To the practical mind peoples move off in history like shadows passing, "like years on the flat plain";[47] but the behavior of the metaphysical is complex and disturbing in the contemplation of a lost time or an imaginatively importunate place.

To assay the known and the unknown, Hart Crane brought

together a vast variety of stubborn materials which his technique fused at high heat. Elinor Wylie, austerely selective by nature, was spare where Crane was profuse. Yet both were subjectively tense. Elinor Wylie's psychological acumen may have been narrower than that of the other poets but surely as swift. She understood the manner and methodology of her antecedents from Donne to Eliot,[48] and she perfected her own metaphysical style.

Although her contrivances sometimes seem too decorative, her quality is far better than picturesque. More often than not the precise images leave a wake of spiritual meaning. While her inspiration was autobiographical rather than universal, like that of Emily Dickinson whose pungency and perception she does not match, her apprehension of life was sufficiently objective to serve the double end of metaphysical poetry. She is a dialectician not so much by a process of argument as by the nice promotion of attitudes. One senses in *Collected Poems* how chronologically, book by book, the poems become progressively more metaphysical. This development, which perhaps reaches its apogee in *Trivial Breath* and parts I and II of *Angels and Earthly Creatures*, involves the first book too, *Nets to Catch the Wind*. Here the distinctive little allegory of the eagle and the mole introduces a key psychological problem of the modern world: personal versus collective consciousness.[49] In this instance the poet chooses the private encounter with the sun and "intercourse / With roots of trees and stones, / With rivers at their source, / And disembodied bones."[50]

The inner experience given in parable and allegory is typical of Elinor Wylie and relates her visionary habit to Blake's as well as Emily Dickinson's. Her clean inward thrust reaches the sanctuary of self built around by blood and bone. "Dead nor living may shake its strength."[51] Indeed, she is so well and intricately inclosed that the self is breathless. But she did not set her life apart from the emotional and intellectual influences of her day, which was lived in the war years and the feverish 1920's. She suffered duality, both social and personal. Love, for instance, is the lion and also the lamb: a piece of true Blakianism.[52] Elinor

Wylie's insight into self is equaled by her insight into death. Her ego reaches for reality in the region of the dead as in the state of the living. This is so true for Emily Dickinson and all metaphysicals to whom no barriers of flesh, grave, space, or time are beyond the eagerness of a ranging imagination. What appear to be contradictory states include varied and reciprocal experiences. At one time the dead are impervious to the sense of peace because they have drunk their fill of it;[53] at another, their sleep is almost sentient and like that of the living, "Not too narrow / And not too deep."[54]

The penetration, as it were, into the domain of the dead is an extension of the acute sense of life. The effort to reckon with the afterlife is equal to the effort to clutch existence itself in an age when both life and immortality have acquired more than ordinary value. Like the tortoise in eternity, the metaphysical poet moves through time before and time after, balancing the enormous universal burden on the sensitive interior self:

> Men's troubled dreams of death and birth
> Pulse mother-o'-pearl to black;
> I bear the rainbow bubble Earth
> Square on my scornful back.[55]

The round world is not more difficult to bear than the inner weight of the heart: "A bright core / To bitter black pain."[56] The poet feeds upon it and yet it grows; it has a grievous flavor and yet is as rewarding as immortal hope. In short sharp words she gives cognate and contrasted traits:

> Eat it I must, I must
> Were it bitter gall.
>
> .   .   .   .   .
>
> Sweet Heaven I shall taste
> Before my death.[57]

The life of feeling and the life of mind, the dead and the animate, are all particularized as if they were germane,[58] as indeed they are in the borderless provinces of metaphysical contemplation. In such indeterminate realms where poetically the expression is actual, mortality takes on theoretic qualities and a concept is equivalent to the sharpest sensation.

> The spiritual savage caged
> Within my skeleton, raged afresh
> To feel, behind a carnal mesh,
> The clean bones crying in the flesh.[59]

This sort of writing is quasi-Dickinsonian. Both women have "thoughts that colour / My soul which slips between; / Thoughts lunar and solar" jutting into the nature of the divine.[60] But neither would relinquish her own imperative "I." As a result, the profound and ironical tension between godliness and mortality, the unknown agent and the self-aware ego, persists:

> He turned His burning eyes on me
>
> . . . . .
> I did not want His company
> Who wanted no one but myself.[61]

These like the following lines are in the key of Emily Dickinson; but more important is the ease of communication between the person and the godhead, the braiding of human things into ineffable texture:

> I have entreated you to grant me Time
> To memorize the pure appointed task;
> Today it is Eternity I ask
>
> . . . . .
> To educate me fitly for your bride.[62]

Both had whimsical tastes, particularly Elinor Wylie with her tenuous exoticism and slightly baroque fancies drawn from remote times and from places of romantic memory.

Her caprices, however, in the manner of the seventeenth century, could touch sublimity and stay on delicately intimate terms with the beyond. A "whim of the glass-blower," the mushroom, the silkworm, are seldom "Stuff too slight to bear the fine / Fingertip of the divine . . ."[63] One expression of metaphysical wit,[64] the fantastic, comes from crossing the normal with the preternatural. This and the restless action between mind and senses—the opposition and convergence of impulses—created the conceit.[65] Where it is not sheer fancy, it achieves intellectual or mystic moments in imagination. Here are two striking conceits that testify to the operation of both types of thinking image, respectively:

> Unswaddled infantile to her
> His soul lies kicking in her lap.[66]

The phenomenon of thought and its ephemeral imprint on time are poignantly indicated:

> Before division of the suns
> Take shears to cut a second's thread,
> The mind must tick ecstatic once
> To prove that it is dead.[67]

Several conceits appear to issue directly out of Donne,[68] such as "A fallen star upon his pointed chin . . . / Wrong as the firstborn of a mandrake root."[69] Elfin fancy, occasional with Donne, is too often indulged by Elinor Wylie. In color, shape, and sound, her elegance affects "jewelled arabesques which adhere to clothe / The outline of your soul";[70] romantic matter in a severely classic setting.[71] Sometimes her "shiny mind is peopled / By brisk goblins,"[72] but when specters of dead lovers disturb her, she neglects the rococo for the dramatic cognitions of the more typical Donne. Then her heart finds "revelation at its lips."[73]

> So one that walks within the air,
> Who loves the ghost below the ground,
> Rejoices fervently to wear
> A body shaken and unsound;
> A brow divided by a wound;
> A throat encircled by a care.[74]

> And what the days, and what the Uranian years
> Shall offer us when you and I are ghosts;
> Forget the festivals and pentecosts
> Of metaphysics, and the lesser fears . . .[75]

Love and extinction (symbolic of being and non-being) are natural protagonists in contemporary poetry, as in the seventeenth century. It is less the fear of death that shadows modern poetry than an obstinate abstract interest. The metaphysical treats the subject as a physician of thought: with realistic respect and imaginative alacrity. The poet regards the body "shrunken to corruption's thread";[76] then commends it to the Mind "swimming somewhere" above.

> Into the hungry coffin and beyond it
> A single uncorrupted drop of youth
> Must live in elegy upon my lips
> When I and chaos shall have come to grips.[77]

The self-aware poet today does not easily surrender to oblivion. In a pyschological rather than religious age, the mysterious substance of the personality seems restive even beyond the grave. Hence the antagonism between death and consciousness, and the poet's repeated raids on both. The mind grapples with two conditions that appear incompatible and yet might be reconciled. From this contention a poetry is made that plays countless nuances of opposition and communion.

The paradoxical love song of the seventeenth century returns in our day at the incentive of rapid changes in society and the harrying forces of annihilation. Life's complexities show up in the very syntax and rhetoric of the verse, whose difficulty everywhere tells the strain of emancipation. Elinor Wylie's personal life and her expatriated years might be a comment on the dislocated times. But in her case the disciplined idiom overcomes obscurity for the most part while pointing up the inner anxiety.

> Although these words are false, none shall prevail
> To prove them in translation less than true
> Or overthrow their dignity . . .
> .   .   .   .
> O love, how utterly am I bereaved
> By Time, who sucks the honey of our days,
> .   .   .   .
> Wherein we flourish, and forget to know
> We must lie murdered by predestined snow.[78]

With her sonnet sequence written for Shelley,[79] and the sequence called "One Person," she illustrates a modern restrained vehe-

mence in the statement of love pulled by psychic tension. In the
tradition of Shakespeare and Donne, these sonnets are related
to the soberer sixteenth- and seventeenth-century locution, compact and cerebral and emotionally exact. She begins with Donne's
frequent abruptness—

> But this is nothing; an eccentric joke,
> The legendary patchwork of a year
>
> .   .   .   .   .
>
> The little sum of my experience
> Remains the sole contrivance I produce
> To weave this mesh, to colour and confuse
> These ragged syllables with soul and sense.
>
> .   .   .   .   .
>
> I have the proper scarlet of my veins,
> The clean involved precision of my mind . . .[80]

The language manifests a characteristic ambivalence suitable
to agitation equally mental and emotive. It has a dry fiery cast
right for feelings constantly tested by thought. The mutual
regard and strife of soul and sense often engender that ambiguous construction seen in Donne and Hopkins, Crane and
Ransom. The verbal statement of passion may tend to be "over-
fine" and intricately

> Knotted about the brain.
>
> Unscrupulous to pinch
> And polish down the thin
> And fire-encasing skin:
> Which pares away an inch
>
> Of valuable soil
> Whereon a god took root,
> Diminishing a brute
> With pumice and with oil.[81]

Expression not quite so concentrated, however, is more usual
with Elinor Wylie. In most of her poems "the slow miracles of
thought / Take shape through patience into grace."[82] She nevertheless chafes to "break the walls of sense in half / And make the

spirit fugitive!"[83] But she respects sensation too much on the one hand and on the other the ruthless discipline of the mind to subordinate either. And she speaks for three elements in man that correspond roughly to Donne's scholastic classification and appear variously in modern psychological forms:[84]

> Then did that fellowship
> Of three, the Body strip;
> Beheld his wounds, and none among them mortal;
> The Mind severe and cool;
> The Heart still half a fool;
> The fine-spun Soul, a beam of sun can startle.[85]

None of these can slough nor "cast his substance off";[86] an illusion that never ceases to intrigue the metaphysical. In an invocation "To a Book," her own, she traces its development from mortal birth: "an aureate grain of mustard / Folding a golden microcosm" and fostered in her bosom to the shape of a "sidereal blossom."[87] Worked out as a symbolic paradox of an uninterrupted quality progressing away from worldliness and still its captive, her imagery is one with her theme. There is a minimum of separation between the poetic texture and the idea—the accomplishment of a successful metaphysical poem.

The poet whose mind, seeking to make the abstract acutely discernible, can represent the pattern of the atmosphere as spherical and climb a "stairway cut from planetary space"[88] has obviously learned from Donne to find objective equivalents for the tenuous apprehensions of the soul. Elinor Wylie acquired the habit of stimulating and efficient conceits like this:

> Stop up my nostrils in default of breath
> With graveyard powder and compacted death,
> And stuff my mouth with ruin for a gag . . .[89]

The coördinates of experience are projected on a "map of Paradise"[88] whose "roots are set profoundly upon trouble";[90] a directional opposition that finds precedent in the seventeenth century and develops its own terms.

> But our palms were welded by a flame
> The moment we came to part,
> And on his knuckles I read my name
> Enscrolled within a heart.[91]

This quatrain recalls two passages in Donne,[92] while his "bracelet of bright haire about the bone"[93] becomes in Elinor Wylie the hand "frayed into a ravelled band / Around a silver ring."[94] It is obvious that she enjoyed "with Donne a metaphysical frolic."[95] Knowing its companion agony quite as sharply, she was intimate with thought of both dissolution and discovery, and pledged to lie "Beside my brother, Thomas Browne."[96] Thus more than once she owned to a kinship not only with Shelley and Plato but with Donne's century. She took what her selective temperament could naturalize and her chaste style convey. "And what delights she tasted as she roved / Are metaphysical, and remain unproved."[97] Another facet of her nature is a little like Herbert's in its palpable religiosity: at once knowing and childlike, pagan and Christian. Whatever is uncompromisingly puritan about Elinor Wylie—and she acknowledged this trait—is not alien.[98] It relates her to Emily Dickinson and to the seventeenth century,[99] which was grafted onto New England.[100] The surprising simplicity of Herbert can be seen again in "The Church-Bell," "Peter and John," and "The Innocents."

The *Collected Poems* compose a crisp portrait of a modern mind whose prototype can be found in another intricate age three hundred years ago. It is the picture of a mind proud of its adventure, clear intransigence, and accepted anguish. This autobiography of "an excessive liveliness of apprehension"[101] objectively sketches a distinct sensibility of our time. Showing an apparently calm and aristocratic exterior, the poetry betrays sheathed tensions. Elinor Wylie is representative not only of a group of agile-minded women poets of her day but of its counterpart among men of a like metaphysical order. She typifies one kind of wit that is for the most part deeper than whim or cleverness. She wore a smile that was curled with "Irony in either

corner";[102] her "archangelic levity"[103] had "austere refracted
angles":[104] she thus mocked herself and the world with sardonic zeal. Her apt epithets imply self-appraisal, a signal stage
in objectifying life. Somewhat brittle but clean and bright, her
wit thrust itself from the soil of her need where she sowed herself
for seed.[105] Because she rose and lived in "the difficult hour,"[106]
"Because the barbarous force of agonies / Broke it, and mended
it,"[107] her aching ecstasy was driven between the poles of antithesis. In sympathy with Dante's and Eliot's proscriptions of the
intermediate attitude which they relegate to limbo, Elinor Wylie
visited the extremes. "The Eagle and the Mole," as also the
following, testifies to this:

> The worst and best are both inclined
> To snap like vixens at the truth;
> But, O, beware the middle mind
>
> .   .   .   .
>
> Beware the moderated soul
> That climbs no fractional inch to fall.[108]

She did not stay at the antipodes of feeling or thought. The metaphysical poet welcomes variously acute instants in which mind
and emotion interact, but skepticism pursues a speculative judgment of one experience against another. Such skepticism created
in her a schooled spirit yet "blown hither and thither / By
trivial breath, over the whole world's length."[109]

"Address to My Soul" signs Elinor Wylie, as it were, in the
metaphysical succession. This piece is a progressive exposition
of the double motif encountered so often in her affiliates. It lacks
Donne's intellectual impact and irresistible distinctions, but it
distills essentials in the Dickinsonian manner and resembles
Eliot's fused structure. The poem is abstract and real in exquisite
proportion. It maintains a strict tension between the animate and
the supernatural, the animistic and the Platonic, sober form and
extravagant imagination. The whole is a medium made of thought
and feeling, and struck to vibration by a touch of metaphysical
misgiving. Within limits of her particular harmonics, the sound
here is almost perfect.

My soul, be not disturbed
By planetary war;

  .   .   .   .   .

Your sustenance is doubt:

  .   .   .   .   .

The universal points
Are shrunk into a flower;

  .   .   .   .   .

Five-petalled flame, be cold:
Be firm, dissolving star:
Accept the stricter mould
That makes you singular.[110]

Of all that amplitude that time explores,
A needle in the sight, suspended north,—
Yielding by inference and discard, faith
And true appointment from the hidden shoal:
This disposition that thy night relates
From Moon to Saturn in one sapphire wheel:
The orbic wake of thy once whirling feet,
Elohim, still I hear thy sounding heel![111]

In contrast, the work of Hart Crane shows us another view of the metaphysical, richly illustrated by this passage. It is romantic and turgid, but also conceptually plausible. The mysticism is cosmic as well as egocentric. Abstraction and physical detail are welded into one meaning within verse that is structurally firm, if often emotionally crowded. Crane was interested in science and God, fact and myth, absolute truth and current matters;[112] potentially interested in everything but always in relation to his own complex personality as an element in the eternal. The intercourse of substance and idea created the theme of his verse. And in all he wrote Crane mirrored the multifarious controversy of the modern soul.

Among our instances of metaphysical vision and technique, we see degrees of clarity and confusion, of tradition and iconoclasm. Elinor Wylie's form is clean and communicable; that of the Fugitives variable and sometimes immoderate; Eliot's a chiaroscuro of vision and contemporary chaos in outline. In perspective modern poets present the violence and process of change. Crane especially manifests this common aspect—in its bitter ebullience and prophetic effort. Repeatedly referring to our mechanical age,[113] he is among the least traditional as to the material of his work for all its many influences: esthetic, ethical, and mystic. Whatever subject matter was taken from American history or from literary impressions was measured against and incorporated into the current spirit of insecurity and experiment. But his "vision was the timeless One of all the seers, and it binds him to the great tradition";[114] it was also his technique that related contemporary "cultural chaos" to the metaphysical fervor of "Possibility."

Crane achieved a remarkable synthesis of the Rimbaud-La-forgue influence, the Donne tradition, and definite indigenous forces. Like his literary cousins Crane was disposed toward both the realism and symbolism of the modern French poets. Their psychological flashes and dark intuitions are also his. "He shares with Rimbaud the device of oblique presentation of theme."[115] He acquired something of the French sense of personalism and the real treatment of objects from Edith Sitwell, Stevens, and Eliot. But more important is that he generally absorbed the symbolist and the metaphysical traditions together. In Crane the Whitmanesque oracular impulse moved with a sort of nervous sensibility; the New England transcendental habit by Dickinsonian strokes of verbal and psychological precision. As a basis for his own experiments, Crane accepted the Eliot idom. With this formula, he readily received the imagist credo concerning immediate and exact diction. "Garden Abstract" is one of several poems cordial to that control.[116] Not an economical poet, Crane managed individual images of pictorial accuracy and compactness. His style of brilliant fragments, closely set, deviated from imagism as a result of his ambitious attempt to relate cosmic principles to the distractions of his age and confusions of his own personality.[117] This endeavor to create an inclusive idiom sent him to much earlier poets. "Crane wields a sonorous rhetoric that takes the reader to Marlowe and the Elizabethans."[118] Texturally pre-Websterian in a sense, the passion of his verse resembles the later Elizabethan drama and its nervous quality has Donne's tension. What appears to be a convergence of eclectic influences,[119] however, is a radiation of the poet's turbulent needs and an audacious stretch to formalize modern changes.

It has been assumed that his frequent failure to coördinate vision and language came not so much from the diversity of his literary inheritance as from the unresolved agonies of our era and his personal life. This assumption finds support in the fact that he stopped his restless career by plunging into the sea from a homeward ship. External forces exacerbated his private disequilibrium; his poetry moved "in a constant swing between ecstasy and exhaustion."[120] Waldo Frank connects Crane's "tendency toward inflation" with the febrile season between 1924 and 1929,[121] which is half the prognostic period covered by MacLeish's collection of poems. Crane's impassioned spirit and chaotic private history stimulated a propensity to experiment with fresh idiom and metaphysical transcription. He strained immensely to see, to tell the continuity between man and the universe; and he certainly came closer in his poetry than in his life to a synthesis of forces: of passion and idea, of doubt and vision. Hunting "a poetic principle to integrate" modern civilization with some basic intent, Crane expresses the metaphysical integer in this "quest but not the finding."[122] Perhaps his truest logic is that of conflicting terms: his "sole clarity is the balance of antithetical movements."[123] Therein Crane sounds the disorder of the social and spiritual condition in his day more flagrantly than most other metaphysical poets, probably because he was also bolder in his try at inclusiveness. Especially in *The Bridge* he meant to synthesize America's history from the strident pioneer days to the machine age and the war years. "Even the failings in execution, since they are due to weakness of the personal focus, help to express the epoch";[121] in him the period has a passionate utterance of its psychological and poetic problems.

Along with such emblems of union and communication as the bridge, the subway, the airplane, Crane deals with the large sym-

bolic life of the sea and with the Indian as allegoric of American
soil. To encompass them all and more than these, the poet seeks
a continuous myth and a principle of oneness. *The Bridge*
develops the myth from Columbus, mystical navigator, to the
near-mystical experience of the contemporary swimmer in the
skies. Beneath the land and the waters, the subway or tunnel
corresponds to the bridge above, which like a parabola spans
river and sea harbor. Although a great breadth of time and a
whole urban civilization are conveyed in tangible imagery,
Crane's themes, "abstractly, metaphysically conceived,"[124] most
often refer to his fundamental symbol of the sea. Because this
primal symbol and his vision are intuitive rather than reasoning, he is perhaps closer to Crashaw in temperament than to
Donne, to Jeffers than to Ransom. Lawrence's symbol of perfect
sexual union and Jeffers' recourse to natural powers are akin to
Crane's compulsion toward the sea. Such creeds and symbols
are elected in "solving the mystic's burden," which is "the organic
continuity between his self and the cosmos."[125] To this extent
Crane bears a resemblance to the obsessed and to visionaries like
Blake, in whom the apocalyptic overwhelms fact and logic. Otherwise, Crane was more metaphysical than mystic when he showed,
contrary to Lawrence, repeated discontent with his own symbols
and used them as a means of further quest.

Conflict is the final reality in his verse. The prophetic and the
rhapsodic are persistently challenged and corrected by ironic
predicament. His purpose is "still one shore beyond desire!"[126]
Crane demonstrates the ordeal of "the dissociation of the modern
consciousness" suffered by Baudelaire and after him by Eliot
and other moderns.[127] Yet had Eliot "written a more ambitiously
unified poem, the unity would have been false" according to
Tate.[128] If understood as an aspect of metaphysical struggle and
query, dissociation is inevitable. The sensibility of metaphysical
poetry is inclusive, but its objective of oneness is symbolized and
approached rather than reached.

The complexity of Crane's private experience and of the world to which he fell heir obviously cried for a supreme effort at integration. Though he never formulated a philosophy or a method of life, he made a dazzling attempt to read himself into the context of the universals.

> My word I poured. But was it cognate, scored
> Of that tribunal monarch of the air
> Whose thigh embronzes earth, strikes crystal Word
> In wounds pledged once to hope—cleft to despair?[129]

"He began, naked and brave, in a cultural chaos. . . . Cities, machines, the warring hungers of lonely and herded men, the passions released from defeated loyalties, were ever near to overwhelm the poet. . . . Crane was a true culture-child; more completely than either Emily Dickinson or Blake, he was a child of modern man."[130] The triple weight of personal maladjustment, the complexity of creative effort, and an urban civilization at cross-purposes confirmed his mysticism while it exaggerated his realism. Interest in the mechanics of modern life and his grandiose intuitions coöperated to form a fascinating poetry. Crane refused no experience in his own life or writing. His eye was exact, his mind inquiring, and his emotions hospitable to all data.[131] The realistic detail and the mood created are rarely divorced from the search for some generic sanction. All his shifting scenes and symbols are threaded on the hope of some form, some truth applicable equally to man, to the devised machine, and to the cosmos. The poet's troubled sense of personal and impersonal existence demanded an organic association between the objective world and the ego, within the abstract aura where they are mysteriously related.

That he was continuously impelled to focus disparate experience shows in his extraordinarily daring imagery. He could visualize "oval encyclicals" or casually "jacket heaven."[132] No contrast was too intimate or sacred, no epithet too violent or technical for his imagination when it worked with the "unfractioned idiom."

> Down Wall, from girder into street noon leaks,
> A rip-tooth of the sky's acetylene . . .[133]

> And now, as launched in abysmal cupolas of space,
> Toward endless terminals, Easters of speeding light—
> Vast engines outward veering with seraphic grace
> On clarion cylinders pass out of sight . . .[134]

Words like "acetylene" and "cylinders" remind us that Crane had very definite ideas as to poetic assimilation of routine life and its mechanics. To him, as to Donne and his kind, the function of poetry includes the naturalization of current practices as well as past effects. In an industrial age particularly, this process demands "an extraordinary capacity for surrender, at least temporarily, to the sensations of urban life."[135] Crane's theory affirms Donne's emphasis on urban materials and the capacity of both to use the accessible science. Yet Crane, recognizing science as the modern deity, had enough large religious feeling to bring spirituality into a dithyramb "To Brooklyn Bridge":

> O harp and altar, of the fury fused,
> (How could mere toil align thy choiring strings!)
> Terrific threshold of the prophet's pledge,
> Prayer of pariah, and the lover's cry . . .
> . . . . . .
> Unto us lowliest sometime sweep, descend
> And of the curveship lend a myth to God.[136]

Coping verbally with perpetual phenomena such as "gravitation's vortex" and the hot stars, Crane nevertheless rejects nothing in the "Years of the Modern!" The past is alive in him, but his spirit feels "Propulsions toward what capes?"[137] Moving with agility from the commonplace to the metaphysical notion, he speaks easily of "interborough fissures of the mind."[138] Neo-Elizabethan passion and localisms of his time and place go coupled. The natural rhetoric of his verse is excitingly enriched in texture by traditional harmonies, then "Striated with nuances, nervosities / That we are heir to":[139]

> Like one whose eyes were buried long ago

> The River, spreading, flows—and spends your dream.
> What are you, lost within this tideless spell?

> You are your father's father, and the stream—
> A liquid theme that floating niggers swell.[140]

Without intellectual control, such imagery could be mere sound full of fury. And Crane has his embarrassing failures, like most audacious writers. For example, he sees Cortez "reining tautly in— / Firmly as coffee grips the taste."[141] But generally the coördinates of past and present, of feeling and figure, are evocatively indicated in "a vast precision."[142] He is capable of counterpointing dissonance: a Pullman breakfaster and an abstraction, early seventeenth-century rhetoric and modern staccato. Extremes are harmonized by Eliot's shuttling technique, the interval filled with the substance of Crane's own dense imagery. A plane flight is mystically projected

> To conjugate infinity's dim marge—
> . . . . .
> The circle, blind crucible of endless space,
> Is sluiced by motion,—subjugated never.
> . . . . .
> Dream cancels dream in this new realm of fact
> From which we wake into the dream of act;
> Seeing himself an atom in a shroud—
> Now hears himself an engine in a cloud![143]

To articulate all his experience, nothing within it must escape the "assessments of the soul."[144] Few poets could see the moon make a "grail of laughter of an empty ash can,"[145] but for Crane all things are dark and "bright insinuations that my years have caught."[146] He captures the continuity of life in unregenerate adult ardor and bitterness, instructed by the painful sensibility of his time and its need for intelligible patterns:

> As silent as a mirror is believed
> Realities plunge in silence by . . .
> . . . . .
> Then, drop by caustic drop, a perfect cry
> Shall string some constant harmony,—
> Relentless caper for all those who step
> The legend of their youth into the noon.[147]

No modern poet, certainly in America, has given a more sumptuous imagery of contrasts brought together with the intention of synthesis: a subliminal or conscious objective of the metaphysical. The material in Crane's experience is a springboard toward some difficult concept. And his adventurous metaphors generally manage the distance. Even Emily Dickinson's vocabulary was less fruitful, if more accessible and efficient. Since the poets of the seventeenth century—Crashaw, Donne, Cleveland—no one, except Hopkins, Yeats, and perhaps Auden or Dylan Thomas, has been more exciting or eccentric in the image. Very few since Vaughan's poetic period have witnessed in the same way a "great wink of eternity,"[148] by which Crane describes the ocean; nor felt, since Donne, the "brain's disk shivered against lust."[149] Crane is indeed a master of the metaphysical thrill, whose vibrations are sometimes too rapid for a ready understanding of his metaphorical truths. The high voltage of sensation is at moments dangerous to the logic of idea. But if the music of his ideas has not been reassuring, the compelling experience of his age at least revealed to Crane the "incunabula of the divine grotesque."[150] The anxiety of a time-troubled generation bred in him occasional paroxysms of poetry and often beautiful plays of the imagination. The following is as transcendental a symbol, in miniature, as Melville's Moby Dick:

> Bind us in time, O Seasons clear, and awe.
> O minstrel galleons of Carib fire,
> Bequeath us to no earthly shore until
> Is answered in the vortex of our grave
> The seal's wide spindrift gaze toward paradise.[151]

The metaphysical "latitudes and levels"[152] of Crane's poetry contrive to implement his symbolism with scientific and technological facts. A willful mind and an era of tribulation extend his subject matter from "what fierce schedules"[153] of the plane to the tears of Christ, and his figurative language from the most intriguing paradox to the rash pun of conceit: "Thy Nazarene and tinder eyes."[154]

It should be evident that Crane's poetic behavior is an im-

portant expression of his time in its social and literary experi-
mentalism. He glowingly exemplifies its struggle for cognition and
the accompanying metaphoric daring. A multiplicity of influences
was therefore congenial to his complex temperament and brilliant endeavor.[155] In Crane's essay on modern poetry, he admits
indirectly his partial derivation from the French symbolists and
their counterparts in English. There is also an incidental reflection
of Hulme's interest in abstract art and Crane's own predilection
for scientific and abstract terminology. Thus not only poetically
but critically he suggests the correlation. He found it indeed

highly probable that the Symbolist movement in French poetry was a
considerable factor in the instigation first, of Impressionism, and later,
of Cubism. Both arts have had parallel and somewhat analogous
tendencies toward abstract statement and metaphysical representation.
. . . Analysis and discovery, the two basic concerns of science, became
conscious objectives of both painter and poet.[156]

Among native symbolist influences on Crane was one whom
he did not acknowledge—Samuel Greenberg. In mystic attitude
and verbal passion, the two poets had innately enough in common for Crane's "Emblems of Conduct" to be routinely accepted
as his own.[157] Actually this poem is a mosaic of Greenberg's lines.
In the obscure young poet who died about 1918, Crane saw "a
quality that is unspeakably eerie and the most convincing gusto.
One little poem is as good as any of the consciously conceived
'Pierrots' of Laforgue."[158] The ease with which Crane could
assimilate and even incorporate lines out of Greenberg without
impairing his own originality indicates their odd resemblance in
poetic instinct and mood. Their bold syntax, dense language
and impacted thought, their spontaneous rebellion against expected diction, show that the two poets freshly attacked the complex problem of consciousness. Conflict worked in both for
spiritual clarification: if without sure syntactical success, at least
with a resulting wealth of vocabulary and meaning, "esoteric and
highly sophisticated."[159] An eager appetite for experience, undisciplined in Greenberg because of meager training, did not
overwhelm the intellectual metaphor or prevent, for Crane, great

technical excellence. Yet for different personal reasons but in a common experience of their civilization, both poets testify to "the frustration of spiritual life by our daily mores."[160]

Crane and Greenberg prove the existence and development of an indigenous style of intensity. It has been claimed that Crane persuaded particularly the decade of poets following Eliot's special disciples—a demonstration of national expression analogous to expatriate influence. This is only obliquely true, since Crane also pastured in Eliot's fields of French symbolists and metaphysicals, and was given to "magnificent Elizabethanisms of epithet and metaphor."[161] Greenberg's similar tastes and tendencies were congenial to Crane. The Blakian Greenberg lived in a "helium of thoughts endowment"[162] and practiced a "sad scrutiny from my warm inner self."[163] He is attractive as a poet who, apart from any established influence, is a symbolist and a mystic by nature and suggests a metaphysical cast of mind. Through one of those strange poetic accidents, he resembles Crashaw, Herbert, and Traherne. What is more, as a figure of the poet personally conditioned ¯toward the metaphysical and independent of current fashion, he recalls Hopkins and Emily Dickinson.

Typical and atypical at once, a poem by Crane epitomizes some common attributes of those metaphysicals whose logic resides in their imaginative and verbal exaltation sooner than in their intellectual coördination and structure. With exceptions that are purely Crane, this poem rings certain particulars of style and spirit in lines by Herbert, Hopkins, Emily Dickinson, and Greenberg.

> Lo, Lord, Thou ridest!
> Lord, Lord, Thy swifting heart
>
> Naught stayeth, naught now bideth
> But's smithereened apart!
>
> Ay! Scripture flee'th stone!
> Milk-bright, Thy chisel wind

Rescindeth flesh from bone
To quivering whittlings thinned—

Swept—whistling straw! Battered
Lord, e'en boulders now out-leap

Rock sockets, levin-lathered!
Nor, Lord, may worm out-deep

Thy drum's gambade, its plunge abscond!
Lord God, while summits crashing

Whip sea-kelp screaming on blond
Sky-seethe, high heaven dashing—

Thou ridest to the door, Lord!
Thou bidest wall nor floor, Lord![164]

Although less critical intellectually than emotionally, Crane felt the abstract with vivid acuteness. The metaphysical is one part realist, one part mystic, and one part intellectual. These proportions often vary to form an asymmetric but dramatically balanced poetry.

NOTES

1. In this connection I submit a tentative graph to indicate the rise, fluctuation, and decline of critical interest in metaphysical verse manifested in this century. Studies concerning metaphysical poetry in general and thirteen seventeenth-century metaphysicals are plotted for every year from 1900 to 1950. See page 244.

The graph gives only approximate inferences. (About 1,500 items are used.) It presents merely a suggestive picture of the concern, in the last fifty years, with seventeenth-century metaphysical poetry and its outstanding exponents. Furthermore, the poets considered must always represent an arbitrary choice. This graph follows in most respects Theodore Spencer's invaluable bibliography of metaphysical studies. To his choice of the following twelve metaphysicals Quarles has been added: Carew, Cleveland, Cowley, Crashaw, Donne, Herbert of Cherbury, George Herbert, King, Marvell, Katherine Philips, Traherne, and Vaughan. An attempt has been made here to rectify some errors in dates (*e.g.:* T. O. Beachcroft's "Mysticism as Criticism," *Symposium,* II, No. 2, belongs to the year 1931 and not 1928 as listed by Spencer), inconsistencies, and omissions. (In his essay Spencer on p. 12 states that he has "omitted many shorter articles, as may be seen by a glance at the accompanying bibliography." Yet several articles longer than some of those included are neglected, *e.g.:* J. E. V. Crofts, "John Donne," *Essays and Studies of the English Association,* XXII, 128-43; A. C. Judson, "The Source of Henry Vaughan's Ideas Concerning God in Nature," *Studies in Philology,* XXIV, 592-606.) In accordance with his bibliography, I included reprints and new editions of the more significant studies because these demonstrate a quickening or continued interest in the subject. For instance, since the publication in 1921 of H. J. C. Grierson's *Metaphysical Lyrics & Poems of the Seventeenth Century,* there have been reprints in 1925, 1928, 1936, 1947; John Hayward's edition of Donne appeared in 1929, 1932, 1934, 1936, and 1949.

Most of the supplemental material is accounted for by the time extension in this graph: its scope being fifty years as against twenty-seven. Spencer studies the span from 1912 to 1938—which compasses the period of greatest activity in work on metaphysical poetry. But it should be noted that several critics and editors showed precocious response to the seventeenth century, for example: H. C. Beeching, G. H. Palmer, A. R. Waller, Bertram Dobell, Edmund Gosse, E. K. Chambers, Louise I. Guiney, George Saintsbury, and Professor Grierson, who published work on that period from 1906. At the other end of the graph are represented works after 1938, such as Austin Warren's study of Crashaw in 1939, a 1940 work on Marvell by M. C. Bradbrook and M. G. L. Thomas, F. E. Hutchinson's 1941 edition of Herbert,

Some Poems & A Devotion by John Donne in the 1941 New Directions series of "The Poet of the Month," a volume of the work of Donne and Blake brought out in 1941, Gladys Wade's *Thomas Traherne*, 1943, Wylie Sypher's provocative item in the *Partisan Review*, 1944, the Italian edition of *La poesia metafisica inglese del seicento* by Mario Praz in 1945. Furthermore, since 1938 there has appeared a host of articles on the individual metaphysicals, Donne in particular. After 1945 interesting books like Rosamond Tuve's *Elizabethan and Metaphysical Imagery* are still to be noted; and Austin Warren's *Rage for Order* in which there are essays on George Herbert, Hopkins, and Yeats among others; Hayward's anthology, *Seventeenth-Century Poetry* in 1948; Leonard Unger's *Donne's Poetry and Modern Criticism*, a 1950 estimate of six major current critiques on the subject.

At best, the decision to indicate or disregard an item is a discretionary matter, subject to inconsistency and personal choice. Raymond M. Alden has an article on the lyrical conceits of the metaphysical poets, which appears in Spencer's bibliography, but an article by the same author on the lyrical conceit of the Elizabethans is omitted. Yet Alden himself admits to the intrinsic connection by writing the article on the metaphysical conceits as a continuation of that on the Elizabethan conceit, the latter subsuming type 3b: logical-metaphysical type. Again, it seems arbitrary of Spencer to name a dubious poem on Vaughan attributed to Siegfried Sassoon and to exclude reviews by T. S. Eliot on books about the metaphysical era, as well as to ignore Eliot's item called "Deux Attitudes Mystiques: Dante et Donne." The bibliography omits also his series of pieces given for *The Listener* in 1930. Another instance is the neglect of *Circumference*, the 1929 anthology that dramatizes the interest in varieties of metaphysical verse. True enough, these poems collected by Genevieve Taggard range from the sixteenth to the twentieth centuries inclusive, but the seventeenth-century group is most prominent. This book seems as worthy of inclusion as Edmund Blunden's *Nature in English Literature,* in which some half-dozen pages on Vaughan apparently justify it as a metaphysical study.

The graph denotes, moreover, as many editions of the metaphysical poets and reviews of metaphysical studies as came to hand. Some of these reviews are listed by Spencer as articles in his bibliography. Others not mentioned by him have been considered in the material for this graph, which uses also the exhaustive bibliography of periodical articles, *John Donne Since 1900,* assembled by William White in 1941 and published in 1942.

2. Eliot, "Donne in Our Time," *A Garland for John Donne,* ed. Spencer, p. 4.

3. *Idem,* "Metaphysical Poetry," I, pp. 1, 2.

4. *Idem,* "John Donne," *The Nation and the Athenaeum* (1923), p. 332.

5. *Idem,* "Donne in Our Time," *A Garland for John Donne,* ed. Spencer, p. 13.

6. *Ibid.,* pp. 17, 18.

NUMBER OF STUDIES IN METAPHYSICAL POETRY--1900-1950

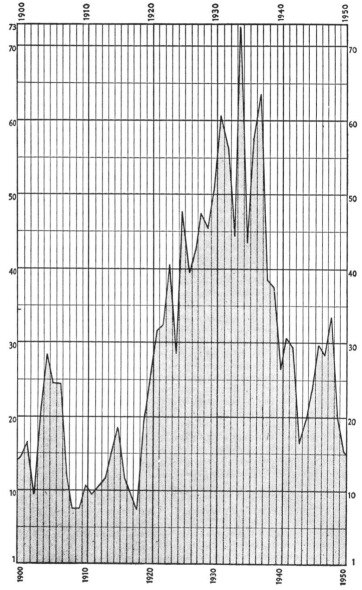

7. "Poets in Their Fame," *The Saturday Review of Literature* (1935), p. 24.

8. *Idem*, "Recent Scholarship in Metaphysical Poetry," *Studies in Metaphysical Poetry*, p. 3.

9. *Ibid.*, pp. 14, 6.

10. *Ibid.*, p. 17.

11. Hugh I'Anson Fausset, "The Poet and His Vision," *The Bookman* (1931), p. 341.

12. Merritt Y. Hughes, "Kidnapping Donne," *Essays in Criticism* (1934), p. 61.

13. F. O. Matthiessen, "Tradition and the Individual Talent," *The Achievement of T. S. Eliot*, p. 12.

14. Her *Nets to Catch the Wind* derives from Webster's line in a song from *The Devil's Law-Case. See* Taggard, ed. *Circumference*, p. 59.

15. Arthur H. Nethercot, "The Reputation of John Donne as Metrist," *Sewanee Review* (1922), p. 463.

16. *See* Samuel Grafton's column "I'd Rather Be Right," *The New York Post*, September 9, 1942, where he writes that "There was nothing to do except retire into one's study and reread John Donne's verse: 'From needing danger, to be good . . . Lord deliver us.'"

17. C. S. Lewis, ironically in a volume dedicated to Grierson in 1938; and Spencer, who has already been mentioned in this connection.

18. John Crowe Ransom, "The Tense of Poetry," *The World's Body*, p. 253.

19. Allen Tate, *Reactionary Essays*, "A Note on Donne," pp. 64, 72.

20. *Ibid.*, "The Profession of Letters in the South," p. 166.

21. Henry W. Wells, "Our Poetic Tradition," *New Poets from Old*, p. 19.

CHAPTER 1

1. "In vain have some Men of late (Transformers of every Thing) consulted upon her [poetry's] Reformation, and endeavoured to abstract her to *Metaphysical* Ideas, and *Scholastical* Quiddities, denuding her of her own Habits and those Ornaments with which she hath amused the World some Thousand Years." ("To his much honoured Friend Dr. Arthur Johnston, Physician to the King," *The Works of William Drummond of Hawthornden.* Edinburgh: Printed by James Watson, 1711, p. 143.)

2. "Johnson's term 'metaphysical' . . . is both more distinctive than any other name . . . and is historically interesting and accurate." (Grierson, "English Poetry," *The First Half of the Seventeenth Century*, p. 156.)

3. *Webster's New International Dictionary of the English Language* (Second edition, unabridged; Springfield, Mass.: G. & C. Merriam Co., 1949).

4. *Three Philosophical Poets.*

5. "Metaphysical Poetry," I, p. 22.

6. *The Lives of the Poets*, vol. IX of *The Works of Samuel Johnson*, ed. Arthur Murphy (London, 1823), p. 19.

7. About Donne: "He affects the metaphysicks, not only in his satires, but in his amorous verses, where Nature only should reign; and perplexes the minds of the fair sex with nice speculations of philosophy, when he should engage their hearts and entertain them with the softnesses of love." ("A Discourse on the Original and Progress of Satire," *The Critical and Miscellaneous Prose Works of John Dryden*, ed. Edmond Malone. London, 1800. III, 79.) Dryden adopted the epithet used by Testi for the school of Marino.

8. Nethercot, "The Term 'Metaphysical Poets' Before Johnson," *Modern Language Notes* (1922), p. 13.

9. "Donne and his Place among Lyrical Poets," *English Literature During the Lifetime of Shakespeare*, pp. 364, 365, 377.

10. "Most commonly the term was used in seventeenth century poetry simply to mean above the material world, supersensible, and hence above 'nature.' . . ." (Robert L. Sharp, "The Pejorative Use of 'Metaphysical,'" *Modern Language Notes*, 1934, p. 503.) This quatrain corroborates:

> Stifle, therefore, my muse, at their first birth
> All thoughts that may reflect upon the earth;
> Be metaphysical, disdaining to
> Fix upon anything that is below.

(Sir Aston Cockain, "A Funeral Elegy on my dear cousin . . ." from *Small Poems of Divers Sorts*, 1658, as quoted in Sharp, "The Revolt Against Metaphysical Poetry," p. 215.)

11. *Idem*, "The Pejorative Use of 'Metaphysical,'" *Modern Language Notes* (1934), p. 505.

12. *Science and the Modern World*, pp. 219, 220, 221. "The two realms are intrinsically inherent in the total metaphysical situation."

13. Whitehead's use of the word "actuality" rather than "reality" is helpful here, since in philosophy the latter term signifies to some what idea, or ideality, does to others. Today the concept of reality is something very tangible. With Plato and Kant, a different meaning obtains.

14. Grierson, ed. *Metaphysical Lyrics*, p. xiii.

15. Eliot apologizes for retaining the popular term "metaphysical" and even plays the devil's advocate for the rejected epithet "fantastic" as subsumed under metaphysical. The seventeenth century is still "metaphysical" to us through confirmed use of the qualification. ("Metaphysical Poetry," I, p. 22.)

16. Grierson, ed. *Metaphysical Lyrics*, p. xiii.

17. W. Bradford Smith, "What is Metaphysical Poetry?" *Sewanee Review* (1934), p. 263.

18. "On Metaphysical Poetry," *Scrutiny* (1933), p. 277.

19. "Prologue to the Succession," *The Donne Tradition*, p. 88.

20. Charles M. Coffin, "Poetry and Science," *John Donne and the New Philosophy,* p. 16.

21. Ed. *Aspects of Seventeenth Century Verse,* foreword to "Metaphysical Verse," p. 177.

22. "Metaphysical Poetry and Propaganda Art," *Modern Poetry and the Tradition,* pp. 39, 42.

23. Joan Bennett, "Introductory," *Four Metaphysical Poets,* pp. 1, 3.

24. *Ibid.,* pp. 7, 8.

25. "The Nature of Metaphysical Poetry," *Reason and Romanticism,* pp. 34, 35.

26. Johnson, *op. cit.,* p. 22.

27. "The Nature of Metaphysical Poetry," *Reason and Romanticism,* pp. 44, 45, 55, 56.

28.
Radical imagery occurs where two terms of a metaphor meet on a limited ground, and are otherwise definitely incongruent. . . . In Radical imagery the minor term is itself of little imaginative value but the metaphorical relation is powerful. . . . The Radical image might be expressed geometrically as a cone. On one end is a point of no imaginative value in itself from which radiate lines of powerful suggestion.

(Wells, "Introduction," "The Radical Image," *Poetic Imagery,* pp. 31, 121, 126.)

29. "Poetry: A Note in Ontology," *The World's Body,* pp. 139, 140.

30. Helen C. White, "Metaphysical Poetry," *The Metaphysical Poets,* pp. 71, 78.

31. Ed. Taggard, "Circumference," *op. cit.,* p. 3.

32. *Ibid.,* p. 6.

33. White, "The Divine Poetry of John Donne," *op. cit.,* p. 148.

34. "The Nature of the Donne Tradition," p. 57.

35. Eliot, "The Metaphysical Poets," *Selected Essays,* pp. 247, 249. "Racine or Donne looked into a good deal more than the heart. One must look into the cerebral cortex, the nervous system, and the digestive tracts." (*Ibid.,* p. 250.)

36. *Ibid.,* p. 250.

37. *Idem,* "Rhyme and Reason: the Poetry of John Donne," *The Listener* (1930), p. 502.

38. *Idem,* "Metaphysical Poetry," I, pp. 7, 12 ff.

39. *Idem, Selected Essays,* "The Metaphysical Poets," "Andrew Marvell," pp. 246, 255, 263.

40. *Ibid.,* "Philip Massinger," p. 185.

CHAPTER 2

1. "Science and Philosophy," *Adventures of Ideas,* pp. 197, 198.

2. *Op. cit.,* p. 23.

3. "The Metaphysical Poets," *Selected Essays*, pp. 241, 242.

4. Ed. *Metaphysical Lyrics*, p. xiii.

5. "On the University Carrier," *The Poetical Works of John Milton*, ed. H. C. Beeching (Oxford University Press, 1925), p. 19. Cf. "Another on the same." (*Ibid.*, pp. 19, 20.) Critical opinion (*see* Grierson's anthology) has named "The Hymn on the Morning of Christ's Nativity" as possibly another metaphysical lyric by Milton. (*Ibid.*, pp. 1-8.)

6. *Op. cit.*, p. 236.

7. Two other groupings, separated by more than two centuries, should help illuminate the problem of the metaphysical category. Among Pope's papers was found a chart placing the following poets in the school of Donne: Cowley, Davenant, Drayton, Overbury, Randolph, Sir John Davis (sic), John Beaumont, Cartwright, Cleveland, Crashaw, Bishop Corbet, and Lord Falkland. *See* Owen Ruffhead, *The Life of Alexander Pope* (London, 1769), p. 424. Peter Quennell, in *Aspects of Seventeenth Century Verse*, selects the following poets for his section on metaphysical verse: Carew, Cartwright, Cowley, Crashaw, Davenant, Donne, Felltham, John Hall, Lord Herbert, Sir Robert Howard, King, Richard Leigh, Marvell, Suckling, and Traherne.

8. Elizabeth Atkins, *Edna St. Vincent Millay and Her Times* (Chicago: University of Chicago Press, 1936).

9. In April, 1937, Miss Millay personally suggested that the young poet study the salutary example of Donne's method.

10. Hopkins' general themes comprise God, Christ, and Mary; death, time, youth, and beauty; love of England. His sources of imagery are the sea, birds, moonlight, the soldier. *See Poems of Gerard Manley Hopkins*, ed. with Notes by Robert Bridges (Second edition, London: Oxford University Press, 1930).

11. Williamson, "The Talent of T. S. Eliot," *The Sewanee Review* (1927), p. 285.

12. *Ibid.*, p. 286.

13. *Idem*, "A Short View of the Tradition," *The Donne Tradition*, p. 237.

14. Elizabeth Drew, "The Logic of the Imagination," *Directions in Modern Poetry*, p. 221.

15. Among the species of knowledge to which he turned were: "Theology, metaphysics, medical lore, mineralogy, military science, law, natural history, animal and human physiology, alchemy. . . ." (George Reuben Potter, "John Donne's Discovery of Himself," *Essays in Criticism*, 1934, p. 6.)

16. J. Smith, *op. cit.*, p. 228.

17. "Metaphysical Poetry," VII, p. 19.

18. J. Smith, *op. cit.*, p. 227.

19. Wells, "The Heritage of Technique," *New Poets from Old*, p. 119.

20. J. Smith, *op. cit.*, p. 227.

21. "The Nature of Metaphysical Poetry," *Reason and Romanticism*, p. 56.

CHAPTER 3

1. "Donne in Our Time," *A Garland for John Donne,* ed. Spencer, p. 16.
2. *Idem,* "Metaphysical Poetry," IV, pp. 21 ff.
3. *Ibid.,* V, p. 2.
4. Raymond M. Alden, "The Lyrical Conceit of the Elizabethans," *Studies in Philology* (1917), p. 137.
5. Eliot, "Metaphysical Poetry," IV, p. 21.
6. Example of sixteenth-century lyrical (verbal) conceit:

> What harvest half so sweet is
> As still to reap the kisses
> Grown ripe in sowing?

(Thomas Campion, "What Harvest," *The Works of Dr. Thomas Campion,* ed. A. H. Bullen. London: Privately Printed at the Chiswick Press, 1889, p. 74.)
Examples of seventeenth-century conceits:
Imaginative type
  a. Simile

> If they be two, they are two so
>   As stiffe twin compasses are two,
> Thy soule the fixt foot, makes no show
>   To move, but doth, if the 'other doe.

(*John Donne,* Dean of St. Paul's: *Complete Poetry and Selected Prose,* ed. John Hayward. London: The Nonesuch Press; New York: Random House, 1936. [First edition, 1929.] "A Valediction: forbidding mourning," p. 37.)

  b. Metaphor

> Since I am comming to that Holy roome,
>   Where, with thy Quire of Saints for evermore,
> I shall be made thy Musique; As I come
>   I tune the Instrument here at the dore,
>   And what I must doe then thinke here before.

(*Ibid.,* "Hymne to God my God, in my sicknesse," p. 320.)

> But O, selfe traytor, I do bring
> The spider love, which transubstantiates all . . .

(*Ibid.,* "Twicknam garden," p. 20.)

  c. Personification

> Thinke then, my soule, that death is but a Groome,
> Which brings a Taper to the outward roome . . .

(*Ibid.,* "Of the Progresse of the Soule: The Second Anniversary," p. 217.)

d. Myth

> Ask me no more if East or West,
> The Phenix builds her spicy nest:
> For unto you at last she flyes,
> And in your fragrant bosome dies.

(Grierson, ed. *Metaphysical Lyrics*, Thomas Carew, "A Song," p. 39.)

Logical type
a. Paradoxical

> Mean while the Mind, from pleasure less,
> Withdraws into its happiness:
> The Mind, that Ocean where each kind
> Does streight its own resemblance find;
> Yet it creates, transcending these,
> Far other Worlds, and other Seas . . .

(*Ibid.*, Andrew Marvell, "The Garden," p. 210.)

b. Logical-metaphysical

> Love is a growing, or full constant light;
> And his first minute, after noone, is night.

(Donne, "A Lecture upon the Shadow," ed. Hayward, *op. cit.*, p. 54.)

Examples of modern conceits:

> The frail ecstatic gnats that move
> Like planets whirling in a sky . . .

(Anna Hempstead Branch, "Under the Trees," *The Shoes that Danced; and Other Poems*. Boston: Houghton Mifflin Co., 1905, p. 181.)

> Concentrical, the universe and I
> Rotated on God's crystal axletree,
>
> I core of the world, a bead in a ball of glass
> So pure that only Nothing could be less.
>
> .   .   .   .   .
> Now cubical upon a fractured pole
> It creaks, scraping the circle of my soul.

(Stanley J. Kunitz, "Geometry of Moods," *Intellectual Things*. Garden City, N. Y.: Doubleday, Doran & Co., 1930, pp. 2, 3.)

> In life I shone with so much death . . .

(José Garcia Villa, "Divine Poems," *Have Come, Am Here*. New York: The Viking Press, 1942, p. 104.)

Pity the strong alone
.   .   .   .   .
Who know, if sounding chord
   To all their thought were given,
If they trod out the wine
   Longed for, from memory's presses,—
The dissonances, poured
   Would sour their own heaven.

(John Wheelwright, *Rock and Shell;* Poems 1923-1933. Boston: Bruce Humphries, 1933. "Mossy Marbles," p. 40.)

I have an hour-glass of years in my
receding hair.

(*Ibid.,* "Gestures to the Dead," p. 74.)

I see a distance of black yews
Long as the history of the Jews.

("Perspectives Are Precipices," *The Collected Poems of John Peale Bishop,* ed. Allen Tate. New York: Charles Scribner's Sons, 1948, p. 49. Cf. Marvell's "To his Coy Mistress.")

Dark clot of speed on pure line, to assert:
Idea the line . . .

(Genevieve Taggard, "Train: Abstraction," *Not Mine to Finish;* Poems 1928-1934. New York: Harper & Brothers, 1934, p. 82.)

And light
That fosters seraphim and is to them
Coiffeur of haloes, fecund jeweller—
Was the sun concoct for angels or for men?
.   .   .   .   .
Light, too, encrusts us making visible
The motions of the mind and giving form . . .

(Wallace Stevens, "Evening without Angels," *Ideas of Order.* New York: Alfred A. Knopf, 1936, pp. 28, 29.)

Flight is intolerable contradiction
We bear the bursting seeds of our return
we will not retreat;   never be moved.
Stretch us onward   include in us the past
sow in us history, make us remember triumph.

(Muriel Rukeyser, "Theory of Flight," *Theory of Flight.* New Haven: Yale University Press, 1935, p. 59.)

Light is the last fact and the first that falls

> On mortal eyes, and while they stare at time,
> Light is a calendar on outdoor walls . . .

(John Holmes, *Address to the Living*. New York: Twayne Publishers, 1949. "Address to the Living," p. 4.)

> . . . body, poised in time and space,
> Remembers the pure right angle of itself to earth,
>
> .   .   .   .
>
> . . . till the blood once more confirms
> The swift and accurate passion of that draughtsmanship.

(*Ibid.*, "The Phoenix Promise," p. 49.)

> And North and South are an intrinsic couple
> And sun and rain a plural, like two lovers
> That walk away as one in the greenest body.

(Stevens, "Notes toward a Supreme Fiction: It Must Change," *Transport to Summer*. New York: Alfred A. Knopf, 1947, p. 130.)

7. Alden, "The Lyrical Conceits of the 'Metaphysical Poets,'" *Studies in Philology* (1920), p. 197.

8. Verbal; imaginative (metaphor-simile, personification, myth); logical (paradox, logical-metaphysical type). (*Idem*, "The Lyrical Conceit of the Elizabethans," *Studies in Philology*, 1917, p. 138.)

⁻9. Raleigh, Greville, Chapman, and at times Sir Philip Sidney anticipated Donne in relatively free and experimental examples of the logical-metaphysical conceit in its earlier stages.

10. Drew, "Poetry and Meaning," *Directions in Modern Poetry*, p. 80.

11. *Seven Types of Ambiguity*, p. 157.

12. Among the more important sources of the conceit, as distinguished from the imagery inherent in all poetry and in language itself, is the Italian poet of Dante's day, who in turn derives from the troubadour. Pound thus went to a good school for imagery and brought his lessons back to the imagists and to Eliot. "The 'concetti metafisici ed ideali' of the *Anatomy of the World* are not more metaphysical . . . than those of the canzone in the *Vita Nuova*. . . ." (Grierson, "English Poetry," *The First Half of the Seventeenth Century*, p. 158.) The English poet also borrowed from the French troubadour when they were related on one soil.

13. Kathleen M. Lea, "Conceits," *The Modern Language Review* (1925), p. 398.

14. *Ibid.*, p. 405.

15. Louis MacNeice, "Imagery," *Modern Poetry*, p. 97.

16. *See* chap. 1, note 28, for definition of the radical image.

17. W. B. Smith, *op. cit.*, pp. 265, 266.

18. "The Garden," *Metaphysical Lyrics*, ed. Grierson, p. 210.

19. "The Second Anniversary," ed. Hayward, *op. cit.*, p. 221.

20. "Sospetto d'Herode," *The Complete Works of Richard Crashaw,* ed. A. E. Grosart (London: The Fuller Worthies' Library, 1872), p. 103.

21.

> And, like Antipodes in shoes,
> Have shod their heads in their canoes.

("Upon Appleton House," *The Complete Works in Verse and Prose of Andrew Marvell,* ed. A. E. Grosart. London: The Fuller Worthies' Library, 1872, p. 41.)

22.

> Each little Pimple had a Tear in it,
> To wail the fault its rising did commit . . .

("Upon the Death of Lord Hastings," *The Poems of John Dryden,* ed. John Sargeaunt. London: Oxford University Press, 1925, p. 176.)

23.

> He's followed by two faithfull fountaines;
> Two walking baths; two weeping motions;
> Portable, & compendious oceans.

("Saint Mary Magdalene or The Weeper," *Metaphysical Lyrics,* ed. Grierson, p. 134.)

24. J. Smith, *op. cit.,* pp. 234, 235.

25. Williamson, "Donne and the Poetry of Today," *A Garland for John Donne,* ed. Spencer, p. 162.

26. C. Brooks, "Metaphysical Poetry and Propaganda Art," *Modern Poetry and the Tradition,* p. 45.

27. Beachcroft, "Mysticism as Criticism," *The Symposium* (1931), p. 217.

28. Matthew W. Black, ed. *Elizabethan and Seventeenth-Century Lyrics,* "The Tribe of Ben," p. 379.

29. *Ibid.,* "The Devotional Lyrists," pp. 485, 486.

30. C. Brooks, *Modern Poetry and the Tradition,* "The Waste Land: Critique of the Myth," p. 169.

31. *Ibid.,* p. 170.

32. *Ibid.,* "The Modern Poet and the Tradition," p. 80.

33. "The Metaphysical Poets," *Selected Essays,* p. 247.

34. *Ibid.,* pp. 248, 249.

35. *Op. cit.,* p. 3.

36. *Ibid.,* p. 74.

37. *Ibid.,* p. 167.

38. *Ibid.,* pp. 281, 282.

39. *Ibid.,* p. 287.

40. *Ibid.,* p. 323.

41. *Ibid.,* p. 298.

42. From another point of view, Winters discusses the ambiguities of modern experimental writers in terms of obscurity which becomes obscurantism under certain conditions. (*See* pp. 16-60 of *Primitivism and Deca-*

dence.) The relevance of his study consists of the examples, drawn chiefly from symbolists and modern poets with whom we have been dealing and whose obscurity or difficulty is noteworthy. Under "grammatical coherence in excess of, or in the absence of, rational coherence" we find instances from Marianne Moore, Crane, Jonson (Crane's model in this connection), Mallarmé, Rimbaud. "Transference of values from one field of experience to another and unrelated field" is seen in Crane's "The Dance" and "Atlantic." Eliot's "Gerontion" and "Burbank with a Baedeker" exemplify "reference to a non-existent plot"; and Alan Porter's "Museum" an "explicit reference to a non-existent symbolic value." Difficulties inherent in much poetry and a reader's limitations of learning make "reference to a purely private symbolic value" a cause of obscurity. Here Winters gives us Blake, Yeats, Shakespeare's sonnets, the mad songs of the sixteenth and seventeenth centuries. Eliot, Pound, Joyce, Laforgue, and Mallarmé serve to show some of the more puzzling—and not always legitimate—effects of "pseudo-reference" and "qualitative progression." A further type of obscurity Winters calls the "double mood," which is certainly one of the characteristic idiosyncrasies of this poetic age. Some examples are given in Byron's style, but also in Laforgue's "Complainte des Printemps," and in Théophile Gautier, from whose *Émaux et Camées* Pound and Eliot have taken either inspiration or actual lines to implement the contrast of moods. Eliot's packed stanzas in "Sweeney among the Nightingales" (often cited for their fusion of past and present, splendor and sordidness) and Pound's "Mauberley" sequence employ the formula of the double mood. Sometimes the two moods are coincident, as in Pound; at other times sequential, as in Gautier and Eliot, and in the irony of Stevens. And these poets change places.

Winters concedes specific values developed by French symbolism and twentieth-century experimentation despite attendant obscurities. In the elaborations of his study he condemns their abuse, which results in preciosity and obscurantism. His departure from Eliot's concept of tradition in poetry appears in his praise of Jones Very, whose poems reprinted by Winters are most uninteresting examples of economy and the uses of poetic tradition.

43. MacNeice, "Obscurity," *Modern Poetry*, p. 161.

44. Thomas McGreevy, *Thomas Stearns Eliot*, p. 56.

45. MacNeice, "Imagery," *Modern Poetry*, p. 96.

46. *Ibid.*, p. 99. "With the acquisition of these qualities—irony, realistic diction, wit—symbolist poetry coalesces with metaphysical." (C. Brooks, "Symbolist Poetry and the Ivory Tower," *Modern Poetry and the Tradition*, p. 61.)

47. Matthiessen, "Tradition and the Individual Talent," *op. cit.*, p. 32.

48. Hopkins, "The Caged Skylark," *op. cit.*, p. 31.

49. "Sweeney among the Nightingales," *Collected Poems* (see chap. 10, note 2), pp. 65, 66.

50. E. M. W. Tillyard, "Preliminary," *Poetry Direct and Oblique*, p. 67.

51. I. A. Richards, *Principles of Literary Criticism*, "The Imagination," p. 250.

52. *Ibid.*, "The Poetry of T. S. Eliot," p. 295.

53. Williamson, "Donne and the Poetry of Today," *A Garland for John Donne,* ed. Spencer, p. 158.

54. Wells, *The Tercentenary of Henry Vaughan* (1922), p. 9.

55. Basil Willey, "Sir Thomas Browne," *The Seventeenth Century Background,* pp. 42, 43.

56. Laurence Binyon, "Gerard Hopkins and His Influence," *University of Toronto Quarterly* (1939), p. 270.

57. Hopkins, "God's Grandeur," *op. cit.,* p. 26.

58. Pp. 58, 101.

CHAPTER 4

1. Matthiessen, "Tradition and the Individual Talent," *op. cit.,* p. 31.

2. "Andrew Marvell," *Selected Essays,* p. 259. Poe's element of surprise in the short story has more meaning for us than in his verse where it is rather mechanical.

3. Willey, "The Heroic Poem in a Scientific Age," *op. cit.,* p. 217.

4. Eliot, "A Note on Two Odes of Cowley," *Seventeenth Century Studies,* p. 239.

5. "Plot," *op. cit.,* pp. 200, 201, 202.

6. Williamson, "Donne and the Poetry of Today," *A Garland for John Donne,* ed. Spencer, pp. 172, 173.

7. *Ibid.,* p. 162.

8. Mark Van Doren, "Seventeenth-Century Poets and Twentieth-Century Critics," *Studies in Metaphysical Poetry,* p. 28.

9. Laura Riding and Robert Graves, "The Humorous Element in Modernist Poetry," *A Survey of Modernist Poetry,* pp. 225 ff.

10. Pierre Legouis insists that the poet of "The Extasie" was well aware of the seducer's tricks he was employing and that behind the serious arguments lurked a smile. (*Donne, the Craftsman.*)

11. "A Note on Two Odes of Cowley," *Seventeenth Century Studies,* p. 242.

12. C. Brooks, "Wit and High Seriousness," *Modern Poetry and the Tradition,* pp. 19, 20.

13. Riding and Graves, "The Problem of Form and Subject-Matter in Modernist Poetry," *op. cit.,* p. 37.

14. Eliot, "Andrew Marvell," *Selected Essays,* p. 255.

15. *Ibid.,* p. 256.

16. *Ibid.,* p. 255.

17. Arthur Clutton-Brock, "Crashaw's Christmas Poems," *More Essays on Religion,* pp. 6, 7.

18. Eliot, "Andrew Marvell," *Selected Essays,* p. 262.

19. *Principles of Literary Criticism,* "Communication and the Artist," p. 29.

20. *Ibid.*, "The Allusiveness of Modern Poetry," p. 219.

21. *Ibid.*, "The Poetry of T. S. Eliot," pp. 290, 291.

22. MacNeice, "Obscurity," *Modern Poetry*, p. 168.

23. W. H. Auden, epigraph to *The Orators; An English Study* (London: Faber & Faber, 1932).

24. Review of *Directions in Modern Poetry* by Elizabeth Drew, *The New York Times Book Review*, May 19.

25. Brooks and Warren offer a defense of alleged ambiguity, allusiveness, and the so-called remote symbolism of modern poetry. They do not require the congruence of the parts of a poem with its total intention. There is an obligation on the part of the reader to grasp the totality of the poet's operative imagination. ("The Reading of Modern Poetry," *The American Review*, 1937, p. 448.)

26. Coleridge's famous characterization of imagination as distinct from fancy (*Biographia Literaria*, ed. With his Aesthetical Essays by J. Shawcross. Oxford: The Clarendon Press, 1907, II, 12) is cited by Eliot ("Andrew Marvell," *Selected Essays*, pp. 256, 257) as applicable to Marvell's images in "To his Coy Mistress" and "The Nymph and the Fawn." The implication in this essay and elsewhere is that the metaphysicals on the whole "satisfy" Coleridge's definition of imagination.

27. Brooks and Warren, *op. cit.*, p. 448.

28. Ransom, "Mr. Empson's Muddles," *The Southern Review* (1938), p. 334.

29. *Idem*, "Shakespeare at Sonnets," *The World's Body*, p. 291.

30. *Ibid.*, pp. 293, 294.

31. To him "a Catholic training is, I believe, more calculated to ensure a proper balance between head and heart." ("Catholicism and International Order," *Essays, Ancient and Modern*, p. 131.)

32. *The Idea of a Christian Society*, p. 61.

33. Eliot, "Hamlet and his Problems," *Selected Essays*, pp. 124, 125.

34. Clutton-Brock, "The Fantastic School of English Poetry," *The Cambridge Modern History*, IV, 767.

35. Coffin, "A Sensible Decay of the World," *op. cit.*, p. 267.

36. Stephen Spender, *"The Ivory Tower* and *The Sense of the Past,"* *The Destructive Element*, p. 105.

37. Tate, "A Note on Donne," *Reactionary Essays*, p. 70.

38. Review of *Baudelaire and the Symbolists* by Quennell, *The Criterion* (1930), pp. 357, 358.

39. *Idem*, "Tradition and the Individual Talent," *Selected Essays*, p. 4.

40. *Poems: 1925-1940* (New York: Random House, 1940), p. 31.

41. "Burnt Norton," *Four Quartets* (*see* chap. 10, note 19), p. 5.

42. Introduction to *Le Serpent* by Valéry, pp. 12, 14.

43. *Idem, Selected Essays*, "Tradition and the Individual Talent," p. 7.

44. *Ibid.*

45. *Ibid.*, pp. 7, 8, 11.

46. *Ibid.*, "Shakespeare and the Stoicism of Seneca," p. 117.

47. Quennell, "Charles Baudelaire," *Baudelaire and the Symbolists,* p. 61.

48. Edmund Wilson, "Symbolism," *Axel's Castle,* p. 2.

49. *Modern Poetry and the Tradition,* "Symbolist Poetry and the Ivory Tower," p. 54.

50. *Ibid.,* "Metaphor and the Tradition," p. 11.

51. Beachcroft, "Traherne and the Doctrine of Felicity," *The Criterion* (1930), p. 305.

52. J. R. Daniells, "T. S. Eliot and his Relation to T. E. Hulme," *The University of Toronto Quarterly* (1933), p. 381.

53. "Filiations with the Metaphysicals," *This Modern Poetry,* p. 184.

54. Fausset claims that Donne is "too mature for that Classic Grace" and "too primitive for Romantic vision." ("Epilogue," *John Donne,* p. 317.) He calls Donne Gothic, but there is no epithet better than metaphysical to characterize his psychological and spiritual sophistication. There is also Grierson's statement: "The Classicism and Puritanism of the seventeenth century banished romance and the fairies." (*The Background of English Literature,* p. 28.) But it must be recalled that the metaphysicals possessed both fancy and vision, romantic traits. For our time, Hulme predicted that "the particular weapon of this new classical spirit, when it works in verse, will be fancy." ("Romanticism and Classicism," *Speculations,* p. 113.) We think at once of an oblique wit, of the Sitwells, Stevens, the Fugitives, and poets of their order.

55. F. L. Lucas, "Fairies and Fungi; or the Future of Romanticism," *The Decline and Fall of the Romantic Ideal,* p. 139.

56. MacNeice, "My Case-Book: Oxford," *Modern Poetry,* p. 74.

57. Riding and Graves, "Conclusion," *op. cit.,* p. 290.

58. Williamson, "Donne and the Poetry of Today," *A Garland for John Donne,* ed. Spencer, pp. 176, 177.

59.

There are reasons why symbolism should suit Eliot's needs peculiarly well. It makes for structural tightness and gives the illusion of fixity, thus fulfilling Eliot's aspirations after "classicism", and it provides an outlet for that desire to expand which, for all his repudiation of the Romantic tradition, he has undoubtedly inherited from it.

(Tillyard, "Symbolism," *op. cit.,* p. 175.)

Symbolism is akin to the metaphysical in its combining efficiency. Eliot compromises equivocally by terming symbolism an "insurgence of something which can hardly be called classicism, which may decently be called Counter-Romanticism." (Review of *Baudelaire and the Symbolists* by Quennell, *The Criterion,* 1930, p. 357.)

60. J. Smith, *op. cit.,* p. 227.

61. Eliot, *Selected Essays,* "Thomas Heywood," p. 158.

62. *Ibid.,* "Ben Jonson," p. 135.

63. *Ibid.,* "Andrew Marvell," p. 256.

64. "Mr. Eliot's Slug-Horn," *The Literary Review* of the *New York Evening Post*, January 20, 1923.

65. Grierson, "The Metaphysical Poets," *The Background of English Literature*, p. 118.

66. John B. Douds, "Donne's Technique of Dissonance," *Publications of the Modern Language Association* (1937), p. 1051.

67. Grierson, ed. *The Poems of John Donne*, II, xxii.

68. "Circumference," *op. cit.*, p. 4.

69. David Daiches, "Thomas Hardy–A. E. Housman–Gerard Manley Hopkins," *Poetry and the Modern World*, p. 32.

CHAPTER 5

1. "The Minor Metaphysicals: from Cowley to Dryden," *The Listener* (1930), p. 641.

2. "Adventure," *Adventures of Ideas*, p. 359.

3. "A Note on Two Odes of Cowley," *Seventeenth Century Studies*, p. 238.

4. "Four American Poets: I. Emily Dickinson," *Reactionary Essays*, pp. 12, 13.

5. Eliot, "Metaphysical Poetry," VIII, pp. 12, 13.

6. *Idem, Selected Essays*, "Andrew Marvell," p. 251.

7. *Ibid.*, "Shakespeare and the Stoicism of Seneca," p. 117.

8. *Ibid.*, p. 119.

9. *Idem*, "Metaphysical Poetry," I, p. 12.

10. Barrett Wendell, "The Development of Prose: The Bible and Bacon," *The Temper of the Seventeenth Century in English Literature*, p. 158.

11. Black, "Donne and the Metaphysicals," *op. cit.*, p. 321.

12. As quoted in L. C. Martin, "Henry Vaughan and the Theme of Infancy," *Seventeenth Century Studies*, p. 245.

13. Translated from the Latin of *Ad Posteros*, 1651. As quoted in Edmund Blunden, "On the Poems of Henry Vaughan," *The London Mercury* (1926), p. 59.

14. Donne, "An Anatomie of the World: The First Anniversary," ed. Hayward, *op. cit.*, p. 202.

15. Grierson, ed. *The Poems of John Donne*, II, xxxviii.

16. Quennell, ed. *Aspects of Seventeenth Century Verse*, introduction, p. 17.

17. White, "The Intellectual Climate," *op. cit.*, p. 41.

18. Whitehead, "The Century of Genius," *Science and the Modern World*, p. 55.

19. *Ibid.*, pp. 56, 57, 65. Cf. Grierson's statement as to "the connexion of 'metaphysical wit' with the complex and far-reaching changes in men's conception of Nature which make the seventeenth century perhaps the

greatest epoch in human thought since human thinking began." (*The Poems of John Donne*, II, v.)

20. "Hooker, Hobbes and Others," *The Times Literary Supplement* (1926), p. 789.

21. *Idem*, "Thinking in Verse: a Survey of Early Seventeenth-Century Poetry," *The Listener* (1930), p. 442. Cf. Rufus M. Jones, "Thomas Traherne and the Spiritual Poets of the Seventeenth Century," *Spiritual Reformers in the 16th & 17th Centuries*, p. 320.

22. Eliot, "Metaphysical Poetry," II, p. 7.

23. Chambers, "The Disenchantment of the Elizabethans," *Sir Thomas Wyatt*, p. 203.

24. Black, "The Courtly Makers," *op. cit.*, p. 51.

25. Chambers, *op. cit.*, p. 183.

26. *Ibid.*, p. 190.

27. Eliot, "Shakespeare and the Stoicism of Seneca," *Selected Essays*, p. 112.

28. *Ibid.*, p. 119.

29. Quennell, ed. *Aspects of Seventeenth Century Verse*, introduction, pp. 19, 20.

30. *See* Geoffrey Bullough, "Bacon and the Defense of Learning," *Seventeenth Century Studies*.

31. Read, "The Nature of Metaphysical Poetry," *Reason and Romanticism*, p. 42.

32. Gosse, "The Last Elizabethans," *The Jacobean Poets*, p. 9.

33. *Notes of Ben Jonson's Conversations with William Drummond of Hawthornden* (London: Printed for the Shakespeare Society, 1842), p. 36.

34. "Jordan," *Metaphysical Lyrics*, ed. Grierson, p. 107.

35. Clutton-Brock, "The Fantastic School of English Poetry," *The Cambridge Modern History*, IV, 760.

36. "An Elegie upon the Death of the deane of Pauls, Dr. John Donne," *Metaphysical Lyrics*, ed. Grierson, pp. 177, 178.

37. This passage is from "To Sʳ Nicholas Smyth" which is "Probably by Sir John Roe, KNT." It appears in Appendix B of Grierson's edition, *The Poems of John Donne*, I, 401, among "Poems attributed to John Donne in the Old Editions (1663-1669) and the principal MS. Collections. . . ." These lines are taken for granted as Donne's by Fausset in his study, *John Donne*, but are not included in the Donne canon by Grierson or Hayward. Even if the verses are not Donne's, they most likely expressed his sentiment.

38. From "Idea" (*Poems, 1619*), *Elizabethan Sonnet-Cycles*, ed. Martha Foote Crow (London: Kegan Paul, Trench, Trubner and Co., 1897), p. 51.

39. *Ibid.*, p. 9.

40. Praz, "Donne's Relation to the Poetry of his Time," *A Garland for John Donne*, ed. Spencer, p. 55.

41. Ed. Hayward, *op. cit.*, pp. 26, 27.

42. *See* Lewis, "Donne and Love Poetry in the Seventeenth Century,"

and Bennett, "The Love Poetry of John Donne," *Seventeenth Century Studies.*

43. Potter, *op. cit.*, p. 7.

44. *Ibid.*, p. 9.

45. Louis I. Bredvold, "The Naturalism of Donne in Relation to Some Renaissance Traditions," *The Journal of English and Germanic Philology* (1923), pp. 471, 493.

46. *Ibid.*, p. 472.

47. Ed. Hayward, *op. cit.*, "Upon Mr. Thomas Coryats Crudities," pp. 139, 140.

48. *Ibid.*, "To Sir H[enry]. W[otton]. At his Going Ambassador to Venice," p. 180.

49. *Ibid.*, Verse Letter "To the Countesse of Bedford," p. 166.

50. Potter, *op. cit.*, p. 17.

51. Ed. Hayward, *op. cit.*, "Of the Progresse of the Soule," p. 266.

52. *Ibid.*, pp. 320, 321.

53. S. Raiziss, "French Influences on Suckling with Special Reference to Voiture." M.A. thesis, New York, Columbia University, 1931.

54. Grierson, ed. *The Poems of John Donne*, II, xxix.

55. Eliot, "The *Pensées* of Pascal," *Selected Essays*, p. 363.

56. Cited in Sharp, "The Revolt Against Metaphysical Poetry," p. 2.

57. T. B. Rudmose-Brown, "A French Précieux Lyrist of the Early Seventeenth Century: Pierre Motin," *Seventeenth Century Studies*, p. 33.

58. Lovelace wrote of him in the poem "Voiture," *Minor Poets of the 17th Century;* Sir John Suckling, Richard Lovelace, Thomas Carew, Lord Herbert of Cherbury, ed. R. G. Howarth (London: J. M. Dent & Sons; New York: E. P. Dutton & Co., 1931. With an Introduction), p. 375.

59.

In French literature the great master of the seventeenth century—Racine—and the great master of the nineteenth—Baudelaire—are in some ways more like each other than they are like anyone else. The greatest two masters of diction are also the greatest two psychologists, the most curious explorers of the soul. . . . Racine or Donne looked into a good deal more than the heart.

(Eliot, "The Metaphysical Poets," *Selected Essays*, pp. 249, 250.)

60. *See* Grierson on the Jesuit poet, Robert Southwell, who learned the antithetic style from the Italians: *Metaphysical Lyrics*, p. xxxix.

61. *See* Clutton-Brock, "Crashaw's Christmas Poems," *More Essays on Religion*, p. 5.

62.

But Giovanni Battista Marino, although in the latter part of the seventeenth century he exercised an extraordinary fascination over the continent of Europe, does not seem to have been much known in England, although Drummond knew him. Moreover, the famous epic of *Adone*, which was the vehicle of that fascination, did not see light in Italy until 1623, when Donne was fifty years of age. . . . [English metaphysical] fondness for extravagant conceits ran parallel with the excesses of Marinism, but that is all we can admit.

(Gosse, "Metaphysical Poetry," *More Books on the Table*, p. 310.)

63. Eliot, "Metaphysical Poetry," VI, p. 22.

64. M. Y. Hughes, "The Lineage of 'The Extasie,' " *The Modern Language Review* (1932), p. 5.

CHAPTER 6

1. Grierson, ed. *Metaphysical Lyrics*, p. lviii.

2. A. E. Taylor, "An Apology for Mr. Hobbes," *Seventeenth Century Studies*, pp. 133 ff.

3. "Aeschylus and . . . ," *Guide to Kulchur* (1938), p. 95.

4. Wendell, "The Later Puritanism," *op. cit.*, p. 258.

5. Eliot, *Selected Essays*, "John Ford," p. 178.

6. *Ibid.*, "Thomas Middleton," p. 146.

7. *Ibid.*, "John Bramhall," pp. 313, 312.

8. Joseph Wood Krutch, "The Phantom of Certitude," *The Modern Temper*, pp. 187, 188.

9. Willey, "The Philosophical Quest for Truth: Descartes," *op. cit.*, p. 85.

10. Ed. Hayward, *op. cit.*, p. 39. This is the doctrine that divides "the world into the three personal elements of matter, soul, and spirit"—and can be compared with a passage in Thomas Mann:

> He sent out of the substance of His divinity spirit to man in this world, that it might rouse from its slumber the soul in the frame of man, and show it, by the Father's command, that this world was not its place, and that its sensual and passional enterprise had been a sin, as a consequence of which the creation of the world was to be regarded..

(Prelude to *Joseph and His Brothers*. New York: Alfred A. Knopf, 1938, I, 39, 40.)

11. Evelyn M. Simpson, "Donne's 'Paradoxes and Problems,' " *A Garland for John Donne*, ed. Spencer, p. 42.

12. Coffin, "A Sensible Decay of the World," *op. cit.*, p. 275.

13. Whitehead, "The Origins of Modern Science," *Science and the Modern World*, pp. 2, 3.

14. The outstanding representatives of the various branches of knowledge might be listed for convenience according to their professed, sometimes multiple, interests: botany—Morison, Grew, Ray, Willughby, Leeuwenhoek, Tournefort, Malpighi; physics—Descartes, Boyle, Newton; mathematics—Descartes, Wallis, Wilkins, Barrow, Newton. Sydenham was the great physician. The instrumental inventions and especially improvements could be summed up as chiefly: the Torricellian barometer, the microscope and the telescope, the thermometer, the compass, the pendulum clock and the spring clock, the magic lantern, the airpump, asbestos, and the weaving loom. Flying was a serious consideration in the mind of Robert Hooke, member of the Royal Society. (Carson S. Duncan, "The New Science," *The New Science and English Literature in the Classical Period*, p. 25.)

15. *Ibid.*, p. 19.

16. In several issues of *The Times Literary Supplement*, XXXVI, 1937, I. A. Shapiro (July 3), M. F. Ashley-Montagu (August 7), W. Fraser Mitchell (August 7), and C. M. Coffin (September 18) carry on a public discussion as to Donne the astronomer's knowledge and references. Shapiro attempts to date Donne's eighth Problem by means of Galileo's discovery of the phases of Venus: January, 1611. But Coffin thinks the poet could have found as good a precedent in Pliny for "Why Venus-star only doth cast a shadow." If Donne derived his suggestion from contemporary work, it must have been rather from Kepler's *Optica* and his 1606 treatise *De Stella Nova*. Our nonpartisan interest is in the poet's astronomical concerns and in the fact that his reading, including Galileo and Kepler, as well as Pliny, provided his work with problems and imagery. *See* his "A Funerall Elegie," ed. Hayward, *op. cit.*, p. 211, for references to Kepler's "pellucid" new star, etc.

17. Williamson, "Mutability, Decay, and Seventeenth Century Melancholy," *A Journal of English Literary History* (1935), p. 133.

18. Ed. Hayward, *op. cit.*, p. 203, *See also ibid.*, "To the Countesse of Huntingdon," p. 169: "If the worlds age, and death be argued well/By the Sunnes fall, which now towards earth doth bend . . ."

19. As quoted in Williamson, "Mutability, Decay, and Seventeenth Century Melancholy," *A Journal of English Literary History* (1935), p. 144.

20. Rudolf Metz, "Bacon's Part in the Intellectual Movement of his Time," *Seventeenth Century Studies*, p. 30.

21. Willey, "Sir Thomas Browne," *op. cit.*, p. 41.

22. Donne, Sermon LXXX, ed. Hayward, *op. cit.*, pp. 673, 674.

23. "Did the poet have an actually realised visual object before him in which he delighted? It doesn't matter if it were a lady's shoe or the starry heavens. . . . The great aim is accurate, precise and definite description." (Hulme, *op. cit.*, pp. 137, 132.)

24. "The Metaphysical Poets," *Selected Essays*, p. 247.

25. Grierson argues that Donne's "Good Friday" echoes Lucretius in lines on the whirling of the spheres, where the word should be "turning" rather than "tuning." ("Donne and Lucretius," *The Times Literary Supplement*, 1929, p. 1032.)

26. Ed. Hayward, *op. cit.*, "The Extasie," p. 39; "Elegie XIII," p. 85; "Obsequies to the Lord Harrington," p. 236; "An Anatomie of the World," p. 202.

27. Charles T. Harrison, "The Ancient Atomists and English Literature of the Seventeenth Century," *Harvard Studies in Classical Philology* (1934), p. 76.

28. "Mathematics as an Element in the History of Thought," *Science and the Modern World*, p. 47.

29. Seventeenth-century mathematics contributed or developed such symbols as the sign X, the decimal system, algebra, analytic geometry, logarithms, and calculus.

30. Sermon LXVIII, *The Works of John Donne, D.D.,* ed. Henry Alford (London: John W. Parker, 1839), III, 205.

31. "You, Andrew Marvell," *Poems, 1924-1933 (see* chap. 12, note 1), p. 58.

32. Coffin, "Figures of Space," *op. cit.,* p. 194.

33. Preface, etc., to the "Lyrical Ballads," *The Poetical Works of William Wordsworth,* ed. Thomas Hutchinson (London: Oxford University Press, 1923), p. 939.

34. Whitehead, "Science and Philosophy," *Adventures of Ideas,* p. 197.

35. Predecessors of the Royal Society were the Society of Antiquaries, 1572 to its termination by James I; the Royal Academy, 1616 and 1635. The Royal Society itself first met in 1645 and 1658 at Gresham as the "invisible college." After its formal establishment in 1660, Charles II, whose court was the last royal concentration of culture in England, had a laboratory installed at Whitehall, notes Samuel Pepys on January 15, 1669.

36. Scientific and mechanical references, with their implications, appear in literature from the Elizabethan Donne to that Restoration apologist for antiquity, Sir William Temple. Similes were taken from *"Meteors, Plants, Beasts* in Natural *Philosophy;* And from the *Starres, Spheres* and their motions in Astronomy; . . . whilst *Mathematicks* were of late in vogue, all similitudes came from *Lines, Circles* and Angles. . . ." (Thomas Blount, 1656, as quoted in Sharp, "The Revolt Against Metaphysical Poetry," pp. 222, 228.) Imagery exploited the telescope, new stars, the rough moon, the Milky Way, and various satellites. Marino praised Galileo as the Columbus of the skies. Herbert, for example, says in "Vanitie"—"The fleet Astronomer can bore,/And thred the spheres with his quick-piercing minde . . ." (*The Works of George Herbert,* ed. F. E. Hutchinson. Oxford: The Clarendon Press, 1941, p. 85.) Donne's first direct reference to the new astronomy in the second part of *Biathanatos* was only the beginning of innumerable allusions in his prose and poetry.

37. Ransom, "Poetry: A Note in Ontology," *The World's Body,* p. 141.

38. Willey, *op. cit.,* "On Scriptural Interpretation," p. 72.

39. Joseph Glanvill desired to "explain how religious the 'science' of the Royal Society really was." (*Ibid.,* "Joseph Glanvill," p. 170.)

40. Grierson, "Holland—Verse and Prose," *The First Half of the Seventeenth Century,* p. 28.

41. *Idem,* "John Milton: The Man and the Poet," *Cross Currents in English Literature of the XVIIth Century,* p. 302. It is not surprising that Marvell, adherent of Cromwell, should be included here, since his political and poetic tone approximated the middle way.

42. One of the apogees of interest in the human drama occurs in the seventeenth-century theater of Spain, England, and France. We have only to cite Ben Jonson, Shakespeare and his successors; Lope de Vega and Calderón; Molière, Corneille, and Racine.

Calderón's mind, or at least his early training, must have resembled Donne's. . . . Like Donne, he had a medieval mind; and as the Middle Ages were, above all, a period in which thought and theology were inextricably entangled, Calderón's ideas were fundamentally theological. . . . The unitary "soul" or "personality" which interests the novelist is for him merely the arena in which the combatants meet: and the "passions" and "desires" of the psycho-analyst have become dramatic *personae* in the plays of Calderón.

(J. B. Trend, "Calderón and the Spanish Religious Theatre of the Seventeenth Century," *Seventeenth Century Studies,* pp. 180, 183.)

43. An individual's personality served as a type of microcosm, a magnified drop of water in which the seventeenth century was so fond of seeing macrocosm illustrated. This relationship was one of the concepts that afforded the metaphysical poet room for exercise and ramification.

The physics of Descartes brought into a single system the stars and the dust of earth, and its effect was to dissolve away the independence of material things and make them mere eddies in the cosmic whirlpool. Although Descartes tried to secure the mind of man against a similar dissolution, yet the growing interest in psychology and the progress of the idea of universal law led naturally to the suggestion that individual minds were immersed in an ocean of mind, perhaps even parts of it.

(L. J. Russell, "Leibniz and the Fitness of Things," *Seventeenth Century Studies,* p. 323.)

44. Whitehead, "Science and Philosophy," *Science and the Modern World,* p. 198.

45. White, "The Divine Poetry of John Donne," *op. cit.,* p. 130.

46. Clutton-Brock, "George Herbert," *More Essays on Books,* pp. 19, 21.

47. White, "Thomas Traherne," *op. cit.,* p. 331.

48. Wendell, "The Later Puritanism," *op. cit.,* p. 263.

49. Michael Roberts, "Psychology and Beliefs," *The Modern Mind,* p. 220.

CHAPTER 7

1. Willey, "The Philosophical Quest for Truth: Thomas Hobbes," *op. cit.,* p. 101.

2. The whole of Shakespeare's dramatic actions and characters can be interpreted "in the light of our own experience and thought, our philosophy of life and the life of man. . . . Goethe, Coleridge, Schopenhauer, the Freudians have all found in Shakespeare grist for their mills." (Grierson, "The Drama: Tragedy," *Cross Currents in English Literature of the XVIIth Century,* p. 127.)

3. R. C. Bald, *Donne's Influence in English Literature,* p. 53.

4. *See* Edwin Arthur Burtt, *The Metaphysical Foundations of Modern Physical Science* (1925).

5. Irwin Edman, "Nostalgia for Tradition," *The Contemporary and His Soul,* pp. 115, 118.

6. Coffin, "Engrafting Old Authors," *op. cit.,* pp. 252, 253.

7. Bonamy Dobrée, "T. S. Eliot," *The Lamp and the Lute,* pp. 108, 109.

8.

Something of this sort has always happened in times of social unrest. The present age has instinctively turned to the seventeenth century, an age of civil disturbance and changing culture. In that century too poetry found itself cut off from a vital relationship with the public life of the time, and turned in upon its own technical problems. . . . But the situation is aggravated for the modern poet. . . .

(Drew, "The Poet and the Community," *Directions in Modern Poetry*, pp. 275, 277.)

9. A possible parallel may be drawn between the Shavian period and the pamphleteering conclusion to the Elizabethan era; between the "mauve decade" and the sonneteering phase which turned sardonic in the hands of Donne.

There is some resemblance between Donne's position at the end of the Elizabethan age and the position of Wilde, Shaw, and others at the end of the Victorian. In both periods there was a reaction from a literature which had been romantic and emotional in its appeal, and a desire for more intellectual display, showing itself in a love of witty paradox. Along with this went a craving for the cynical and the morbid. . . ."

(Simpson, "Donne as a Man of Letters," *A Study of the Prose Works of John Donne*, p. 57.) *See also* Spencer, "Donne and His Age," *A Garland for John Donne*, ed. Spencer, p. 197: Chapman, Greville, and Donne are considered as counterparts of the realistic and moral satire of the 1890's.

10. Fausset, "Epilogue," *John Donne*, p. 313 ff.

11. Whitehead, *Adventures of Ideas*, p. viii.

12. *Idem*, "Mathematics as an Element in the History of Thought," *Science and the Modern World*, p. 50.

13. "The Secular Masque," *The Poems of John Dryden*, p. 203.

14. Quennell, ed. *Aspects of Seventeenth Century Verse*, introduction, p. 16.

15. Harold J. Massingham, ed. *A Treasury of Seventeenth Century English Verse*, p. xix.

16. Tate, "A Note on Elizabethan Satire," *Reactionary Essays*, p. 81.

17. Ruth Bailey, *A Dialogue on Modern Poetry*, p. 81.

18. George Every, review of *Poetry and Prose of John Donne*, ed. A. Desmond Hawkins, *Purpose* (1938), p. 233.

19. "T. E. Hulme and T. S. Eliot," *op. cit.*, p. 104.

20. Amos N. Wilder, "Contemporary Perdition," *The Spiritual Aspects of the New Poetry*, p. 97.

21. Daiches, "T. E. Hulme and T. S. Eliot," *op. cit.*, p. 105.

Chapter 8

1. Eliot, "Religion Without Humanism," *Humanism and America*, ed. Norman Foerster, p. 112.

2.

Classicism vs. romanticism in culture, individualism vs. statism, internationalism vs. racism in statecraft, humanism vs. materialism, Christianity vs. paganisms of self, race, blood, science, or nation—these dark dilemmas torment and oppress the spirit of every man, civilized or uncivilized, consciously or unconsciously, in the world of today.

(Frederick H. Young, review of *Metapolitics* by Peter Viereck, *The New York Times Book Review*, June 7, 1942.)

3. "The Ultimate Plato with Picasso's Guitar," *The Harvard Advocate* (1940), p. 13.

4. George N. Shuster, review of *Basic Verities* by Charles Péguy, *The New York Times Book Review*, February 28, 1943.

5. Auden, "Criticism in a Mass Society," *The Intent of the Critic*, ed. Donald A. Stauffer, pp. 135, 136.

6. Van Wyck Brooks, "What a Set!" *Opinions of Oliver Allston*, p. 252.

7. *Out of the Jewel*; Poems (New York: Charles Scribner's Sons, 1942), pp. 124, 125.

8. Foreword to *Ruins and Visions*; Poems 1934-1942 (New York: Random House, 1942), p. 12.

9. Warren, "John Crowe Ransom: A Study in Irony," *The Virginia Quarterly Review* (1935), p. 113.

10. Thus in the twenties the stress was on introspection and sex; in the thirties on material hungers—a transfer of allegiance, so to speak, from Freud to Marx. The individual spirit has more recently regained its ascendancy. Variations of attitude throughout this whole period have been rapid and manifold, with the colors sometimes repeating.

Its arc of alternating protest and reaction, experiment and conformity, of liberalism at odds with orthodoxy, and thus through the progressive emancipation, confusion, and decline of the individual in an age of rising social claims [still changes]. . . . The processes of poetic experience have shifted from courage to fear, from ecstasy to skepticism, and animal unfaith, from the contempt of society to its triumph, and now from abject demoralization to the splendor of a "new-world objective."

(Morton D. Zabel, "Poets of Five Decades," *The Southern Review*, 1936, pp. 161, 162.)

11. Edwin Muir, "Contemporary Poetry," *Transition*, p. 185.

12. "The point of view here, then, is that historicism, scientism, psychologism . . . [express] a spiritual disorder. That disorder may be briefly described as a dilemma." (Tate, "The Present Function of Criticism," *Reason in Madness*, p. 4.)

13. Edman, "The Soul of Man under Modernism," *op. cit.*, pp. 4 ff.

14. V. W. Brooks, *On Literature Today*, pp. 20, 25, 26.

15. Spencer, "The Later Poetry of W. B. Yeats," *Literary Opinion in America*, ed. Zabel, p. 269.

16. Eliot's scattered interest in oriental wisdom ("The Waste Land") came by way of studies in anthropology and comparative religions. "We see

one cause for the attraction the Upanishads and other Eastern scripture exert upon certain types of modern consciousness. The Hindu mystic's denial of personality, his pantheism . . . and fatalism" (Wilder, "Mr. Conrad Aiken and the Self," *op. cit.,* p. 68) might well suit Eliot's tenet of impersonality, suggested perhaps by Hulme's anti-humanism and admiration for the Byzantine. Another hypothesis to account for the modern interest in Eastern literature is that its meticulous, imagistic, spare wisdom and poetic form attract the bombast-weary Western mind. The Easterner has his cosmic references that compose an aura, an extension of the "little" poetic stroke. Apparently the yearning for a unity of mind and emotion finds congenial the economically reduced oriental picture, which at the same time is suggestive of otherness. We are likely to notice, then, that "whenever poetry finds the uses of its special world gone flat and stale, it is very apt indeed . . . to turn its eyes to the exhaustless East. . . . It isn't the vastness or the mystery of the East that this time exercises its old compulsion. . . . That which does allure it in the East is an amazing tininess and finesse. . . ." (John Livingston Lowes, "The Hardening of Conventions, and Revolt," *Convention and Revolt in Poetry,* p. 165.)

17. White, "Thomas Traherne," *op. cit.,* p. 334.
18. "Byzantium gives us perhaps the best architecture, or at least the best inner structure that we know, I mean for proportion. . . ." (Pound, "Mediaevalism," *Make It New,* p. 347.)
19. "A Programme," *op. cit.,* pp. 55, 57.
20. Tillyard, "Oblique Statement of What?" *op. cit.,* p. 47.
21. *Gaudier-Brzeska,* p. 22.
22. As quoted in *ibid.,* p. 116.
23. Eliot, "The Golden Ass of Apuleius," *The Dial* (1928), p. 255.
24. *The Idea of a Christian Society,* p. 62.
25. *Ibid.*
26.
There are three main alternatives for thinking people in an age of uncertainty. They can repudiate the contemporary state of mind and take refuge in religious or political authority; they can take refuge in elaborately constructed private solutions . . . or they can make up their minds to put up with uncertainty, to suspend judgment.
(Tillyard, "The Contemporary Moral," *op. cit.,* p. 274.)

Each of these choices, two of which are reactions in the form of escape, is characteristic of one or more poets in whom we are interested. The metaphysical poet has been religious (Dante, Donne, Herbert, Crashaw, Vaughan, Traherne, Hopkins, Eliot, etc.), and/or he has turned to some other particular authority or panacea (Dante and Eliot again); he has resorted to local or private remedies (Donne, Baudelaire, Rimbaud, Yeats, the Fugitives); he has suspended judgment (Donne generally and many of these same poets who continue the tone of conflict).

27. It is "striking that metaphysical successes and failures are about the

same distance from the Elizabethan metaphor: they represent expansion, contraction, analysis, or some other progressive development." (Sharp, "Observations on Metaphysical Imagery," *The Sewanee Review*, 1935, p. 470.)

28. Krutch, *op. cit.*, "The Genesis of a Mood," pp. 24, 26.

29. *Ibid.*, "Love—or the Life and Death of a Value," p. 113.

30. *Ibid.*, "The Phantom of a Certitude," pp. 194, 195.

31. Wilson, "Symbolism," *op. cit.*, pp. 5, 6.

32. Riding and Graves, *op. cit.*, "Modernist Poetry and the Plain Reader's Rights," pp. 31, 32.

33. *Ibid.*, "Modernist Poetry and Civilization," p. 173.

34. Tate, *Reason in Madness*, "Tension in Poetry," p. 67.

35. *Ibid.*, "Understanding Modern Poetry," pp. 89, 97.

36. Howard Baker, "Add This to Rhetoric," *The Harvard Advocate* (1940), p. 16.

37. Archibald MacLeish, "Nevertheless One Debt," *Poetry: A Magazine of Verse* (1931), pp. 213, 214.

38. *Primitivism and Decadence*, "Poetic Convention," p. 75.

39. *Ibid.*, "Primitivism and Decadence," p. 89.

40. "Diction," "Conclusion," *Modern Poetry*, pp. 152, 205.

41. "T. S. Eliot," "Ezra Pound," *Aspects of Modern Poetry*, pp. 99, 178.

42. Richards, "Figurative Language," *Practical Criticism*, p. 196.

43. Whitehead, "The Eighteenth Century," *Science and the Modern World*, p. 80.

44. Cecil Day Lewis, "A Hope for Poetry," *Collected Poems*, p. 73.

45. Matthiessen, "The Integrity of a Work of Art," *op. cit.*, p. 111.

46. Preface to *Homage to John Dryden*, p. 9.

47. *Idem*, "John Donne," *The Nation and The Athenaeum* (1923), p. 332.

48. *Idem*, *Selected Essays*, "Christopher Marlowe," pp. 100, 101.

49. *Ibid.*, "John Dryden," p. 274.

50. Bailey, *op. cit.*, p. 42.

51. As quoted in *ibid.*, p. 86.

52. Dilys Powell, "Edith Sitwell," *Descent from Parnassus*, p. 119.

53. "An Elizabethan Poet and Modern Poetry," *The Edinburgh Review* (1913), pp. 374 ff. and p. 377.

54. Riding and Graves, "Modernist Poetry and Dead Movements," *op. cit.*, p. 119.

55. *Ibid.*, pp. 120, 121.

56. MacNeice, "A Change of Attitude," *Modern Poetry*, p. 8.

57. Daiches, "Thomas Hardy—A. E. Housman—Gerard Manley Hopkins," *op. cit.*, pp. 33, 55.

58. *Ibid.*, "Poetry in the 1930's—I: Cecil Day Lewis," p. 193.

59. The Steinesque fad, the ultimate abstract, the perverse obscurity of the Dada craze, and *outré* surrealism are representative extremes. They pass into the history of literary thought and style as the early or late phases of an important movement.

60. Amy Lowell insisted that free verse derived from the French symbolists; but there are sufficient precedents in Meredith, Whitman, Stephen Crane, and even Milton's "Lycidas."

61.
That is to say, at a particular date in a particular room, two authors . . . decided that the dilutation of *vers libre*, Amygism, Lee Masterism, general floppiness had gone too far and that some counter-current must be set going. . . . Remedy prescribed "Émaux et Camées." . . . Rhyme and regular strophes. Results: Poems in Mr. Eliot's *second* volume . . . also "H. S. Mauberley."

(Pound, "Harold Monro," *Polite Essays*, p. 14.)

Le rythme ["Mauberley"] est celui des *Émaux et Camées* que Pound et Eliot avaient décidé d'utiliser et de donner comme modèles aux poètes américains qui abusaient du vers libre. . . . L'exactitude et la dureté sont qualités recherchées par les artistes de 1914, qui se révoltent contre l'abandon des formes pratiqués par les impressionistes et les symbolistes.

(René Taupin, "La Poésie d'Ezra Pound," *Revue Anglo-Américaine*, 1931, p. 231.)

62. Introduction to *Savonarola* by Charlotte Eliot, p. xi.
63. Tate, "Milton: Paradise Lost," *Invitation to Learning*, p. 310.
64. "A Note on the Verse of John Milton," *Essays and Studies of the English Association* (1935), p. 36.
65. Eliot, Binyon, Praz, for example.
66. Pound, "Notes on Elizabethan Classicists," *Pavannes and Divisions*, p. 202.
67. Praz, "Milton and Poussin," *Seventeenth Century Studies*, pp. 203, 204.
68. *Polite Essays*, "Hell," "Prefatio Aut Cimicium Tumulus," pp. 29, 138.
69. *Ibid.*, "Note on Dante," p. 199.
70. *Milton and His Modern Critics* (1940).
71. Among more recent defenses of Milton is the very interesting article by Wylie Sypher which ingeniously attempts to include both Donne and Milton in one baroque tradition—a tradition of seventeenth-century art and poetry—comprising also Crashaw, Herbert, Cleveland, and Dryden. "Donne, then, stands in genuine relationship with Milton. Both must be seen against the authentic 'movement' of the seventeenth century. When thus seen, Milton is the greatest of the baroque poets, the most polyphonic." ("The Metaphysicals and the Baroque," *Partisan Review*, 1944, p. 17.)
72. Richards, "Sentimentality and Inhibition," *Practical Criticism*, p. 269.

CHAPTER 9

1. Edgar Foxall, "The Politics of W. H. Auden," *The Bookman* (1934), p. 475.
2. Hulme, "Reflections on Violence," *op. cit.*, pp. 259, 260.

3. *Ibid.*, p. 258.

4. Spender, *The Destructive Element*, "T. S. Eliot in his Poetry," p. 142.

5. *Ibid.*, "Epilogue," p. 278.

6. Eliot, "Modern Education and the Classics," *Selected Essays*, p. 458.

7. Daiches, "T. E. Hulme and T. S. Eliot," *op. cit.*, p. 98.

8. Riding and Graves, "The Humorous Element in Modernist Poetry," *op. cit.*, p. 226.

9. MacNeice, "A Change of Attitude," *Modern Poetry*, p. 10.

10. Daiches, "Thomas Hardy—A. E. Housman—Gerard Manley Hopkins," *op. cit.*, p. 36.

11. "The Noble Rider and the Sound of Words," *The Language of Poetry*, ed. Tate, p. 116.

12. Franz Werfel gave in *The Song of Bernadette* one of those indirect expressions of our unhappy experience of destruction: "a polemic of this war."

No one understands this war who still believes that it is a war for living space, a war for the victory of certain economic or social forms. . . . On the one side stands radical nihilism which no longer regards the human being as the image of God but as an amoral machine in a completely meaningless world. On the other side, on our side, stands the metaphysical, the religious concept of life, the conviction that this Cosmos was created by the spirit and that a spiritual meaning lives and breathes in every atom. It is indeed a war between the principles of spiritual life and spiritual death.

("Writing 'Bernadette,'" *The Commonweal*, 1942, p. 126.)

13. As quoted in Spender, "The School of Experience in the Early Novels of Henry James," *The Destructive Element*, p. 32.

14.

For the past twenty years distinguished writers in England and in the United States have been aware of the potential existence of another world war, and they have warned their readers of its hidden forces long before its actual events took place, and in that sense most of the best poetry written in the present generation continues to be "war poetry."

(Horace Gregory, "Fare Forward, Voyager," review of *Four Quartets* by Eliot, *The New York Times Book Review*, May 16, 1943.)

15. Muir, *The Present Age from 1914*, "General Background," pp. 33, 34.

16. Wyndham Lewis, as quoted in *ibid.*, "Poetry," p. 117.

17. Edith Batho and Dobrée, "Poetry," *The Victorians and After*, p. 73.

18. Pound, "Harold Monro," "Mr. Eliot's Solid Merit," *Polite Essays*, pp. 4, 7, 8, 99.

19. "I don't see that anyone save a sap-head can now think he knows any history until he understands economics." ("Date Line," *Make It New*, p. 19.)

20. *Science and the Modern World*, "The Romantic Reaction," pp. 105, 106, 115.

21. *Ibid.*, "The Origins of Modern Science," pp. 3, 4.

22. "False Categories," *op. cit.*, p. 32.

NOTESNOTES 271

23. "Hulme was always haunted by a suspicion of the futility of logic. This is at the bottom of his interest in Bergson, and equally of his somewhat contradictory enthusiasm for Dr. Moore's objective ethics, and of his distrust of Cartesian principles. . . ." (Read, introduction to *Notes on Language and Style* by Hulme, p. 7.)

24. Wilson, "Marcel Proust," *op. cit.*, p. 157.

Proust insisted that one of his principal concerns was to discover the real resemblances between things which superficially appeared different. And we remember that the far-fetched comparisons of the poetry of the age of Gongora and Crashaw, to which the poetry of the Symbolists seems akin, have been defended as indicating relations where none had previously been perceived.

(*Ibid.*, p. 158.)

25. Riding, *Contemporaries and Snobs*, "Escapes From The Zeitgeist: The Poetic Absolute," p. 38.

26. *Ibid.*, "T. E. Hulme, The New Barbarism, & Gertrude Stein," p. 184.

27. A. C. Partridge, *T. S. Eliot*, p. 18.

28. *Op. cit.*, "A Programme," pp. 59, 62.

29. *Ibid.*, "Reflections on Violence," p. 257. *See also* "Modern Art and its Philosophy," p. 80.

30. Krutch presents the three-cornered modern conflict among primitivists, humanists, and the religious metaphysicians. (*Op. cit.*, "The Paradox of Humanism," p. 41.) In preference to a return to pre-Renaissance metaphysical systems, Krutch suggests—as a concomitant to advancing scientific proficiency—the acknowledgment "that metaphysics has a right to conclusions independent of and even contrary to the conclusions of science." (*Ibid.*, "The Phantom of Certitude," p. 202.)

31. *Ibid.*, p. 214.

32. *Ibid.*, p. 230. When confronted, "certain of its proponents like G. K. Chesterton and T. S. Eliot seek immediate refuge in Roman or Anglican Catholicism, whose dogmas, if accepted without argument, provide the basis which pure reason cannot discover." (*Ibid.*, pp. 228 ff.)

33. Eliot, *Selected Essays*, "Second Thoughts About Humanism," p. 435.

34. *Ibid.*, "The Humanism of Irving Babbitt," p. 426.

35. *Ibid.*, "Second Thoughts About Humanism," p. 437.

36. *Idem*, Choruses from "The Rock," *Collected Poems*, pp. 181, 182.

37. *Idem*, *Selected Essays*, "Thomas Middleton," p. 142.

38. *Ibid.*, "Baudelaire," p. 372.

39. *Ibid.*, pp. 375, 378, 379.

40. *Ibid.*, p. 381.

41. *Idem*, *After Strange Gods*, p. 61.

42. *Idem*, "Second Thoughts About Humanism," *Selected Essays*, p. 438.

43. Santayana, "Goethe's Faust," *op. cit.*, p. 167.

44. "Inferno," *La Divina Commedia*, Italian text ed. H. Oelsner, English version by Dr. J. A. Carlyle (London: J. M. Dent & Sons, Temple Classics, 1933), Canto XXVI, p. 292, lines 94-99.

45. Simpson, "Donne's 'Paradoxes and Problems,'" *A Garland for John Donne*, ed. Spencer, p. 35.

46. "Obscurity," *Modern Poetry*, p. 177.

47. "Henry James and the Contemporary Subject," *The Destructive Element*, p. 194.

48. R. P. Blackmur, "Emily Dickinson: Notes on Prejudice and Fact," *The Expense of Greatness*, p. 125.

49. Tate, "Four American Poets: Emily Dickinson," *Reactionary Essays*, pp. 5, 6.

50. Spender, "The School of Experience in the Early Novels of Henry James," *The Destructive Element*, pp. 41, 42.

51. R. T. S. Lowell, "Homage to T. S. Eliot," *The Harvard Advocate* (1938), p. 20.

52. MacNeice, "The Personal Factor," *Modern Poetry*, p. 85.

53. Wilson, "T. S. Eliot," *op. cit.*, p. 102.

54. *Ibid.*, pp. 105, 106.

55. Matthiessen, "Tradition and the Individual Talent," *op. cit.*, pp. 8, 9.

56. "The Poetry of T. S. Eliot," *The Atlantic Monthly* (1933), p. 64.

57. Hulme, "The Religious Attitude," *op. cit.*, p. 70.

58. *Selected Essays*, "Thoughts After Lambeth," p. 322.

59. *Ibid.*, p. 342.

60. *Ibid.*, "Francis Herbert Bradley," p. 403.

61. Ransom, "Yvor Winters: the Logical Critic," *The New Criticism*, p. 214.

62.

The Emersonian and allied doctrines differ in their moral implications very little from any form of Quietism or even from the more respectable and Catholic forms of mysticism. If we add to the doctrine the belief in pantheism . . . we have the basis for the more or less Freudian mysticism of the surrealistes. . . .

("The Experimental School in American Poetry," *Primitivism and Decadence*, p. 42.)

63. "The New Reformation," *Adventures of Ideas*.

64. Krutch, "The Genesis of a Mood," *op. cit.*, p. 16.

65. Eliot, "An Emotional Unity," *The Dial* (1928), p. 110.

66. Spender, "T. S. Eliot in his Criticism," *The Destructive Element*, p. 164.

67. Blackmur, "T. S. Eliot," *The Double Agent*, pp. 200, 201.

68. Before Freud had been popularized, the time spirit impelled men like Proust "to perceive that the passions, too, have their rationale. . . . What Henry James sought all his days to do, to approfundize his own sensations, . . . this nervous Parisian laboriously achieved." (Paul Rosenfeld, "Marcel Proust," *Men Seen*, pp. 117, 121.) In the case of Joyce also, Italo Svevo would prove that Freudianism as such did not influence his work, since in 1915 he was unaware of psychoanalysis. And by this time, *Ulysses* and his other books "had already been conceived." In Zurich Joyce learned of this "new science" and was partly won over, but in 1919 Svevo found

him rebelling against it. Nevertheless, the work of Joyce is in itself a rich field for psychoanalytic study. (*See* Italo Svevo, *James Joyce; A Lecture Delivered in Milan in 1927, And now translated by Stanislaus Joyce for James Laughlin as a keepsake for his friends and those of New Directions. Christmas, 1950.*)

69. "A Sketch for a Psychology," *Principles of Literary Criticism*, pp. 81, 83.

70. Empson, *op. cit.*, p. 16.

71. "Grâce à la psychologie moderne, on savait que le symbole, s'il etait total, était l'expression la plus directe qui fut." (Taupin, "Théories imagistes," *L'Influence du Symbolisme français sur la Poésie américaine*, p. 120.)

72. Ransom says also of Eliot that he has "a special version of psychologistic theory. . . . Eliot would be saying in effect that a poem has a central logic or situation or 'paraphrasable core' . . . the poem has also a context of lively local details to which other and independent interests attach. . . ." ("Criticism as Pure Speculation," *The Intent of the Critic*, ed. Stauffer, pp. 97, 98, 110, 118.)

73. Roberta Morgan and Albert Wohlstetter, "Observations on 'Prufrock,' " *The Harvard Advocate* (1938), p. 28.

74. *Ibid.*, p. 34.

75. *Ibid.*, p. 28.

76. Spender, "The Airman, Politics and Psycho-analysis," *The Destructive Element*, p. 262.

77. "History," *op. cit.*, p. 38.

78. Walter Prichard Eaton, as quoted in Halford E. Luccock, "Morning After an Earthquake," *Contemporary American Literature and Religion*, p. 20.

79. Kenneth Burke, "Psychology and Form," *Counter-Statement*, p. 41.

80. V. W. Brooks, "Coterie-Literature," *Opinions of Oliver Allston*, p. 243.

81. "The Origins of Modern Science," *Science and the Modern World*, p. 23.

82. "The Science of the nineteenth century seemed to expel Poetry with a brandished test-tube; the Science of the twentieth reopens the door to her with a bow." (Lucas, "Fairies and Fungi; or the Future of Romanticism," *The Decline and Fall of the Romantic Ideal*, p. 145.)

83. Edman, "The Soul of Man under Modernism," *op. cit.*, pp. 15, 16.

84. At the time Eliot wrote this poem, "some of the more approving critics said that I had expressed the 'disillusionment of a generation,' which is nonsense. I may have expressed for them their own illusion of being disillusioned, but that did not form part of my intention." ("Thoughts After Lambeth," *Selected Essays*, p. 324.)

85. We have witnessed "psychoanalytic interpretations of Marxism, and Marxian interpretations of psychoanalysis. There have also been biological interpretations of theology, and mathematical interpretations of art." (Muir, "General Prose," *The Present Age from 1914*, p. 165.)

86. Richards, "The Neutralization of Nature," *Science and Poetry*, p. 58.

274   THE METAPHYSICAL PASSION

87. Relativity was an appropriate word for poetry to borrow from science in telling the atomic epic of the mind and the world. (Riding, "Poetry & the Literary Universe," *op. cit.*, pp. 23, 24.)
88. "Contemporanea," *The Egoist* (1918), p. 84.
89. *Idem, The Idea of a Christian Society,* p. 62.
90. "Antheil," *Antheil and the Treatise on Harmony,* p. 52.
91. "I think that, more important than the invention of a new machine, is the creation of a temper of mind in people such that they can learn to use a new machine rightly." (*The Idea of a Christian Society,* p. 103.)
92. Rosenfeld, "Guillaume Apollinaire," *op. cit.*, p. 80.
93. Tate, "A Note on Donne," *Reactionary Essays,* p. 72.

CHAPTER 10

1. Léonie Adams, James Agee, Ben Belitt, John Peale Bishop, Louise Bogan, Angelico Chavez, Helen Cornelius, Malcolm Cowley, Adelaide Crapsey, Harry Crosby, Richard Eberhart, Dudley Fitts, Hildegarde Flanner, Charles Henri Ford, E. S. Forgotson, Samuel B. Greenberg, Horace Gregory, Louise Guiney, Hazel Hall, Raymond Holden, John Holmes, Rolfe Humphries, Jeremy Ingalls, Randall Jarrell, Stanley J. Kunitz, Marjorie Meeker, Josephine Miles, Clarence Millspaugh, Elder Olson, Kenneth Patchen, Alan Porter, Frederic Prokosch, Phelps Putnam, Carl Rakosi, Kenneth Rexroth, Theodore Roethke, Delmore Schwartz, Karl Shapiro, Theodore Spencer, Mark Turbyfill, Parker Tyler, Ernest Walsh, Eda Lou Walton, Glenway Westcott, John Wheelwright, Oscar Williams, Yvor Winters, George Zabriskie, Louis Zukofsky.

A commentary on present crosscurrents, and on labels in general, is J. G. Fletcher's discussion of "intellectual" poets in his article on "two elements in poetry." He adduces Léonie Adams, Marianne Moore, Eliot, Read, the Sitwells, and Valéry; names the Fugitives Ransom, Warren, Davidson, Tate, and those connected with them in earlier days: Mark Van Doren, Laura Riding, Hart Crane; and cites also on the side of intellectualist poetry Lucretius, Dante, Goethe, Donne, Herbert of Cherbury, Chapman, and Blake.

2. "For Ezra Pound *il miglior fabbro*," dedication to "The Waste Land," *Collected Poems: 1909-1935* (New York: Harcourt, Brace & Co., 1936), p. 67. This phrase is taken from Dante (*op. cit.*), "Purgatorio," Canto XXVI, p. 328. Guido Guinicelli's words about Arnaut Daniel are quoted by Pound in "Il Miglior Fabbro," *The Spirit of Romance,* p. 14.
3. "Isolated Superiority," *The Dial* (1928), pp. 4, 5, 6.
4. "Und Drang," under "Poems Published Before 1911," *Lustra;* with Earlier Poems (New York: Alfred A. Knopf, 1917), p. 145.
5. "The Love Song of J. Alfred Prufrock," *Collected Poems,* p. 11.
6. "A Draft of XXX Cantos," *The Cantos of Ezra Pound* (Norfolk, Conn.: New Directions, 1948), p. 13.

7. "Mr. Apollinax," *Collected Poems*, p. 35.
8. "A Draft of XXX Cantos," *The Cantos of Ezra Pound*, pp. 24, 25.
9. *Ibid.*, p. 26.
10. *Ibid.*, p. 28.
11. "The Waste Land," *Collected Poems*, p. 90.
12. *Personae, The Collected Poems of Ezra Pound* (Norfolk, Conn.: New Directions, 1949), "Moeurs Contemporaines," p. 178.
13. *Ibid.*, "Villanelle: the Psychological Hour," p. 158.
14. *Ibid.*
15. "The Love Song of J. Alfred Prufrock," *Collected Poems*, pp. 12, 15.
16. The Ezra Pound period from 1910 to 1920, especially between 1912 and 1919, was riddled with literal and figurative blasts that emancipated poetry and the other arts from subservience, and gathered at one time and often in one place a formidable number of future fames. Iris Barry describes the year 1916. "At that time his name stood in England, along with that of the sculptor Epstein, for all that was dangerously different, horridly new." ("The Ezra Pound Period," *The Bookman*, 1931, p. 159.)
17. In Pound's poetic experiences are "none of Mr. Eliot's complex intensities of concern about soul and body: the moral, religious and anthropological preoccupations are absent." (F. R. Leavis, "Ezra Pound," *New Bearings in English Poetry*, p. 140.)
18. Eliot, "The Naming of Cats," *Old Possum's Book of Practical Cats* (New York: Harcourt, Brace & Co., 1939), p. 10.
19. "East Coker," *Four Quartets* (New York: Harcourt, Brace & Co., 1943), p. 17.
20. *The Family Reunion* (New York: Harcourt, Brace & Co., 1939), p. 31.
21. *Murder in the Cathedral* (New York: Harcourt, Brace & Co., 1935), p. 13.
22. *The Family Reunion*, p. 29.
23. "East Coker," *Four Quartets*, p. 14.
24. See pp. 29, 41, 155.
25. *The Family Reunion*, pp. 21, 105, 59, 85, 57, 34.
26. *Murder in the Cathedral*, p. 43, 23.
27. "These are only hints and guesses, / Hints followed by guesses . . ." ("The Dry Salvages," *Four Quartets*, p. 27.)
28. "The Waste Land," *Collected Poems*, p. 69.
29. *Murder in the Cathedral*, p. 83.
30. *Ibid.*, p. 24.
31. *Ibid.*, p. 72.
32. See discussion, pp. 26-28.
33. Interlude, Part I, *Murder in the Cathedral*.
34. *Collected Poems*, "Ash Wednesday," pp. 110, 112, 118.
35. *Ibid.*, "The Love Song of J. Alfred Prufrock," p. 17.
36. *Ibid.*, "Gerontion," p. 45.
37. *Four Quartets*, "Little Gidding," p. 37.
38. *Ibid.*, "East Coker," pp. 11, 17.

39. *Collected Poems,* "The Rock," p. 209.
40. *Ibid.,* p. 192.
41. *Ibid.,* p. 187.
42. *Ibid.,* p. 186.
43. *Ibid.,* pp. 206, 207.
44. *Ibid.,* "Mr. Eliot's Sunday Morning Service," p. 64.
45. *Ibid.,* "Five-finger exercises," p. 169.
46. *The Family Reunion,* pp. 28, 29.
47. "The Rock," *Collected Poems,* p. 191.
48. "East Coker," *Four Quartets,* p. 16.
49. *The Family Reunion,* p. 31.
50. *Murder in the Cathedral,* p. 68.
51. *The Family Reunion,* pp. 88, 107.
52. "Burnt Norton," *Four Quartets,* p. 7.
53. *Collected Poems,* "Preludes," p. 25.
54. *Ibid.,* "The Hollow Men," p. 104.
55. *Ibid.,* "Animula," p. 129.
56. *Ibid.,* "The Love Song of J. Alfred Prufrock," p. 12.
57. *Murder in the Cathedral,* p. 76.
58. *The Family Reunion,* p. 67.
59. *Murder in the Cathedral,* p. 65.
60. *The Family Reunion,* p. 101.
61. *Murder in the Cathedral,* p. 17.
62. *Ibid.,* p. 66.
63. *The Family Reunion,* pp. 110, 101.
64. "East Coker," *Four Quartets,* p. 16.
65. "Gerontion," *Collected Poems,* pp. 45, 46.
66. The Sweeney quatrains are also related to Marlowe, Shakespeare, Webster, Donne, Dryden; "Prufrock," "Gerontion," "The Cooking Egg," "Conversation Galante"; "To his Coy Mistress," Jonson's *The Poetaster,* and others.

Tudor and Jacobean poetry in general will explain the kind of exaggeration, the kind of rhetorical stress, the kind of ferocious humor, and above all the kind of self-dramatisation in these poems. . . . The surface world of Jonson, the force of Marlowe, the seriousness of Marvell, and the wit of Dryden . . . suggest the nature of what Mr. Eliot does in his own poems. . . . Hence certain lines acquire a kind of breathless density of texture. The feeling is made final but utterly precarious. . . . This is wit at the height of seriousness; and what requires emphasis there is that the wit more than the metre is the form. . . . They are a train of facts, the passage of which stirs up certain feelings. Or if you like they are conceits about facts of observation. They are almost concepts of facts. . . .

(Blackmur, "T. S. Eliot," *The Hound & Horn,* 1928, pp. 205, 206, 209.)
67. *Collected Poems,* "Whispers of Immortality," p. 62.
68. *Ibid.,* "The Rock," p. 198.
69. "Burnt Norton," *Four Quartets,* p. 4.
70. This in "Prufrock" (*Collected Poems,* p. 11) is not the only instance

of the use of anesthesia in his work. For example: "His soul stretched tight
across the skies . . ." (*ibid.*, "Preludes," p. 25); "The partial anaesthesia of
suffering without feeling . . ." (*The Family Reunion*, p. 29).

71. *See* discussion, pp. 21 ff.
72. *Collected Poems*, "The Waste Land," p. 70.
73. *Ibid.*, "Preludes," p. 26.
74. *Ibid.*, "Rhapsody on a Windy Night," p. 27.
75. *Ibid.*, "The Hollow Men," p. 103.
76. *Ibid.*, "The Waste Land," p. 74.
77. *Ibid.*, "A Song for Simeon," p. 127.
78. *The Family Reunion*, p. 106.
79. "Burnt Norton," *Four Quartets*, p. 6.
80. "Burnt Norton," "East Coker," "The Dry Salvages," and "Little Gidding." "Burnt Norton" maintains a noticeable arc connecting the first lines
and the last, with quasi-refrains between:

> Time present and time past
> Are both perhaps present in time future,
> And time future contained in time past.
> . . . .
> Quick now, here, now, always—
> Ridiculous the waste sad time
> Stretching before and after.

(*Four Quartets*, pp. 3, 8.) In a syllogistic movement the poem develops
essential paradoxes about certain metaphysical themes.

81. To exemplify the classic structure of a metaphysical lyric, one might
also cite Donne's "Lovers infinitenesse" among the secular, and among the
divine poems the seventeenth holy sonnet. (Ed. Hayward, *op. cit.*, pp.
11, 287.)
82. Of *The Family Reunion* it has been said that "this is the finest verse
play since the Elizabethans." (Jack, *The New York Times Book Review*,
April 9, 1939.)
83. "Burnt Norton," *Four Quartets*, p. 4.
84. "The Extasie," ed. Hayward, *op. cit.*, p. 38.
85. "East Coker," *Four Quartets*, p. 14.
86. "Ascension-Hymn," *Metaphysical Lyrics*, ed. Grierson, pp. 149, 150.
87. Eliot, "The Love Song of J. Alfred Prufrock," *Collected Poems*, p. 15.
88. *Metaphysical Lyrics*, ed. Grierson, p. 74.
89. *Collected Poems*, pp. 78, 79.
90. *Metaphysical Lyrics*, ed. Grierson, p. 74.
91. Eliot, *Collected Poems*, "Five-finger exercises," p. 168.
92. *Ibid.*, "Ash Wednesday," p. 109.
93. *See* Eliot's exalted analysis of the Bishop in "Lancelot Andrewes,"
Selected Essays, pp. 297 ff.
94. "It is also worth noting that there is very considerable spiritual
affinity (and perhaps even direct influence) between Donne's *First Anniversary* and *The Waste Land*." (Bald, *op. cit.*, p. 61.)

95. Dante has written his signature across Eliot's poetry spiritually and verbally. In "The Waste Land," Eliot alludes to him specifically on pp. 71, 83, 89, 90. (All pages refer to *Collected Poems*.) Two of the distinctive images that occur with symbolic frequency throughout Eliot are apparently Dantean in origin: the purgatorial figure of the stairs, and the key in the door. The two are combined in the following examples: "I mount the stairs and turn the handle of the door / And feel as if I had mounted on my hands and knees." ("Portrait of a Lady," p. 21.) "Memory! / You have the key, / The little lamp spreads a ring on the stair. / Mount." ("Rhapsody on a Windy Night," pp. 29, 30.) The stairs appear also in "A Song for Simeon" (p. 128), "The *Boston Evening Transcript*" (p. 32), "Burbank with a Baedeker" (p. 48), and "Ash Wednesday," whose whole structure is built around stairs: "Struggling with the devil of the stairs who wears / The deceitful face of hope and of despair." (P. 114.) In the same poem Dante is echoed in "Our peace in His will . . ." (p. 121). Among repeated symbols is one akin to Dante's figure of the river, such as "Or che di là dal mal fiume dimora . . ." (*op. cit.*, "Purgatorio": Canto I, p. 8). This symbol is to be found in a number of Eliot poems, e.g.: "The Wind Sprang up at Four O'clock" (p. 166). Another symbol Dantesque in character is that of light, and its companion shadow. "Looking into the heart of light, the silence" is a felt presence for Eliot ("The Waste Land," p. 70), while in Dante the divine spirit "col suo lume sè medesmo cela." (*Op. cit.*, "Purgatorio": Canto XVII, p. 206.) The source of the first line of "Animula" (p. 129) is Dante's "Esce di mano a lui . . . l'anima semplicetta . . ." (*op. cit.*, "Purgatorio": Canto XVI, p. 196). If Eliot drew on other sources for Tiresias, Philomela, the desert scene, the symbol of the dice, etc., it must nevertheless be noted that they also occur in Dante. Borrowed lines and suggested imagery are less important than the religious attitude, the psychological understanding, and the metaphysical passion.

96. The extracts given below are taken from poems reprinted in *The Harvard Advocate*, 1938, pp. 11-16. They were originally published in this undergraduate magazine, as the dates indicate, when Eliot was a student at Harvard. The tone and imagery quite remarkably anticipate later poems like "Prufrock," "Portrait of a Lady," and the French pieces—translated and adapted from or composed in French. At this point in Eliot's precocious career, he had already immersed himself in French symbolist literature, as "Nocturne," "Humoresque" (after Laforgue), and "Spleen" palpably illustrate. He himself says: "the form in which I began to write, in 1908 or 1909, was directly drawn from the study of Laforgue together with the later Elizabethan drama; and I do not know anyone who started from exactly that point." (Introduction to *Selected Poems* by Ezra Pound, p. viii.)

> She stands at evening in the room alone.
> . . . .
> The parrot on his bar, a silent spy,
> Regards her with a patient curious eye.
>   ("On a Portrait," January 1909)

Romeo, *grand serieux* . . .
. . . in the usual debate
Of love, beneath a bored but courteous moon . . .

. . . . .

Behind the wall I have some servant wait,

. . . . .

. . . in my best mode oblique . . .
("Nocturne," November 1909)

Evening, lights, and tea!
Children and cats in the alley;

. . . . .

And Life, a little bald and gray,
Languid, fastidious, and bland,
Waits, hat and gloves in hand,
Punctilious of tie and suit
(Somewhat impatient of delay)
On the doorstep of the Absolute.
("Spleen," January 1910)

97. "That is to say, we must affirm the eternal against the transient. . . . We are obviously at the end of an age, oppressed by the sense of corruption and decay, and fearful of the kinds of change which may come, since some change must. . . . The extremes, however, may meet." (Eliot, "Literature and the Modern World," *An Approach to Literature,* ed. C. Brooks, pp. 168, 169.)

CHAPTER 11

1. *The Fugitive,* I, No. 2 (June 1922), anon., "Caveat Emptor," p. 34.
2. *Ibid.,* Henry Feathertop, "Cul-de-Sac," p. 52.
3. *Ibid.,* No. 3 (October 1922), p. 76: changed by only three words in his *Poems: 1922-1947* (New York: Charles Scribner's Sons, 1948).
4. *The Fugitive,* I, No. 3 (October 1922), pp. 66, 68.
5. *Ibid.,* "Whose Ox," No. 4 (December 1922), pp. 99, 100.
6. *Ibid.,* anon., "Merely Prose," II, No. 7 (June-July 1923), p. 66.
7. *Ibid.,* No. 5 (February-March 1923), pp. 24, 25.
8. *Ibid.,* No. 9 (October 1923), p. 131.
9.

But dissolution clutched me
Descanting in Mme. Atelie's salon
Of balls at Nice and coursing at L'Enprix.
I sipped my tea with marked exactitude . . .

(*Ibid.,* No. 8, August-September 1923, p. 106.)
10. *Ibid.,* No. 10 (December 1923), p. 178. This line appears on p. 147 in *Poems: 1922-1947,* as "Of a body vanished into a thought."
11. *The Fugitive,* III, Nos. 5, 6 (December 1924), p. 133. The translation

is given again in *Poems: 1922-1947*, p. 205: "Perfumes and colors and sounds correspond."

12. "One Escape from the Dilemma," *The Fugitive*, III, No. 2 (April 1924), pp. 34, 35, 36.

13. *Idem, Poems: 1922-1947*, "Ode to Fear," p. 104.

14. *Ibid.*, "The Cross," p. 126.

15. *Ibid.*, "The Eagle," p. 114.

16. *Ibid.*, "The Oath," p. 108.

17. *Ibid.*, "The Wolves," p. 110.

18. *Ibid.*, "Records: I. A Dream," p. 44.

19. *Ibid.*

20. *Ibid.*, "Elegy," p. 89.

21. *Ibid.*, "The Ancestors," p. 9.

22. *Ibid.*, "Ode to the Confederate Dead," pp. 20, 22.

23. *Ibid.*, pp. 19, 22.

24. *Ibid.*, "The Mediterranean," p. 4.

25. Cf. Eliot's epigraph to "A Cooking Egg," *Collected Poems*, p. 52, with Tate's to "Fragment" in *Selected Poems* (New York: Charles Scribner's Sons, 1937), p. 39. *Idem, Poems: 1922-1947*, "Fragment of a Meditation," p. 83.

26. *Ibid.*, pp. 83, 87.

27. *Ibid.*, "The Twelve," p. 117. Cf. Eliot's "Journey of the Magi," *Collected Poems*, p. 126.

28. Cf. Donne's Holy Sonnet VII: "At the round earths imagin'd corners, blow / Your Trumpets, Angells, and arise, arise . . ." (ed. Hayward, *op. cit.*, p. 282).

29. Tate, *Poems: 1922-1947*, "Sonnets at Christmas: II," p. 51.

30. *Ibid.*, "Message from Abroad: I," p. 11.

31. *Ibid.*, II, p. 12.

32. Tate admits: "I have had only two Masters, and one of them is T. S. Eliot." ("Homage to T. S. Eliot," *The Harvard Advocate*, 1938, p. 41.)

33. *Idem*, "Idiot," *Poems: 1922-1947*, p. 158.

34. *Idem*, "Epistle," *Selected Poems*, employs the image of a sick eagle once and that of a crab twice.

35. Tate writes an "Epistle to Edmund Wilson," *Selected Poems*, p. 75, and mentions him and *Axel's Castle* in "The Ivory Tower," *The Mediterranean and Other Poems* (New York: The Alcestis Press, 1936), p. 56; he addresses Landor in "Unnatural Love," *Poems: 1922-1947*, p. 140—cf. "To a Young Beauty," *The Collected Poems of W. B. Yeats* (New York: The Macmillan Co., 1949), p. 159; he writes a "Horatian Epode to the Duchess of Malfi," *Poems: 1922-1947*, p. 71, and cites Kyd in "Causerie," *ibid.*, p. 77, where, by mentioning Ransom and Warren as well as Wilson again, he relates them and himself to the Elizabethan tone in which this dramatic monologue is written; he is impressed by Pound's and Eliot's crowded library:

> For now the languid stertorous
> *Pale verses of Propertius*

And the sapphire corpse undressed by Donne
(Prefiguring Rimbaud's etymon),
Have shrunk to an apotheosis
Of cold daylight after the kiss.

("The Progress of Œnia: V. Epilogue to Œnia," *ibid.*, p. 148.)

36. *Ibid.*, pp. 120, 122.

37. *Ibid.*, "Obituary," "Death of Little Boys," "The Anabasis," "Elegy," "Mother and Son," "Inside and Outside," and of course the fine "Ode to the Confederate Dead."

38. *Ibid.*, "The Wolves," p. 110.

39. *Ibid.*, p. 111.

40.

"I suppose I belong," he writes, "to what is at present known, and I think improperly known, as the modern metaphysical school of poetry. . . . I should imagine that our best contemporary instance is the work of Yeats, with plenty of room for Eliot and Pound in the immediate background, and going back, in this country, to Dickinson and Poe. More remotely but no less powerfully the seventeenth-century metaphysicals would stand as the historical justification of this contemporary school."

(Tate, as quoted in Fred B. Millett, *Contemporary American Authors,* pp. 609, 610.)

41. *Poems: 1922-1947*, "Death of Little Boys," p. 131.

42. *Ibid.*, "The Eagle," p. 113.

43. For example, "the thick and the fast / Whirl of the damned in the heavenly storm . . ." (*ibid.*, "The Twelve," p. 117).

44. Donne might have said that "love so hates mortality . . ." (*ibid.*, "The Cross," p. 125).

45. *Ibid.*, "Obituary," p. 162.

46. *Ibid.*, "The Subway," p. 59.

47. The dedication is omitted in *Selected Poems.*

48. "The Traveller," *Poems: 1922-1947*, pp. 105, 106.

49. Dedicated to R. P. W., obviously Robert Penn Warren, in *Poems: 1928-1931* (New York: Charles Scribner's Sons, 1932). *See also Poems: 1922-1947*, "Causerie," p. 79.

50. *Ibid.*, "Last Days of Alice," pp. 115, 116.

51. *Ibid.*, "Inside and Outside," pp. 129, 130.

52. *Ibid.*, "The Paradigm," pp. 48, 49.

53. *Ibid.*, "Pastoral," pp. 136, 137.

54. *Ibid.*, "Causerie," p. 81.

55. *Ibid.*, pp. 79, 80.

56. *Ibid.*, "Ignis Fatuus," p. 153.

57. *Ibid.*, "To the Lacedemonians," pp. 15, 16, 14, 18.

58. Warren, *Selected Poems, 1923-1943* (New York: Harcourt, Brace & Co., 1944), "Monologue at Midnight," p. 58.

59. *Ibid.*, "Bearded Oaks," pp. 59, 60.

60. "To Lucasta," *Metaphysical Lyrics*, ed. Grierson, p. 58.

61. Poem XIX, *The Complete Poems of Emily Dickinson* (Boston: Little, Brown & Co., 1926), p. 190.

62. Warren, "Love's Parable," *Selected Poems*, pp. 65-67.

63. Ed. Hayward, *op. cit.*, "A Valediction: forbidding mourning," p. 37.

64. *Ibid.*, "Extasie," pp. 38, 39.

65. *Selected Poems*, "Picnic Remembered," pp. 61, 62.

66. In a very earthy regional ballad, Warren weaves parenthetical commentary into the story. The contrapuntal method enriches the racy tale with notes of a haunting metaphysical depth. These notes are played in a minor key on the motif of time, whose "innocent savagery" and "unwinking eye" he invokes with ironic stress. The poet refers the "hero" of the story to everyman whose "implacable thirst of self" drinks of his "deep identity" from birth to death: "For the beginning was definition and the end may be definition . . ." (*ibid.*, "The Ballad of Billie Potts," pp. 4, 7, 9, 17).

67. *Ibid.*, "Original Sin: A Short Story," p. 24.

68. *The Family Reunion*, p. 58.

69. *Selected Poems*, "Revelation," p. 46.

70. *Ibid.*, "Crime," p. 25.

71. *Ibid.*, "End of Season," p. 38.

72. *Ibid.*, "Terror," p. 19.

73. *Ibid.*

74. *Ibid.*, "Pursuit," p. 22.

75. *Ibid.*, "Terror," p. 18.

76. *Ibid.*, "Question and Answer," pp. 34, 35.

77. *Ibid.*, "Pursuit," p. 21.

78. *Ibid.*, "Terror," p. 20.

79. *Poems: 1922-1947*, "To the Lacedemonians," p. 15.

80. *Ibid.*, "Sonnets at Christmas: I," p. 50.

81. *Selected Poems*, "Terror," p. 19.

82. *Ibid.*, "Pursuit," pp. 21, 22.

83. *Ibid.*, "The Last Metaphor," p. 91.

84. *Ibid.*, "So Frost Astounds," p. 90.

85. *Ibid.*

86. *Ibid.*, "The Return: An Elegy," p. 75.

87. *Ibid.*, "Kentucky Mountain Farm: I. Rebuke of the Rocks," p. 79.

88. *Ibid.*, "VI. Watershed," p. 82.

89. *Ibid.*, "II. At the Hour of the Breaking of the Rocks," p. 80.

90. *Ibid.*, "Calendar," p. 95.

91. *Ibid.*, "Problem of Knowledge," p. 97. Cf. Warren's "spider contemplation" with Donne's "spider love," from "Twicknam Garden," ed. Hayward, *op. cit.*, p. 20.

92. Warren, "To One Awake," *Thirty-Six Poems* (New York: The Alcestis Press, 1935), p. 66.

93. *Selected Poems*, "Croesus in Autumn," p. 89.

94. *Ibid.*, "History," p. 32.

95. *Ibid.*, "Letter from a Coward to a Hero," pp. 27, 28.

96. *Idem,* "Resolution," *Thirty-Six Poems,* p. 34.
97. *Idem, Selected Poems,* "Letter to a Friend," p. 43.
98. *Ibid.,* "Late Subterfuge," p. 68.
99. Ransom, *The Fugitive,* II, No. 6 (April-May 1923), "Agitato Ma Non Troppo," p. 56.
100. *Ibid.,* No. 7 (June-July 1923), "Nocturne," p. 82. Later in *Chills and Fever* (New York: Alfred A. Knopf, 1924).
101. *Idem, Poems about God* (New York: Henry Holt & Co., 1919), pp. v, vi.
102. *Ibid.,* "Geometry," p. 27.
103. *Ibid.,* p. 29.
104. *Ibid.*
105. *Ibid.,* "Worship," p. 39.
106. *Ibid.*
107. *Metaphysical Lyrics,* ed. Grierson, "Job XIII, XXIV," p. 116.
108. *Ibid.,* "The Collar," pp. 111, 112.
109. Ransom, "Sickness," *Poems about God,* p. 75. Cf. seventeenth-century poems: "Hymne to God my God, in my sicknesse" by Donne, "A Hymn to my God in a night of my late Sicknesse" by Sir Henry Wotton, *Metaphysical Lyrics,* ed. Grierson, pp. 91, 93. Herbert's childlike anguish appears again as modern irony in MacLeish:

> At the Last Day, at the Judgement, the Lord God
> Will say to you that sit on his right hand,
> Come unto me ye blessed and be glad,
>
> . . . . . .
>
> But unto us, Ye others, ye that looked
> Dazzled in your own eyes and saw me not,
>
> . . . . . .
>
> Go find the thing ye seek and still alone
> Seek on, seek on forever. Go your way.
>
> And we will turn to go and one will say
> Which are the chosen, Lord?

("Question in Time of Eternity," *Streets in the Moon,* p. 91. *See* chap. 12, note 32.)
110. "The Second Anniversary," ed. Hayward, *op. cit.,* p. 221.
111. "Judith of Bethulia," *Selected Poems* (New York: Alfred A. Knopf, 1935), p. 25.
112. *Poems about God,* "The Bachelor," p. 46.
113. *Ibid.,* "The Cloak Model," p. 42.
114. "Elegie VIII: The Comparison," ed. Hayward, *op. cit.,* pp. 74, 75.
115. Cf. also "If you go on, my soul, in this broad-leaved acre / Your fingers will sprout leaves between the digits." (Taggard, "Evening Love-of-Self," *Not Mine to Finish,* p. 47.)
116. *Selected Poems,* "Winter Remembered," p. 1.
117. *Chills and Fever,* "Two Sonnets," p. 20.

118. *Ibid.*, "To a Lady Celebrating Her Birthday," pp. 22, 23.
119. Cf. Donne.
120. Cf. Carew.
121. Cf. Lovelace.
122. Cf. Suckling.
123. *Selected Poems*, "Vaunting Oak," p. 13.
124. *Ibid.*, p. 14.
125. *Chills and Fever*, "Fall of Leaf," p. 32.
126. *Ibid.*, "Night Voices," p. 73.
127. *Ibid.*, "Lichas to Polydor," p. 68.
128. *Ibid.*, "Plea in Mitigation," pp. 82, 83.
129. *Ibid.*, "Adventures This Side of Pluralism," pp. 74, 75.
130. "I remember a slice of lemon, and a bitten macaroon." (Eliot, "Mr. Apollinax," *Collected Poems*, p. 36.)
131. *Selected Poems*, "Good Ships," p. 10.
132. *Ibid.*, "Philomela," p. 29.
133. *Ibid.*, "Survey of Literature," pp. 61, 62.
134. *Ibid.*, "Philomela," p. 28.
135. *Two Gentlemen in Bonds* (New York: Alfred A. Knopf, 1927), "Persistent Explorer," p. 44.
136. *Ibid.*, "Miller's Daughter," p. 12.
137. *Selected Poems*, "Dog," p. 58.
138. Van Doren's statement facing title page, *Two Gentlemen in Bonds*.
139. *Selected Poems*, "Eclogue," pp. 38, 39.
140. *Ibid.*, "Captain Carpenter," pp. 31-33.

CHAPTER 12

1. MacLeish, *Poems, 1924-1933* (Boston: Houghton Mifflin Co., 1933), p. 31.
2. In MacLeish we see the impress of Pound, Eliot, Crane, Gertrude Stein, together with attitudes and techniques of the poets whom they espoused: Poe, Rimbaud, St.-J. Perse *(Anabasis)*, Laforgue *(Hamlet)*, Valéry, etc.
3. Prosody is relevant to the problem of metaphysical expression. In general, metaphysical poetry has been accompanied by experimentation because the pounding impact of thought or the suggestiveness of feeling demands an often wrenched and special rhetoric. In America particularly, where fresh idiom is likely to develop, the incidence of metaphysical poetry is associated with experimental vigor and variety. Breaking through in the time of Emily Dickinson and Whitman, the crisp and sometimes violent unconventionality of verse forms has been much extended in our century. Pound, Eliot, and half the imagists were American in origin and background, though (like Gertrude Stein and Laura Riding also) they transplanted their experiments to Europe. There, theory and new practice further adapted

the effects of French and English experimentation. Such growth and exchange were developed by the expatriates abroad and, in the United States, by the Fugitives chiefly. The story of metaphysical poetry in America and among Americans in Europe is obviously allied to modern changes in rhetoric and prosody.

4. *See* pp. 15-19.

5. MacLeish, "Speech to a Crowd," *Public Speech;* Poems (New York: Farrar & Rinehart, 1936).

6. After rejecting the spirit of expatriation, MacLeish wrote "The Aristocracy of Wealth and Talents / Moved out: settled on the Continent: / Sat beside the water at Rapallo . . ." (*America Was Promises.* New York: Duell, Sloan & Pearce, 1939, p. 14).

7. "The Garden," *Metaphysical Lyrics,* ed. Grierson, p. 210.

8. ". . . let the silence of / Green be between us / And the green sound." ("Words to be spoken," *Public Speech.*) Cf. his earlier: "And let the old remembering wind think through / A green intelligence or under sea . . ." ("Einstein," *Poems, 1924-1933,* p. 70).

9. *The Fall of the City;* A Verse Play for Radio (New York: Farrar & Rinehart, 1937), p. 3.

10. Title poem, *The Happy Marriage;* And Other Poems (Boston, Houghton Mifflin Co., 1924), pp. 38, 39.

11. *Land of the Free;* Photographs Illustrated by a Poem (New York: Harcourt, Brace & Co., 1938), pp. 49, 82.

12. *Panic;* A Play in Verse (Boston: Houghton Mifflin Co., 1935), pp. 95, 33.

13. *Ibid.,* pp. 39, 88.

14. *The Happy Marriage,* pp. 24, 37, 15.

15. *Nobodaddy;* A Play (Cambridge, Mass.: Dunster House, 1926), foreword.

16. *Ibid.,* p. 18.

17. *Ibid.,* p. 30.

18. *Ibid.,* p. 62.

19. *See* MacLeish's foreword to *Nobodaddy,* written and first published in Paris, 1925, before *The Pot of Earth* which was subsequently included in his *Poems, 1924-1933.*

20. "The Pot of Earth," *Poems, 1924-1933,* pp. 101, 110.

21. *Ibid.,* p. 110.

22. *Ibid.,* pp. 114, 115.

23. *Ibid.,* p. 113.

24. *Ibid.,* p. 115.

25. "But he never achieves the dramatic fusion of opposed attitudes . . . he has never succeeded in unifying these alter egos; but there is a good deal to be said for having a John Fletcher loose among the metaphysicals." (Arthur Mizener, "Archibald MacLeish," *We Moderns,* p. 46.)

26. "The Hamlet of A. MacLeish," *Poems, 1924-1933,* pp. 12, 24.

27. "Coriolanus and His Mother: The Dream of One Performance, a

narrative poem," *In Dreams Begin Responsibilities* (Norfolk, Conn.: New Directions, 1938).

28. "Lines for a Prologue," *Poems, 1924-1933*, p. 34.

29. "The World," *The Works of Henry Vaughan*, ed. L. Cyril Martin (Oxford: The Clarendon Press, 1914), p. 466.

30. *Poems, 1924-1933*, "You, Andrew Marvell," pp. 58, 59.

31. *Ibid.*, "L'An Trentiesme de mon Eage," pp. 40, 41. Cf. *Personae, The Collected Poems of Ezra Pound*, p. 187; Eliot, *Collected Poems*, p. 52; Tate, *Selected Poems*, p. 39.

32. "History," *Streets in the Moon* (Boston: Houghton Mifflin Co., 1926), p. 100.

33. *Poems, 1924-1933*, "Le Secret Humain," p. 42.

34. *Ibid.*

35. *Ibid.*, "Voyage," p. 44.

36. *Ibid.*, "Interrogate the Stones," p. 61.

37. Such as "Cinema of a Man," "Signature for Tempo," "Salute," "Seafarer," etc., *ibid.*

38. *See* discussion of the "metaphysical shudder," pp. 6, 48, 54 ff.

39. *Poems, 1924-1933*, "Mother Goose's Garland," p. 85.

40. *Ibid.*, "Einstein," pp. 70, 73.

41. *Ibid.*, p. 73.

42. *Ibid.*, p. 75.

43.

> Dos that saw the tyrants in the lime
> Ernest that saw the first snow in the fox's feather
>
> Stephen that saw his wife
> Cummings his quick fillies
> Eliot the caul between the ribs of life
> Pound—Pound cracking the eggs of a cock with the beautiful
> sword of Achilles . . .

(*Ibid.*, "Sentiments for a Dedication," pp. 77.)

44. *Ibid.*, "Immortal Helix," p. 82.

45. *Ibid.*, "The End of the World," p. 93.

46. MacLeish, as interviewed by Robert Van Gelder, *The New York Times Book Review*, May 10, 1942.

47. *Idem*, "Conquistador," *Poems, 1924-1933*, p. 270.

48. Not in the opinion of Cleanth Brooks: "But of course Miss Cornelius is no more a metaphysical poet than is Miss Wylie. . . . The important thing is that the reasoning . . . is not done through the images. The reasoning is merely the string on which the bright hard images are strung." ("Poets and Laureates," *The Southern Review*, 1936, p. 394.)

49. Auden's work is a serious inquiry, with ironic overtones, into this contemporary issue. Cf. his summary epigram, p. 43.

50. *Collected Poems of Elinor Wylie* (New York: Alfred A. Knopf, 1933), "The Eagle and the Mole," p. 4.

51. *Ibid.,* "Sanctuary," p. 14.
52. *Ibid.,* "The Lion and the Lamb," p. 15. *See also* the Blake-like "Pity Me," *ibid.,* p. 85.
53. *Ibid.,* "Bells in the Rain," p. 19.
54. *Ibid.,* "Fire and Sleet and Candlelight," p. 28.
55. *Ibid.,* "The Tortoise in Eternity," p. 34.
56. *Ibid.,* "Incantation," p. 35.
57. *Ibid.,* "Valentine," pp. 41, 42.
58. *See* discussion of the objective equivalent, pp. 40-42, 44, 45, 50.
59. *Collected Poems,* "Full Moon," p. 47.
60. *Ibid.,* "Song," p. 52.
61. *Ibid.,* "The Good Birds," p. 54.
62. *Ibid.,* "One Person," p. 185.
63. *Ibid.,* "To a Lady's Countenance," p. 232.
64. *See* chap. 4.
65. *See* pp. 21-26.
66. *Collected Poems,* "Demon Lovers," p. 74.
67. *Ibid.,* "Hospes Comesque Corporis," p. 124.
68. "Goe, and catche a falling starre, / Get with child a mandrake roote." ("Song," ed. Hayward, *op. cit.,* p. 4.)
69. *Collected Poems,* "King Honour's Eldest Son," p. 71.
70. *Ibid.,* "Unfinished Portrait," p. 86.
71. *See* pp. 50-54.
72. *Collected Poems,* "Lilliputian," p. 94.
73. *Ibid.,* "Last Supper," p. 164.
74. *Ibid.,* "Lament for Glasgerion," p. 165.
75. *Ibid.,* "One Person," p. 189.
76. *Ibid.,* "Lament for Glasgerion," p. 165.
77. *Ibid.,* "Dedication," p. 109.
78. *Ibid.,* "One Person," pp. 171, 179.
79.
Poetically Elinor had two masters. The first was Shelley. . . . Later on, Elinor read a great deal of Donne. Her poems shew his influence, but I think their two minds were naturally akin. . . . Elinor carried everywhere with her the complete poetical works of Donne, and she read them again and again. The subjects he chose were subjects which she too would have chosen, and her treatment of a theme was often oddly like his.

(Edith Olivier, tribute in *Last Poems of Elinor Wylie.* New York: Alfred A. Knopf, 1943, pp. xii, xiv.)
80. *Collected Poems,* "A Red Carpet for Shelley," pp. 156, 158.
81. *Ibid.,* "Minotaur," p. 114.
82. *Ibid.,* "O Virtuous Light," p. 199.
83. *Ibid.*
84. *See* pp. 84, 85 and chap. 6, note 10.
85. *Collected Poems,* "This Corruptible," p. 204.
86. *Ibid.,* p. 206.

87. *Ibid.*, "To a Book," p. 162.

88. *Ibid.*, "One Person," pp. 173, 188.

89. *Ibid.*, "Malediction Upon Myself," p. 118.

90. *Ibid.*, "True Vine," p. 120.

91. *Ibid.*, "The Puritan's Ballad," p. 139.

92. "Our hands were firmely cimented / With a fast balme . . ." (ed. Hayward, *op. cit.*, "The Extasie," p. 38); "My name engrav'd herein, / Doth contribute my firmness to this glasse . . ." (*ibid.*, "A Valediction: of my name, in the window," p. 17).

93. *Ibid.*, "The Relique," p. 46.

94. *Collected Poems*, "The Madwoman's Miracle," p. 260.

95. *Ibid.*, "Portrait in Black Paint, With a Very Sparing Use of White-wash," p. 276.

96. *Ibid.*, "Letter to V——," p. 302.

97. *Ibid.*, "Little Eclogue," p. 289.

98.

> Down to the Puritan marrow of my bones
> There's something in this richness that I hate.
> I love the look, austere, immaculate . . .

(*Ibid.*, "Wild Peaches," p. 12. *See also ibid.*, "Sonnet," p. 308.)

99. A Jacobean would have felt at home with the following conceit:

> God cure your cold,
> Whether it be but a cold in the head
> Or the more bitter cold which binds the dead.

(*Ibid.*, "To a Cough in the Street at Midnight," p. 220.)

You might take for mood, cadence, and imagery Elinor Wylie's lines:

> I shall go shod in silk,
> And you in wool,
>
> .   .   .   .
> We shall step upon white down,
> Upon silver fleece,
> Upon softer than these.
>
> .   .   .   .
> We shall walk in the snow.

(*Ibid.*, "Velvet Shoes," p. 40.)

Against the above set this seventeenth-century stanza:

> O lull me, lull me charming air,
> My senses rock with wonder sweet;
> Like snow on wool thy fallings are,
> Soft like a spirit's, are thy feet . . .

(William Strode, "In Commendation of Music," *Aspects of Seventeenth Century Verse*, ed. Quennell, p. 152.)

100. *See* discussion of this theory, pp. 149-151.

101. William Rose Benét, foreword to *Collected Poems of Elinor Wylie*, p. vi.

102. Wylie, *Collected Poems*, "Preference," p. 63.
103. *Ibid.*, "To a Book," p. 162.
104. *Ibid.*, "Self-portrait," p. 69.
105. *Ibid.*, "Hymn to Earth," p. 202.
106. *Ibid.*, "One Person," p. 174.
107. *Ibid.*, p. 173.
108. *Ibid.*, "Nonsense Rhyme," p. 218.
109. *Ibid.*, "Self-portrait," p. 69.
110. *Ibid.*, "Address to My Soul," pp. 160, 161.
111. *The Collected Poems of Hart Crane*, ed. with an Introduction by Waldo Frank (New York: Liveright Publishing Corporation, 1933), "Ave Maria," p. 8.
112.
The poet's concern must be . . . the articulation of the contemporary human consciousness *sub specie aeternitatis*, and inclusive of all readjustments incident to science and other shifting factors related to that consciousness. . . . The familiar contention that science is inimical to poetry is no more tenable than the kindred notion that theology has been proverbially hostile—with the "Commedia" of Dante to prove the contrary.

(*Ibid.*, "Modern Poetry: An Essay," appendix B, pp. 175, 176, 178.)
113. He said that "unless poetry can absorb the machine, i.e., *acclimatize* it as naturally and casually as trees, cattle, galleons, castles and all other human associations of the past, then poetry has failed of its full contemporary function." (*Ibid.*, p. 177.)
114. *Ibid.*, Frank, introduction, p. x.
115. Tate, foreword to *White Buildings; Poems by Hart Crane* (New York: Horace Liveright, 1926), p. xv.
116. "The apple on its bough is her desire,— / Shining suspension, mimic of the sun." (*The Collected Poems*, p. 70.) But Crane by temperament was obliged to enrich graphic scenes and natural objects transcendentally—to go beyond the merely explicit or decorative methods of imagism, e.g.: "Royal Palm," "North Labrador." In the last stanza of "The Air Plant" he calls it "Angelic Dynamo! Ventriloquist of the Blue!" And he questions its destiny. (*Ibid.*, p. 122.)
117. "The poet's concern must be, as always, self-discipline toward a formal integration of experience." (*Ibid.*, "Modern Poetry: An Essay," p. 175.)
118. Tate, foreword to *White Buildings*, p. xiv.
119. The Bible, Plato, Dante, the Elizabethans, Donne, Blake, Emerson, Whitman, Poe, Dickinson, Melville, Rimbaud, Laforgue, Pound, Eliot, Stevens, Fletcher, Richard Aldington, Edith Sitwell, Sherwood Anderson, Samuel Greenberg.
120. Frank, introduction to *The Collected Poems*, p. xiv.
121. *Ibid.*, p. xxvii.
122. *Ibid.*, p. xiv.
123. *Ibid.*, p. xv.

124. Tate, foreword to *White Buildings*, p. xi.
125. *The Collected Poems*, Frank, introduction, pp. xvii, xiii.
126. *Ibid.*, Crane, "The Bridge," p. 8.
127. Tate, foreword to *White Buildings*, p. xii.
128. *Ibid.*, p. xiii.
129. *The Collected Poems*, Crane, "The Broken Tower," p. 136.
130. *Ibid.*, Frank, introduction, p. x.
131. "Objective reality exists in these poems only as an oblique moving-inward to the poet's mood. But the mood is never, as in imagist or romantic verse, given for and as itself." (*Ibid.*, p. xv.)
132. *Ibid.*, Crane, "The Broken Tower," pp. 135, 136.
133. *Ibid.*, "To Brooklyn Bridge," p. 4.
134. *Ibid.*, "Cape Hatteras," p. 39.
135. *Ibid.*, "Modern Poetry: An Essay," p. 177.
136. *Ibid.*, "To Brooklyn Bridge," p. 4.
137. *Ibid.*, "Cape Hatteras," pp. 36, 38.
138. *Ibid.*, "The Tunnel," p. 51.
139. *Ibid.*, "For the Marriage of Faustus and Helen," p. 97.
140. *Ibid.*, "The River," p. 17.
141. *Ibid.*, "Van Winkle," p. 11.
142. *Ibid.*, "The River," p. 17.
143. *Ibid.*, "Cape Hatteras," pp. 36, 32.
144. *Ibid.*, "Praise for an Urn," p. 68.
145. *Ibid.*, "Chaplinesque," p. 74.
146. *Ibid.*, "Voyages," p. 105.
147. *Ibid.*, "Legend," pp. 61, 62.
148. *Ibid.*, "Voyages," p. 102.
149. *Ibid.*, "Recitative," p. 91.
150. *Ibid.*, "For the Marriage of Faustus and Helen," p. 97.
151. *Ibid.*, "Voyages," p. 103.
152. *Ibid.*, p. 106.
153. *Ibid.*, "Cape Hatteras," p. 34.
154. *Ibid.*, "Lachrymae Christi," p. 85.
155. In *The Collected Poems* there are tributes to Plato, Marlowe, Goethe, "To Shakespeare," to the metaphysical novelist in "At Melville's Tomb"; songs in praise of Whitman in "Cape Hatteras," Emily Dickinson in "Quaker Hill" and "To Emily Dickinson," and in memory of Harry Crosby: the "Cloud Juggler."
156. *Ibid.*, "Modern Poetry: An Essay," p. 176.
157. This poem is a mosaic of Greenberg's lines from "Conduct," "The Laureate," "Immortality," "Perusal," "Daylight" (Nos. 61, 50, 63, 51, 60 of "Sonnets of Apology"). *See Poems from The Greenberg Manuscripts; A Selection from the Work of Samuel B. Greenberg*, ed. with a Commentary by James Laughlin (Norfolk, Conn.: New Directions, 1939).
158. As quoted in Philip Horton, "Identity of S. B. Greenberg," *The Southern Review* (1936), p. 423.

159. Horton, "The Greenberg Manuscript and Hart Crane's Poetry," *The Southern Review* (1936), p. 151.
160. *Ibid.*, p. 158.
161. *Ibid.*, p. 149.
162. *The Greenberg MSS.*, "Memory," p. 369.
163. *Ibid.*, "Words," p. 370.
164. Crane, "The Hurricane," *The Collected Poems*, pp. 124, 125.

PARTIAL BIBLIOGRAPHY
OF CRITICAL WORKS FROM 1900

Aiken, Conrad. "Emily Dickinson," *The Bookman* (London), LXVII, No. 397 (October 1924), 8-12.

———. *Scepticisms;* Notes on Contemporary Poetry. New York: Alfred A. Knopf, 1919.

Alden, Raymond Macdonald. "The Lyrical Conceit of the Elizabethans," *Studies in Philology* (Chapel Hill, N. C.), XIV, No. 2 (April 1917), 129-52.

———. "The Lyrical Conceits of the 'Metaphysical Poets,'" *Studies in Philology* (Chapel Hill, N. C.), XVII, No. 2 (April 1920), 183-98. (Carew, Donne, Cowley.)

Aldington, Richard. "Cowley and the French Epicureans," "The Poetry of T. S. Eliot," in his *Literary Studies and Reviews.* London: George Allen & Unwin, 1924. Pp. 103-12, 181-91.

Bagguley, William H., ed. *Andrew Marvell, 1621-1678;* Tercentenary Tributes. London: Oxford University Press, 1922. (Essays by Augustine Birrell, T. S. Eliot, Cyril Falls, Edmund Gosse, H. H. Henson, Harold J. Massingham, J. C. Squire, Edward Wright.)

Bailey, Ruth. *A Dialogue on Modern Poetry.* London: Oxford University Press, 1939.

Bald, R. C. *Donne's Influence in English Literature.* Morpeth: St. John's College Press, 1932.

Barber, C. L. "T. S. Eliot After Strange Gods," *The Southern Review* (Baton Rouge, La.), VI, No. 2 (Autumn 1940), 387-416.

Barry, Iris. "The Ezra Pound Period," *The Bookman* (New York), LXXIV, No. 2 (October 1931), 159-71.

Batho, Edith, and Bonamy Dobrée (*q.v.*). *The Victorians and After; 1830-1914*, vol. IV of *Introductions to English Literature*, ed. Dobrée. London: The Cresset Press, 1938. (With a Chapter on the Economic Background by Guy Chapman.)

Beachcroft, T. O. "Mysticism as Criticism: A Conversation at the School for Critics," *The Symposium* (Syracuse, N. Y.), II, No. 2 (April 1931), 208-25.

———. Review of *The Poems of John Donne*, ed. H. J. C. Grierson, 1929; and *John Donne; Complete Poems and Selected Prose*, ed. John Hayward, 1929. *The Criterion* (London), IX, No. 37 (July 1930), 747-50.

———. "Traherne and the Doctrine of Felicity," *The Criterion* (London), IX, No. 35 (January 1930), 291-307.

Bennett, Joan. *Four Metaphysical Poets:* Donne, Herbert, Vaughan, Crashaw. Cambridge: Cambridge University Press, 1934.

Binyon, Laurence. "Gerard Hopkins and His Influence," *University of Toronto Quarterly*, VIII, No. 3 (April 1939), 264-70.

————. "A Study of Donne," *The Bookman* (London), LXVII, No. 400 (January 1925), 201-2.

Black, Matthew W., ed. Introductions to *Elizabethan and Seventeenth-Century Lyrics*. Philadelphia: J. B. Lippincott Co., 1938.

Blackmur, R. P. *The Double Agent;* Essays in Craft and Elucidation. New York: Arrow Editions, 1935.

————. *The Expense of Greatness*. New York: Arrow Editions, 1940.

————. "T. S. Eliot," *The Hound & Horn* (Cambridge, Mass.), I, No. 3 (March 1928), 187-213; No. 4 (June 1928), 291-319.

Blunden, Edmund. "On the Poems of Henry Vaughan," *The London Mercury*, XV, No. 85 (November 1926), 59-75. Reprinted as *On the Poems of Henry Vaughan;* Characteristics and Intimations. London: R. Cobden-Sanderson, 1927.

————. "The Unknown God: Vaughan, Wordsworth, Coleridge, Shelley," in his *Nature in English Literature*. London: Leonard & Virginia Woolf (The Hogarth Press), 1929. Pp. 60-88.

The Bookman (London), LXXIX, No. 474 (March 1931), 341-47. "In Memory of John Donne." (Articles by Hugh I'Anson Fausset, Frank R. Leavis, Christopher Saltmarshe, Cyril Tomkinson.)

Bredvold, Louis I. "The Naturalism of Donne in Relation to Some Renaissance Traditions," *The Journal of English and Germanic Philology* (Urbana, Ill.), XXII, No. 4 (October 1923), 471-502.

————. "The Religious Thought of Donne in Relation to Medieval and Later Traditions," in *Studies in Shakespeare, Milton, and Donne* (University of Michigan Publications, Language and Literature, I, 193-232). New York: The Macmillan Co., 1925.

Brenner, Rica. *Poets of Our Time*. New York: Harcourt, Brace & Co., 1941.

Brinkley, Roberta F., ed. Prefaces to *English Poetry of the Seventeenth Century*. New York: W. W. Norton & Co., 1936.

Brittin, Norman A. "Emerson and the Metaphysical Poets," *American Literature* (Durham, N. C.), VIII, No. 1 (March 1936), 1-21.

Brooke, Rupert. "John Donne, the Elizabethan," review of *The Poems of John Donne*, ed. Grierson, 1912. *The Nation* (London), XII, No. 20 (February 15, 1913), 825-26.

Brooks, Cleanth. *Modern Poetry and the Tradition*. Chapel Hill: University of North Carolina Press, 1939. (Includes "Three Revolutions in Poetry," from *The Southern Review*, 1936: I. "Metaphor and the Tradition," II. "Wit and High Seriousness," III. "Metaphysical Poetry and Propaganda Art." Also "The Modern Poet and the Tradition," from *The Virginia Quarterly Review*, 1935; "The Waste Land: Critique of the Myth," from *The Southern Review*, 1937.)

————. "Poets and Laureates," *The Southern Review* (Baton Rouge, La.), II, No. 2 (Autumn 1936), 391-96.

————, J. T. Purser, and R. P. Warren, eds. *An Approach to Literature;* A Collection of Prose and Verse with Analyses and Discussions. Baton Rouge: Louisiana State University Press, 1936. Revised ed., New

York: F. S. Crofts & Co., 1939, etc. (Includes Eliot's "Literature and the Modern World.")

——, and Warren. "The Reading of Modern Poetry," *The American Review* (New York), VIII, No. 4 (February 1937), 435-49. (Paper read at the meeting of the Modern Language Association: Richmond, December 1936. Article erroneously attributed to Allen Tate in *Purpose,* London, X, No. 1, January-March 1938, 31-41.)

——, and ——, eds. *Understanding Poetry.* New York: Henry Holt & Co., 1938.

Brooks, Van Wyck. *On Literature Today.* New York: E. P. Dutton & Co., 1941.

——. *Opinions of Oliver Allston.* New York: E. P. Dutton & Co., 1941.

Brown, Alec. "The Lyric Impulse in the Poetry of T. S. Eliot," in *Scrutinies,* II. London: Wishart & Co., 1931.

Brown, E. K. "Mr. Eliot and Some Enemies," *University of Toronto Quarterly,* VIII, No. 1 (October 1938), 69-84.

Burgum, Edwin Berry, ed. *The New Criticism;* An Anthology of Modern Æsthetics and Literary Criticism. New York: Prentice-Hall, 1930. (Includes essays by Croce, Eliot, Fernandez, Fry, Haldane, Muir, etc.)

Burke, Kenneth. *Counter-Statement.* New York: Harcourt, Brace & Co., 1931.

——. *The Philosophy of Literary Form.* Baton Rouge: Louisiana State University Press, 1941.

Burtt, Edwin Arthur. *The Metaphysical Foundations of Modern Physical Science;* A Historical and Critical Essay. London: Kegan Paul, Trench, Trubner & Co.; New York: Harcourt, Brace & Co., 1925.

Cairns, Huntington, Allen Tate, and Mark Van Doren. *Invitation to Learning.* New York: Random House, 1941. (Talks over Columbia Broadcasting System.)

Chambers, E. K. "The Disenchantment of the Elizabethans," in his *Sir Thomas Wyatt;* and Some Collected Studies. London: Sidgwick & Jackson, 1933. Pp. 181-204.

Chapin, Christina. "Henry Vaughan and the Modern Spirit," *The Nineteenth Century and After* (London), CXIV, No. 681 (November 1933), 619-28.

Clough, Benjamin C. "Notes on the Metaphysical Poets," *Modern Language Notes* (Baltimore, Md.), XXXV, No. 2 (February 1920), 115-17. (Donne, Carew, Dryden, Butler.)

Clutton-Brock, Arthur. "Crashaw's Christmas Poems," in his *More Essays on Religion.* London: Methuen & Co., 1927; New York: E. P. Dutton & Co., 1928. Pp. 1-10.

——. "Donne's Sermons," in his *Essays on Books.* London: Methuen & Co.; New York: E. P. Dutton & Co., 1920. Pp. 78-91.

——. "The Fantastic School of English Poetry," in *The Cambridge Modern History,* eds. A. W. Ward, G. W. Prothero, and Stanley Leathes.

New York: The Macmillan Co.; Cambridge: Cambridge University Press, 1906. IV, chap. 26, 760-75.

———. "George Herbert," "Marvell and Vaughan," in his *More Essays on Books*. London: Methuen & Co.; New York: E. P. Dutton & Co., 1921. Pp. 14-23, 134-48.

Coffin, Charles Monroe. *John Donne and the New Philosophy*. New York: Columbia University Press, 1937.

Cogan, Isabel. "John Donne: Poet and Metaphysician," *The Poetry Review* (London), XX, No. 3 (May-June 1929), 183-94.

Collin, W. E. "T. S. Eliot," *The Sewanee Review* (Tenn.), XXXIX, No. 1 (January-March 1931), 13-24.

———. "T. S. Eliot the Critic," *The Sewanee Review* (Tenn.), XXXIX, No. 4 (October-December 1931), 419-24.

Courthope, W. J. "The Intellectual Conflict of the Seventeenth Century," in his *A History of English Poetry*. London: Macmillan & Co., 1903. III, chaps. 6, 8, 10, 11, 12.

Cowley, Malcolm, ed. *After the Genteel Tradition; American Writers Since 1910*. New York: W. W. Norton & Co., 1937.

Crofts, J. E. V. "John Donne," *Essays and Studies of the English Association*, XXII (1936), 128-43. Oxford: The Clarendon Press, 1937.

Daiches, David. *Poetry and the Modern World; A Study of Poetry in England Between 1900 and 1939*. Chicago: University of Chicago Press, 1940.

Daniells, J. R. "T. S. Eliot and his Relation to T. E. Hulme," *University of Toronto Quarterly*, II, No. 3 (April 1933), 380-96.

Daniels, R. Balfour. *Some Seventeenth-Century Worthies in a Twentieth Century Mirror*. Chapel Hill: University of North Carolina Press, 1940.

Day Lewis, Cecil. "A Hope for Poetry," in his *Collected Poems, 1929-1933*. New York: Random House, 1935. Pp. 161-256.

De La Mare, Walter. "An Elizabethan Poet and Modern Poetry," review of *The Poems of John Donne*, ed. Grierson, 1912; and *Georgian Poetry, 1911-1912*. *The Edinburgh Review*, CCXVII, No. 444 (April 1913), 372-86.

Deutsch, Babette. *Potable Gold; Some Notes on Poetry and This Age*. New York: W. W. Norton & Co., 1929.

———. *This Modern Poetry*. New York: W. W. Norton & Co., 1935; London: Faber & Faber, 1936.

———. "T. S. Eliot and the Laodiceans," *The American Scholar* (New York), IX, No. 1 (Winter 1939-1940), 19-30.

Dobrée, Bonamy, ed. *Introductions to English Literature*. London: The Cresset Press, 1938, 1939.

———. "T. S. Eliot," in his *The Lamp and the Lute; Studies in Six Modern Authors*. Oxford: The Clarendon Press, 1929. Pp. 107-33.

Doggett, Frank A. "Donne's Platonism," *The Sewanee Review* (Tenn.), XLII, No. 3 (July-September 1934), 274-92.

Douds, John B. "Donne's Technique of Dissonance," *P M L A, Publications of the Modern Language Association of America* (New York), LII, No. 4 (December 1937), 1051-61.

Drew, Elizabeth. *Directions in Modern Poetry.* New York: W. W. Norton & Co., 1940. (In Collaboration with John L. Sweeney.)

———. *Discovering Poetry.* New York: W. W. Norton & Co., 1933.

Duncan, Carson S. *The New Science and English Literature in the Classical Period.* Menasha, Wis.: George Banta Publishing Co., 1913. (The Collegiate Press.)

Dunn, Esther Cloudman, "First Aid to Moderns," review of *Themes and Conventions of Elizabethan Tragedy* by M. C. Bradbrook. *The Saturday Review of Literature* (New York), XII, No. 1 (May 4, 1935), 22.

Edman, Irwin. *The Contemporary and His Soul.* New York: Jonathan Cape & Harrison Smith, 1931.

Eliot, T. S. *After Strange Gods; A Primer of Modern Heresy.* London: Faber & Faber; New York: Harcourt, Brace & Co., 1934. (The Page-Barbour Lectures, University of Virginia, 1933.)

———. "Andrew Marvell," review of his *Miscellaneous Poems. The Nation and the Athenaeum* (London), XXXIII, No. 26 (September 29, 1923), 809.

———. "The Borderline of Prose," *The New Statesman* (London), IX, No. 215 (May 19, 1917), 157-59.

———. "Contemporanea," *The Egoist* (London), V, No. 6 (June-July 1918), 84-85.

———. "Dante as a 'Spiritual Leader,'" review of *Dante* by Henry D. Sidgwick. *The Athenaeum* (London), CLII, No. 4692 (April 2, 1920), 441-42.

———. "Deux Attitudes Mystiques: Dante et Donne," *Chroniques,* No. 3 (1927), 149-71. *Le Roseau d'Or—Oeuvres et Chroniques:* 14. Paris: Librarie Plon, 1927. (Translated by Jean de Menasce.)

———. "The Devotional Poets of the Seventeenth Century: Donne, Herbert, Crashaw," *The Listener* (London), III, No. 63 (March 26, 1930), 552-53. (Published by the British Broadcasting Corporation.)

———. *Elizabethan Essays.* London: Faber & Faber, 1934.

———. "An Emotional Unity," *The Dial* (New York), LXXXIV, No. 2 (February 1928), 109-12.

———. *Essays Ancient and Modern.* London: Faber & Faber; New York: Harcourt, Brace & Co., 1936.

———. *Ezra Pound;* His Metric and Poetry. New York: Alfred A. Knopf, 1917.

———. *For Lancelot Andrewes;* Essays on Style and Order. London: Faber & Gwyer, 1928; Garden City, N. Y.: Doubleday, Doran & Co., 1929.

———. "George Herbert," *The Spectator* (London), CXLVIII, No. 5411 (March 12, 1932), 360-61.

———. "The Golden Ass of Apuleius," review of The Adlington-Elizabethan

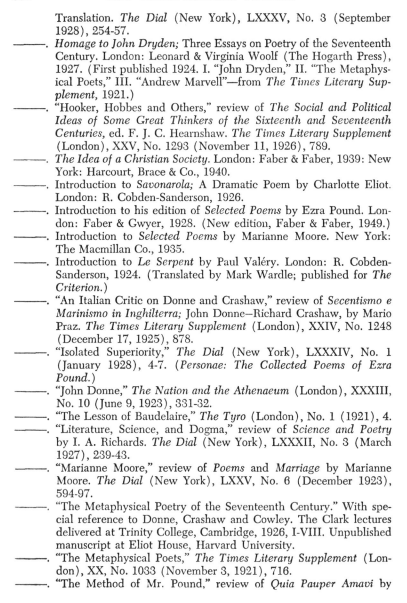

Translation. *The Dial* (New York), LXXXV, No. 3 (September 1928), 254-57.

———. *Homage to John Dryden;* Three Essays on Poetry of the Seventeenth Century. London: Leonard & Virginia Woolf (The Hogarth Press), 1927. (First published 1924. I. "John Dryden," II. "The Metaphysical Poets," III. "Andrew Marvell"—from *The Times Literary Supplement,* 1921.)

———. "Hooker, Hobbes and Others," review of *The Social and Political Ideas of Some Great Thinkers of the Sixteenth and Seventeenth Centuries,* ed. F. J. C. Hearnshaw. *The Times Literary Supplement* (London), XXV, No. 1293 (November 11, 1926), 789.

———. *The Idea of a Christian Society.* London: Faber & Faber, 1939: New York: Harcourt, Brace & Co., 1940.

———. Introduction to *Savonarola;* A Dramatic Poem by Charlotte Eliot. London: R. Cobden-Sanderson, 1926.

———. Introduction to his edition of *Selected Poems* by Ezra Pound. London: Faber & Gwyer, 1928. (New edition, Faber & Faber, 1949.)

———. Introduction to *Selected Poems* by Marianne Moore. New York: The Macmillan Co., 1935.

———. Introduction to *Le Serpent* by Paul Valéry. London: R. Cobden-Sanderson, 1924. (Translated by Mark Wardle; published for *The Criterion.*)

———. "An Italian Critic on Donne and Crashaw," review of *Secentismo e Marinismo in Inghilterra;* John Donne–Richard Crashaw, by Mario Praz. *The Times Literary Supplement* (London), XXIV, No. 1248 (December 17, 1925), 878.

———. "Isolated Superiority," *The Dial* (New York), LXXXIV, No. 1 (January 1928), 4-7. (*Personae: The Collected Poems of Ezra Pound.*)

———. "John Donne," *The Nation and the Athenaeum* (London), XXXIII, No. 10 (June 9, 1923), 331-32.

———. "The Lesson of Baudelaire," *The Tyro* (London), No. 1 (1921), 4.

———. "Literature, Science, and Dogma," review of *Science and Poetry* by I. A. Richards. *The Dial* (New York), LXXXII, No. 3 (March 1927), 239-43.

———. "Marianne Moore," review of *Poems* and *Marriage* by Marianne Moore. *The Dial* (New York), LXXV, No. 6 (December 1923), 594-97.

———. "The Metaphysical Poetry of the Seventeenth Century." With special reference to Donne, Crashaw and Cowley. The Clark lectures delivered at Trinity College, Cambridge, 1926, I-VIII. Unpublished manuscript at Eliot House, Harvard University.

———. "The Metaphysical Poets," *The Times Literary Supplement* (London), XX, No. 1033 (November 3, 1921), 716.

———. "The Method of Mr. Pound," review of *Quia Pauper Amavi* by

Ezra Pound. *The Athenaeum* (London), CLI, No. 4669 (October 24, 1919), 1065-66.

———. "The Minor Metaphysicals: from Cowley to Dryden," *The Listener* (London), III, No. 65 (April 9, 1930), 641-42.

———. "Mystic and Politician as Poet: Vaughan, Traherne, Marvell, Milton," *The Listener* (London), III, No. 64 (April 2, 1930), 590-91.

———. "A Note on Poetry and Belief," *The Enemy* (London), I, No. 1 (January 1927), 15-17.

———. "A Note on the Verse of John Milton," *Essays and Studies of the English Association*, XXI (1935), 32-40. Oxford: The Clarendon Press, 1936.

———. "Note sur Mallarmé et Poe," *La Nouvelle Revue Française* (Paris), XXVII, No. 158 (November 1, 1926), 524-26. (Translated by Ramon Fernandez.)

———. "On a Recent Piece of Criticism," *Purpose* (London), X, No. 2 (April-June 1938), 90-94. (G. W. Stonier's "The Mystery of Ezra Pound.")

———. "The Preacher as Artist," review of *Donne's Sermons; Selected Passages.* With an Essay, by Logan Pearsall Smith. *The Athenaeum* (London), CLI, No. 4674 (November 28, 1919), 1252-53.

———. Preface to his translation of *Anabasis; A Poem* by St.-J. Perse, pseud. (Aléxis Saint-Léger Léger). London: Faber & Faber, 1930.

———. "Prose and Verse," *The Chapbook* (London), IV (?), No. 22 (April 1921), 3-10.

———. "Reflections on *Vers Libre*," *The New Statesman and Nation* (London), VIII, No. 204 (March 3, 1917), 518-19.

———. "Religion Without Humanism," *Humanism and America; Essays on the Outlook of Modern Civilisation*, ed. Norman Foerster. New York: Farrar & Rinehart, 1930. Pp. 105-12.

———. Review of *Baudelaire and the Symbolists* by Peter Quennell. *The Criterion* (London), IX, No. 35 (January 1930), 357-59.

———. Review of *God: Being an Introduction to the Science of Metabiology* by J. Middleton Murry. *The Criterion* (London), IX, No. 35 (January 1930), 333-36.

———. Review of *Reason and Romanticism* by Herbert Read; and *Messages* by Ramon Fernandez. *The New Criterion* (London), IV, No. 4 (October 1926), 751-57.

———. "Rhyme and Reason: The Poetry of John Donne," *The Listener* (London), III, No. 62 (March 19, 1930), 502-3.

———. *The Sacred Wood; Essays on Poetry and Criticism.* London: Methuen & Co., 1920; New York: Alfred A. Knopf, 1921.

———. *Selected Essays;* New Edition. New York: Harcourt, Brace & Co., 1950. (Original edition, 1932.)

———. "Shakespearian Criticism: From Dryden to Coleridge," in *A Companion to Shakespeare Studies*, eds. Harley Granville-Barker and

302   THE METAPHYSICAL PASSION

G. B. Harrison. Cambridge: Cambridge University Press; New York: The Macmillan Co., 1934. Pp. 287-99.

———. "The Silurist," review of *On the Poems of Henry Vaughan* by Edmund Blunden. *The Dial* (New York), LXXXIII, No. 3 (September 1927), 259-63.

———. "Swinburne and the Elizabethans," review of *Contemporaries of Shakespeare* by A. C. Swinburne, ed. Edmund Gosse. *The Athenaeum* (London), CLI, No. 4664 (September 19, 1919), 909-10.

———. "Thinking in Verse: a Survey of Early Seventeenth-Century Poetry," *The Listener* (London), III, No. 61 (March 12, 1930), 441-43.

———. "Ulysses, Order, and Myth," review of *Ulysses* by James Joyce. *The Dial* (New York), LXXV, No. 5 (November 1923), 480-83.

———. *The Use of Poetry and the Use of Criticism;* Studies in the Relation of Criticism to Poetry in England. Cambridge, Mass.: Harvard University Press; London: Faber & Faber, 1933. (The Charles Eliot Norton Lectures for 1932-1933.)

Ellis, Havelock. "Cowley," *The New Statesman* (London), O. S. XIII, No. 327 (July 12, 1919), 369-71.

Empson, William. "Henry Vaughan, An Early Romantic," *The Cambridge Review* (London), L, No. 1241 (May 31, 1929), 495-96.

———. *Seven Types of Ambiguity.* London: Chatto & Windus, 1930; New York: Harcourt, Brace & Co., 1931. (Second edition, revised, 1947.)

———. *Some Versions of Pastoral.* London: Chatto & Windus, 1935. (Includes "Marvell's 'Garden,'" from *Scrutiny*, 1932.)

Every, George [G. E.]. Review of *Poetry and Prose of John Donne,* ed. A. Desmond Hawkins. *Purpose* (London), X, No. 4 (October-December 1938), 232-34.

Fausset, Hugh I'Anson. *John Donne; A Study in Discord.* London: Jonathan Cape, 1924.

———. *The Modern Dilemma.* London: J. M. Dent & Sons; New York: E. P. Dutton & Co., 1930.

Fergusson, Francis. "T. S. Eliot and His Impersonal Theory of Art," in *The American Caravan; A Yearbook of American Literature,* eds. Van Wyck Brooks, Alfred Kreymborg, Lewis Mumford, Paul Rosenfeld. New York: The Macaulay Co., 1927. Pp. 446-53.

Fitts, Dudley. "Music Fit for the Odes," review of *A Draft of XXX Cantos* by Ezra Pound, 1930. *The Hound & Horn* (New York), IV, No. 2 (January-March 1931), 278-89.

———. "Two Anthologies," review of *Circumference,* ed. Genevieve Taggard, and *Olive, Cypress and Palm,* comp. Mina Curtiss. *The Hound & Horn* (New York), IV, No. 1 (October-December 1930), 149-54.

Fletcher, John Gould. "Two Elements in Poetry," *The Saturday Review of Literature* (New York), IV, No. 5 (August 27, 1927), 65-66.

Forgotson, E. S. "The Poetic Method of Robert Penn Warren," *American Prefaces* (Iowa City), VI, No. 2 (Winter 1941), 130-46.

Forster, E. M. "T. S. Eliot and His Difficulties," *Life and Letters* (London), II, No. 13 (June 1929), 417-25.

Foxall, Edgar. "The Politics of W. H. Auden," *The Bookman* (London), LXXXV, No. 510 (March 1934), 474-75.

Frost, A. C. "Donne and a Modern Poet," *The Cambridge Review* (London), L, No. 1239 (May 17, 1929), 449-50. (T. S. Eliot.)

The Fugitive. Nashville, Tenn.: The Fugitive Publishing Co., April 1922 to December 1925. (Poetry and criticism by Ransom, Tate, Warren, Laura Riding, etc.)

Garrod, H. W. "Cowley, Johnson, and the 'Metaphysicals,'" in his *The Profession of Poetry; and Other Lectures.* Oxford: The Clarendon Press, 1929. Pp. 110-30.

George, Robert E. G. *Outflying Philosophy;* A Literary Study of the Religious Element in Donne, Sir Thomas Browne, Henry Vaughan . . . by Robert Sencourt, pseud. Hildesheim, Germany: F. Borgmeyer, 1924; London: Simpkin, Marshall, Hamilton, Kent & Co., 1925.

Gosse, Edmund. *The Jacobean Poets.* New York: Charles Scribner's Sons; London: J. Murray, 1894, 1899.

————. "Metaphysical Poetry," in his *More Books on the Table.* London: William Heinemann; New York: Charles Scribner's Sons, 1923. Pp. 307-13.

————. *Seventeenth Century Studies;* A Contribution to the History of English Poetry. London: Kegan Paul, Trench & Co., 1883. (Included as vol. I in *Collected Essays.* London: William Heinemann, 1913; New York: Charles Scribner's Sons, 1914.)

Grafton, Samuel. "I'd Rather Be Right," *The New York Post,* September 9, 1942.

Greenlaw, Edwin. "The New Science and English Literature in the Seventeenth Century," *The Johns Hopkins Alumni Magazine* (Baltimore, Md.), XIII, No. 4 (June 1925), 331-59.

Gregory, Horace. "American Poetry 1930-1940," *Decision* (New York), I, No. 1 (January 1941), 24-29.

————. "Fare Forward, Voyagers," review of *Four Quartets* by T. S. Eliot. *The New York Times Book Review,* May 16, 1943.

Grierson, Sir Herbert J. C. *The Background of English Literature;* and Other Collected Essays & Addresses. London: Chatto & Windus, 1925; New York: Henry Holt & Co., 1926. (Chap. 1, "The Metaphysical Poets," a reprint of his introduction to *Metaphysical Lyrics & Poems.*)

————. *Cross Currents in English Literature of the XVIIth Century;* or The World, The Flesh, & The Spirit, Their Actions & Reactions. London: Chatto & Windus, 1929. (Messenger Lectures, Cornell University, 1926-1927.)

————. "Donne and Lucretius," *The Times Literary Supplement* (London), XXVIII, No. 1453 (December 5, 1929), 1032.

————. *The First Half of the Seventeenth Century,* vol. VII of *Periods of*

European Literature, ed. George Saintsbury. Edinburgh: William
Blackwood & Sons; New York: Charles Scribner's Sons, 1906.
————, ed. Introductions & Commentary to *The Poems of John Donne.*
Oxford: The Clarendon Press, 1912. (Reprinted, Oxford University
Press, 1929, 1933, 1938.) Vol. II.
————, ed. Introduction to *Metaphysical Lyrics & Poems of The Seven-
teenth Century;* Donne to Butler. Oxford: The Clarendon Press,
1921. (Reprinted 1925, 1928, 1936.)
————. "John Donne," in *The Cambridge History of English Literature,* eds.
A. W. Ward & A. R. Waller. Cambridge: Cambridge University
Press; New York: G. P. Putnam's Sons, 1909. IV, chap. 11, 196-223.
————. Review of *Donne the Craftsman* by Pierre Legouis. *The Review of
English Studies* (London), VI, No. 22 (April 1930), 214-16.
————. " 'What Is Truth?' " Review of *The Seventeenth Century Back-
ground* by Basil Willey. *Scrutiny* (Cambridge, Eng.), III, No. 3
(December 1934), 294-303.
Guiney, Louise Imogen. "Lovelace and Vaughan: A Speculation," *The Cath-
olic World* (New York), XCV, No. 569 (August 1912), 646-55.
————. "Milton and Vaughan," *The Quarterly Review* (London and New
York), CCXX, No. 439 (April 1914), 353-64.
Hamilton, George R. "Wit and Beauty: A Study of Metaphysical Poetry,"
The London Mercury, XIV, No. 84 (October 1926), 606-20. (Donne
and Francis Thompson.)
Harrison, Charles T. "The Ancient Atomists and English Literature of the
Seventeenth Century," *Harvard Studies in Classical Philology,* XLV,
1-70. Cambridge, Mass.: Harvard University Press, 1934.
The Harvard Advocate (Cambridge, Mass.), CXXV, No. 3 (December
1938), 3-42, 45-48. "For T. S. Eliot." (Notes, Observations, and
Homage To T. S. Eliot—A Symposium—by Conrad Aiken, Howard
Baker, R. P. Blackmur, R. W. Church, Richard Eberhart, Lawrence
Leighton, R. T. S. Lowell, Archibald MacLeish, F. O. Matthiessen,
Merrill Moore, Roberta Morgan and Albert Wohlstetter, George
Marion O'Donnell, Frederic Prokosch, Theodore Spencer, Wallace
Stevens, Allen Tate, W. G. Tinckom-Fernandez, Robert Penn War-
ren, William Carlos Williams. With Eight Poems by Eliot, pp.
11-16.)
————, CXXVII, No. 3 (December 1940), 3-44. "Wallace Stevens Num-
ber." (Articles and Statements by Howard Baker, Cleanth Brooks,
John Finch, Harry Levin, F. O. Matthiessen, Marianne Moore,
Delmore Schwartz, Hi Simons, Theodore Spencer, Allen Tate,
Robert Penn Warren, William Carlos Williams, Morton Dauwen
Zabel. With Poems, 1899-1940, by Stevens.)
Hebel, J. William. *English Seventeenth Century Literature;* A Brief Working
Bibliography. New York: Columbia University Press, 1929. (With
Frank A. Patterson; assisted by C. M. Coffin.)
Heywood, Terence. "Hopkins' Ancestry," *Poetry: A Magazine of Verse*

(Chicago), LIV, No. 4 (July 1939), 209-18; No. 5 (August 1939), 271-79.

Hodgson, Geraldine E. "Anglo-Catholic Mystics and Others," in her *English Mystics*. London: A. R. Mowbray & Co.; Milwaukee: The Morehouse Publishing Co., 1922. Pp. 208-72.

Horton, Philip. "The Greenberg Manuscript and Hart Crane's Poetry," *The Southern Review* (Baton Rouge, La.), II, No. 1 (Summer 1936), 148-59.

———. "Identity of S. B. Greenberg," *The Southern Review* (Baton Rouge, La.), II, No. 2 (Autumn 1936), 422-24.

Hughes, Glenn. *Imagism & the Imagists; A Study in Modern Poetry.* Stanford, Calif.: Stanford University Press; London: Oxford University Press, 1931.

Hughes, Merritt Y. "Kidnapping Donne," *Essays in Criticism* (University of California Publications in English, Second Series, IV, 61-89). Berkeley, Calif.: University of California Press, 1934.

———. "The Lineage of 'The Extasie,'" *The Modern Language Review* (Cambridge, Eng.), XXVII, No. 1 (January 1932), 1-5.

Hulme, T. E. *Speculations; Essays on Humanism and the Philosophy of Art,* ed. Herbert Read. London: Kegan Paul, Trench, Trubner & Co.; New York: Harcourt, Brace & Co., 1924. (Includes as Appendix A "The Translator's Preface to Sorel's 'Reflections on Violence,'" from *The New Age*, 1915. Second edition, 1936.)

Hutchinson, F. E. "George Herbert: A Tercentenary," *The Nineteenth Century and After* (London), CXIII, No. 673 (March 1933), 358-68.

———. "The Sacred Poets," in *The Cambridge History of English Literature,* eds. A. W. Ward & A. R. Waller. Cambridge: Cambridge University Press; New York: G. P. Putnam's Sons, 1911. VII, chap. 2, 26-47.

Jack, Peter Monro. Review of *Directions in Modern Poetry* by Elizabeth Drew. *The New York Times Book Review*, May 19, 1940.

———. Review of *Eleven Poems on the Same Theme* by R. P. Warren. *The New York Times Book Review*, April 26, 1942.

———. Review of *The Family Reunion* by T. S. Eliot. *The New York Times Book Review*, April 9, 1939.

James, D. G. *Scepticism and Poetry; An Essay on the Poetic Imagination.* London: George Allen & Unwin, 1937.

Jones, Richard F. "Science and English Prose Style in the Third Quarter of the Seventeenth Century," *P M L A, Publications of the Modern Language Association of America* (New York), XLV, No. 4 (December 1930), 997-1009.

Jones, Rufus M. "Thomas Traherne and the Spiritual Poets of the Seventeenth Century," in his *Spiritual Reformers in the 16th & 17th Centuries.* London: Macmillan & Co., 1914. Pp. 320-35.

Judson, Alexander Corbin. "Abraham Cowley in Arcadia," *The Sewanee Review* (Tenn.), XXXI, No. 2 (April-June 1923), 220-26.

———. "The Source of Henry Vaughan's Ideas Concerning God in Nature,"

306   THE METAPHYSICAL PASSION

Studies in Philology (Chapel Hill, N. C.), XXIV, No. 4 (October 1927), 592-606.

Kemp, Violet A. "Mystic Utterance in Certain English Poets," *The Hibbert Journal* (London), XXVI, No. 3 (April 1928), 474-83.

Knight, G. Wilson. *The Christian Renaissance;* With Interpretations of Dante, Shakespeare and Goethe, And a Note on T. S. Eliot. Toronto: The Macmillan Co., 1933.

Krutch, Joseph Wood. *The Modern Temper;* A Study and a Confession. New York: Harcourt, Brace & Co., 1929.

Laboulle, M. J. J. "T. S. Eliot and some French Poets," *Revue de Littérature comparée* (Paris), XVI, No. 2 (April-June 1936), 389-99.

Lea, Kathleen M. "Conceits," *The Modern Language Review* (Cambridge, Eng.), XX, No. 4 (October 1925), 389-406.

Leavis, Frank R., ed. *Determinations;* Critical Essays. London: Chatto & Windus, 1934. (Essays by Ronald Bottrall, William Empson, James Smith, etc. With an Introduction.)

———. *How to Teach Reading;* A Primer for Ezra Pound. Cambridge, Eng.: Gordon Fraser, The Minority Press, 1932.

———. "Mr. Eliot, Mr. Wyndham Lewis and Lawrence," review of *After Strange Gods* by T. S. Eliot. *Scrutiny* (Cambridge, Eng.), III, No. 2 (September 1934), 184-91.

———. *New Bearings in English Poetry;* A Study of the Contemporary Situation. London: Chatto & Windus, 1932.

———. *Revaluation;* Tradition & Development in English Poetry. London: Chatto & Windus, 1936. (Includes "English Poetry in the Seventeenth Century," from *Scrutiny*, 1935, as chap. 1: "The Line of Wit.")

Legouis, Pierre. *Donne the Craftsman;* An essay upon the structure of the *Songs and Sonets.* Paris: Henri Didier; London: Oxford University Press, 1928.

———. "Sur un vers de Donne," *Revue Anglo-Américaine* (Paris), X, No. 1 (October 1932), 49-50; No. 3 (February 1933), 228-30.

Leishman, James B. *The Metaphysical Poets;* Donne, Herbert, Vaughan, Traherne. Oxford: The Clarendon Press, 1934.

Loudon, K. M. *Two Mystic Poets;* and Other Essays. Oxford: Basil Blackwell, 1922. (Crashaw and Vaughan.)

Lowes, John Livingston. *Convention and Revolt in Poetry.* London: Constable & Co.; Boston: Houghton Mifflin Co., 1919, etc. (Revised edition, 1930.)

Lucas, F. L. *Authors Dead and Living.* London: Chatto & Windus, 1926. (Essays on Donne, Vaughan, Marvell, etc.)

———. *The Decline and Fall of the Romantic Ideal.* Cambridge: Cambridge University Press; New York: The Macmillan Co., 1936.

Luccock, Halford E. *American Mirror;* Social, Ethical and Religious Aspects of American Literature, 1930-1940. New York: The Macmillan Co., 1940.

———. *Contemporary American Literature and Religion*. Chicago: Willett, Clark & Co., 1934.

MacCarthy, Desmond. *Criticism*. London: G. P. Putnam's Sons, 1932.

McGreevy, Thomas. *Thomas Stearns Eliot; A Study*. London: Chatto & Windus, 1931.

MacLeish, Archibald. As interviewed by Robert Van Gelder, *The New York Times Book Review*, May 10, 1942.

———. "Nevertheless One Debt," *Poetry: A Magazine of Verse* (Chicago), XXXVIII, No. 4 (July 1931), 208-16.

MacNeice, Louis. *Modern Poetry; A Personal Essay*. London: Oxford University Press, 1938.

Massingham, Harold J., ed. Introduction to *A Treasury of Seventeenth Century English Verse; From the Death of Shakespeare to the Restoration* (1616-1660). London: Macmillan & Co., 1919.

Masters, Charlie. "Some Observations on 'Burnt Norton,'" *American Prefaces* (Iowa City), VI, No. 2 (Winter 1941), 99-112; No. 3 (Spring 1941), 212-31.

Matthiessen, F. O. *The Achievement of T. S. Eliot; An Essay on the Nature of Poetry*. New York: Oxford University Press, 1947. (Revised and enlarged from 1935 edition.)

Mégroz, R. L. "The Wit and Fantasy of Donne," *The Dublin Magazine*, N. S. I, No. 2 (April-June 1926), 47-51.

Melton, Wightman Fletcher. *The Rhetoric of John Donne's Verse*. Baltimore: J. H. Furst Co., 1906.

Millett, Fred B. *Contemporary American Authors; A Critical Survey and 219 Bio-Bibliographies*. New York: Harcourt, Brace & Co., 1940. (Based on J. M. Manly and E. Rickert's *Contemporary American Literature*, 1922.)

Mitchell, F. L. "Jack Donne, the Pagan: Doctor John Donne, the Divine," *The Bookman's Journal* (London), XIV, No. 55 (April 1926), 15-18.

Moore, John F. "Scholasticism, Donne, and the Metaphysical Conceit," *Revue Anglo-Américaine* (Paris), XIII, No. 4 (April 1936), 289-97.

Moore, Marianne. "If a Man Die," review of *The Coming Forth by Day of Osiris Jones* and *Preludes for Memnon* by Conrad Aiken. *The Hound & Horn* (New York), V, No. 2 (January-March 1932), 313-20.

———. "A Machinery of Satisfaction," review of *Marina* by T. S. Eliot. *Poetry: A Magazine of Verse* (Chicago), XXXVIII, No. 6 (September 1931), 337-39.

Moore, Merrill, comp. *The Fugitive; Clippings and Comment about the* magazine and the members of the group that published it. Boston, 1939. (With a Post-Script by John Crowe Ransom.)

Moorman, F. W. "Cavalier Lyrists," in *The Cambridge History of English Literature*, eds. A. W. Ward & A. R. Waller. Cambridge: Cambridge University Press; New York: G. P. Putnam's Sons, 1911. VII, chap. 1, 21-25.

More, Paul Elmer. "The Cleft Eliot," review of *Selected Essays* by T. S. Eliot. *The Saturday Review of Literature* (New York), IX, No. 17 (November 12, 1932), 233, 235.

Morley, Christopher. "Courting John Donne," *The Saturday Review of Literature* (New York), XVI, No. 1 (May 1, 1937), 10, 16.

Muir, Edwin. *The Present Age from 1914*, vol. V of *Introductions to English Literature*, ed. Dobrée. London: The Cresset Press, 1939.

———. *Transition;* Essays on Contemporary Literature. New York: The Viking Press, 1926.

Murry, J. Middleton. *Aspects of Literature*. London: W. Collins Sons & Co.; New York: Alfred A. Knopf, 1920.

Naylor, Edward W. "Three Seventeenth Century Poet-Parsons and Music," *Proceedings of the Musical Association* (London), 54th Session, 1927-28 (March 27, 1928), pp. 93-113. (Herbert, Herrick, and Traherne.)

Nethercot, Arthur H. "The Attitude toward 'Metaphysical Poetry' in Neo-Classical England." (Unpublished Ph.D. dissertation, University of Chicago, 1922.)

———. "Milton, Jonson, and the Young Cowley," *Modern Language Notes* (Baltimore, Md.), XLIX, No. 3 (March 1934), 158-62.

———. "The Reputation of John Donne as Metrist," *The Sewanee Review* (Tenn.), XXX, No. 4 (October 1922), 463-74.

———. "The Reputation of the 'Metaphysical Poets' during the Age of Johnson and the 'Romantic Revival,'" *Studies in Philology* (Chapel Hill, N. C.), XXII, No. 1 (January 1925), 81-132.

———. "The Reputation of the 'Metaphysical Poets' during the Age of Pope," *Philological Quarterly* (Iowa City), IV, No. 1 (January 1925), 161-79.

———. "The Reputation of the 'Metaphysical Poets' during the Seventeenth Century," *The Journal of English and Germanic Philology* (Urbana, Ill.), XXIII, No. 2 (April 1924), 173-98.

———. "The Reputation of Native vs. Foreign 'Metaphysical Poets' in England," *The Modern Language Review* (Cambridge, Eng.), XXV, No. 2 (April 1930), 152-64.

———. "The Term 'Metaphysical Poets' before Johnson," *Modern Language Notes* (Baltimore, Md.), XXXVII, No. 1 (January 1922), 11-17.

Newbolt, Sir Henry, ed. Introduction to *Devotional Poets of the XVII Century*. London: Thomas Nelson & Sons, 1929. (Donne, Herbert, Crashaw, Herrick, Vaughan, Traherne.)

Nicolson, Marjorie. "The 'New Astronomy' and English Literary Imagination," *Studies in Philology* (Chapel Hill, N. C.), XXXII, No. 3 (July 1935), 428-62.

———. "The Telescope and Imagination," *Modern Philology* (Chicago), XXXII, No. 3 (February 1935), 233-60.

Orange, U. M. D. "The Poetry of George Herbert," *The Poetry Review* (London), XXIV, No. 2 (March-April 1933), 118-27.

Oras, Ants. *The Critical Ideas of T. S. Eliot.* Tartu, Esthonia: K. Mattiesen, 1932.

Osmond, Percy H. *The Mystical Poets of the English Church.* London: Society for Promoting Christian Knowledge; New York: The Macmillan Co., 1919.

Parkes, Henry Bamford. *The Pragmatic Test;* Essays on the History of Ideas. San Francisco: The Colt Press, 1941.

Partridge, A. C. *T. S. Eliot.* (Publications of the University of Pretoria, Series No. III: Arts and Social Sciences No. 4.) Pretoria, South Africa, 1937.

Pinto, V. de Sola. *The English Renaissance;* 1510-1688, vol. II of *Introductions to English Literature,* ed. Dobrée. London: The Cresset Press, 1938. (With a Chapter on Literature and Music by Bruce Pattison.)

Potter, George Reuben. "John Donne's Discovery of Himself," *Essays in Criticism* (University of California Publications in English, Second Series, IV, 3-23). Berkeley, Calif.: University of California Press, 1934.

——. "Milton's Early Poems: The School of Donne, and the Elizabethan Sonneteers," *Philological Quarterly* (Iowa City), VI, No. 4 (October 1927), 396-400.

Pottle, Frederick A. *The Idiom of Poetry.* Ithaca, N. Y.: Cornell University Press, 1941. (Second edition, revised, 1946.)

Pound, Ezra. *Antheil and the Treatise on Harmony.* Paris: Three Mountains Press, 1924. (Chicago: Pascal Covici, 1927. With Supplementary Notes.)

——. *Culture;* The Intellectual Autobiography of a Poet. Norfolk, Conn.: New Directions; (*Guide to Kulchur*) London: Faber & Faber, 1938.

——. "Drunken Helots and Mr. Eliot," *The Egoist* (London), IV, No. 5 (June 1917), 72-74.

——. *Gaudier-Brzeska;* A Memoir Including the Published Writings of the Sculptor, and a Selection from his Letters. London: John Lane, The Bodley Head, 1916. (Laidlaw & Laidlaw, 1939.)

——. *Instigations.* New York: Boni & Liveright, 1920. (Together with An Essay on the Chinese Written Character by the late Ernest Fenollosa.)

——. *Make It New;* Essays. London: Faber & Faber, 1934; New Haven: Yale University Press, 1935.

——. *Pavannes and Divisions.* New York: Alfred A. Knopf, 1918.

——. *Polite Essays.* Norfolk, Conn.: New Directions, 1940. (Includes *How to Read*, 1931, and sections from *Active Anthology*, 1933.)

——. *The Spirit of Romance;* An Attempt to Define Somewhat the Charm of the Pre-Renaissance Literature of Latin Europe. London: J. M. Dent & Sons; New York: E. P. Dutton & Co., 1910.

Powell, Dilys. *Descent from Parnassus.* London: The Cresset Press; New York: The Macmillan Co., 1934.

Praz, Mario. "Mysticism or Advocatus Diaboli," *The Criterion* (London), VIII, No. 32 (April 1929), 460-79.

——. "T. S. Eliot and Dante," *The Southern Review* (Baton Rouge, La.), II, No. 3 (Winter 1937), 525-48.

Quennell, Peter, ed. Introduction and Forewords to *Aspects of Seventeenth Century Verse*. London: Jonathan Cape, 1933. (Revised edition, Home & Van Thal, 1947.)

——. *Baudelaire and the Symbolists;* Five Essays. London: Chatto & Windus, 1929.

Quiller-Couch, Sir Arthur. "Some Seventeenth Century Poets," in his *Studies in Literature*. Cambridge: Cambridge University Press; New York: G. P. Putnam's Sons, 1918. (First Series. Includes Donne, Herbert and Vaughan, Traherne, Crashaw, etc., pp. 96-167.)

Ramsay, Mary P. *Les Doctrines médiévales chez Donne;* le Poète métaphysicien de l'Angleterre. London: Oxford University Press, 1916 (with thesis note), 1917. (Second edition, 1924.)

Ransom, John Crowe. "Mr. Empson's Muddles," *The Southern Review* (Baton Rouge, La.), IV, No. 2 (Autumn 1938), 322-39.

——. *The New Criticism*. Norfolk, Conn.: New Directions, 1941. (Includes "Eliot and the Metaphysicals," from *Accent*, as Section 5 of "T. S. Eliot: the Historical Critic.")

——. "T. S. Eliot as Dramatist," *Poetry: A Magazine of Verse* (Chicago), LIV, No. 5 (August 1939), 264-71.

——. "T. S. Eliot on Criticism," review of *The Use of Poetry and the Use of Criticism* by Eliot, 1933. *The Saturday Review of Literature* (New York), X, No. 36 (March 24, 1934), 574.

——. *The World's Body*. New York: Charles Scribner's Sons, 1938. (Includes "Shakespeare at Sonnets," from *The Southern Review*.)

Read, Herbert. *In Defence of Shelley;* & Other Essays. London: William Heinemann, 1936. (Includes "Obscurity in Poetry," from *The Bookman*, 1933.)

——. Introduction to his edition of *Notes on Language and Style* by T. E. Hulme. Seattle: University of Washington Book Store, 1929. (University of Washington Chapbooks, ed. Glenn Hughes, No. 25.)

——. *Reason and Romanticism;* Essays in Literary Criticism. London: Faber & Gwyer, 1926. (Includes "The Nature of Metaphysical Poetry," from *The Criterion*, 1923.)

Rees, Garnet. "A French Influence on T. S. Eliot: Rémy de Gourmont," *Revue de Littérature comparée* (Paris), XVI, No. 4 (October-December 1936), 764-67.

Richards, I. A. *Coleridge on Imagination*. New York: Harcourt, Brace & Co., 1935.

——. *The Philosophy of Rhetoric*. New York: Oxford University Press, 1936. (The Mary Flexner Lectures on the Humanities, III.)

——. *Practical Criticism;* A Study of Literary Judgment. London: Kegan

Paul, Trench, Trubner & Co.; New York: Harcourt, Brace & Co., 1929.

———. *Principles of Literary Criticism.* London: Kegan Paul, Trench, Trubner & Co.; New York: Harcourt, Brace & Co., 1924.

———. *Science and Poetry.* London: Kegan Paul, Trench, Trubner & Co.; New York: W. W. Norton & Co., 1926.

Riding, Laura. *Contemporaries and Snobs.* London: Jonathan Cape; Garden City, N. Y.: Doubleday, Doran & Co., 1928.

———, and Robert Graves. *A Survey of Modernist Poetry.* London: William Heinemann, 1927; Garden City, N. Y.: Doubleday, Doran & Co., 1928.

Roberts, Michael. *The Modern Mind.* London: Faber & Faber, 1937.

Rosenfeld, Paul. *Men Seen;* Twenty-Four Modern Authors. New York: Lincoln MacVeagh, The Dial Press, 1925.

Ross Williamson, Hugh. *The Poetry of T. S. Eliot.* London: Hodder & Stoughton, 1932; New York: G. P. Putnam's Sons, 1933. (Includes "A Commentary on T. S. Eliot's 'The Waste Land,'" from *The Bookman,* 1932.)

———. "T. S. Eliot and his Conception of Poetry," *The Bookman* (London), LXXIX, No. 474 (March 1931), 347-50.

Rugoff, Milton Allan. *Donne's Imagery;* A Study in Creative Sources. New York: Corporate Press, 1939. (Ph.D. dissertation, Columbia University, 1939.)

Rylands, George. "The Metaphysical Poets," *The Cambridge Review* (London), LVI, No. 1365 (October 26, 1934), 46-47.

Saintsbury, George, ed. Introductions to *Minor Poets of the Caroline Period.* Oxford: The Clarendon Press, 1905-1921. (Vols. I: Benlowes, K. Philips, etc.; II: Kynaston, Hall, Godolphin, etc.; III: Cleveland, King, Stanley, Flatman, etc.)

———. "Lesser Caroline Poets," in *The Cambridge History of English Literature,* eds. A. W. Ward & A. R. Waller. Cambridge: Cambridge University Press; New York: G. P. Putnam's Sons, 1911. VII, chap. 4, 72-94.

———. "The Metaphysical Poets," *The Times Literary Supplement* (London), XX, No. 1032 (October 27, 1921), 698; No. 1034 (November 10, 1921), 734.

———. *Prefaces and Essays.* London: Macmillan & Co., 1933. (Includes introductions to his edition of *Seventeenth Century Lyrics,* 1892, etc., and to E. K. Chambers' edition of *The Poems of John Donne,* 1926.)

Sampson, Ashley. "The Resurrection of Donne," *The London Mercury,* XXXIII, No. 195 (January 1936), 307-14.

Sampson, John. "A Contemporary Light upon John Donne," *Essays and Studies of the English Association,* VII (1921), 82-107. Oxford: The Clarendon Press, 1921.

Santayana, George. *Three Philosophical Poets;* Lucretius, Dante, and Goethe. Cambridge, Mass.: Harvard University Press, 1927.

Schelling, Felix E. "Devotional Poetry in the Reign of Charles I," in his *Shakespeare and "Demi-Science";* Papers on Elizabethan Topics. Philadelphia: University of Pennsylvania Press, 1927. Pp. 138-57.

———. "Donne and his Place among Lyrical Poets," in his *English Literature During the Lifetime of Shakespeare.* New York: Henry Holt & Co., 1910. Pp. 357-77.

Scrutinies; Critical Essays by Various Writers. Vol. II. London: Wishart & Company, 1931. (Collected by Edgell Rickword. Includes two essays on Eliot, and others on Huxley, Joyce, Lawrence, the three Sitwells, etc., by Alec Brown, William Empson, Peter Quennell, etc.)

Seventeenth Century Studies. Presented to Sir Herbert Grierson. Oxford: The Clarendon Press, 1938. (Under editorship of John Purves. Essays by R. I. Aaron, Joan Bennett, Laurence Binyon, Geoffrey Bullough, T. S. Eliot, F. E. Hutchinson, Pierre Legouis, C. S. Lewis, L. C. Martin, Rudolf Metz, Mario Praz, T. B. Rudmose-Brown, L. J. Russell, C. J. Sisson, A. E. Taylor, E. M. W. Tillyard, J. B. Trend, Basil Willey.)

The Sewanee Review (Tenn.), LVI, No. 3 (Summer 1948), 365-476. "Homage to John Crowe Ransom." (Essays on his Work as Poet and Critic, Prepared and here Collected in Honor of his Sixtieth Birthday by Allen Tate and Robert Penn Warren: Cleanth Brooks, Randall Jarrell, Robert Lowell, Andrew Lytle, F. O. Matthiessen, Howard Nemerov, William Van O'Connor, Robert Wooster Stallman, Donald A. Stauffer, Wallace Stevens.)

Sharp, Robert Lathrop. *From Donne to Dryden;* The Revolt Against Metaphysical Poetry. Chapel Hill: The University of North Carolina Press, 1940.

———. "Observations on Metaphysical Imagery," *The Sewanee Review* (Tenn.), XLIII, No. 4 (October-December 1935), 464-78.

———. "The Pejorative Use of 'Metaphysical,'" *Modern Language Notes* (Baltimore, Md.), XLIX, No. 8 (December 1934), 503-5.

———. "The Revolt Against Metaphysical Poetry; A Study in the Development of Neo-Classicism in England." (Unpublished Ph.D. dissertation, Harvard University, 1932.)

———. "Some Light on Metaphysical Obscurity and Roughness," *Studies in Philology* (Chapel Hill, N. C.), XXXI, No. 4 (October 1934), 497-518.

Shuster, George N. Review of *Basic Verities* by Charles Péguy. *The New York Times Book Review,* February 28, 1943.

Simpson, Evelyn M. "John Donne and Sir Thomas Overbury's 'Characters,'" *The Modern Language Review* (Cambridge, Eng.), XVIII, No. 4 (October 1923), 410-15.

———. *A Study of the Prose Works of John Donne.* Oxford: The Clarendon Press, 1924.

Sitwell, Edith. *Aspects of Modern Poetry.* London: Gerald Duckworth & Co., 1934.

Smith, G. C. Moore. "Donniana," *The Modern Language Review* (Cambridge, Eng.), VIII, No. 1 (January 1913), 47-52.

Smith, James. "On Metaphysical Poetry," *Scrutiny* (Cambridge, Eng.), II, No. 3 (December 1933), 222-39.

Smith, Logan Pearsall. "Donne's Sermons," in his *Reperusals and Re-Collections.* London: Constable & Co., 1936; New York: Harcourt, Brace & Co., 1937. Pp. 222-55. (Same as essay in his edition of *Sermons: Selected Passages* by John Donne, 1919.)

———. *Milton and His Modern Critics.* London: Oxford University Press, 1940; Boston: Little, Brown & Co., 1941.

Smith, W. Bradford. "What is Metaphysical Poetry?" *The Sewanee Review* (Tenn.), XLII, No. 3 (July-September 1934), 261-72.

Sparrow, John. "Donne's Table-Talk," *The London Mercury*, XVIII, No. 103 (May 1928), 39-46.

———. *Sense and Poetry;* Essays on the Place of Meaning in Contemporary Verse. New Haven: Yale University Press, 1934.

Spencer, Theodore, ed. *A Garland for John Donne; 1631-1931.* Cambridge, Mass.: Harvard University Press, 1931. (Essays by Thomas Stearns Eliot, John Hayward, Mario Praz, Mary Paton Ramsay, Evelyn M. Simpson, John Sparrow, Theodore Spencer, George Williamson.)

———. "The Poetry of T. S. Eliot," *The Atlantic Monthly* (Boston), CLI, No. 1 (January 1933), 60-88.

———. "Poets in Their Fame," review of *The Metaphysical Poets* by James B. Leishman, and *Four Metaphysical Poets* by Joan Bennett. *The Saturday Review of Literature* (New York), XII, No. 1, (May 4, 1935), 22, 24.

———. "Recent Scholarship in Metaphysical Poetry," in his *Studies in Metaphysical Poetry.* New York: Columbia University Press, 1939. (Two Essays and a Bibliography. With Mark Van Doren, *q.v.*)

Spender, Stephen. *The Destructive Element;* A Study of Modern Writers and Beliefs. London: Jonathan Cape, 1935; Boston: Houghton Mifflin & Co., 1936.

Spurgeon, Caroline F. E. *Mysticism in English Literature.* Cambridge: Cambridge University Press; New York: G. P. Putnam's Sons, 1913.

Stauffer, Donald A., ed. *The Intent of the Critic* by Edmund Wilson, Norman Foerster, John Crowe Ransom, and W. H. Auden. Princeton: Princeton University Press, 1941. (With an Introduction.)

Stevens, Wallace. "A Poet that Matters," article on *Selected Poems* by Marianne Moore. *Life and Letters Today* (London), XIII, No. 2 (December 1935), 61-65.

———. Preface to *Collected Poems* by William Carlos Williams. New York: The Objectivist Press, 1934.

Symons, Arthur. *The Symbolist Movement in Literature.* New York: E. P.

314   THE METAPHYSICAL PASSION

Dutton & Co., 1919. (Revised and enlarged from the earlier London edition of 1899.)

Sypher, Wylie. "The Metaphysicals and the Baroque," *Partisan Review* (New York), XI, No. 1 (Winter 1944), 3-17.

Taggard, Genevieve, ed. Preface to *Circumference;* Varieties of Metaphysical Verse (1456-1928). New York: Covici Friede Publishers, 1929.

———. "John Donne: A Link between the Seventeenth and the Twentieth Centuries," *The Scholastic* (Dayton, O.), XXIV, No. 8 (March 24, 1934), 11-12.

Tate, Allen. "American Poetry Since 1920," *The Bookman* (New York), LXVIII, No. 5 (January 1929), 503-8.

———. "Elinor Wylie's Poetry," review of *Collected Poems of Elinor Wylie,* ed. William Rose Benét. *The New Republic* (New York), LXXXII, No. 107 (September 7, 1932), 107.

———. "Emily Dickinson," *The Outlook* (New York), CXLIX, No. 16 (August 15, 1928), 621-31.

———, ed. *The Language of Poetry* by Philip Wheelwright, Cleanth Brooks, I. A. Richards, and Wallace Stevens. Princeton: Princeton University Press; London: Oxford University Press, 1942.

———. "Modern Poets and Convention," *The American Review* (New York), VIII, No. 4 (February 1937), 427-35.

———. "Post-Symbolism," review of *Axel's Castle* by Edmund Wilson. *The Hound & Horn* (New York), IV, No. 4 (July-September 1931), 619-24.

———. *Reactionary Essays on Poetry and Ideas.* New York: Charles Scribner's Sons, 1936. (Includes "Hart Crane and the American Mind," from *Poetry*, 1932; "In Memoriam: Hart Crane: 1899-1932," from *The Hound & Horn*, 1932; "Irony and Humility," review of Eliot's *Ash Wednesday*, from *The Hound & Horn*, 1931; "New England Culture and Emily Dickinson," from *The Symposium*, 1932.)

———. *Reason in Madness;* Critical Essays. New York: G. P. Putnam's Sons, 1941.

Taupin, René. "The Classicism of T. S. Eliot," *The Symposium* (Syracuse, N. Y.), III, No. 1 (January 1932), 64-82. (Translated by Louis Zukofsky.)

———. *L'Influence du Symbolisme français sur la Poésie américaine (de 1910 à 1920).* Paris: Librairie Ancienne Honoré Champion, 1929.

———. "La Poésie d'Ezra Pound," *Revue Anglo-Américaine* (Paris), VIII, No. 3 (February 1931), 221-36.

Thompson, Elbert N. S. "Mysticism in Seventeenth Century Literature," *Studies in Philology* (Chapel Hill, N. C.), XVIII, No. 2 (April 1921), 170-231.

Tillyard, E. M. W. *Poetry Direct and Oblique.* London: Chatto & Windus, 1934. (Revised 1945; reprinted 1948.)

Turnell, G. M. "Tradition and T. S. Eliot," *The Colosseum* (London), I, No. 2 (June 1934), 44-54.

Tuve, Rosemond. *Elizabethan and Metaphysical Imagery; Renaissance Po-etic and Twentieth-Century Criticism.* Chicago: University of Chicago Press, 1947.

Unger, Leonard. *Donne's Poetry and Modern Criticism.* Chicago: Henry Regnery Co., 1950.

——. "Notes on *Ash Wednesday*," *The Southern Review* (Baton Rouge, La.), IV, No. 4 (Spring 1939), 745-70.

Van Doren, Mark. "Seventeenth-Century Poets and Twentieth-Century Critics," in *Studies in Metaphysical Poetry.* New York: Columbia University Press, 1939. (With Theodore Spencer, *q.v.* Included in *The Private Reader* by Mark Van Doren, 1942.)

Walton, Geoffrey. "Abraham Cowley and the Decline of Metaphysical Poetry," *Scrutiny* (Cambridge, Eng.), VI, No. 2 (September 1937), 176-94.

Warren, Robert Penn. "John Crowe Ransom: A Study in Irony," *The Virginia Quarterly Review,* XI, No. 1 (January 1935), 93-112.

——. "The Reading of Modern Poetry," *The American Review* (New York), VIII, No. 4 (February 1937), 435-49. (With Cleanth Brooks, *q.v.*)

Wells, Henry W. *New Poets from Old; A Study in Literary Genetics.* New York: Columbia University Press, 1940.

——. *Poetic Imagery; Illustrated From Elizabethan Literature.* New York: Columbia University Press, 1924.

——. *The Tercentenary of Henry Vaughan.* New York: Hudson Press, 1922.

We Moderns. (1920-1940.) New York: Gotham Book Mart, 1940. (Catalogue No. 42. With introductions, articles, comments by Conrad Aiken, W. H. Auden, John Peale Bishop, e. e. cummings, Richard Eberhart, Dudley Fitts, Arthur Mizener, Kenneth Patchen, Ezra Pound, Samuel Putnam, Paul Rosenfeld, Delmore Schwartz, Gertrude Stein, Genevieve Taggard, Allen Tate, William Carlos Williams, Edmund Wilson, etc.)

Wendell, Barrett. *The Temper of the Seventeenth Century in English Literature.* New York: Charles Scribner's Sons, 1904. (Clark Lectures at Cambridge, 1902-1903.)

Werfel, Franz. "Writing 'Bernadette,' " *The Commonweal* (New York), XXXVI, No. 6 (May 29, 1942), 125-26.

White, Helen C. *The Metaphysical Poets; A Study in Religious Experience.* New York: The Macmillan Co., 1936. (Donne, Herbert, Crashaw, Vaughan, Traherne.)

Whitehead, Alfred North. *Adventures of Ideas.* New York: The Macmillan Co., 1933.

——. *Science and the Modern World.* New York: The Macmillan Co., 1925. (Lowell Lectures, 1925. Reprinted 1926, etc.)

Wilder, Amos N. *The Spiritual Aspects of the New Poetry.* New York: Harper & Brothers, 1940.

Willey, Basil. *The Seventeenth Century Background;* Studies in the Thought of the Age in Relation to Poetry and Religion. London: Chatto & Windus, 1934. (New York: Columbia University Press. Reprinted 1942, 1946, 1950.)

Williams, Charles. *Poetry at Present.* Oxford: The Clarendon Press, 1930.

Williamson, George. "The Donne Canon," *The Times Literary Supplement* (London), XXXI, No. 1594 (August 18, 1932), 581.

———. *The Donne Tradition;* A Study in English Poetry from Donne to the Death of Cowley. Cambridge, Mass.: Harvard University Press, 1930. (Includes "The Nature of the Donne Tradition," from *Studies in Philology,* 1928.)

———. "The Libertine Donne: Comments on 'Biathanatos,'" *Philological Quarterly* (Iowa City), XIII, No. 2 (July 1934), 276-91.

———. "Mutability, Decay, and Seventeeth Century Melancholy," *E L H, A Journal of English Literary History* (Baltimore, Md.), II, No. 2 (September 1935), 121-50.

———. "The Talent of T. S. Eliot," *The Sewanee Review* (Tenn.), XXXV, No. 3 (July-September 1927), 284-95. (Expanded and reprinted as *The Talent of T. S. Eliot;* A Study of Donne's Influence. Seattle: University of Washington Book Store, 1929. University of Washington Chapbooks, ed. Glenn Hughes, No. 32.)

Wilson, Edmund. *Axel's Castle;* A Study in the Imaginative Literature of 1870-1930. New York: Charles Scribner's Sons, 1931.

———. "The Canons of Poetry," *The Atlantic Monthly* (Boston), CLIII, No. 4 (April 1934), 455-62.

Winters, Yvor. *Maule's Curse;* Seven Studies in American Obscurantism. Norfolk, Conn.: New Directions, 1938.

———. "Poets and Others," review of *Poems* by Allen Tate. *The Hound & Horn* (New York), V, No. 4 (July-September 1932), 675-79.

———. *Primitivism and Decadence;* A Study of American Experimental Poetry. New York: Arrow Editions, 1937.

———. "The Symbolist Influence," review of *L'Influence du Symbolisme français* by René Taupin, 1929. *The Hound & Horn* (New York), IV, No. 4 (July-September 1931), 607-18.

———. "T. S. Eliot: The Illusion of Reaction," *The Kenyon Review* (Gambier, O.), III, No. 1 (Winter 1941), 7-30, 221-39.

Woolf, Virginia. "Donne after Three Centuries," in her *The Common Reader;* Second Series. London: Leonard & Virginia Woolf (The Hogarth Press), pp. 24-39; *The Second Common Reader.* New York: Harcourt, Brace & Co., 1932. Pp. 20-37.

Wylie, Elinor. "Mr. Eliot's Slug-Horn," review of *The Waste Land* by T. S. Eliot, 1922. *The Literary Review* of the *New York Evening Post,* January 20, 1923.

Yeats, William Butler. *A Packet for Ezra Pound.* Dublin: The Cuala Press, 1929.

Young, Frederick H. Review of *Metapolitics* by Peter Viereck. *The New York Times Book Review*, June 7, 1942.

Zabel, Morton Dauwen, ed. *Literary Opinion in America;* Essays Illustrating the Status, Methods, and Problems of Criticism in the United States Since the War. New York: Harper & Brothers, 1937. (Essays by Irving Babbitt, R. P. Blackmur, Van Wyck Brooks, T. S. Eliot, Marianne Moore, Paul Elmer More, John Crowe Ransom, Philip Blair Rice, George Santayana, Theodore Spencer, Allen Tate, Charles K. Trueblood, Edmund Wilson, Yvor Winters, Morton Dauwen Zabel, etc. With an Introduction. Revised 1951.)

——. "The Mechanism of Sensibility," *Poetry: A Magazine of Verse* (Chicago), XXXIV, No. 3 (June 1929), 150-55.

——. "Poets of Five Decades," *The Southern Review* (Baton Rouge, La.), II, No. 1 (Summer 1936), 160-86.

Zukofsky, Louis. "The Cantos of Ezra Pound," *The Criterion* (London), X, No. 40 (April 1931), 424-40.

INDEX OF NAMES

319

322 INDEX OF NAMES